THE ROLLS-ROYCE MOTOR CAR
AND THE BENTLEY SINCE 1931

THE
ROLLS-ROYCE
MOTOR CAR
AND THE BENTLEY SINCE 1931

ANTHONY BIRD, IAN HALLOWS and
BRENDAN JAMES

SIXTH REVISED EDITION

B T BATSFORD

Picture facing title page: Frederick Henry Royce, 1863–1933.

First published 1964
Second edition 1966, Reprinted 1968
Third edition 1972
Fourth edition 1975
Fifth edition 1984
Sixth edition 2002

Illustrations supplied with kind permission by The Sir Henry Royce
Memorial Foundation

ISBN 07134 8749 6

A CIP catalogue record for this book is available from the British
Library.

Printed in Portugal by Printer Portuguesa Lda.
Typeset in Baskerville
for the publishers

B T Batsford
64 Brewery Road
London N7 9NY
England
www.batsford.com

A member of Chrysalis Books plc

Distributed in the United States and Canada by:
Sterling Publishing Co., Inc.
387 Park Avenue South
New York, NY 10016

FOREWORD TO THE SIXTH EDITION

DURING the thirty-eight years since the publication of the first edition of this book, a great many works have been published on various aspects of the history of the Rolls-Royce motor car – some of which are of lasting value. As a result, a few minor points have been corrected in this edition, including an adjustment to the total number of Phantom IIs built, where the figures given by Raymond Gentile in his pioneering book *The Rolls-Royce Phantom II Continental* have been accepted as more authentic than my original figures.

Some changes to Tony Bird's text have been made, particularly where the passage of time has affected dates or periods that he mentioned, and new changes to Rolls-Royce activities since his death have been added.

In Part Two, a chapter explaining the international 17-digit vehicle identification numbering system and eight other chapters covering models built from 1980 to 2001 have been added.

Thanks to Phillip Hall, CEO of The Sir Henry Royce Memorial Foundation, The Rolls-Royce & Bentley Picture Archive, and to Ian Rimmer BSc Tech for his patient help in correcting mistakes, adding information, identifying pictures and reading the manuscript.

BMJ

PREFACE TO THE FIRST EDITION

FOR half a century the Rolls-Royce has been called 'The Best Car in the World', not only by its makers but by nearly all of their customers and by vast numbers of ordinary people who had little hope of riding in a Rolls until their final journey in some long obsolete model, re-bodied as a hearse, and relegated in old age to the humble, necessary task of carrying the dead in decorous silence to the grave.

A great number of words have been written about the Rolls-Royce, but as yet no definitive history has appeared, and no writer has yet succeeded in explaining why the makers can get away with this apparently arrogant and indefensible claim that theirs is the best car in the world. As it would be a brave man who would attempt even to define what constitutes 'best' it may seem to be flying rather high to attempt to distil the essence of Rolls-Royce upon paper; but, at least, this attempt should be made.

Published material, apart from short articles in specialist journals of small circulation, is conspicuously lacking in any real attempt to fit the cars, particularly the early ones, into their background, and unless one is fortunate enough to have driven, say, an early Napier, Lanchester or De Dion no standard of comparison is available. Indeed, in nearly all the early books on Rolls-Royce, information about the cars themselves is disappointingly scanty. In 1926 the Company commissioned Massac Buist, one of the best motoring journalists of the day, to write *Rolls-Royce Memories*. In this book, now very rare; no attempt was made at a definitive history; it is, nevertheless, an admirable work which has been extensively pillaged, without acknowledgment, by many later writers.

Claude Johnson, Managing Director and *éminence grise* of Rolls-Royce in the formative years, wrote *The Early History of Motoring* in the mid-twenties. This, again, is a most readable book but C. J. finished his story in 1902 and the only information on Rolls-Royce cars in the book is in a supplement compiled after his death. In any case, though Claude Johnson was eminently qualified to treat of the early motoring scene in general, he did not lay claim to any particular technical knowledge. After Royce's death in 1933 only one biography appeared; *The Life of Sir Henry Royce* by the late Sir Max Pemberton. This is an excellent book, but, once more, there is little in it about the motor-cars and nothing at all which shows them in comparison with their contemporaries. Other works, notably Harold Nockold's *The Magic of a Name*, contain considerable information about the earlier cars and a great deal of miscellaneous material, technical and historical, is to be found in a variety of journals published during the last sixty years. However, the reader who wanted a complete picture of the early history and technical development of all the cars built by Rolls-Royce from 1904 to the present day has hitherto had to seek his information from various sources and to fill a number of gaps from his own knowledge or intuition. The attempt has been made by Anthony Bird in Part One of this book to provide a complete account of the very remarkable Rolls-Royce motor-cars and the equally remarkable men who designed, made and sold them.

The Specifications which form Part Two and which will be, the Authors hope, of great value to Rolls-Royce owners and enthusiasts, have been compiled by Ian Hallows. Minor modifications have been excluded from these specifications, which would otherwise have required a volume of their own, but it is believed that all changes of importance in the production life of each model have been included. In the compilation of the specifications, a great deal of assistance has been received from members of Rolls-Royce Ltd. and from private owners. Thanks are particularly due to Stanley Bull for making available the Company's records of post-war cars; to Dennis Miller-Williams for arranging access to the Conduit Street photographic files and for other help; to John Sumpter for advice and suggestions; to Ron Haynes for much assistance, particularly on post-war cars; to W. A. Robotham for information on experimental cars; to Robin Barnard for helpful comments on Silver Ghost details; to Tess Hillman for patient help with the manuscript; and to Michael Symmons for checking post-war car statistics.

Many other knowledgeable people have helped with information and advice; amongst them Stanley Sears and John Bolster must be particularly mentioned for their helpful letters, and George A. Oliver for his outstanding generosity in making available various notes on Rolls-Royce history which he had compiled over a long period. Michael Sedgwick and Michael Ware, curator and librarian of the Montagu Motor Museum, gave their time to find little-known photographs. Harry Fergusson-Wood of Jack Barclay (Service) Ltd. has also given his valuable assistance with information and photographs. Thanks must also go to Michael Vivian and Air Commodore H. V. Rowley for reading the proofs and making valuable suggestions.

Finally, the authors and publishers join in thanking Rolls-Royce Ltd., not only for the information and help they gave but also for kindly reading the manuscript.

Contents

PART ONE

'I am rarely tempted into the realms of prophecy, but I venture to say Messrs. Rolls and Co. will make a high reputation for themselves through their all British-made cars'.

Motor News, December 1904

1

Royces are born in Cooke Street

B Y 1904 the infant motor-car had become a fairly lusty child, and in the next ten years before the first German War it was to reach maturity. The first practical experiments with mechanical road vehicles had been made in 1769–70 by Joseph Cugnot, one of whose steam wagons is still to be seen in Paris; and had it not been for punitive toll charges, later reinforced by restrictive legislation, the steam coaches developed in England between 1820 and 1840 might well have achieved commercial success. Had they done so it is almost certain that the motor-car, in the sense of a light machine for personal use, as opposed to the goods vehicle or omnibus, would have been born early in Queen Victoria's reign rather than towards the end of the nineteenth century.

For all practical purposes the motor industry may be said to date from 1887, in which year Carl Benz sold one of his 3-wheeled, belt-driven, gas-engined horseless carriages to Emile Roger of Paris and at the same time assigned to him sole agency rights for France. Although Benz was by no means first in the field with an internal-combustion vehicle his was the first concern to sell motor-cars, made to a set pattern, to the public. From about 1892 onwards his improved 4-wheeled models, which were altered only in detail during the next ten years, sold in quite impressive quantities, and the design was copied by a number of firms in Germany, France, England and America. Until 1894–5, when demand and output began to grow, the number of Benz cars sold probably did not amount to more than a dozen a year from Benz's own works plus, perhaps, another dozen assembled by Roger, but production increased greatly during the last five years of the century, and so sound was the design within its limitations that there is very little difference between a Benz 'Velo' of 1893 and a Benz 'Ideal' of 1901.

Of all the many concerns or individuals in France who tried their hands at motor-car design before 1900 three are pre-eminent: Panhard et Levassor, Peugeot, and De Dion et Bouton. Panhard et Levassor were the French licensees for Daimler engines and to them goes the credit of evolving the formula on which the 'conventional' twentieth-century car was based. This was done by Levassor in 1891 when he placed the new Daimler V-twin engine vertically in the front of a wooden chassis, with its crankshaft in the longitudinal line, and coupled it via a pedal-controlled friction clutch to a sliding-pinion change-speed gear, the motion from which was taken by bevel-geared countershaft and chain to the hind wheels. The merit of this arrangement, which in itself contained nothing new, was that it was capable of almost unlimited improvement, whereas the Benz type of carriage could not be developed much beyond the point it had reached with the first production models. Peugeot also used and developed the Daimler type of engine (bought from Panhard et Levassor initially) in a series of successful rear-engined models. De Dion et Bouton's contribution was that they produced, in 1895, the first really high-speed petrol engine and by 1896 their standard engines (used at first for tricycles) ran at 1,500 r.p.m. and developed 7 h.p. per litre: this was twice the speed and output of the Daimler or Panhard engines and nearly four times faster and more efficient than those of Benz.

Although it would be wrong to ignore the contributions of many scores of individuals and firms in Europe, England and America the *système* Panhard and the high-speed engine were the twin bases of the twentieth-century motor-car.

By 1900 the Panhard et Levassor layout was being copied by most builders of cars in the medium to large range; even the Daimler Motoren Gesellschaft had adopted the formula and in the next year were to bring it right up to date with the first Mercedes. The house of Peugeot, Panhard's chief rivals in the early years, were on the point of throwing away the rear-engined design which had served them so well for nine years, but it would have been a rash man to have asserted that the *système* Panhard would prevail or even that the internal combustion engine would triumph over steam.

In England, motoring hardly existed before 1896 when a handful of enthusiasts prevailed upon a reluctant government to pass the Locomotives on Highways Act which replaced the 4 m.p.h. speed limit, and three-persons-in-attendance, restrictions of 1865, with a speed limit of 12 m.p.h. and allowed mechanical vehicles to be used without being preceded by a man with a red flag. Since 1878, in fact, the red flag had been unnecessary, but since the walking attendant was still insisted upon, the warning banners were still commonly carried in front of traction engines and road rollers. For the first few years after the 'Emancipation' Act was passed, progress in England was held up by the financier, Harry Lawson, who attempted to control the whole industry by buying up and licensing every available motor patent. By the end of the century the trade in England was almost exclusively in the hands of a number of firms importing, or copying, European cars. Foremost among the copyists were the English Daimler Company, who made a fairly straightforward copy of the Daimler-engined Panhard, the Napier which, again, started life as a Panhard with an English design of engine, and firms like International, Star, Arnold and Marshall which followed Herr Benz down the cul-de-sac of the belt-driven horseless carriage. Wholly English-born were the remarkably advanced Lanchester, which did not reach the production stage until, late 1900, and the Wolseley voiturette designed by Herbert Austin.

The *système* Panhard had plenty of rivals, particularly in the small car or voiturette field. There was, to start with, a rich variety of quadricycles, fore-cars, tandem tri-cars and similar strange and terrible devices, most of which had evolved out of the De Dion-Bouton motor tricycle which had had great success since its introduction five years earlier. Most of these machines were powered by De Dion, or De Dion type, engines, as were a host of small scale 'conventional' cars of which the most important, historically speaking, was the Renault. Louis Renault's contribution was the combination of a gearbox arranged to give a direct drive on the top gear, and a bevel-geared live axle mounted on springs and driven by a jointed propeller shaft. This arrangement was widely copied on small machines, but final drive by chain remained common on large cars for some years. Renault's was by no means the first example of a gear-driven live axle as Lanchester had already built live-axle cars, using his famous hour-glass worm gear, and Hiram Percy Maxim had also used a bevel-geared live axle on his 1898 design for the Columbia Cycle and Carriage Co. of Hartford, Conn. Other pioneers were not far behind, but in most early instances the live axle was unsprung, to avoid the complication of universal joints in the transmission shaft, which was soon found to be a mistake.

The De Dion company brought out their first 4-wheeled vehicle in 1899 and this admirable design of rear-engined voiturette was deservedly successful: it was copied in England, Germany and America, though most of the copies fell far short of the original as the plagiarists did not use the ingenious, 'fool-proof' constant-mesh and expanding clutch system of change speed mechanism, or the famous De Dion final-drive arrangement which has recently come to the fore again.

Although the archetype of the American 'gas-buggy' type of runabout, the curved-dash Oldsmobile, was not to appear until 1901 it was already apparent that American designers were not then ready to adopt the Panhard layout, of which, indeed, few examples existed in America at that time. But by 1900 the native pattern was already emerging, and the centrally mounted, slow running, horizontal engine was more favoured than the European type of (relatively) fast running vertical affair. Also the first of those frail but entrancing American steamers was already well established: the Stanley brothers had sold their design to Locomobile in 1898 and many would-be motorists were tempted by the silence, flexibility and (apparent) simplicity of the Locomobile type of light steamer. They were mostly to regret their purchases sooner or later, but improved and sturdier types of steam cars were serious rivals to the best petrol vehicles for some years.

The period from 1900 to 1904, when Henry Royce's first car took the road, was one of growth and consolidation. A rich variety of new designs came on the market, ranging from the technically advanced Lanchester to the palpably absurd Sunbeam-Mabley. Although there were to be many exceptions to the rule for many years to come, the *système* Panhard gained ground yearly even in the voiturette class. De Dion-Bouton, Decauville and many others abandoned their rear-mounted engines in favour of the big car style with the engine vertically and longitudinally mounted under a bonnet over the front axle. The belt-driven Benz finally became extinct in 1902–3, and with the introduction of the first Mercedes in 1901 the Daimler Motoren Gesellschaft made most of their rivals look old-fashioned. The American industry, having got off to a late start, was making enormous strides and a very great number of manufacturers were following closely and respectfully behind Winton, Packard, Olds, etc., in producing a modernised and Americanised concept of the Benz-inspired horseless vehicle. The typical American motor-car of this period was technically uninspired, with its large, heavy, slow running, centrally mounted horizontal engine, 2-

speed epicyclic transmission and final drive by central chain to a live axle, but it was simple and cheap to make, easy to drive and keep in order, and what it lacked in performance it compensated for by running with a degree of quietness that put many of the best European cars to shame. Like the Benz of ten years earlier, however, this type of car was incapable of much development; consequently the leading American makers began to fall in line with European practice. In many instances this was unashamedly done by straightforward copying; thus the re-styled Packards derived from Mors, the new Locomobile petrol cars from Berliet, the Thomas from Brasier, the Pierce from De Dion, the Simplex from Mercedes and so on.

One of the most talked-of innovations on the English market was the 6-cylinder Napier which appeared towards the end of 1903. Despite the shrill assertions of S. F. Edge, whose flair for publicity lay behind much of Napier's success, this was neither the first 6-cylinder car to be made nor did it provide the final answer to the shortcomings of the petrol motor-car – noise, vibration and inflexibility. Though the early 6-cylinder Napiers were undeniably fine cars by 1904 standards, it was apparent that the 6-cylinder engine posed new problems of design and construction; these problems were not solved for a few years and one of Henry Royce's most important attainments was to improve and refine the multi-cylinder engine so as to achieve the 'silky' running which has been the hall-mark of a fine 6-cylinder car for the past half-century.

Early motor-cars were by no means so crude, noisy and unreliable as they are usually made out to be. True enough, there were a number of pretty horrible devices offered to an unsuspecting and unknowledgeable public. This was particularly the case in the cheap light car market in which a number of get-rich-quick operators, owners of small engineering concerns, bicycle factors and so on took advantage of the boom in motors, and the ignorance of the public, and assembled small batches of single-cylinder cars from imported proprietary components or, indeed, from rejected components from the reputable makers or mere shoddy imitations. The De Dion-Bouton Company, in particular, suffered much from imitators who not only produced unlicensed copies of the famous engines, but bogus De Dion sparking-plugs, contact-breakers and other specialised components. Most of these fly-by-night concerns lasted but little longer than the short time it took their sordid productions to shake and rattle themselves into oblivion.

There were, however, a great number of firms offering sound, well-engineered cars at prices varying between £150 and £2,500 naturally, the customer got what he paid for, and at the £150 end of the scale he would have to be content with a fairly stark and under-powered single-cylinder runabout which would need a good deal of humouring and tinkering, which, at its best, would do scarcely more than 20 m.p.h., and which would be reduced to a low-gear crawl at walking pace up any but the gentlest slope. At £200 to £300 there were a number of much more refined, faster and longer-lived vehicles; single-cylindered mostly but some with 2-cylinder engines. Reputable makers such as De Dion, Wolseley, Renault, and many more were also beginning to develop larger models to supplement their voiturettes and light cars which had already earned the reputation of being reliable and well finished. Also at about £200 (in Great Britain that is; they were, naturally, cheaper in the U.S.A.) were the single-cylinder Oldsmobiles, Cadillacs and other American runabouts which remained relatively unaltered until the Model T Ford came to dominate the cheap car market in America.

For the motorist with £300 to £500 to spend there was a wide choice of admirable 2- and 3-cylinder cars (the 3-cylinder vogue lasted, roughly, from 1903 to 1906); the larger models in this class could seat four or five people in comfort and travel at 30 to 40 m.p.h. under favourable conditions. The 4-cylinder market, broadly speaking, started at £500 in 1904, though there were a few small 4-cylinder models available for rather less. The £500-and-over class ranged from the 12 h.p. Star at £500 to the 60 h.p. Mercedes at £2,500: this was the most expensive, but not the most powerful car listed in 1904. The few 6-cylinder cars available cost between £1,000 and £2,000.

The over-£500 range included the bigger steam cars and the electric town carriages; the little American steamers and electric runabouts of the early years had cost considerably less but were, by now, dying out in favour of sturdier and more practical vehicles.

The motorist with £1,500 and more to spend expected, and got, a vast and impressive chain-drive monster propelled by an engine of between eight and fourteen litres capacity. Though far from smooth running and quiet by our standards, such cars were then thought the last word in luxury and they were, indeed, roomy, luxuriously upholstered, well sprung and fast: the finish of all the parts would be considered good by any standard, and design had come a long way since the beginning of the century. They were capable of speeds up to 65 or 70 m.p.h. (perhaps even more if lightly bodied) at the expense of a truly terrifying tyre bill. They were mostly propelled by gargantuan 4-cylinder engines but by the middle of 1904 a few firms, such as Brooke, Napier, Sunbeam, Spyker and Panhard, were offering 6-cylinder models.

The unreliability of early motor-cars has been much exaggerated. Roadside stoppages were commonplace indeed, but the majority of these were occasioned by the extreme frailty of the pneumatic tyres of those days, or by some quite trivial cause, such as a choked carburettor jet or faulty electrical connection. The pioneer motorists were, generally, unacquainted with any machine more complicated than a bicycle and were consequently unable to diagnose the simplest ailments from which their motors might suffer.

The most valid criticisms of the first petrol cars were on the score of inflexibility (which made frequent gear-changing necessary), noise and vibration. These last two vices were particularly apparent when standing with the engine running, and lent a great deal of ammunition to the horse-loving opponents of 'those noisy, palpitating abominations'. Steam and electric cars did not suffer from these defects, but the delightful performance of a good steamer was bought at the expense of the great skill required in driving (despite the apparent simplicity), the constant work needed in maintenance, high fuel and water consumption and very rapid depreciation. The electric carriage was vibrationless, odourless, silent, safe and simple to drive. Alas! it was expensive to run and maintain, very heavy, slow, and bedevilled by its limited range of operation.

It is Henry Royce's first triumph that, starting relatively late, he developed by 1906 a machine which combined the lively performance and stamina of a fine petrol car with the effortless running of a good steamer and the silent flexibility of an electric brougham.

*   *   *

*Frederick Henry Royce was born on 27 March 1863 at Alwalton in Lincolnshire, where his father ran a water-powered flour mill. Millers are usually fairly rich or, at least, well-to-do, but this does not seem to have been the case with Royce's father, and some ill-defined financial difficulties obliged him to move to London with his sons when Henry (as he was generally called) was four years old. Both he and his elder brother had to contribute to the purse, and Henry's first job was as a newspaper boy for W. H. Smith & Sons at Clapton and, after, at Billingsgate.

The 'Newspaper Boy to Millionaire' background of so many eminent men has been so much publicised that newspaper selling is looked upon as almost the only ingredient needed for success in life. But it is too easy to overlook the stultifying effects of too much work, too little food, and scanty education which were the lot of the poor a century ago. Exceptional strength of character was needed to overcome these handicaps.

Henry Royce's father died in 1872 and the next five years were particularly hard. The boy could go to school only irregularly (at the Croydon British School), the family's usual food was bread and jam, enlivened occasionally by bread and milk; meat was the rarest of treats and new clothes an unheard-of luxury. Newspaper deliveries were succeeded by work as a telegraph messenger.

A break in the lean years came when he was fourteen years old and spending a brief, rare, holiday with an aunt at Fletton, near Peterborough. She thought it a pity that so promising a boy should not have a chance to get out of the rut and, having a tiny income as well as a kind heart, she arranged for her nephew to be bound apprentice to the Great Northern Railway works at Peterborough, and undertook to pay £20 a year for his apprenticeship as well as to provide enough for his board and lodging.

For three years all went well, and Royce was particularly fortunate in his lodgings which were with a Mr. and Mrs. Yarrow. Together with his son, Yarrow also worked in the railway repair shops and was able to keep a fatherly eye on his lodger's progress. More important still, he had a backyard workshop quite comprehensively equipped with a lathe and a fair selection of hand tools, and here in the evenings Royce and young Yarrow were able to practise turning, fitting and the proper handling of tools. This was a valuable extension of their work in the railway shops, and it seems that Mr. Yarrow as a teacher was both strict and skilled: the foundation of Royce's consummate craftsmanship was laid during this period.

Financial disaster struck again and the generous aunt could no longer afford to keep him. His mother by this time was supporting herself by working as a housekeeper and so had no home to offer; consequently at the age of seventeen Henry Royce set out on foot to find work in the north of England. This was far from easy, for 1879 was a year of slump;

* His first name is spelt Fredrick in the Church baptismal register at Alwalton.

factories and mills everywhere had closed and half-trained apprentices were not wanted. Eventually he got a job with a Leeds tool-making concern at the miserable wage of eleven shillings for a fifty-four-hour week. Even in 1880 this was barely enough to live upon, but Royce somehow managed and even found time and energy to study the elements of the new-born science of electrical engineering.

Some chance brought to his notice an advertisement for a tester with the Electric Light and Power Company in London; with little more than the clothes he stood in, the price of a third-class ticket, and the most rudimentary knowledge of a subject which was then wrapped in mystery, Royce took the plunge, applied for the job and got it.

Although the electric arc-light had been known for more than half a century, the cost of operation, from primary batteries, had kept it at the level of a scientific toy. The incandescent electric lamp was something quite new, and the whole business of generating electricity by means of the dynamo had hardly advanced beyond the stage reached by Faraday in 1830. Electric telegraphy and electroplating were well established, but these derived their current from chemical batteries, and the Electric Light and Power Company was one of the first concerns in England to attempt to supply the mysterious electric fluid for lighting streets and public buildings. The work was fascinating, as all pioneer work is, and fraught with hazards, not the least of which was to prevent the dynamos running too fast if the load decreased. When an electrically lit theatre, for example, closed for the night and the manager started to switch off the lights the engineer at the power house had to keep a sharp eye on his dynamo and a ready hand on the engine throttle or the remaining lights left burning would glow with unearthly radiance for a few glorious seconds before burning out.

In addition to working long hours for the power company, Henry Royce studied electrical theory under Professor Ayrton and also attended classes at the new Polytechnic Institute. His employers thought so well of him that he was appointed first electrician at a subsidiary, the Lancashire Maxim and Western Electric Company; considering his youth and lack of formal education this was an achievement and Royce took up his new post in Liverpool with enthusiasm. As in London, the company was chiefly concerned with supplying public buildings, theatres and entertainment halls. In towns and villages where gas was available the conservative British preferred to stick to the devil they knew, and electric light for private houses was then confined to the country mansions of rich men who could afford to install their own generating plant. The Lancashire Maxim and Western Electric Company was a little ahead of its time and had to go into liquidation after about eighteen months.

At the age of twenty Royce was again out of work, but he was not dismayed for he had at his command technical and practical knowledge of a new trade of great potential. He also had the self-confidence which comes of bearing responsibility early, and no less than £20 of capital. Furthermore, he had a friend, E. A. Claremont, who shared his enthusiasm for electricity and who had the even more princely sum of £50 to play with. With their combined capital the two friends set up in business as electrical engineers in a small workshop in Cooke Street, Manchester. This was in 1884 when Royce was just twenty-one.

With only £70 behind them the new firm of F. H. Royce and Company had little stamina, and when they had bought tools and equipment there was not much left for development, or even for food. They lived a rather hand-to-mouth existence making lamp-holders and filaments for larger concerns, and sleeping in a little room over the workshop. Meals, such as they were, were taken at the work bench and the partners' only amusement, according to Harold Nockolds,* was a game called 'grab', which is described as 'a combination of all-in wrestling and strip-poker'.

The first tentative step on the road to prosperity was taken when Royce designed a little electric bell outfit for domestic use which could be sold for one-and-sixpence. This comprised a very neat trembler bell, a push-button for the door post and a sufficiency of cotton-covered wire. The purchaser had to buy, or make, his own Leclanché cells. These sets caught the public fancy, for although electric light was still regarded with suspicion, an electric door bell had become a 'must' for fashionable householders. The profit at eighteen pence a time was derisory, but at least it was enough to pay their trade creditors and give scope for better things.

With the bread-and-butter work on lamp-holders, filaments, bell sets and sundries steadily increasing, Royce turned his genius for refining the work of others to the problem of improving the crude dynamos of that time. Dynamo 'brushes' really were brushes then and consisted of bundles of fine copper wire 'bristles' bound together and gripped in suitable holders. These bristles wore quickly and caused constant sparking at the commutator and rapid burning of the segments. The problem was kept within bounds by limiting the voltage, but it was appreciated that if the arcing could be reduced, the voltage, and therefore the efficiency, could be increased.

This is no place for a history of electrical engineering, fascinating though that story is. By unceasing work and experiment in the intervals of his normal work, with odd sausages or sandwiches snatched at the bench, and often working until he fell asleep at his table in the small hours of the morning F. H. Royce was able to break into the dynamo market in 1891 with a 'sparkless' drum-wound dynamo which was a great advance on existing types. The name 'dynamo' was then used indiscriminately for generators and electric motors, and the same principle of sparkless commutation made Royce motors safe for use in coal-mines, flour-mills and other places where the Catherine wheel effect of most contemporary machines could not be tolerated.

Royce dynamos were soon selling well and earned the reputation for complete reliability and longevity which has been characteristic of every Royce product since then. A modest degree of prosperity and security came to the little factory; more workpeople were engaged and in 1893, nine years after they had started, both partners were able to marry. Even in their choice of wives they were in harmony, and each married a daughter of a Mr. Alfred Punt. With marriage and a little prosperity the days of sleeping in the workshop were over, and the Royces bought a house at Knutsford where, soon after, Royce brought his mother to live.

Another fortunate contact was made in the same year when a young man was engaged as cashier and book-keeper: his name was John de Looze, and in addition to being a sound man of business he soon developed the qualities of admiration and loyalty which were felt

* *The Magic of a Name*, by Harold Nockolds, G. T. Foulis & Co. Ltd., (1938).

by most of the people who worked for Henry Royce. Very soon after starting work he was to be found not only chasing his employer with invoices to sign or accounts to approve, but with glasses of milk or sandwiches. Royce would still work for twenty hours at a stretch without food or rest if left to himself.

The two chief events of 1894 were that the business was made into a limited company, under the name of 'Royce Ltd., Electrical and Mechanical Engineers and Manufacturers of Dynamos, Motors and Kindred Articles', and electric cranes were added to their products. This new development soon became the most profitable they had ventured upon. The first directors of the company were Royce, Claremont and a friend of Claremont's who had some capital to spare. The Secretary was John de Looze who was to occupy that post in Rolls-Royce Ltd. from 1906 to 1943.

Royce cranes soon became well known; like the dynamos they were reliable and long-lived. Mines, quarries, mills and factories all use lifting tackle of one sort and another, and in the 1890s, apart from a few small pneumatic or hydraulic hoists, there was no alternative to the steam crane with its bulky boiler. This meant that all the many lifting jobs which did not warrant the installation of steam power were done by pulley-hauley, block and tackle or laborious hand-cranked crane. There was plenty of work for the adaptable new electric cranes and hoists to perform. The other sides of the business expanded too, but growth was quickest in the crane department where the orders rose from £6,000 in 1897 to £20,000 in 1899, when the capital of the business was increased to £30,000 to allow for growth. Expansion from a £70 partnership to a £30,000 public company in fifteen years is not, perhaps, as spectacular as some business successes have been, but it is no small achievement, and the concern was sound enough to withstand the slump which set in as the new century dawned and the Boer War dragged on interminably. Rival firms were not slow to join in the profitable business of making electric cranes and dynamos, and many of these rivals were financially stronger and better equipped than the relatively small Royce Ltd. Nor were they so scrupulous about quality: despite their undercutting, and a drop in profits, Royce refused to budge from his high standards. Cutting production costs by devising better methods was always one of his main objectives, but nothing would tempt him to deviate from his maxim: 'The quality remains after the price is forgotten'.

With business in the doldrums the time was clearly ripe for branching out in some new direction, but it seems to have been largely fortuitous that Henry Royce became interested in motor-cars at about this time. It is usually said that his associates were divided between tolerant amusement and serious concern that their chief engineer spent most of his time in the early part of 1903 tinkering about with a second-hand motor-car. This may be a case of reading history backwards, as it is easy to say, now, that the early enthusiasts for the motor-car were invariably regarded as cranks, and the car itself as a rich man's plaything which could have no future. This would have been true in 1893 but by 1903 the new-born motor industry had come a long way. Many small concerns had burnt their fingers, but the well-established and reputable motor manufacturers had well-filled order books. Whether Royce was already toying with the idea of motor manufacture it is not possible to say, and it is probable that, at first, he was concerned to explore the possibility of making electric ignition components for others. Though his fellow directors might pull his leg, and the foreman might swear when men were taken from their jobs, it soon became apparent that Henry Royce's passionate interest in his 2-cylinder 10 h.p. Decauville was more than a passing whim.

It has been said so often, in general histories of the motor-car, that Royce was disgusted with the coarseness, noisiness and unreliability of his Decauville and it has become an article of faith that motor-cars in general, and Decauvilles in particular, were coarse, noisy and unreliable. This distorts the perspective, as the stature of Royce, and the Rolls-Royce cars, does not need to be artificially enhanced by exaggerating the defects of contemporary cars. It is also unjust to Decauville which was one of the better makes of small car. The Société Decauville was an old-established engineering concern in a large way of business; they had taken up motor building as a side-line in 1898 when they put a very neat little tubular-framed voiturette on the market. This had a rear mounted 2-cylinder, $3^1/2$ h.p. air-cooled engine, derived originally from coupling two $1^3/4$ h.p. De Dion tricycle engines on a common crankcase, and though the live rear axle was unsprung, this little car was one of the first to be produced with independent front wheel suspension.

Despite the crudity of exposed change-speed and final-drive gearing the little Decauvilles were reliable and speedy; with the clatter of their high-speed exposed engines and the snarl of uncased straight-toothed gears they were, it must be said, notoriously noisy and, after developing a 5 h.p. water-cooled version of the same type, the firm brought out a much refined 'conventional' car in 1900. This had a forward-mounted engine, properly enclosed 3-speed gearbox, jointed propeller shaft and an extremely well-designed, and quiet, live axle. One of these cars ran for 1,000 miles without stopping the engine at the Crystal Palace in 1901; this was no mean achievement at that time. A larger 4-speed model rated at 10 h.p. soon supplemented the 3-speed 8 h.p. Decauville, and it was on a 10 h.p. type that Royce started his experiments.

Because the most obvious characteristic of the first Royce car was its comparative silence, it is as well to take a look at the reasons why early petrol cars offended the public with their din. To start with, of course, not all were noisy; the old belt-driven Benz had been notably quiet and many of the larger cars were not too offensive, particularly when they were pulling. Many of the single- and twin-cylinder light cars were, however, given to providing a sort of anvil chorus from their exposed valve gear, with a background diapason composed of barking exhaust, snorting atmospheric inlet valves and snarling spur gears. It was noticeable that all petrol cars, particularly the small ones, made much more noise when standing with the engines running than when under way; and as most carriage folk and horsemen insisted on their privilege of halting motor-cars (by raising the right hand) as they drove past, they were given plenty of opportunity to complain of the din of 'those horrible motors'. Early petrol engines were not capable, generally, of being throttled down to a gentle tick-over: this was partly a legacy from the nineteenth-century practice of regarding the petrol engine as a constant-speed affair, which, indeed, it was in the days of atmospheric inlet valves, hot-tube ignition, crude carburettors without throttles, and speed control by centrifugal governor, the business of which was merely to prevent the engine racing when

21

the load was removed. Even when electric ignition, mechanical inlet valves, and throttle control supplanted the earlier arrangements, the carburettors of the time were far from automatic and engines consequently could only be coaxed to run slowly by deft manipulation of throttle, spark and air-inlet control levers. When called upon to stop the average driver usually had neither time nor skill to attend to these things, nor did he wish to risk stalling his engine which was therefore usually left to chatter away at a rapid rate.

The same shortcoming of imperfect carburation and gas distribution which made the engines reluctant to run slowly also made them relatively inflexible under load, and a speed range of about 500 to 1,500 r.p.m. was thought exceptionally good. Consequently variations of car speed called for constant gear-changing which was a difficult, and usually noisy, operation.

Even the best 4- and 6-cylinder cars were relatively rough running by today's standards, as poor gas distribution and variations in ignition timing between one cylinder and another were added to the bad effects of ill-balanced (or unbalanced) reciprocating parts, heavy flywheels, and the torsional vibration of over-long 'whippy' crankshafts. When pulling at

C. S. Rolls at the wheel of Royce's first car in December, 1904, driving the Duke of Connaught on army manoeuvres. Lord Brabazone is about to turn the starting handle, and a member of the Motor Volunteer Group stands at the rear.

moderate speed, most of these shortcomings were not apparent in the bigger engines, but the most avid admirer of veteran motor-cars must concede that the twin- and single-cylinder light cars vibrated intolerably. The only vibrationless petrol engine was the extraordinary 4¼-litre Lanchester with its ingenious but complex arrangement of two cylinders, two pistons, and two counter-rotating crankshafts linked together by six connecting rods.

These vices of mechanical noise and vibration were present in Royce's Decauville, though much less so than in many of its contemporaries, and they were precisely the vices most likely to offend a craftsman of his sensibility. After several months of experimenting, chiefly on the carburation and ignition, he announced his intention of building a batch of three light cars to his own design.

*   *   *

The first Royce model was built largely by Henry Royce himself with the help of two apprentices, Platford and Haldenby, who were later to become famous in Rolls-Royce affairs. The Decauville had inevitably suffered a loss of reliability while being used as a mobile experimental station but as the design was basically sound Royce copied many of its features. Here he was following the path he had already trodden and was often to follow in the future. He never claimed to be an inventive man (though perhaps he was overly modest), but he was a superb craftsman who combined sound engineering sense with the eye of an artist, and his particular genius lay in his ability to improve and refine the work of his contemporaries.

The Royce specification was, therefore, completely conventional and, indeed, included many bought-out or imported components finished and improved in the Cooke Street works to Royce's exacting requirements. The engine was a vertical tandem 2-cylinder, rated at 10 h.p., with dimensions of 95 mm bore and 127 mm stroke. Cylinder barrels and heads were integral, but exceptionally large water spaces, with detachable covers, were provided. The mechanically operated inlet valves were inverted over the exhaust valves. It is sometimes said that this i.o.e. lay-out was a Royce innovation but it had been almost universal in the days of the atmospheric inlet valve as it was convenient and allowed the valve 'pocket' to be kept small. When mechanical operation was extended to the inlet valves, the i.o.e. arrangement was retained by many makers for some years until, in the interests of simplicity and silence, the less efficient T-head or L-head side valve arrangement became usual. In common with most of its contemporaries, the push-rod and rocker mechanism of Royce's engine was entirely exposed, but it was unusually quiet in action thanks to meticulous fit and finish of the moving parts.

The crank throws were placed at 180° to one another which provides good mechanical balance at the expense of uneven power impulses; expressed simply, the firing sequence of a vertical 2-cylinder 4-stroke engine so arranged is 'Bang-Bang-Silence-Silence', whereas with the crank throws in line and the two pistons rising and falling together the impulses are evenly spaced – 'Bang-Silence-Bang-Silence'. One of the disadvantages of the 180° crank arrangement was that during the two successive idle strokes the petrol level rose in the carburettor jet so that the first cylinder to draw, on its inlet stroke, received a richer dose of mixture than its fellow which drew immediately after. This defect was so marked on some 2-cylinder engines that they would refuse to fire on both cylinders below a certain speed, and some manufacturers consequently preferred the less easily balanced type, with the crank throws in line, which not only gave slightly more even torque but also kept the demand on the carburettor more constant. Being determined to keep vibration to the minimum Royce adopted the plan which allowed the better balance, and dealt with the problem of uneven distribution by suitably 'tuning' the inlet tracts.

The most noticeable differences between the Royce engine and its contemporaries lay in the 'plumbing', which was planned more carefully than usual. Considering how much was already known about the behaviour of gases, it is something of a mystery why the majority of early engines were hampered by unnecessarily long and tortuous exposed inlet pipes, by constricted and sharply radiused induction passages, and by absurdly small-bore exhaust systems. But so it was; and the well-planned manifolding, and clear run for the exhaust, on Royce's engine were very much ahead of current practice. In its size of silencer the car almost equalled the 'curved dash' Oldsmobile which was famous in its day for its prodigious exhaust box and the decorous gentle chuffing of its slow-running horizontal engine.

The commonest source of trouble on early cars was the imperfection of the ignition system. Electricity was little understood, batteries and coils were often temperamental and the commonly used trembler-coil system left much to be desired, particularly on multi-cylinder engines. On this system, the rotating 'wipe' contact and distributor merely closed the primary circuit and the necessary 'make and break' to induce the secondary current was performed by an electro-magnetic trembler, on the coil itself, which vibrated as long as the primary circuit was kept closed by the wipe contact. It was the usual practice for each cylinder to have its own coil and trembler (though Napier made a step forward with his new synchronised system in 1903), and it was extremely difficult to tune the tremblers so that all should vibrate at the same speed. In practice this meant that one cylinder might receive a weaker, and consequently later, spark than its fellows which made fine tuning difficult and contributed to noise and roughness. The more cylinders there were to fire, the greater the difficulty, obviously. Other types of ignition available then were the De Dion type of mechanical contact breaker and non-trembler coil (from which the present-day system derives), the low-tension magneto which was excellent but required the complication of moving contacts inside the combustion chambers, and the high-tension magneto which was just becoming a practical proposition. The trembler-coil system had the merit that at hand cranking speeds the primary circuit was closed for long enough to allow a stream of sparks to pass the gap at each sparking plug; this made for easy starting, and multi-cylinder engines would often stand for hours and yet retain sufficient vapour in the cylinders to 'start on the switch' in the most obliging fashion.

Electric ignition posed no problems for Royce the electrician, who made his own commutators, distributors and contacts to such a degree of nicety that they functioned with the accuracy of a chronometer. The first experimental cars had Carpentier trembler coils, but the subsequent production Rolls-Royce models had coils of Royce's design and manufacture.

Much the same may be said of the carburettor – the Achilles heel of most early engines. Nearly all the leading makers were experimenting to make their carburettors automatic; that is, so that variations in engine speed would not require manual adjustment of the gas/air proportions. The first two cars had French Longuemare carburettors, considerably modified, but the third was fitted with Royce's own carburettor, based upon the Krebs which was widely used in France but, as with the ignition system, the details were so improved and the workmanship so fine that truly automatic carburation was at last achieved. This meant that shutting the throttle on the 2-cylinder Royce instantly reduced engine speed to a tick-over with no fear of stalling and no need for fumbling with an air control lever to enrich the mixture. Conversely the engine could be accelerated suddenly, and would pick up smoothly, without the concomitant juggling with air levers, spluttering and misfiring which were then so common. This instant response to the throttle, which we now take for granted, was conspicuously absent from most engines of 1904.

Transmission was by cone clutch, 3-speed and reverse gearbox, open propeller shaft, and bevel-geared live axle. The only difference between the Royce and its contemporaries was that all the parts were so justly proportioned and finely made that they functioned with the minimum of noise and mechanical loss.

The cone clutch has come in for a lot of lambasting from various writers. Harold Nockolds* says 'The average clutch of that time was apt to present only two positions, in or out, a fact which made getting away from a standstill an affair of rapid but short-lived acceleration and traffic driving a thing to be avoided. The Royce clutch provided an infinite variety of intermediate positions, so that the car glided away from a standstill with fascinating smoothness.' Opinions of this sort have been stated so often, without full knowledge of the facts, that it has become an article of faith that 'cone clutches are fierce'.

This is a little unfair. Nockolds was writing before the Second World War when the cult of old cars was in its infancy, and when the few veteran machines which were preserved more or less intact appeared in public they were usually in very poor condition. Also they were brought out largely as a joke, and any kangaroo-like propensities were exaggerated to raise a laugh.

Provided it is properly made there is no reason why a cone clutch should not be as gentle in action as any other variety. Apart from certain fundamental rules governing the angle of the cones according to the nature of the facing material (rules which were, admittedly, sometimes ignored in cheap machines), the essential requirement is that the bases of the cones shall meet before the apices. The only basic weakness of the cone clutch is that wear of the mating faces after prolonged use (or less prolonged misuse) permits the narrow parts of the cones to engage before the wider parts touch. When this happens the thing does, indeed, become intractably fierce; hence the prevalent modern belief that too-sudden engagement is an inherent weakness of the type. The fallacy should be disproved by the fact that Rolls-Royce, and many other fine cars, were fitted with cone clutches until relatively late. Their sweetness of action left nothing to be desired.

The 3-speed and reverse gearbox of the Royce followed conventional French practice, but thanks to careful tooth formation it contented itself with the gentlest of whining noises in place of the clamorous growl so often heard then. The gear-change was of the progressive (the so-called 'quadrant') type as pioneered by Panhard et Levassor. Most English manufacturers at that time were following the Cannstatt-Daimler example and

* *The Magic of a Name*, by Harold Nockolds, C. T. Foulis & Co. Ltd., n.d. (1938).

using the much superior selective or 'gate' control. The French, however, would have none of it; largely, one suspects, because they could not stomach the thought of paying royalties to a German firm.

Decauville practice was most clearly seen in the live rear axle of the Royce; for one of the talking points of the re-fashioned Decauvilles of 1901 had been a new type of live axle in which the hub bearings revolved upon the fixed axle tubes, and the half shafts were merely called upon to transmit torque and were not required to carry the weight of the car. This 'fully floating' type of axle was an improvement on the ordinary variety, not only because it was more efficient mechanically, but because it spared the motorist the embarrassment of losing a hind wheel if a half-shaft broke.

The engines were carefully run-in and tested on the bench (a practice which still obtains at Rolls-Royce) and, as one would expect of an electrical engineering concern, the testing was done electrically. That is, the engine was coupled to a dynamo and run at full power for some hours while fuel consumption and output were recorded. The figure for the first engine worked out at 1.7 pence per kilowatt hour.

It is difficult to be certain exactly how much of the three Royce cars, and the first Rolls-Royces, was actually made in the Cooke Street works and how much was made elsewhere to specification. Over the years the belief has gained ground that practically every component was made in the Royce works and just as a certain type of worshipper of the olde-worldy will aver, in the teeth of the evidence, that the best Sheraton furniture was personally constructed by Mr. Sheraton, so a myth is growing up that Royce himself made each piece of his early cars.

There is obviously much exaggeration in this, although it is true that everything had to pass Royce's critical eye. All other considerations apart it is obvious that Cooke Street was not equipped for such tasks as heavy forging, spring making and so forth. It has been said, for instance, that even the cylinder blocks were cast on the premises, but it is extremely doubtful whether the little foundry at Cooke Street could have coped with such a task and it is certainly established that when the first Silver Ghosts were in production four years later, a Rugby foundry supplied the cylinder castings. It was typical of Royce, incidentally, that when one of these castings failed on a car he was testing (one of the hemispherical cylinder ends blew off into the water jacket, doubtless because of a weak section thickness or a misplaced core) he immediately examined a batch of eleven blocks cast from the same pattern and machined ready for fitting, demolished the lot with a hammer and gave the foreman patternmaker instructions to put diagonal ribs outside the combustion chambers so as to avoid any possibility of further failure. The actual chance of the mishap being repeated was small, and most firms would have let the batch through and contented themselves, at the most, with modifying subsequent castings. But that was not Royce's way of doing business.

By the time the first engine was ready to install in the first chassis the whole factory was, naturally, agog for the first trial trip. Royce, however, would not hurry or skimp any part. Everything had to be tested and re-tested. The slightest evidence of poor workmanship would lead to the scrapping of a complete assembly, to the accompaniment of a fairly vitriolic address to the offending workman from 'Pa' Royce. This happened, as Platford recalled many years later, with the front axle which was found to have a slight discrepancy in the angles of the respective king-pin eyes. Royce found one of the men attempting to correct the error by giving a slight twist to the axle tube; this rough and ready procedure would have passed muster in most factories but would not do for Royce, and back went the axle to the company who had made it.

With various delays of this sort therefore it was 1 April 1904 before the first trial run took place though for some years the 'official' date was given as 31 March, to avoid the tedious waggishness of the anti-motoring fraternity. Just as, in the North of England, the engineering apprentice who finishes his time is 'hammered out' by his mates, so the Royce car was 'hammered out' into Cooke Street. Every employee in the place seized some tool or bar and belaboured the nearest bench, anvil or floor as the little car set off on its first journey, Royce at the wheel, followed by Platford and Holdenby in the old Decauville. This triumphant tintinnabulation completely drowned the gentle 'putter-putter, putter-putter' of the Royce's engine.

With the Decauville in attendance, quite unnecessarily, Royce drove to his house at Knutsford without a hitch. So carefully had everything been tested and adjusted that the barest minimum of final tuning was needed, and within a week the chassis was stripped of its rough test-rig and sent to a local coachbuilder to have a 2-seater body fitted. The other two chassis were finished, tested, and bodied soon after.

Fully equipped with body and accessories the first 10 h.p. cars weighed '$14\frac{1}{2}$ cwt. This was fairly heavy by comparison with most contemporary cars of comparable size. It is very often said that the secret of the Royce's excellent performance lay in its having a better power-to-weight ratio than its rivals, but this is just not true. Royce abhorred clumsy and needlessly heavy components, and the various light alloys developed by Rolls-Royce Ltd. are famous, but though he was a master at combining strength with lightness the safety factor had always to come first, and in his first cars it is not unjust to say he erred on the side of safety. This did not prevent the 10 h.p. Royce, and its successors, from out-performing their rivals. The lively and willing performance came from high mechanical efficiency of the running gear, the exceptional flexibility of the engine and the harmonious relationship between the engine's range of speed and the gear ratios. A measure of this harmony is shown by the figures recorded at a Veteran Car Club rally in 1959, during which one of the surviving 10 h.p. Rolls-Royces climbed Prescott Hill in 1 min. 56 sec. The course is half a mile long, not particularly well surfaced, rises 165 feet with a maximum gradient, at a hairpin bend, of 1 in 6. By contrast a 1904 Tony Huber of approximately the same engine capacity and wheelbase, but weighing 2 cwt. less, took 3 min. 8 sec. The explanation of the big difference is that after negotiating the hairpin the driver of the Rolls-Royce was able to change up into second speed and to accelerate steadily for the rest of the hill, whereas the Tony Huber (like most cars of the period), being once committed to low gear had to stay in low gear until reaching almost-level ground. In the years ahead it was flexibility and well- chosen gear ratios which so often gave Rolls-Royce cars the advantage.

Some few details of Royce's first cars might be criticised today. Engine lubrication by the then common splash system, with visible drip feeds on the dash-board to which the oil was forced by exhaust pressure, left much to be desired and soon became obsolete on good quality cars. The bolted-on front dumb-irons might occasion some head-shaking, too, but the technique of steel pressing was relatively new (indeed, many contemporary chassis were still constructed of wood reinforced with iron flitch-plates) and many designers objected to the curvature necessary to make the dumb-irons integral with the chassis side members. And, at least, when any part of a Royce structure was bolted to any other part, the holes were reamed to be an exact engineering fit to the bolts. Unfortunately the apt simile with which Royce stigmatised the usual fit, or lack of it, of bolt to bolt hole cannot be recorded in these polite pages.

The least happy feature of early Royce engines is that the lower halves of the main bearings are attached to the lower half of the crankcase. This indefensible arrangement had been criticised in the technical press as early as 1902; but Royce was in good company, for Ettore Bugatti made his engines in this obsolete fashion for some years. In April/May 1906, however, for the heavy 20 and all post-60500 30s, Royce adopted the modern arrangement of the main bearings which allows greater accuracy and rigidity in this vital heart of the engine.

After more than one hundred years of development it is easy enough to point the finger of scorn at certain infelicities of design, but it must be remembered that precision engineering on a large scale only developed with the motor industry; in 1903–4 accuracy of fit, and fine finish, depended on the skill of the craftsman. This made simplicity, sometimes to the point of crudity, a much more desirable quality than it is now, and seen in the context of its time the first Royce model was an admirable compromise. It was refined to a degree scarcely equalled by the most expensive of its contemporaries, and yet simple enough to be relatively inexpensive. Neither complex machining operations nor unduly costly forgings or castings were employed in it, yet the car as a whole was so near perfect as to win the support of one of the most knowledgeable and exacting enthusiasts of the day – Charles Rolls.

2

Rolls and the Tourist Trophy

———•─•─•———

Iɴ late Victorian England engineering was considered no fit occupation for a gentleman. Though the whole wealth and influence of Great Britain depended upon her industrial supremacy, and though the Victorians were justly proud of the native inventiveness, and considered British railways, steamships, bridges and other engineering works second to none, the upper and middle classes on the whole thought of commerce as fit only for counter-jumpers and regarded the world of mechanical knowledge as a province occupied only by uncouth and greasy-handed artisans.

Yet the spirit of an older, more liberal-minded, society lingered on, and the gifted amateurs, the dilettanti, men of the sort who had produced the Royal Society and fostered and financed every kind of technical innovation from the mid-seventeenth century onwards, were still active. The class-consciousness of the time produced the paradox that many of these gifted amateurs came from the extreme upper echelons of the class structure. The respectable, wealthy, upper-middle class Victorian who lived on tenterhooks lest any taint of 'trade' should be discovered in his connections, dared not show interest in anything but sport, but the aristocrat had no fear of being thought eccentric, or being mistaken for a mechanic, and could do as he pleased. Although amateurs of this sort had no need to practise the avocations which interested them, whether engineering or photography, astronomy or sewage-disposal, they very frequently were better qualified than the professionals.

It was men of this sort, scientific amateurs in the best sense, who first made motoring possible and acceptable in England. Men like the Hon. Evelyn Ellis, son of Lord Howard de Walden and a considerable public figure, the Earl of Winchilsea, Sir David Salomons, second-generation City baronet (a type which, thanks to the Prince of Wales, was no longer excluded by the stuffier elements of Society) and a scientist of no mean stature and, most importantly, the Hon. C. S. Rolls.

Charles Stewart Rolls was the third son of Lord Llangattock; he was born in 1877 and was therefore still a young man, indeed, still at Cambridge, when he began to take an interest in the new Continental pastime of motoring. He quickly became far more knowledgeable of the mechanics of his hobby than most pioneer motorists for he was studying engineering, for which he had a natural flair, and he eventually qualified as an M.I.M.E. In 1896 he imported a $3\frac{1}{2}$ h.p. Peugeot from France though there seemed little point in owning a car in England as the 4 m.p.h. speed limit was still in force; but Evelyn Ellis had paved the way by bringing to England the Panhard he had bought two years before for use in France.

The Daimler-engined Peugeot, driven in defiance of legal restrictions.

Ellis, and a few other enthusiasts, realised that a new industry was about to be born and that England would be left behind unless the Government could be cajoled and manœuvred into rescinding some of the more absurd restrictions. As a preliminary step Ellis proposed to drive his motor car about without the attendance of the 'Red Flag' man, and without observing the 4 m.p.h. speed limit: by flouting the law in this way he expected to be prosecuted and so to have an opportunity of exposing the stupidity of the law. Unfortunately he was so respected a public figure that the police left him alone and he often drove his Panhard at 12 m.p.h. or more through the streets of Windsor without being called to account.

In a similar fashion Rolls drove his Peugeot in defiance of the legal restrictions. He too seems to have been left alone by the police, though the University authorities in Cambridge took umbrage at first, and the well-known photograph of Rolls in his Peugeot, preceded by a man carrying an enormous flag, was faked up for publicity purposes in the drive of his father's house. On the public highways he followed Ellis's example and deliberately broke the law.

Sir David Salomons followed suit, and not only brought his car to England but also staged the first 'Motor Show' in England in the grounds of his house near Tunbridge Wells. Though there were only six exhibits this affair attracted quite a lot of notice and was good publicity for Sir David's newly formed Self Propelled Traffic Association which he had founded to bring pressure to bear on the Government.

These and other efforts gradually prevailed, and the Locomotives on Highways Act was passed to become effective on 14 November 1896. Motoring in England was now legalised at the dizzy pace of 12 m.p.h. (a speed already safely exceeded threefold in France), and 'Light Locomotives' were no longer bound by the 'three persons in attendance' rule.

In celebration of Emancipation Day, that wily but far-sighted company promoter, H. J. Lawson, organised the London to Brighton Celebration Run. Organised is not, perhaps, the right word for, in common with most of Lawson's schemes, a strong element of chaos and farce permeated the affair. But the seed had been planted and motoring began to flourish in England.

From this point onward the name of Rolls is to be found in conjunction with every important motor-car event, both at home and on the Continent. Gradually, too, the name of Claude Goodman Johnson came to be prominently associated with the automobile movement.

Two of Lawson's early manœuvres in his plan to control the entire motor industry had been the foundation of the Motor Car Club in 1895 and an exhibition of horseless carriages at the Imperial Institute in the spring of 1896. Claude Johnson, then a minor official at the Institute, helped to organise this exhibition which owed its success very largely to his grasp of business and attention to detail.

England is the land of clubs, and nearly all the pioneer motorists became members of Lawson's Motor Car Club, only to discover that it was no more than a disguised trading organisation the chief function of which was to puff Lawson's grandiose (and sometimes near-fraudulent) company flotations. In 1897 a new organisation, completely non-commercial, was started by Harrington Moore and F. R. Simms who was the original licensee of the Daimler patents in England. At the inaugural meeting 163 members broke away from the Motor Car Club, and the Automobile Club of Great Britain and Ireland (now the R.A.C.) got off to a flying start. With memories of his successful organisation of the Imperial Institute show in mind the founders appointed Claude Johnson as Secretary.

During the next three years the Automobile Club grew in stature. Rallies, hill-climbing contests, brake and manœuvrability tests, demonstrations to police and local authorities were staged by Johnson and, being well run and strictly controlled, went a long way to allay public suspicion of the new-fangled motors. At nearly all of these functions Charles Rolls was a prominent figure. His title, his enthusiasm, his skill as a driver and his real knowledge of engineering matters made him an indispensable part of the early motoring scene.

The Automobile Club's 1,000 Miles Trial of 1900 was a triumph for the club, for Johnson and for Rolls. The club, and the automobile movement in general, scored because the trial convincingly demonstrated to the public that the motor was more than a mere mechanical toy for rich eccentrics. Johnson scored because his organisation of this extremely complex affair

C. S. Rolls at the wheel of a 1902, 10 h.p. Panhard-Levassor, with the Prince of Wales (later George V) beside him. Panhard-Levassor were the French licensees for Daimler engines.

was beyond all praise. Rolls scored because his performance with his 12 h.p. Panhard, in all sections of the trial including the hill climbing and speed contests, was so much better than that of any other competitor that a special gold medal was struck in his honour.

In 1903, though he continued to drive as an amateur in races and trials, Charles Rolls became a 'professional' in that he set up in business as a motor dealer and importer. New Panhard et Levassor and Minerva cars were his main preoccupations but he also sold Whitlock-Asters, Mors, Gardner-Serpollet steam cars and a few good quality second-hand machines of other makes; after almost a year in business on his own he managed to persuade Claude Johnson to join him in partnership. Not, one imagines, that Johnson needed much persuasion for he and Rolls had been firm friends since the days of the Trial, and the job of Secretary to the Automobile Club was becoming irksome. The Committee had unwittingly allowed the club to become a stamping ground for rival commercial interests, those of Danny Weigel and S. F. Edge principally, and the atmosphere of horse-coping which had driven the founders to secede from the Motor Car Club threatened, for a while, to submerge its successor.

The summer of 1904, therefore, found Rolls and Johnson firmly engaged in motor-dealing with offices and showrooms in Brook Street, Mayfair (the Conduit Street premises opened in 1905), repair shops off Lillie Road, Fulham, and a well-filled order book. The stars of Rolls and Royce were just about to move into conjunction.

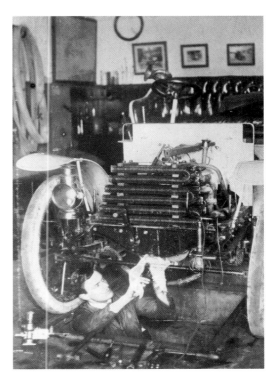

Right and left: C.S. Rolls in his workshop, in a role more usually associated with Royce.

*　　*　　*

Of the three original Royce cars, the first was retained by Royce himself, the second went to E.A. Claremont and became a trial horse for various modifications and improvements as a result of which, like the old Decauville before it, its reliability declined sharply: fortunately Mr. Claremont was an exceptionally patient man. The third car went to Henry Edmunds, who had become a director of the company in 1903, and who was himself an experienced and enthusiastic motorist, a committee member of the Automobile Club, and donor of the Henry Edmunds Hill-Climbing Trophy. He was just the man to appreciate the niceties of the little Royce and, more importantly, he was enough of a business-man to see the importance of finding the right sort of sales outlet if Royce Ltd. were to embark on motor manufacture seriously. Too many promising cars had failed for want of the right men to market them. Rolls and Johnson would be ideal, he decided, if only they could be persuaded to add the Royce to their list.

This was not altogether easy. Royce had little thought for anything but the workshop, he was a reserved man, ill-at-ease in company and slow to make acquaintances; above all he was very reluctant to go to London to meet Rolls. Edmunds, however, was convinced that Rolls and Royce would respect each other's qualities if they did meet, but Rolls was as little anxious to go to Manchester as Royce was to journey to London. From his experience of the motor world, and his knowledge of English taste, Rolls knew that quietness and smooth running were the qualities most likely to appeal in this country and he did not see how a 2-cylinder light car could meet these needs. Rather against his better judgement, therefore, he allowed himself to be persuaded into making the trip, with Edmunds, to Manchester where they were joined by Royce at the Midland Hotel.

After lunch the moment came to inspect and test the car. At first sight there was nothing to distinguish the machine from others of its kind. The famous 'Grecian' radiator still lay in the future and Rolls' expert eye doubtless noted that many features of the Royce were unashamedly borrowed from existing sources. For example, the radiator was markedly similar to that of the contemporary Alldays and Onions, whilst the bonnet itself was scarcely to be distinguished from a Gladiator. But from the instant the engine was started it was obvious that this was not just another 2-cylinder runabout, and the behaviour of the car on the road soon showed that it was in a class of its own. A very short trial run sufficed to turn Rolls from a lukewarm critic to a wholehearted enthusiast; here was a car he need have no hesitation in offering to the most exacting customer. Furthermore, over lunch, Royce had mentioned his hopes for producing 3-, 4-, and 6-cylinder cars if an outlet could be found for them. If the 2-cylinder Royce was as refined as this, then surely a 6-cylinder version must be something no discriminating motorist could resist?

A few days later, arrangements were made for Claude Johnson to have a trial trip and he succumbed to the charm of the Royce as completely as his partner had done. Though there was no thought then of regarding the Royce as anything but an extra string for their bow, Johnson and Rolls were equally anxious to have exclusive rights in selling this enchanting newcomer, and an agreement was negotiated for C. S. Rolls and Co., to take all the motor cars made by Royce Ltd.

Whilst Johnson was attending to the business arrangements Rolls was urging Royce to prepare as much as possible for him to exhibit at the Paris Salon to be held early in December. By all-out effort the Cooke Street works managed to provide a complete 10 h.p. car for giving demonstration runs, a 10 h.p. polished 'show' chassis and engine, a 15 h.p. chassis, a 20 h.p. car and a 30 h.p. 6-cylinder engine. The 20 h.p. 24264 car was part complete and the 15 h.p. was without an engine, but the beautiful finish of the Royce products was there for all to see and the demonstration car was kept busy giving the motoring press and public a foretaste of what the name Rolls-Royce was to signify. For the agreement between the two companies, though not actually signed until December 23rd, had been modified since the first tentative discussions to include a clause stipulating that the cars should be called 'Rolls-Royce'.

This was a stroke of genius in which one detects the hand of Johnson. The name 'Royce' alone meant nothing to the motor world, but Rolls stood shoulder to shoulder with such famous pioneers as Camille Jenatzy, René de Knyff, Charles Jarrott, S. F. Edge, Fernand Charron and other notabilities. Also it is demonstrably true that double-barrelled names have always been associated with the finest products of the motor industry; names like Panhard et Levassor, De Dion et Bouton, Sheffield-Simplex, Delaunay-Belleville, Hispano-Suiza and many more spring instantly to mind.

Apart from the change of name three major differences are to be discerned between the 10 h.p. Royces and the 10 h.p. Rolls-Royces. In the first place much more attention to external finish was given on the production cars than on the prototypes. Royce was never given to lavishing unnecessary spit-and-polish on externals, and the fine appearance of Rolls-Royce machinery is inherent in its design and construction, in marked contrast to some early car engines which concealed poor design and rough workmanship of essentials beneath a lavish display of burnished brass and copper or elaborately 'snailed' aluminium housings. But Royce was business-man enough to appreciate how the lay public are always seduced by external appearances and the production models were given a greater degree of effulgence than their predecessors. The second change was of much greater importance and involved completely redesigning the crankshaft and its bolted-on balance weights.

The third change was the most significant as far as the public were concerned for the famous 'Grecian' radiator, in rather embryonic form, replaced the more commonplace cooler of the Royce cars after 20150 and 20151, the first two production cars. In anticipation of the formal agreement the complete 10 h.p. car made ready for the Salon had been adorned with a Rolls-Royce radiator and name.

There is a theory that the classic radiator outline was derived from an obscure make of car called the Norfolk which was made by Blackburn and Co., textile machine manufacturers, of Cleckheaton. Towards the end of 1903 very large orders for looms for South America decided this concern to give up the car business as factory space could no longer be spared for it, and, it is said, that some of their redundant car workers were taken on by Royce and Co. and passed on to their new employers the plan of the Norfolk radiator. Despite the air of improbability of this tale, which Rolls-Royce Ltd. neither confirm nor deny, it is undeniable that the surviving Norfolk motor car has a radiator which strongly resembles the shape made famous by Rolls-Royce. The chief difference is one of detail, in that the Norfolk's filler cap is surmounted by an affair like the lantern of a lighthouse in which a fountain plays to indicate that the water pump is working, and it took a man of Royce's artistic sensibility to apply the ancient principle of entasis which entails making the apparently flat surfaces slightly convex. This optical trick is necessary in order to deceive the human eye which, at a slight distance, 'sees' flat surfaces as being slightly concave.

The formal agreement provided for immediate production of four types: the 10 h.p. twin cylinder, of which a first batch of twenty was put in hand at once, a 3-cylinder 15, h.p., a 4-cylinder 20 h.p. and a 6-cylinder of 30 h.p. Production was to be simplified by the fact that cylinder dimensions and general layout were practically the same on all four models, and many of the major components such as cylinder blocks (except for the 3-cylinder), pistons, connecting-rods, valves, etc., were the same for all. The 2-cylinder engines had the cylinder bores increased to 100 mm, and these larger dimensions were given to most of the 20 h.p. engines and to all the 3-cylinder and 6-cylinder ones.

For many years, except for some two-stroke units and certain diesel engines, 3-cylinder engines struck an odd note, but there was a considerable vogue for them *c.* 1905–7. With

35

Rolls and Johnson before the start of the Paris–Boulogne Race, organised by the Automobile Club de France, in 1898.

the cranks angled at 120° they were free from the inherent harmonic vibration of the 4-cylinder engine whilst giving almost the same regularity of torque, and, as the crankshafts could be kept short and stiff, the torsional vibration which bedevilled so many early 6-cylinder engines could also be avoided. Although only six 3-cylinder Rolls-Royce cars were made, they were quite successful and the engines were notably lively and willing. It is often said that they were unsatisfactory and were consequently withdrawn. This seems to be argument from the wrong premises. They were discontinued partly because it could already be seen that the problems associated with 4- and 6-cylinder engines were on the way to being solved and that, in consequence, there would only be a limited future for the 3-cylinder; a more cogent reason was that they did not fit into the pattern of production which presented headaches enough in the tiny factory. Two of the 'paired' cylinder blocks served for the 20 h.p. engine, and three could be coupled on a common crankcase to make up the 30 h.p. 6-cylinder unit, but the 3-cylinder engine, which had separate cylinders, was odd man out. Also, despite its freedom from some of the problems of the 4- and 6-cylinder engines, it cannot be denied that the 3-cylinder posed special problems in balancing. Royce overcame this, as far as possible, by the use of a carefully balanced crankshaft, but on the evidence of the surviving 3-cylinder car it is clear that he had good reason to feel that there was room for improvement.

The 4-cylinder models were ready for the market almost as soon as the first production twins, and one was shown at Olympia in February 1905. Although the name was not given until later this was the 'Heavy Twenty', heavy only by comparison with the Tourist Trophy type 'Light Twenty' which was evolved from it; but it was certainly an exceptionally sturdy and rigid chassis by the standards of 1905 as Rolls had realised many buyers would choose to have lofty and heavy closed bodies. Many of the early closed bodies, though very well made as a rule, soon gave trouble with loosened joints and rattling doors or windows because the typically 'whippy' chassis of the time were not rigid enough to protect them from twisting strains. Also they were often quite unnecessarily massive and designed with insufficient forethought so that it was necessary to drill holes or attach brackets at most unsuitable points on the chassis. Both Rolls and Royce realised the importance of avoiding these faults and the Rolls-Royce policy of imposing stringent specifications on their coachbuilders stems from this period.

The Rolls-Royce prices in 1905 (chassis only) were: 2-cylinder 10 h.p., £395; 3-cylinder 15 h.p., £500; 4-cylinder 20 h.p., £650 and the 6-cylinder 30 h.p., £890. To these figures must be added the cost of bodywork, lamps, tools and so on which ranged from about £80 for the simplest 2-seater to some £500 for the most luxurious enclosed coachwork for a large

Rolls-Royce 1905 10 h.p. 2-cylinder SU13 Chassis No. 20165.

chassis. It is often said that Rolls-Royce cars were much more expensive than their contemporaries from the start, but this is not true. The 10 h.p. Decauville on which the Royce had been based was admittedly much cheaper at £360 for the complete 2-seater but many comparable cars were about the same price or dearer. For instance, the smallest model of Panhard, the 7 h.p. 2-cylinder, cost £360 for the chassis without tyres; that very antiquated and lethargic machine the 2-cylinder 10 h.p. M.M.C. cost the same as the Rolls-Royce, whilst the two models of 2-cylinder Renault (both rated at 10 h.p. and very similar in specification and performance to the R-R.) cost £380 for the smaller and £410 for the larger chassis. In the 3-cylinder class a 15 h.p. Belsize chassis cost £495 a 15 h.p. Panhard cost £460 (without tyres) but the 16 h.p. Dürkopp was £50 more than the Rolls-Royce. In the 4-cylinder class most comparable cars were dearer: both the Panhard and the Daimler chassis of similar specification were £100 more at £750 apiece. The 6-cylinder models showed the same trend in that the cheapest 6-cylinder Napier chassis cost £1,050 and the 40 h.p. Spyker, complete with open body but without lamps or tools, was no less than £1,600.

During the spring and summer of 1905 Rolls and Johnson had no difficulty in selling all the cars which came from the Cooke Street works. As the specifications in Part Two show production was very small; indeed it could not be otherwise considering the limited space and resources of the factory. It says much for Royce's organising ability that production was not even less, for the cars were only a side-line and cranes' electric motors, dynamos, 2- and 4-cylinder cars, the first of the 6-cylinder models and a number of experimental cars all competed for workshop space, and fitters' time, under Royce's hand and eye. The Rolls-Royce method of close scrutiny of every component of every chassis was already firmly established.

Similarly, the Rolls-Royce was still only a side-line for Rolls and Johnson who continued to sell Minervas and Panhards (the latter were dropped later in the year), and who furthermore added another make to their list. This was the New Orleans, a well-made and attractive light car made at Twickenham by Messrs. Burford and Van Toll who had started, in 1899, by building a Belgian voiturette called the Vivinus under licence. Their American-sounding name for the English Vivinus was inspired by the address of their factory in Orleans Road.

Though only a newcomer, and a fairly puny one by comparison with such well-established British makes as Napier, Lanchester, Wolseley and Argyll, the Rolls-Royce was warmly praised by all who owned or drove in one, and it clearly deserved to be better known. Then as now there was no better form of advertisement than to win distinction in racing and Rolls prevailed upon Royce to prepare two specially lightened and modified 20 h.p. cars for him to enter in the Tourist Trophy Race to be held in the Isle of Man in September, 1905.

* * *

The first real motor race in the world had taken place on 11–13 June 1895; it was organised by the Automobile Club de France over the formidable distance of 732 miles from Paris to Bordeaux and back, and it was a triumph for Emile Levassor who drove the

4-cylinder 20 h.p. Rolls-Royce; 40 were produced in 1905–6. The body is by Barker and Company.

whole distance himself in a 4 h.p. 2-cylinder car of his own design. With only brief intervals, he remained at the tiller for the entire period of $48^3/_4$ hours, averaging 15 m.p.h. and outdistancing the next car home, a Peugeot, by nearly six hours.

From this point onward the sport of motor racing quickly grew in popularity and importance. The first cars to compete were practically indistinguishable from those their makers hoped to sell to the public but inevitably the rival competing manufacturers evolved special machines powered by special engines, and the first, and most obvious, expedient in the search for more speed was merely to fit larger and larger engines. The niceties of engine design in general, and metallurgy in particular, were not advanced enough to produce machines capable of developing more than about 4 or 5 h.p. per litre, but it was easy enough to make bigger and bigger motor-cars propelled by ever larger and more monstrous engines. The Automobile Club de France realised the situation was getting out of hand and tried to curb the spawning of monsters by imposing a weight limit of 1,000 kg. in 1902. This praiseworthy attempt failed at first as the manufacturers merely exercised their ingenuity in constructing even bigger engines, of the least possible weight, and placing them in chassis of such tenuous proportions that the 1,000 kg. limit was not exceeded. This process resulted in the folly, the splendid folly, of the 13 litre, 4-cylinder, 70 h.p. Panhard of 1902 and similar fleet but frail and frightening machines.

Road racing in England was impossible: it was so far beyond the wildest flights of imagination that Authority would grant permission that, in fact, Authority was never asked. The speed limit of 12 m.p.h. was commonly exceeded after 1900 and the Motor Car Act of 1903 grudgingly increased the figure to 20 m.p.h., but the new limit was much more rigorously enforced. Speed contests had to take the form of one-car-at-a-time sprints over short distances on private roads: these were of little interest to anybody but the participants.

In 1902 S. F. Edge won the Gordon Bennett Trophy for England by virtue of being the sole survivor with his 30 h.p. Napier. The French regarded the contest as of minor importance and another win for France as a certainty; consequently the Gordon Bennett Race was run concurrently with the year's big event, the Paris–Vienna Race (in which, incidentally, Rolls drove a 60 h.p. Mors), and only four of the 137 competitors in the main event were competing for the Gordon Bennett Trophy. The relatively small Napier was, naturally, slower than the 70 h.p. Panhard, the 60 h.p. C.G.V. and the 60 h.p. Mors driven by the other Gordon Bennett competitors but it was much better able to withstand pounding over rough Austrian roads, and consequently when the final-drive-pinion of de Knyff's Panhard broke 30 miles from the finish (the Mors and the C.G.V. having failed earlier), Edge had only to drive gently on to Innsbruck in order to win. This he had no difficulty in doing – unless one has sufficient credulity to accept the legend (which first became current some twenty years after the event) that he and his mechanic were obliged to change all four tyres with their bare hands, having lost their tools and jack during the descent of the Arlberg.

The outcome of this victory was that the English regulating body, the Automobile Club, was obliged under the rules to arrange the 1903 Gordon Bennett event. The English club determined, if possible, that the affair should take place on British territory and eventually a special Act of Parliament was passed which allowed roads to be closed and the race to be run in a sparsely populated part of Ireland. This left the club the necessity of finding a course on which to run the Eliminating Trials and this, in turn, led to the interesting discovery that it was possible to close roads and race motorcars in the Isle of Man without fuss of any kind. That happy island, having its own legislature, could do as it pleased and it pleased the Manxmen to do anything to bring trade to their island.

The Eliminating Trials held there in 1903–5 were so successful that the Automobile Club decided to stage a full-scale race in the Isle of Man. They were not, however, in the least interested in a competition for 90 m.p.h., 100 h.p. monsters in the Continental tradition, but were concerned to find a formula which could help improve the breed of ordinary touring cars. Prototypes would be allowed, but they were to be of ordinary touring type and were not to weigh less than 1,300 or more than 1,600 lb. Full scale 4/5 seater touring bodies were to be fitted and, in addition to the driver and mechanic, ballast of equivalent weight to two adults was required. In order to prevent any crafty manufacturer from concealing an engine of gargantuan proportions beneath an innocuous exterior only a limited amount of fuel was to be allowed.

As soon as the race was announced and the conditions were outlined Rolls determined that this event would give just the opportunity needed for the Rolls-Royce to prove itself before the public; his entry was the first to be received by the Club and Royce and his leading craftsmen busied themselves in preparing two 20 h.p. cars for the race. It is a measure of the relative unimportance of the Rolls-Royce at this stage that Charles Rolls also entered a 16 h.p. Minerva for the Tourist Trophy; this incidentally had the same arrangement of overdrive fourth speed as the Rolls-Royce.

By the time he had the Tourist Trophy cars in hand Royce had begun using nickel steel for chassis and axle forgings. This innovation, not adopted outside England for some while, allowed considerable weight-saving and no special means were needed to keep well below the prescribed maximum. Though both engines were perfectly standard (apart from more-than-ordinarily careful testing and tuning) it was decided to provide one with the smaller bore cylinders, 95 mm against the usual 100 mm: the stroke remained unaltered at 127 mm. The decision to use the slightly smaller engine for one entrant was taken because the exact petrol allowance to be granted was not made known until very late in the day, and it was feared the larger engine might disqualify itself by having too great a thirst.

The major differences between the T.T. cars and their predecessors lay in the gearboxes which had four speeds instead of the three previously used. But the fourth speed was a geared-up overdrive and the direct drive remained on the third speed. This was done in the interest of fuel economy and not to provide a higher maximum speed, but the geared-up fourth was given the charming, if slightly misleading, title of 'the sprinting gear'. It was by no means the first time such an arrangement had been used and, indeed, many early cars were so high geared anyway that the top speed, whether direct or indirect, could only be 'thrown in' on a dead level or downhill road. Colonel Siddeley laid claim to anticipating Royce in the combination of a direct-drive third and overdrive fourth, and in their entry for the 1905 T.T. the Vauxhall Company went a stage further and provided a 2-speed final drive which, in effect, gave the driver a choice of six ratios. Unfortunately they had no opportunity to demonstrate the merit of this device as entanglement with a tree put the Vauxhall out of the race in the second lap.

The Automobile Club had announced that the amount of petrol allowed would be '. . . determined by the Club according to the nature of the course selected and the conditions of the road surface on the day of the Race'. This was not very helpful, and only slightly more enlightening was the further proviso that the permitted fuel consumption would be '. . . equivalent to the allowance of one gallon of petroleum spirit for every 25 miles of dry average road – the term "average road" signifying a course similar to the road from London to Oxford, via Uxbridge, High Wycombe and Stokenchurch'. The equation of this well-surfaced and not very hilly 'dry average road' with the rough mountain roads in the Isle of Man, where it is generally wet, was left to the ingenuity of the competitors, and the club's final decision on the actual petrol allowance was not disclosed until the day before the race.

In May Rolls took a Grey Ghost over to the Isle of Man, as a TT car was not ready, to make sure the gear ratios were suited to the job, and a petrol consumption test was carried out on the London–Oxford road. The result of this showed that even the larger-engined car ran $27\frac{1}{2}$ miles to a gallon of fuel on this 'dry average road' and this was thought to provide a sufficient margin for the more strenuous work to come. In the event the allowance was finally fixed at $22\frac{1}{2}$ m.p.g. so the margin erred on the side of safety. Both cars were given a 500-mile non-stop reliability test.

The Tourist Trophy type of Rolls-Royce, of which about fifty were built, is considered to be the finest thing Royce did before the Silver Ghost. It has been compared with the contemporary 18/28 h.p. Mercedes which had a slightly larger engine (100×130 mm) in a very similar chassis, but those who have had the good fortune to drive both find the balance comes down hard on the Rolls-Royce side. The Mercedes has fractionally the better performance in terms of outright speed and scores high marks (as all Mercedes did, and do) for its admirable gear-change: the early Rolls-Royce, though good, was not as easy as some largely because of Royce's cautious insistence on 'latching-in' each speed by a notch in the gate. But on all other counts the Rolls-Royce scores handsomely; despite its overhead inlet valves the engine is very much quieter than the T-head side-valve Mercedes which emits mangle-like growlings and clankings from its exposed straight-toothed timing wheels. The Rolls-Royce, though slightly slower, would probably come out best in average speed over a given distance as its steering and road-holding are beyond praise, whereas the Mercedes steering is somewhat lacking in precision and delicacy.

The Mercedes was a chain-driven car with a 'dead' rear axle, and the advocates of chain drive, quite rightly, claimed the system reduced the unsprung weight by comparison with a live axle; theoretically therefore it made for better road-holding and less tyre wear to offset the disadvantages of noise and rapid wear. But the live axle on the Rolls-Royce was admirably light, the casing being largely made of aluminium, and it was located by a tubular triangulated torque arm, in the Renault manner, which relieved the springs of all driving and braking torque. The rear springing was of the kind known as 'platform suspension' in which the normal longitudinal semi-elliptic springs were shackled at their rearward ends, not to the chassis in the usual way, but to a third inverted semi-elliptic spring running transversely across the back of the frame, to which it was attached at its highest point. This system was extremely popular at that time as it relieved the rear part of the chassis of twisting strains at the expense, on some examples, of a tendency to roll at speed. This drawback was avoided in the Rolls-Royce by the expedient of attaching the axle not at the central points of the side springs, but midway between centre and rear extremity, so that the part of the spring aft of the axle was relatively inflexible and tended to act as an anti-roll member. Though present-day motor pundits sneer at what they are pleased to miscall 'cart springs' the Rolls-Royce system worked admirably.

The competitors and their staffs, together with officials, journalists and onlookers began to assemble in the Isle of Man about a week before race-day, 14 September, and in addition to the two competing cars a 30 h.p. 6-cylinder Rolls-Royce was brought over by Claude Johnson for the race officials to use. The 20 h.p. cars aroused interest but no great enthusiasm as it was generally thought that their silence and docility could hardly be compatible with the 'guts' needed to put up any great speed. When Rolls covered a practice lap of the rough and hilly 52 miles circuit (which rose to 1,350 feet above the starting point) at an average speed of 33 m.p.h. and 26 m.p.g. the *cognoscenti* began to hedge their bets.

The 54 entries, reduced to 42 by the usual crop of non-starters, included single-, twin-and 3-cylinder cars though the 4-cylinder type predominated. There were no 6-cylinder models, even Napiers being content with a 4-cylinder 18 h.p., for the excellent reason that no 6-cylinder cars then made were capable of so small a fuel consumption as the regulations specified. The two Arrol-Johnstons were particularly favoured, and in *The Magic of a Name**these are described as 'brand new 2-cylinder jobs with rakish lines and wire wheels'. The matter was not quite as simple as that, for although the Arrol-Johnston engine certainly had but two cylinders it also had four pistons as its makers had been exponents of the opposed-piston principle since 1898. The cylinders were horizontally disposed, one behind the other, and set transversely across the frame and each contained two pistons working outwardly from a common combustion chamber in the centre. Each piston was coupled by a short connecting rod to the top of a rocking lever from the lower end of which another, longer, connecting rod gave motion to the crankshaft which lay below the cylinders. This arrangement was known as the 'Scotch motion' and it was revived in recent years with great success for a highspeed Diesel lorry engine; it provided good mechanical balance, high thermal efficiency, and allowed the advantage of a long stroke without the disadvantage of high piston speed. With its automatic inlet valves, low-tension ignition, and hit-and-miss governor the Arrol-Johnston engine may have seemed old-fashioned but it was undeniably efficient and of well-proven stamina. The designer, John Napier, allied the old engine with an admirably light but rigid chassis, a four-speed gearbox and a live back axle. Opinion may have been slightly biased in favour of this unconventional car as only a few months before an opposed-piston Gobron-Brillié car, of 110 h.p., had been the first car ever to exceed 100 m.p.h.

*   *   *

The Club's officials waited until the last day before the race to announce their decision on the actual amount of petrol to be allowed. Had the 25 m.p.g. figure been adhered to, each car would have been allowed 8.34 gallons for the 208½ miles, but the Club decided the difference between the London–Oxford road and the Isle of Man Circuit warranted allowing each car 9¼ gallons, which increased the permitted consumption to 22.54 m.p.g. Understandably enough, the competitors were aggrieved that this had not been announced earlier.

There was a certain amount of bickering on other points too. The regulations called for suitable drain taps to the tanks, pipes and carburettors so that all fuel systems could be completely drained before the permitted 9¼ gallons were poured in by an official and the filler cap sealed. It was also specified that the vent pipe or hole in the tank cap (or elsewhere) should not be more than $\frac{1}{32}$in in diameter so as to preclude any dishonest competitors from surreptitiously pouring in more fuel through the vent: this was fair enough but, at first, the officials insisted that all cars must have vented petrol systems which, of course, was nonsense for those makes which relied upon pressure-fed systems.

The Magic of a Name, by Harold Nockolds, G. T. Foulis & Co. Ltd., n.d. (1938).

The checking and filling of tanks and weighing the cars (chassis and bodies separately, bodies had to be attached with no more than six bolts), the competing drivers and mechanics, and the ballast was a tedious business which occupied most of the day. No weighbridge was available and the cars had to be weighed on an ingenious but makeshift contrivance rigged up for the purpose. This came in for some fairly scathing comment and it does, indeed, appear to have been as capricious in action as its operator was high-handed in manner to those who ventured to question its accuracy. There was some tittle-tattle, apparently unjustified, about concealed petrol supplies, double-bottomed tanks and so on, and many of the competing cars were criticised for the way in which they had been ruthlessly lightened in order to scrape through the maximum weight limit. It was hardly proper, observed *The Autocar*, to describe as a standard chassis something which consisted largely of holes. Some cars even had bits of rag tied over the hubs in lieu of the proper brass caps and at least one had a cardboard bonnet. No such expedients were needed for the Rolls-Royce, nor is it conceivable that Royce would have allowed them.

The race started punctually at nine o'clock on the 14th. All the cars were towed by horses to the starting line, to conserve petrol, and pushed off downhill one at a time at one-minute intervals. Rolls had been allocated No. 1 (chassis No. 26358) and was therefore first away, followed by two Napiers, two Speedwells and two New Orleans which, though privately entered, had been supplied by Rolls and Co. The slightly smaller-engined Rolls-Royce, carrying No. 22 (chassis No. 26357), started in seventeenth place driven by Percy Northey who was soon to become famous as the leading official Rolls-Royce driver and demonstrator; at this period, however, he was still described as an amateur. The two Arrol-Johnstons were last away, in forty-first and forty-second places, numbered 53 and 54 respectively. John Napier, their designer, drove No. 53.

In the very first lap of its first race Rolls-Royce No. 1 went out of action. This occurred, according to *The Motor*, when Rolls had 'only just got past the railway and there stopped. He had tried to get his third speed in, and could not, so he tried his fourth, and coming back again to the third, there was A CRACK, AND THE GEARS HAD PARTED, putting him out of the race in the first mile'.

With or without the capital letters, which *The Motor* was then apt to sprinkle about in unexpected places, this was an irretrievable disaster, and there have been a great number of theories, including the suggestion of sabotage, to account for it. The simplest explanation is probably the correct one. In the early days of the governed engine it was accepted practice to coast down hills with the gear engaged but the clutch held out*; by 1905, though governed engines were going out of fashion and the merits of throttle control and engine braking were beginning to be appreciated, old habits died hard and most drivers still 'flew' their hills. This was certainly done, in order to save petrol, by the majority of the T.T. competitors, Rolls included, who not only declutched but also put the gears into neutral in order to reduce internal friction in the gearbox whilst coasting. It also appears that his

* On the majority of early cars, particularly those originally based on the Panhard et Levassor, the brakes and clutch were interconnected: it was possible to declutch without braking, but impossible to brake without declutching.

engine was switched off while the car was coasting and, naturally enough, re-engaging gears with a dead engine and no synchromesh can only safely be done at a walking pace. In the excitement of the race even so fine a driver as Rolls could become impatient and try to mesh a revolving gear wheel with a stationary one at too high a speed. That the engine *was* stationary we know from Rolls's own account. The suggestion of sabotage arose when the first hasty examination revealed some chewed-up nuts, which could not be accounted for, amongst the debris in the gearbox, but full investigation showed that these had come from one of the smashed gear wheels which had been bolted to a flanged sliding sleeve. Despite this, the allegations of sabotage have been repeated from time to time; this seems unnecessarily hard upon the motoring fraternity which has certainly never been free from chicanery but which, surely, did not stoop quite as low as that.

With Rolls out of the race (accompanied, it may be said, by more than half the field before the affair was done), Rolls-Royce hopes were transferred to Northey on No. 22 which was doing splendidly, running a very close second, on time, to John Napier on the Arrol-Johnston. Indeed, on the third lap Northey was seen to have made best time of the day at 1 hour 31 min. 41 sec., which equalled 34.1 mph., and as he was first home in the fourth and final circuit a quick calculation of the lap times seemed to indicate him as the winner. When the aggregate times were finally calculated, however, it was found that the order was:

1st.   John S. Napier (Arrol-Johnston). Average speed 33.9 m.p.h.
2nd.   Percy Northey (Rolls-Royce). Average speed 33.7 m.p.h.
3rd.   Norman Littlejohn (Vinot et Deguingand). Average speed 33.3 m.p.h.

The second Arrol-Johnston came in fourth, which made it a day of triumph for the old-established firm with its unconventional engine, but Northey's win of second place was a relatively greater triumph for the new and little-known Rolls-Royce, particularly as the margin was so honourably small – though it might have been a little greater if Napier had not been obliged to stop to re-fix a loosened silencer just before the finish. The Rolls-Royce made, therefore, the fastest non-stop run.

The final test was to see how much petrol was left in the tanks and, again, the order was Arrol-Johnston first with 8.3 pints, and Rolls-Royce second with 6.8 pints.

Although an outright win had eluded them, everybody concerned with the Rolls-Royce cars was justifiably pleased with the result which, really, was of greater importance in the history of Rolls-Royce than appears at first sight. Without this near-victory it is extremely likely that Rolls-Royce cars would have continued to occupy a minor place in Johnson's mind, but as it was he immediately busied himself with exploiting the success in every possible way, and the fine performance of the 20 h.p. undoubtedly caused the partners to move the newcomer to first place in their estimation. This in turn led to its occupying the only place.

At the beginning of the year, when the T.T. entries were preparing, one A. H. Briggs, an astute Yorkshire business-man who was a friend of Johnson's and himself the happy owner of one of the first twenties, had pointed out the dangers of diversifying and the importance of concentrating on one, or at most, two, of the best makes. After the race he raised the matter again and suggested a closer connection between Rolls and Co. and Royce Ltd.; the partners needed little persuasion to see the force of his arguments. They had, in any event, already dropped the Panhard-Levassor (for which they were only sub-agents), and during the spring of 1906 the New Orleans, Minerva and other concessions were sold and, under the guidance of Mr. Briggs, a new company known as Rolls-Royce Ltd. was registered on 16 March with a capital of £60,000. Claremont became chairman, de Looze was secretary, and the directors were Rolls, Royce, Johnson and Briggs. C. S. Rolls and Co. ceased to exist but the new company only took over the motor-car business from Royce Ltd., which, as electrical equipment makers, remained a separate entity until it was wound up soon after Henry Royce's death in 1933.

The year 1906 was of outstanding importance to the new marque. It saw the formation of the Company, which meant that Rolls and Johnson (particularly the latter) gave all their time and talents to Rolls-Royce affairs; it saw a Rolls-Royce win the second Tourist Trophy Race and it saw the birth of the Silver Ghost.

But before leaving the events of 1905 the following appreciation of the 20 h.p. car Northey drove in the race is worth quoting. It was written ten months after the event by Henry Swindley, owner of *The Autocar*, who bought the car soon after the race. He wrote:

'With the exception of grinding one exhaust valve the engine has been untouched, always excepting periodical scraping of the deposit from the piston heads and combustion chamber walls . . . this job is a mere trifle . . . With but one exception, and that due to lack of acquaintance with the idiosyncrasies of the ignition system, the writer has never heard the engine misfire . . . The remarkable sweetness of the clutch provokes the driver to regard himself as a very artist in clutch manipulation. Of the flexibility of the engine too much cannot be said; so perfectly does it pull away at any speed that the third, direct, speed can be retained during a long drive through the maziest intricacies of London traffic . . . But it is the human-like manner in which the car obeys the slightest variation of the throttle-pedal which endears the little carriage to anyone who cares for and delights in the refinement of driving. With the pedal alone one can almost make the car play cat's-cradle.'

3

Brief Flirtation with Folly

THE logical development of the Rolls-Royce, from the 10 h.p. twin, via the 20 and 30 h.p. models, to the Silver Ghost could be taken as a continuous process were it not for the intrusion of a 'sport', in the biological sense, which had little commercial significance but which cannot be ignored.

Soon after the 1905 Tourist Trophy Race Claude Johnson arranged a dinner party at the Trocadero in honour of Northey and Royce. Many prominent motorists were invited as well as representatives of the trade and the press. and after presentation of silver cigar boxes, congratulatory speeches, and toast-drinkings Johnson announced that earlier in the year he had asked Royce to design a luxury town car which should have all the advantages of an electric carriage with none of its drawbacks. The requirements were that it was to be driven by a petrol engine but that the engine was to be completely unobtrusive and as far removed from the passenger space as possible; it was to provide plenty of room and yet have a short wheelbase, to make for manœuvrability in traffic, consequently it was to be 'bonnetless'; finally it was to be noiseless, odourless, vibrationless and smokeless and able to run from 3 m.p.h. to 20 m.p.h. on its top gear. After this introduction Henry Royce rose and described how he had fulfilled these requirements.

It has often been said that this bonnetless town carriage was a unique conception of Royce's but this is complete nonsense, although the way in which he tackled the job showed great originality and ingenuity. A number of the leading firms of the period listed bonnetless cars, usually fitted with landaulet or brougham bodies, which outwardly resembled the fashionable electric carriages; indeed the Napier Company, Rolls-Royce's most formidable rival in their early years, had announced their new motor brougham a few weeks earlier. Such well-known makers as Argyll, Minerva, Standard, Austin and Singer also trod the cul-de-sac of the petrol-brougham, and the plan most generally adopted was to use a normal, vertical engine, placed rather further back in the chassis than usual so that steering column and controls could be brought right to the front of the car with the driver's seat above the engine casing.

Understandably enough, this arrangement was not without certain snags, of which the inconvenient height of the driver's seat, inaccessibility of the engine, and intrusion of noise and fumes into the rear compartment were not least. On some examples, the Argyll for instance, the great length of the gear-levers which the lay-out necessitated, made gear changing a more than ordinarily difficult business – particularly as the hapless chauffeur of an Argyll was apt to receive a sharp rap over the knuckles from the heavy brass gear-lever knob dithering wildly on the end of its five-foot stalk.

A fairly large and extremely vocal minority of motorists and manufacturers in England had always denounced the Continental style and deplored the 'ugly motor bonnet', and such firms as N.E.C., and James and Browne were staunch adherents to the horizontal engine which lent itself more readily than the vertical to being hidden away under the floor

The V-8 engine (incomplete) designed for the bonnetless town-carriages and Legalimits.

of a bonnetless car, but despite the validity of their arguments it soon became apparent that the minority could not convert the majority, and the demand for bonnetless cars was small and short-lived. The Lanchesters, as ever, provided an exception to this general rule for the Lanchester cars, though certainly bonnetless, were in a class apart from the hybrid petrol-broughams or landaulets; but in general it was seen that those who wanted an electric carriage would buy (or, more generally, hire) an electric carriage not a petrol car in disguise, whilst those who wanted a petrol car wanted it to look like a petrol car. And the longer the bonnet the better. This attitude of mind led to the absurdity of horizontal-engined cars like the Cadillac, the Oldsmobile, the Adams-Hewitt and many more being furnished with imposing bonnets which served only as repositories for a tool-box or the chauffeur's secret hoard of bottled beer.

Royce's ingenious solution of the problem lay in the use of a V-formation 8-cylinder engine which was so shallow and compact that it could be placed below the floor, on the nearside of the frame with the steering-gear, pedal cross-shafts and gear change mechanism conveniently placed beside it. Accessibility, merely by lifting the floor, was better than on many conventional cars and the great flexibility of the engine, coupled with a low-geared back axle, made the car almost independent of its three-speed gearbox. In order to abolish the then-prevalent plume of blue smoke Royce adopted full-scale pressure lubrication in place of the drip-feed and splash system he had hitherto used. Although Lanchester and one or two other manufacturers had already led the way with lubricating under pressure through a hollow crankshaft, the majority clung to the drip-feed system, with all its hazards, for a number of years. Consequently most motorists learnt the hard way that the dividing line between excessive and insufficient oiling was very finely drawn, erred on the side of safety, and laid a nauseous smokescreen behind them.

There was, of course, nothing new in the V-shaped engine, as the famous Daimler V-twin had powered all Panhard and Peugeot cars from 1891 to 1895; Emile Mors had used an advanced V-4 engine in 1897 and a remarkable V-12 unit for motor boats was marketed by Craig Dorwald in 1904. There was also the Adams Eight, which appeared at about the same time as Royce's design, which had a V-8 engine based upon the Antoinette used by Santos-Dumont in his airship. But Royce's V-8 was so neat and compact, with such admirably planned accessories, that it might well have been designed in 1930 rather than 1905.

One use for the bonnets of early motor-cars might well have been to accommodate the swarms of bees hatched by the self-styled experts of the period. For reasons which do not stand much examination most 'experts' thought it essential for the valves of a petrol engine to be vertical, and horizontal or inclined engines with the valve-stems likewise horizontal or inclined were condemned out of hand no matter how well they worked. Though Royce was not the sort of man to be swayed by ill-digested theorising it will be seen that though the cylinders of the V-8 were necessarily inclined (at 90 degrees) the valves were, indeed, vertical. Although this necessitated having two camshafts it made possible a very clean run for the exhausts and short, smoothly contoured valve ports. A separate trembler coil and distributor served each bank of cylinders, with the two distributor rotors superimposed in a common housing and driven by a vertical shaft from the train of timing wheels at the front of the engine. With the V-8 Royce broke away from the obsolete 'main bearing lower-halves attached to crankcase' structure; the cranks were angled at 180° which, in conjunction with evenly spaced power impulses, must have resulted in a severe transverse couple.

With its well-planned porting, short and rigid crankshaft and admirable carburation this short-stroke 8-cylinder engine (83 mm bore and stroke) fulfilled the requirements of smooth, silent and flexible operation. It suffered, as all new designs do, from teething troubles, principally it seems to have thrown oil on to its sparking plugs, but it was a lively engine capable of better things than the humdrum task of competing with the electric vehicle. One other task was, in fact, assigned to it but this was even more of an *ignis fatuus* than the town carriage.

This task was to propel a car of outwardly conventional appearance which was branded with the unhappy title of the 'Legalimit'. This was primarily intended for the owner driver and was so geared as to be incapable of exceeding the legal speed limit of 20 m.p.h. (though, a high-geared version capable of 26 m.p.h. was listed in the 1906 catalogue, but none of these was made). With its engine conventionally placed and covered by a low, wide bonnet of admirable proportions the only 'Legalimit' known to have been finished (to the order of

Sir Alfred Harmsworth* who allowed the company to exhibit it at the Motor Show) was as handsome as it was silent and flexible; but it soon became clear that there would be little demand for an expensive and potentially sprightly 8-cylinder car which could never show its paces. This despite the protestations of an unco' guid minority of motorists who wrote to the motoring press from time to time to advocate fitting cars with devices which would compel their weaker brethren to abide by the letter of the law.

Even if the arrival of the Silver Ghost in the following year, and the adoption of a one-model policy, had not put a stop to the V-8 cars before they were fairly started lack of demand would have brought about their demise fairly soon. The 'Legalimit' was doomed from the start, whilst the experiences of other manufacturers soon showed that the bonnetless town-carriage style of car was no more than an uneasy and uneconomic compromise. In 'invisible engine' or 'visible' form the V-8 cars represent one of the few occasions when Claude Johnson's commercial acumen was at fault. Technically they were of great interest and constructionally they can fairly be described by D. B. Tubbs's aphorism of: 'Rolls-Royce . . . even their mistakes are beautifully made.'

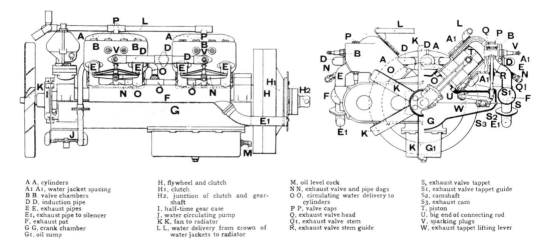

A A, cylinders	H, flywheel and clutch	M, oil level cock	S, exhaust valve tappet
A1 A1, water jacket spacing	H1, clutch	N N, exhaust valve and pipe dogs	S1, exhaust valve tappet guide
B B, valve chambers	H2, junction of clutch and gear-shaft	O O, circulating water delivery to cylinders	S2, camshaft
D D, induction pipe	I, half-time gear case	P P, valve caps	S3, exhaust cam
E E, exhaust pipes	J, water circulating pump	Q, exhaust valve head	T, piston
E1, exhaust pipe to silencer	K K, fan to radiator	Q1, exhaust valve stem	U, big end of connecting rod
F, exhaust pot	L L, water delivery from crown of water jackets to radiator	R, exhaust valve stem guide	V, sparking plugs
G G, crank chamber			W, exhaust tappet lifting lever
G1, oil sump			

The V-8 engine.

* *The Hyphen in Rolls-Royce* by W. J. Oldham, G. T. Foulis & Co Ltd, 1967. George Clegg's comment on this was 'No Noise, no smell, no fumes and no speed.' Henry Fleck drove it for Harmsworth, but it was never photographed.

4

Rolls-Royce: a New Model and a New Factory

The great motor topic of the period when the Rolls-Royce was beginning to make its way in the world was the 'battle of the cylinders'. This battle was in reality an affair of shadow boxing carried on by S. F. Edge, the doughty and vociferous, but not always scrupulous, *eminence grise* of the Napier Company, who had been the most active and successful (though not, as Edge claimed, the first) exponents of the 6-cylinder motor-car which had first been marketed late in 1903.

At this distance of time it is difficult to say whether the pro- or anti-6-cylinder partisans were the more ridiculous in their assertions, but the controversy certainly added spice to the pages of the motor journals and the contending parties, in the main, appear to have enjoyed pricking each other's bubbles; though, as one plaintively observed, it was hard to venture an opinion if Mr. Edge was immediately going to demand the deposit of £1,000 with the Automobile Club as stake money in some wager or contest so ingeniously framed that the Napier was bound to win. One clear fact which does emerge from the fog of verbiage is that, disregarding the technical pros and cons, the richer section of the English motor fraternity valued silence and flexibility above all else. As the six-in-line engine could be made to score on these points by comparison with a 4-cylinder engine of comparable power the manufacturers who wished to cater for the 'carriage trade' were constrained to produce 6-cylinder models.

Though the first 6-cylinder cars were warmly praised for their flexibility and freedom from vibration a critic today would find them rough and coarse. They certainly possessed good torque at low speed (a quality also beginning to be given to the contemporary 4-cylinder engines by improvements in carburation, ignition and gas-distribution), but the silky-smoothness of running now associated with the 6-cylinder type eluded them.

Various factors contributed to this: to avoid unevenly cooled cylinders, which led to distortion and cracking, it was usual for them to be cast singly or in pairs, consequently the early 6-cylinder engines were very long. A long engine necessarily has a long crankshaft and the majority of them were, to the modern eye, alarmingly tenuous and 'whippy'. In order to keep rubbing-speeds low, so that splash lubrication would suffice, the crank-pins and journals were very long but of very small diameter by modern standards; with the large flywheels of the period one can visualise these long, frail, shafts winding and unwinding like the elastic of a toy aeroplane. Finally, the 6-cylinder engine was at first conceived as three 2-cylinder units coupled, with the crank throws usually angled at 180° throughout the length of the shaft, though a few were tried with 60° crank angles. Torsional vibration and the risk of broken shafts were inherent in engines built on these lines.

The advocates of the six-in-line engine, S. F. Edge in particular, argued that the overlapping impulses of the six cylinders solved all the drawbacks of roughness, vibration and inflexibility associated with the petrol engine: this view was too optimistic, as engineers soon discovered. Every crankshaft and flywheel assembly, as was well known, has a natural frequency of torsional vibration; this is irrespective of the number of crank throws or cylinders but only an in-line 6-cylinder engine has the additional complication of a disturbing torque due to the motion of the pistons which follow an almost pure sine wave of considerable size. When this disturbing torque, oscillating three times per revolution, reaches the point of resonance, which it does when the rotational speed of the engine is one-third of the natural frequency of the shaft, something has to happen. And what usually happens is that the engine goes to smash and scatteration, as Mark Twain said in another context, if it is allowed to run at this critical speed for more than a few seconds. Before the nature of the problem was fully understood the many broken shafts on early 6-cylinder engines were usually attributed to faulty material. Apart from the possibility of damping the oscillations by some means (which at best is only a partial, though important, palliative) the usual solution lies in designing the crankshaft so that its natural frequency, and therefore its critical speed, lies outside the normal r.p.m. range of the engine; a matter which is much more easily said than done.

It would be agreeable for the historian to record that Henry Royce avoided these stumbling blocks with his first 6-cylinder cars, but truth must prevail and the 30 h.p. Rolls-Royces of 1905–6 were, relatively, less successful than the 4-cylinder 20 h.p. models. Royce himself was dissatisfied with them, and he and his assistants threw themselves energetically into the search for improvement. Confirmation that the 30 h.p. model was not free from crankshaft vibration came from that great Rolls-Royce expert and collector, Stanley Sears, who restored to running order the only known survivor of the thirty-seven which were made.

Claude Johnson had been anxious to have a 6-cylinder model on the market as soon as possible because he and Rolls clearly saw where fashion was heading. The chassis of the 30 h.p. model was virtually the same as that of the original 20 h.p. type, which, by 1906, was called the 'Heavy Twenty' to distinguish it from the T.T. or 'Light Twenty' model; following the Tourist Trophy success the overdrive fourth speed was fitted to all the 4- and 6-cylinder cars. The 30 h.p. engine, as we have seen, was based upon the use of components which were common to the 2- and 4-cylinder engines. Allowing for slightly different bore dimensions therefore the cylinder blocks, pistons and connecting-rods were common to all three types, and consequently the journal and crank-pin dimensions of the 30 h.p. engine were the same as those of the 2-cylinder 10 h.p. though the crankshaft itself was more than three times as long. In accordance with the usual practice of the day the shaft was carried in seven main bearings which mitigated, to a large extent, the evils of its nature. It did not take an engineer of Royce's calibre long to realise that though it was logical and satisfactory to make a 4-cylinder engine by pairing a couple of twins it was fundamentally unsound to carry the process further. He saw that a brace of triplets could more easily live in harmony than a trio of twins.

The outcome of Royce's experiments and observations on 6-cylinder engines during 1905 was the development of a much larger unit, of 114 mm bore and stroke, which was conceived as two 3-cylinder engines, using two cylinder blocks with the cranks placed at 120° instead of 180°. This lay-out is not, as it is sometimes described, two 3-cylinder engines coupled in line, but in reality, two such units coupled front to back: that is, the third and fourth crank pins (and pistons) rise and fall together.

This is the crank arrangement now almost universal for 6-cylinder-in-line engines and though it does not solve the torsional vibration problem (which is, indeed, insoluble) it is the one which allows the best possible combination of expedients to raise the critical speed of the shaft. Although antedated by Lanchester, and, indeed, by the Wolseley Company who had built a prodigious marine engine to this plan in 1904, Royce's adoption of this form of crankshaft, coupled with the other outstanding qualities of his new engine, marked a new phase in the development of the motor-car.

The diameters of the crank-pins and journals were almost double those of the earlier 6-cylinder engine, and the increase in peripheral speed which this entailed was catered for by a full-pressure lubrication system similar to that used on the V-eights. During his experiments Royce had observed that the 'rocking couple' takes effect principally in the centre and at the extremities of a long crankshaft, and extra long bearings were provided at these points. The shaft was extraordinarily massive and rigid by the standards of 1906 and made most of its contemporaries look like mangled fence-wire.

In most other aspects the engine design conformed to the practice of the time. That is, the cylinder heads were not detachable and the overhead inlet valves were given up in favour of the newly fashionable L-head side-valve arrangement. The tappet-ends valve stems, guides, and springs were not enclosed; even in 1906 this was a trifle old fashioned but Royce maintained that most manufacturers enclosed the valve motion only to keep the noise at bay, and that properly designed and finished valve gear should be able to suffer exposure in silence. As with his earlier engines the tappets were adjustable: it may seem extraordinary, today, to have to remark upon this but, incredible though it may seem, the only way of adjusting valve clearances on the majority of contemporary engines was by brazing bits on to the valve stems, or grinding bits off.

The carburettor was similar in principle to that of the earlier cars and, as always with a Royce design, the manifolding, porting and exhaust-run were very carefully planned. As on the later 4-cylinder models the ignition was duplicated with the synchronised trembler coil system reinforced by an H.T. Eisemann magneto. Each ignition had its own sparking plugs, and the firm recommended using both together, for starting and slow running in traffic, but in order to conserve the accumulators it was usual to switch the coil ignition off when running normally.

In outward appearances the new Rolls-Royce engine was less advanced than, say, the clean-cut Hermes designed by Ettore Bugatti at about the same time. It was also less 'interesting' than, say, the contemporary Lanchester with its horizontal overhead valves closed by flat blade springs. Also the output of the engine, 48 h.p. at 1,250 r.p.m., was nothing out of the ordinary. Consequently many critics and writers during the last fifty years have gleefully repeated L. H. Pomeroy senior's gibe of 'a triumph of workmanship over design'. Another typically splenetic remark, often heard, was 'Ah yes, wonderful car – if you can afford to use thirty horse power to silence the fifteen which do the work'. Sneers such as these are easily made but are quite beside the point. Royce never claimed to be an inventive man, or to have developed anything particularly new in engine design; nor was he trying to build a racing car or to extract the greatest possible output from a given capacity. He was concerned to design a motor-car of better-than-average performance which should be as robust, trouble-free, long-lived, economical, smooth-running and silent as human ingenuity could make it. In this he succeeded brilliantly.

The new engine was allied to a chassis very similar to that of the 30 h.p. model but larger, stronger and with many detail improvements. The leather-faced cone clutch, four-speed gearbox with the direct drive on third, bevel-geared back axle, and the platform rear-suspension were all much as before, suitably scaled-up for the extra work they had to do. A minor difference was that the back axle was attached nearer to the centre point of the rear longitudinal springs, and frictional rebound-dampers of Royce's own design were used both front and back. A typical example of the designer's passion for improving details lay in the arrangement for compensating the pull on the back-wheel brakes (side brakes in the language of the day), for in place of the usual adequate but untidy whippletree device, was a complete miniature differential gear coupling the two halves of a divided brake cross-shaft, the whole thing neatly encased in a beautifully finished aluminium housing.

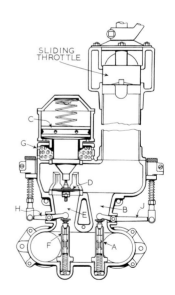

Rolls-Royce carburettor for the 40/50 h.p. engine.

One of the great merits of the 40/50 Rolls-Royce was its uncanny flexibility, even better than that of its predecessors, which derived largely from its near-perfect carburation. The original Royce carburettor was an improved version of the Krebs (one of the first successful semi-automatic car-burettors, designed by Commandant Krebs, a director of Panhard et Levassor), which depended upon a suction-operated extra-air inlet valve to balance the mixture when depression in the inlet tract was at maximum with the engine running fast, but lightly loaded, with the throttle partly closed. On engine speed falling under increased load, but with the throttle opened wider, the induction vacuum would be lessened whereupon the extra-air valve would tend to close, thereby enriching the mixture. Though rather crude

* The first few 40/50 h.p. cars had single-jet carburettors of the original Royce type.

the Krebs was an improvement upon most early carburettors which relied upon manual control of the extra-air supply, and in his adaptation of the principle Royce had greatly improved upon the original design by meticulous fit and finish of the moving parts, and by careful design of the gas-passages to ensure unimpeded flow.

Good though the early Royce carburettor was, it was not flexible enough to cope automatically with a very wide r.p.m. range, by present-day standards, and the redesigned instrument for the 40/50 engine was, as the drawing on p. 54 shows, a double jet* affair with the smaller jet and choke tube calibrated to provide a sufficient gas flow for slow running, balanced as before by the automatic extra-air valve; at higher speeds and loads the larger jet came into action. A hand control on the dashboard provided for enriching or weakening the supply from both jets to provide for cold starting or variations brought about by changes of altitude or fuel density.

The arrangement worked to a nicety; not only was the 40/50 Rolls-Royce exceptionally economical by the standards of its day, but it was able to accelerate smoothly from 3 to 60 m.p.h. in top gear without hesitation or spluttering. By contrast other leading manufacturers were seeking to provide automatic carburation by empirical means which ranged from the ingenious but complicated hydraulic control used by Napier to the absurd and inefficient 'single lever' system adopted by Daimler at about this time. The 'single lever' in question was mounted on the steering column and Daimler cars had no foot throttle; moving the lever simultaneously opened the throttle, admitted extra air and advanced the ignition. This was well enough for accelerating away under fairly light load but was very wasteful when ticking over in traffic or running down hill with the throttle nearly shut, and wholly left out of account the occasions when an engine calls for full throttle but retarded spark and enriched mixture.

A minor function of the accelerator pedal on the 40/50 Rolls-Royce, on the last third of its travel, was to open a valve to allow a supply of oil to be fed direct from the pump to the cylinder walls. The whole lubricating system was very carefully designed; the only trifling fault a modern eye could discern was that the only way of checking the oil level in the sump was by means of a try-cock at the side of the crank chamber. Curiously enough very many early cars were not even furnished with level plugs or try-cocks, and the simple but much maligned dip stick did not materialise until about 1912, therefore there was no way for the driver to determine whether he had enough oil in his engine. In a series of Hints and Tips written in 1905, Lieut. Windham, a well-known pioneer motorist, advocated draining out the oil into a tin, and carefully measuring the amount, on first collecting a new car from the works as, he said, 'The makers, as a rule, know how much should be used'. The words 'as a rule' add a nice touch and say all that needs to be said. Despite Lieut. Windham's good advice, however, by far the commonest practice was merely to pour or pump oil into the engine until a nauseous smoke screen advised the motorist that although he might expect oiled-up sparking plugs, choked silencer, and heavily carboned combustion chambers he was reasonably secure from seized bearings. The later 40/50 engines were given neat float-operated level indicators in place of the rather messy try-cocks.

By superhuman efforts the Cooke Street works managed to finish two of the new 40/50 h.p. machines in time for the Motor Show at the end of 1906; one was a stripped and polished chassis and the other was a Pullman-bodied limousine. They created the usual amount of interest provoked by any new model, but the full impact of Royce's achievement was not felt until press and public were able to see, hear and savour the new model in action. Once this was done, early in 1907, it was apparent that the new Rolls-Royce was as much in advance of all existing 6-cylinder cars, including its 30 h.p. forebear, as the original 2-cylinder Royce had been of the old Decauville.

*   *   *

Quite apart from designing the new model Henry Royce had been busier than ever during 1906. Following the 1905 T.T. success, orders for Rolls-Royce cars had steadily increased, experimental work and training his picked team occupied enough time for any ordinary man, but there were in addition such trifles as pouncing upon, stripping and examining components or even complete chassis during assembly, testing and tuning completed cars picked at random, supervising the electrical machinery business, and, to crown it all, the little task of planning the design and layout of a new factory.

It had been apparent for a long while that the Cooke Street works were bursting out at the elbows and Johnson knew very well what happened to thriving little motor firms who fell too far behind in their deliveries. He and Royce were both agreed that a move was essential and that the new site must be big enough to allow for expansion. Most of the business of finding a suitable site fell to Claude Johnson and many places were investigated; finally the choice lay between Leicester and Derby which were both equally suitable as far as space, communication and nearness to the chief sources of materials and components were concerned. A judicious offer of cheap electrical power by the Derby Corporation decided the matter and a site of $12^2/_3$ acres was bought. Here, Royce's part in the affair started in earnest (though he had shown himself a shrewd judge of land values), and much of the actual design of the factory buildings, as well as the planning of their interior economy, was done by him.

The cost of this expansion was met by increasing the nominal capital to £200,000 and by making the concern a public company. On 11 December 1906 subscriptions were invited for preferred and ordinary shares to the value of £100,000. Although the Rolls-Royce car had earned a splendid reputation in two years it was still a newcomer, and the company was a pygmy alongside Napier, Panhard et Levassor, Mercedes and similar big concerns; also many investors had had their fingers badly burnt after the motor boom of 1901–2 when far too many unstable companies had been floated. The Rolls-Royce flotation very nearly failed. The minimum subscription had been set at £50,000 and when the due date was near the figure had reached only £41,000 and the flow of subscriptions had almost stopped. Under the terms of the issue it appeared that the flotation must be abandoned and the subscriptions returned, but John de Looze tried a last chance. He took a train to Harrogate and put the problem to Mr. Briggs, knowing that he was not only a

56

director of Rolls-Royce and an enthusiastic Rolls-Royce driver but one of the richest, as well as one of the shrewdest, businessmen in Yorkshire. Arthur Briggs unhesitatingly agreed to take £10,000 worth of shares himself and by so doing he saved Rolls-Royce Ltd. from the embarrassment, indeed the disaster, of under-subscription.

The prospectus provided for the following appointments: F. H. Royce as chief engineer and works director at £1,250 a year plus 4% of the annual profits after the first £10,000; the Hon. C. S. Rolls as technical managing director at £750 and 4% of the surplus profits; C. G. Johnson as commercial managing director on the same scale as Rolls, and E.A. Claremont as chairman at £250 a year and 2% of the surplus profits. John de Looze remained secretary, and one of the first new shareholders was the erstwhile apprentice, Platford, who invested ten pounds – or perhaps one should say sovereigns when writing of that high and far off time when Britons clinked gold coins in their pockets.

The birth of the new model 40/50, not yet christened 'Silver Ghost', gave point and purpose to these developments.

*   *   *

Since the autumn of 1905 Rolls and Johnson had taken every opportunity to put the Rolls-Royce in the public eye. Johnson had contrived to get a full-page advertisement in *The Autocar* on the day after the T.T. Race (and elsewhere soon after) in which with considerable cunning, he made the point that the Rolls-Royce, driven by an amateur, '. . . beat all other cars having vertical cylinders'. But indirect advertisement was better and

Claude Johnson at the wheel of a 30 h.p. 6-cylinder, 1906.

cheaper than announcements of this sort, and one of Rolls' most impressive demonstrations of the Light Twenty's versatility was to steal the record in May 1906 for the Monte Carlo–London journey set up by Charles Jarrott a year earlier.

Jarrott had done this in a specially prepared 40 h.p. Crossley, and had said afterwards that he did not think his time could be equalled by any ordinary touring car. Whereupon in an ordinary touring car of half the rated horse-power Rolls showed him how wrong he was despite running into a blinding storm, losing the route more than once, and suffering a delay of 3 hours 11 min. on the quay at Boulogne. The chief part of the trip, from Monte Carlo to Boulogne (771 miles), was made at an average speed of 27.3 m.p.h. against the Crossley's 24.2 m.p.h. This amounted to a gain of 3 hours 21 min. over Jarrott, nearly all of which was lost in the delay of waiting for the boat; Jarrott had had no delay. Further time was lost after leaving Dover as Rolls took a wrong turning but insisted on continuing against the advice of his navigator, H. Massac Buist. The result was that the 20 h.p. Rolls-Royce beat the 40 h.p. Crossley by only a minute and a half; but the smaller car had gained $3^{1}/_{2}$ hours over the larger on the most testing part of the run.

Claude Johnson himself did not often take part in competition work, though he was a fine and sensitive driver, and while Rolls was chiefly concerned with the sporting proclivities of the Light Twenty, with which he competed at hill climbs and trials of various kinds, Johnson put in good work demonstrating the virtues of his particular love, the 30 h.p. 6-cylinder model. Consequently he found himself embroiled in the 'battle of the cylinders' which led to his accepting a challenge made by Captain H. P. P. Deasy, who was then engaged in making a series of extremely meritorious observed runs in that fine car the 30-40 h.p. 4-cylinder Martini, a Swiss make for which Deasy was then concessionaire.

Deasy's challenge was for a reliability and performance competition between his 4-cylinder and a 6-cylinder of equal capacity, and it was arranged that he and Johnson should each enter a car for the Scottish Reliability Trials, which were fairly formidable, and that in addition to the 671 miles of the Trial itself the journey to and from Scotland should be taken into account and should be made under the scrutiny of Automobile Club observers who would award points for speed, hill-climbing, fuel consumption, reliability and the number of gear-changes required. The relative silence and freedom from vibration were to be judged by a committee of members of the Stock Exchange. At first sight this seems a little odd until one reflects that, in the intervals of exchanging improper stories and broking stock, stockbrokers are apt to be very good judges of quality whether in wine or women, mouse-traps or motor-cars.

The outcome was most satisfactory for Johnson and the 30 h.p. Rolls-Royce. Though beaten for speed on some of the hills by a small margin the Rolls-Royce won the battle of the cylinders by 396 points: in fairness it must be said that the Martini lost 390 points through a simple, but exasperating, failure of the petrol pressure feed system. However, reliability was one of the points at issue. The only adjustment the Rolls-Royce needed was to the foot-brake which was a matter of 40 sec., and *The Autocar* observed of the Scottish Trial itself: 'The only 6-cylinder car to complete the course without a stop was the Rolls-Royce which ran very quietly and perfectly throughout.' The only adverse criticism came from a 'Mr. Jackson' who wrote to *The Autocar* to point out how unfavourably the Rolls' consumption of 11.63 m.p.g. compared with the Martini's 13.98. Johnson replied that the disappointing figure was because his carburettor had been out of adjustment, and that he did not risk altering it for fear of making it worse. He added that if Mr. Jackson could establish his bona fides as a private motorist and was not, as he suspected, a member of a rival firm, he would be happy to demonstrate that a 30 h.p. Rolls-Royce, complete with closed body, could cover any 100-mile course at 16 mpg. There was no reply.

As soon as any particular make of car begins to do well there are, and always have been, a host of acidulous critics ready to leap up and say that some contest was not fair, or that if so-and-so had happened, or not happened, the such-and-such would have done better. This type of criticism was levelled at the Rolls-Royce soon after the 1905 T.T. when it was said that the 'sprinting gear' was only an expedient to save fuel and was positively a disadvantage for the ordinary driver as it entailed raising the other gear ratios to such a degree that the car could not possibly start on a steep hill with its full load. The 20 h.p. car was certainly very high geared, delightfully so, but this criticism did not take into account the amazing low-speed torque of the engine which resulted from its excellent carburation; enough weight was, however, attached to the matter for the 1906 T.T. regulation to include a rule requiring each car to be driven over a level half mile at 12 m.p.h., or less, on its direct drive, and then to stop and restart with full load on a 1-in-6 gradient. Rolls and Johnson sprang joyfully on this as soon as it was announced, and the two 1905 T.T. cars were taken to the Mall early one morning and there driven over a half mile, under the scrutiny of Automobile Club officials, at 9.04 and 8.31 m.p.h. respectively. With the gear-ratios and tyre sizes employed this meant that the engine of the slower car was pulling at only 180 r.p.m. The cars were then taken to Jasper Road, Sydenham, which provided the necessary 1-in-6 gradient and Johnson made a stop and restart with nine passengers clinging on by their fingernails and eyebrows. Nothing more was heard about Rolls-Royces being unable to start on steep hills.

In addition to this new 'low-speed' test the 1906 T.T. regulations abolished the maximum chassis-weight condition and stipulated a definite 25 m.p.g. limit early in the proceedings. Once again, two Rolls-Royce cars were entered, to be driven by Rolls and Northey, and this year both had engines of 100 mm (4 in.) bore and wire wheels were used in place of the wood-spoked artillery type of the previous year. Two Arrol-Johnstons were again entered, indeed they seem to have been the actual 1905 cars, but one was too badly damaged in practice to compete.

The preliminaries of the race went forward without a hitch, and the weighing and petrol-measuring arrangements were much better than in 1905. The 'half-mile at 12 m.p.h.' part of the business demonstrated very clearly that few engines were capable of pulling at so low a speed as the Rolls without protest. *The Autocar* reported: ' . . . it really was very painful to see the visitors to Douglas watching the unfortunate cars as they were forced along with their engines knocking . . . many of the spectators did not understand that all the cars could run delightfully at 12 m.p.h. on their low speeds, and must have regarded them as the most shameful collection of noisy, jerky machines they had ever seen.' Even as late

Claude Johnson about to re-start 26358 on the 1-in-6 gradient of Jasper Road, Sydenham, 1906.

as 1906 the petrol engine, generally, was an intractable beast when asked to run slowly, and the astute Mr. Coleman, English concessionaire for the White steam cars, scored heavily on this occasion. Debarred from competing in the race itself as they could not hope to run 25 miles on a gallon of fuel, Mr. Coleman had placed a small fleet of his steamers at the Club's disposal for officials to use, and their silent effortless progress when shepherding the competitors through their slow running test was applauded by the crowd.

The first lap of the race was a sort of mirror image of the 1905 event, with Northey out of the running with a broken front spring, and Rolls, carrying No. 4, leading Napier's Arrol-Johnston by a short head on time. In the second lap Napier lost an hour and eighteen minutes through tyre troubles – two punctures, one nipped tube and one burst – as a result of which Rolls felt justified in dropping his speed slightly so as to conserve petrol and keep something in reserve. In spite of running on a flat tyre for almost the whole circuit Napier managed to cover his final lap at 40.2 m.p.h. which was exactly the same speed as Rolls' first lap; it was, furthermore, the fastest lap time in the race. Final results were:

1st.   C. S. Rolls (Rolls-Royce). Average speed 39.3 m.p.h.
2nd.   P. Bablot (Berliet). Average speed 35.4 m.p.h.
3rd.   A. Lee Guinness (Darracq). Average speed 34.2 m.p.h.

The gallant Arrol-Johnston scored an honourable seventh place at 30 m.p.h. Its actual running time was 4 hours 4 min. 1 sec., or almost two minutes *less* than the Rolls-Royce, but had the Arrol-Johnston not dropped so far behind Rolls would not have lowered his speed.

It was entirely characteristic of Charles Rolls that his reply to a message of congratulation from Harry Swindley of *The Autocar* was, 'I would like to thank *The Autocar* for its congratulations, but as I had nothing to do but sit there and wait until the car got to the finish the credit is obviously due to Mr. Royce the designer and builder.'

In October, while Royce and Johnson were busying themselves about the new factory, Rolls introduced the *marque* to America by taking Northey's T.T. car to compete in the 5-mile race for cars under 25 h.p. at the Empire City Track in New York. This was won by the Rolls-Royce, and when the event was over Rolls gave demonstration runs to members of the American trade and press. He also visited some of the American factories and made arrangements with a Mr. Martin to represent Rolls-Royce Ltd. in the States.

On his return to England he gave a press interview during which he praised some aspects of American design, but criticised some other aspects: in particular, he said the American industry did not do enough to fill the gap between the horizontal-engined runabouts, which were of admitted excellence but limited in performance and obsolete in design, and vast, fuel-hungry 4-cylinder cars. This remark angered E. R. Thomas, of Thomas Flier fame, who promptly offered to match his 60 h.p. 4-cylinder machine against the Rolls-Royce in a race from New York to Chicago and back. As he stipulated that this should take place within thirty days, knowing quite well that there was no Rolls-Royce car available in the States at that time, Rolls declined the challenge, but expressed his willingness to take part in a suitable competition in which reliability, flexibility, silence and fuel consumption should be taken into account as well as speed. He concluded with a hint that Mr. Thomas might take part in the next T.T. contest, but charitably refrained from pointing out that the renowned Thomas Flier was an American-built copy of the French Brasier.

1906 Tourist Trophy Race. Rolls' winning car during practice.

Rolls-Royce Light Twenty trophy car at Florida Beach.

5

The Silver Ghost Triumphant

———◆●◆———

Iɴ the two years since making its first bow at the Paris Salon the Rolls-Royce had come a long way, and 1907 opened with work advancing well on the new factory, orders coming in faster than they could be met (including some from America), and a new model on the stocks which was destined to raise the make head and shoulders above all competitors.

As soon as the 40/50 model had been rigorously tested it was obvious to Claude Johnson that this was *the* car, and he set about proving it in typically Johnsonian fashion. The chassis he took for the purpose (the twelfth made, No. 60551) was fitted with a 4/5 seater touring body, painted with aluminium paint and adorned with silver-plated lamps and fittings. A handsome silver-plated cast brass plate on the dash carried the name 'Silver Ghost', and with this first Silver Ghost Johnson set out to demonstrate that a quiet car need not be slow, and that a fast and luxurious carriage could set a standard of reliability (and consequently economy) that was quite beyond the reach of most of its contemporaries.

The first step was to make a 2,000 miles run under R.A.C. observation (the Automobile Club had acquired the prefix Royal shortly before) early in May. After the run the principal parts of the car were examined by the R.A.C. and the 2,000 miles included the course of the forthcoming Scottish Reliability Trial; it also had the flavour of a pleasure trip about it for the Silver Ghost was accompanied by Frederick Coleman on a 30 h.p. White steamer, and the R.A.C. observers were hard put to it to choose between Coleman and Johnson as ideal companions either in the car or at the dinner table.

Complete with four occupants and equipment the Silver Ghost weighed $39\frac{1}{4}$ cwt. With 880×120 mm tyres the gear speeds at 1,000 r.p.m. were: first, 13 m.p.h.; second, 22 m.p.h.; third, 38 m.p.h.; overdrive fourth, 47 m.p.h. Petrol consumption worked out at 20.86 m.p.g. on the London–Glasgow road, and 17.8 m.p.g. for the whole 2,000 miles, which included some very heavy going in Scotland. The journey from Bexhill to Glasgow was made throughout on the overdrive and third speeds, and on the direct drive the car showed itself capable of accelerating from 3.4 m.p.h. to 53 m.p.h. without any trace of jerk or snatch. At the end of the trip the R.A.C. officials were only able to find a trace of wear in the planet pins of the differential gear and slight movement of the piston rings in their grooves. But all this was little more than a preliminary canter, for it was proposed that the car should be entered for the Scottish Trials and then should be driven on a set route, still under scrutiny, between Glasgow and London night and day (Sundays excepted) until 15,000 miles had been covered, whereupon it was to be completely dismantled and every part examined and measured so as to ascertain the amount of wear, and expense, the private owner might expect after the equivalent, then, of three years' use.

It is often thought that this long-distance trial was a complete novelty but this is not so, for similar trials had been held before and only a few weeks earlier a 40 h.p. Siddeley (or Wolseley Siddeley – the names were indiscriminately used) had completed a 10,000 miles trial, and a 6-cylinder 50 h.p. Hotchkiss was actually running a somewhat similar test, at the same time as the Rolls-Royce, which ultimately extended to over 20,000 miles – though not without a fairly large number of involuntary stops. It is probably because the R.A.C. observers on the Hotchkiss just could not stomach the thought of being shuttled back and forth like the Flying Dutchman for all time that the limit for these tests was set at 15,000 miles shortly after this affair had at last drawn to a close. It is also sometimes said that the official observation and recording of all repairs and adjustments was a mere formality which failed to record many quite major operations. This, too, is untrue and S. C. H. Davis*, who took part in many such affairs, writes:

'They were not popular, these observers, mainly because they seemed to possess superhuman knowledge of competitors' tricks. For example we were on official test to prove that a Sheffield-Simplex could travel from Land's End to John o' Groat's using top gear only. Every single thing which had to be adjusted en route was recorded. Now, the brakes needed adjustment, a fact which we preferred should remain secret. So we suggested the car should be washed and cleaned. By cleaning vigorously around the hand adjustment of the brake rods, under cover of a large rag, we were able to give the adjustment a good twiddle. That the observer sitting on a box at the other side of the car could see this was incredible. Judge therefore our fury when the observer's sheet for the day's run contained the simple sentence . . . "brakes adjusted".'

The 'novelty' of the Silver Ghost's trial lay in its greater severity and outstanding results. The only involuntary stop occurred at the 629th mile, during the Scottish Trial (in which the car won a gold medal), when the petrol tap, being a little too loose, shook itself into the closed position causing a delay of one minute. There was a certain amount of magneto trouble but as the engine had dual ignition no involuntary stoppage resulted and the magnetos were changed at the scheduled halts; in any event, as the Eisemann magneto was one of the few 'bought out' components, this failure reflected no discredit on Rolls-Royce Ltd. After the Scottish Trial was over the car started on its series of return journeys between Scotland and London, via Glasgow, Edinburgh, Durham, Leeds, Bradford, Huddersfield, Manchester, Newport and Coventry. Johnson, Rolls, Platford and Macready took it in turns to drive and a sister car carrying reporters joined them after the Siddeley's record of 7,089 miles without involuntary stoppage had been broken. On the night of the 8th of August the 15,000th mile was reached when 23 miles north of London on the last homeward run, and the car was duly driven in to the R.A.C. garage to be dismantled.

The non-stop distance stood at 14,371 miles, more than double that of the Siddeley, and when the car was stripped and examined its condition was seen to be truly amazing.

* 'The Memory be Green', by S. C. H. Davis, *The Motorist's Bedside Book*, B. T. Batsford, Ltd., 1962.

Rolls-Royce Silver Ghost with a Barker body in the Pyrenees.

The slight movement of the differential planet pins in their carrier, noted after the 2,000 mile preliminary canter, had grown no worse, the valves were slightly pitted and needed grinding but otherwise the only components in need of attention were as follows:

Replace steering pivot pins – worn 0.005 in. inch.

Refit universal joint in magneto driving shaft.

Replace sphere in pendulum lever of steering arm – worn 0.005 in. inch (ball joint of steering drop-arm in present day terminology).

Refit socket of steering tube.

Replace pin at end of cross steering rod (track-rod).

Repack water pump spindle.

Under ordinary conditions these things could have been left for many more miles, but Claude Johnson ordered them to be seen to so as to bring the car to 'as new' condition, and the cost of the new parts was a derisory £2 2s. 7d. No measurable wear could be found in any of the engine or transmission bearings, or the cylinder bores, and it was a particular triumph that the final-drive bevel gears were still running at the exact depth-tolerance specified in erection and with machining marks still visible on the teeth. This should have silenced, but did not, all those critics who never tired of asserting that the gear-driven live axle was utterly wrong in principle for all but the lightest of runabouts; for the chain-driven Siddeley had carried a spare pair of chains which had been used turn-and-turn about with those on the car, and both pairs of chains, together with the sprocket wheels, were due for renewal at the end of the Siddeley's run.

The theory that the chain-driven car was necessarily lighter on tyres than the shaft and live-axle type was also exploded, for the average tyre life on the Siddeley had worked out at the abysmal figure of 631 miles per tyre against more than 2,500 miles per tyre for the

Silver Ghost Rally.

Silver Ghost on test. Full production did not start until completion of a 15,000-mile trial.

Rolls-Royce. With 920 × 120 mm covers at £10 apiece (of 1907 money) this made the Siddeley's progress an expensive business though, no doubt, the terrible rate of tyre consumption was partly accounted for by the use of a patent anti-puncture preparation called Elastes of which, understandably enough, little more was heard after this essay. The cost of running the Rolls-Royce, including tyres, was calculated by the R.A.C. as $4\frac{1}{2}d$. a mile which made Rolls-Royce travelling about the cheapest luxury on the market.

Two of the new 40/50 h.p. cars had been displayed at the 1906 Motor Show but it was April 1907 before Johnson invited press representatives to a trial run in the Silver Ghost; May saw the preliminary canter of 2,000 observed miles and the famous 15,000 miles trial did not take place until July–August, and it was only after this had been done that production started in earnest at the rate of four chassis a week. So determined were the partners that the car should be as near perfect as possible that the delay was considered unimportant by comparison with the rigorous tests carried out on various components during the early part of the year. Also production of the other models had to be given priority and work was going on the whole time in connection with the new factory.

The 15,000 mile test, naturally, made the best possible advertisement for the new model but neither Rolls nor Johnson was given to resting on his laurels and the Silver Ghost was not the only Rolls-Royce to be kept in the public eye. A 20 h.p., for instance, performed with distinction at the Ormond Beach Races in 1907 and broke the World's five-mile record for cars up to 60 h.p.; it was also awarded the Bronze Statue for the World's International Touring Car Championship – a dignity which would have carried even greater weight had the doyen of Motor Clubs, the Automobile Club de France, afforded it their recognition: but France, as ever, declined to believe that anything which happened outside her shores was of the least importance. A seven-seater 40/50 h.p. Rolls-Royce was also voted the handsomest exhibit at the New York Motor Show in the autumn of 1907.

This car, as well as those exhibited at the London show, had certain minor modifications and improvements by comparison with the prototype, and Royce's meticulous attention to detail resulted in many slight alterations as time went on. In the summer of 1908 a more significant experiment, which indirectly foreshadowed the New Phantom of the 'twenties, was made when cars 707, 726, 737 and 751 were furnished with overhead inlet valve engines of higher compression and greater output than the standard units. These engines developed 70 b.h.p. against the 48 of the production models, but because they did not quite attain Royce's standards of refinement the design was laid aside; though some of the lessons learnt from them doubtless influenced the development of the longer stroke 40/50 h.p. engines which were used after 1909.

Two of the 70 h.p. cars, named White Knave and Silent Rogue, were entered for the International Touring Car Trial. White Knave suffered a broken piston but the other car, driven by Percy Northey, won its class handsomely and made fastest time on Kirkstone Pass and Shap Fell. The last part of the Trial led by a devious route to the newly opened Brooklands Track where each competitor had to cover 200 miles against the watch; a proviso which had provoked some outraged opposition from some would-be competitors who held that touring cars had no business to be subjected to an outright speed contest. By the time he reached the course Northey had so much in hand, on aggregate time, over his rivals that a comparatively leisurely average speed of 53.6 m.p.h. on the track was enough. To demonstrate just how much he had in hand he and Johnson took the two cars to Brooklands again a few weeks later and covered twenty laps, under R.A.C. observation, at 65.9 m.p.h. and 65.84 m.p.h. respectively; speeds which would not be despicable even today. If one disregards the mishap of the broken piston it is clear that the 'seventies', though non-standard, were as durable as every other Rolls-Royce. One covered a great many miles (usually at top speed) carrying a King's Messenger about France during the War until it eventually succumbed to enemy action. After being returned to the works and repaired it was furnished with twin rear wheels and a truck body and served as a works hack until 1920 when, in the characteristic phrase, it was 'reduced to produce'.

The principal events of 1908 for the company were the board meeting on March 13th at which Claude Johnson persuaded his fellow directors to agree to a 'one-model' policy, which had, in reality, been in operation for over a year, and the formal opening of the new factory on July 9th. This function was, naturally enough, attended by most of the notabilities of the motor world and, after a speech by the Hon. C. S. Rolls, a luncheon, more speeches and a tour of the works, Lord Montagu of Beaulieu switched on the current and 'the most perfectly equipped motor works in the kingdom' sprang to life.

Though the importance of the fine new factory, which, clearly, necessitated a vigorous sales policy if it were to pay its way, cannot be denied it was probably of less moment in the development of the company than the 'one-model' policy. Claude Johnson belonged to that rare type of business-man who brings common sense to bear upon common problems, and one of the besetting sins of most manufacturers was not lost upon him. This was the tendency, so often apparent in the early years, of countering competition or declining sales by putting an ever larger variety of models into production. A glance at the fortunes of many once-famous firms shows how few managements realised the self-destruction implicit in this process. Those firms who concentrated upon two or three well-proven types usually did well, but to carry the process to its logical conclusion was a very bold stroke indeed and, at first, Johnson's fellow directors (and Royce himself) had been reluctant to drop the 2- and 4-cylinder models which were doing so well. Consequently a loophole was left and it was announced, at first, that for 1909 the 40/50 would be the only model made. What would follow in later years was left for time to decide.

Although a few other manufacturers of the period, Georges Richard of Unic fame for one, also embarked upon one-model policies the only important maker to cling to the policy with consistency and success equal to that of Rolls-Royce was Henry Ford: there is a curious parallel between the birth dates and life spans of those two famous cars the Silver Ghost Rolls-Royce and the Model T Ford. Catering for vastly different markets each was splendid value in its sphere.

If the production of the Silver Ghost had not been supported by adequate service it would not have succeeded as it did, and the growth of the company's service and repair departments, school for drivers and system of annual inspection, if needed, at the customers' homes were as important as the car itself. Between 1907 and the first German War what are now called customer relations between Rolls-Royce owners and the company were established on that high, almost mystic, plane which has survived the social upheaval of the last half century. The essence is very simple; Rolls-Royce cling firmly to the belief now curiously old fashioned, that their customers are entitled to the best possible value for money.

It must not be thought, however, that Rolls-Royce have ever been servile or grovelling to their clients; indeed, there have, at times, been criticisms of a 'holier-than-thou' attitude. On examination it will usually be found that complaints of this sort originated with splenetic journalists or disgruntled chauffeurs. On the whole the system worked, and works, admirably and one may dismiss as apocryphal the story of the owner of an early Silver Ghost who resisted the company's suggestion, after the annual report had been made by the travelling inspector, that his car should be returned to Derby for the latest modification to be made to some part of the chassis. And he continued to resist, but at last was left without his car, disconsolately writing out one hundred times: 'I must not argue with Rolls-Royce . . .'

A Rolls-Royce was again entered for the 1907 T.T. but was withdrawn, partly because Claude Johnson (and many others) thought the fuel consumption part of the business had outlived its usefulness, partly because Charles Rolls's interest was being increasingly drawn to flying, but principally because everybody concerned was just too busy, and no more 20 h.p. models were being made. Having made their mark, indeed, the Rolls-Royce company did not officially enter cars for pure speed events after 1907 though their Spanish agent won the 1913 Spanish Grand Prix, other forms of public trial and contest were practised, and private entrants for events of various kinds were always able to count on the works for

C. S. Rolls demonstrating the steering lock on a 40/50 Rolls-Royce.

support. On the whole, however, Rolls-Royce Ltd. worked on the 'good wine needs no bush' principle, and direct advertising of any kind was relatively small and unimportant by comparison with the indirect advertising which every Rolls-Royce owner gave them.

As Ian Hallows' specifications show there were a number of minor alterations and improvements made to the Silver Ghost during its long production life, but only three fundamental changes were made which affected the engine, the gearbox and the rear suspension.

Late in 1909 the engine stroke was increased from $4^{1}/_{2}$in. to $4^{3}/_{4}$in.: this increased the capacity from 7,036 c.c. to 7,428 c.c. and raised the output to about 60 b.h.p. With these increases a slight roughness at certain engine speeds became apparent which was attributable to crankshaft vibration, and from 1911 onwards the engines were equipped with the well-known frictional type of torsional vibration damper. This was, at first, mounted externally at the forward end of the crankshaft and was known as the 'slipper flywheel', but after 1912 the damper was enclosed and made part of the timing gear whereupon it was re-christened the 'slipper drive'.

A slight degree of mystery attaches to the genesis of the crankshaft damper, at least as far as Rolls-Royce is concerned. In *Rolls-Royce Memories** Massac Buist wrote of the original 30 h.p. 6-cylinder cars: 'Of course crankshaft vibration was a fault which, though it was generally deemed inevitable, had only to be pondered by Mr. Royce for him to consider it unpardonable. After sleepless nights and several attempts each of which resulted in disappointment he evolved the "slipper flywheel" which was actually standardised on the 30 h.p. 6-cylinder cars which were issued to the public as far back as 1906. . . . This is put on record because some four years later a master patent was granted for a much-discussed crankshaft vibration damper; whereas Mr. Royce had found out that remedy and applied it as a routine part of his factory programme without ever troubling to patent the idea.'

The patent to which Massac Buist refers was granted to Dr. Frederick Lanchester in 1910 covering the damper he had designed the year before in his capacity as consultant to the Daimler Company who were experiencing a great deal of crankshaft trouble with their newly introduced 6-cylinder models. Different varieties of this device were then fitted to Daimler engines and to Lanchester's own 6-cylinder models. With all possible respect to Massac Buist and his *Rolls-Royce Memories* it appears that his own memory, or information, must be at fault, for the 'slipper flywheel' was *not* standardised on the 30 h.p. models although many were the subject of experiments aimed at curing torsional vibration. Certainly the surviving 30 h.p. Rolls-Royce was innocent of any such refinement until Stanley Sears fitted a damper as a palliative for the vibration period from which it undeniably suffered.

According to C. W. Morton*, who has investigated many aspects of Rolls-Royce history with tireless erudition, the crankshaft vibration on the 30 h.p. cars manifested itself chiefly by causing rattle from the timing gears. To cure this, small additional flywheels were fitted to the forward ends of the crankshafts; this reduced the rattle, but by concentrating the torsional effect towards the centres of the shafts it was found that the extra flywheels were apt to induce fatigue fractures. Consequently they were reduced in weight and a reasonable compromise was reached. It was then observed that one car was notably free from timing gear rattle and investigation showed that the small flywheel was slightly loose on its key and that the small amount of radial play allowed it in effect to perform the part of a vibration damper: from his observations and experiments with this Royce evolved his 'slipper flywheel'. The sequel to which was that Frederick Lanchester started negotiations with Rolls-Royce Ltd., and with Royce in particular, claiming priority and insisting on payment of royalty. According to the memories of various employees as examined by Morton (for no written evidence can be found), Royce then had no difficulty in proving that it was a genuine case of great minds thinking alike and that Rolls-Royce cars, fitted with the slipper flywheel, had been in customers' hands before the granting of the Lanchester patent (which could thereby have been upset). Whereupon it was agreed that Rolls-Royce would not claim priority in the invention and Lanchester would not claim royalties.

This story is plausible enough for nothing is commoner in the history of engineering than to find two or more minds producing the same ideas, or similar answers to similar problems, quite independently. On closer view, however, it seems that certain

* *Rolls-Royce Memories*, by H. Massac Buist, privately published, 1926.
* For a more detailed discussion, see *A History of Rolls Royce Motor Cars*, volume 1 by C.W. Morton, G.T. Foulis & Co Ltd.

discrepancies have yet to be explained, because, without further evidence, it is impossible to reconcile the details of C. W. Morton's account with the known dates of the grant of the Lanchester patent and the fitting of 'slipper flywheels' to Rolls-Royce engines. Also, Dr. Lanchester's brother, George, who was in close collaboration with him at the time, stated quite categorically that there were no negotiations between Lanchester and Royce. All of which proves, if proof were needed, that even after three-quarters of a century the exact historical truth is difficult to ascertain in default of reliable contemporary written evidence. Unfortunately Massac Buist's statement that the 30 h.p. cars were fitted with the 'slipper flywheels' has gained wide credence, together with his statement (about the 30 h.p.) 'Moreover, in these cars no crankshaft broke in service', which is misleading as it conceals the fact that some broke on test.

The ghost of torsional vibration has been laid for so long now (or, rather, kept under control), and nowhere more firmly laid than in the 40/50 Rolls-Royce, that Dr. Lanchester's observations are worth repeating. In the Thomas Hawksley Lecture delivered to the Institution of Mechanical Engineers in 1937 Lanchester said:

'The second trouble, which first became noticeable in the six-cylinder engine, was due to torsional crankshaft vibrations: the long six-throw crankshaft could not in practice be made sufficiently stiff, and when any of the applied frequencies due to piston inertia or torque intermittence synchronised with a natural frequency period of the shaft (with its attached masses) "thrashing points" were experienced which were not only intolerable to the occupants of the car but were fatal to the crankshaft itself. A crankshaft put to run at one of its critical speeds fractured after a test of only two hours' duration, although made from a forging of 65-ton steel and normally not carrying a higher stress than 5 or 6 tons per sq. in. in shear, calculated maximum combined stress. When this trouble first arose no one appeared to have any conception of the magnitude of the oscillations set up, which to my knowledge sometimes amounted to as much as 8 degrees. In the first six-cylinder Lanchester car I overcame this difficulty by fitting the flywheel at the front end of the engine instead of at the rear end and employing a well lubricated multi-disk clutch which acted as a damper*. I had to face this problem again in connexion with a firm (Daimler) who had rushed into the production of six-cylinder cars and had a stock of cars on their hands which were not marketable owing to the serious nature of the vibration. It was then that I introduced my vibration damper which took the form of a secondary flywheel at the front of the engine, driven by a multi-disk friction coupling always in action. The application of this invention immediately released something like £20,000 worth of 'frozen assets'. This torsional damper has since become an essential part of the modern multicylinder engine . . . .'

Late in 1909 the 4-speed gearbox with the overdrive fourth gear was replaced by a

---

* The Lanchester engine was 'oversquare' (4in. bore × 3in. stroke) as a further means of reducing torsional vibration.

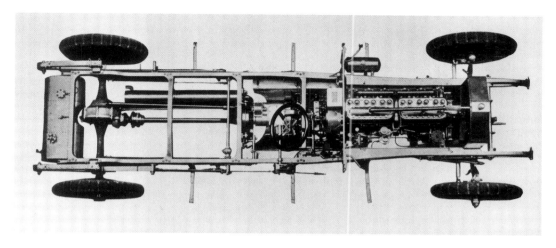

Rolls-Royce Silver Ghost chassis of 1910 in elevation and plan.

normal 3-speed box with the direct drive on the top gear. Several writers have said that this change was made only because the overdrive made a slight humming sound, and as the company could not prevent their customers from using it at low speeds, which made the sound apparent (the extreme flexibility of the engine made this possible), they 'took the overdrive away from them'. Although the present writer supported this theory in the past, further consideration makes it seem probable that although the noise of the 'sprinting gear' was a contributory factor the chief reason for the change lay elsewhere.

From the start of motoring history gear changing was regarded as the chief bugbear by most motorists; even after the adoption of 'synchromesh' it remained the *pons asinorum* for many. In the very early days, when atmospheric inlet valves, hot-tube ignition and the other design features of the period made the motor engine virtually a constant speed affair, controlled only by centrifugal governor the duty of which was merely to prevent the exhaust valves from opening, thereby checking the speed, when r.p.m. rose to a

73

predetermined rate, the most skilful driver could not avoid making ugly noises when changing speed. This was particularly so when changing from a low gear to a higher one as, once declutched, the governed engine tended to accelerate to its permitted maximum. The pioneer drivers looked upon the graunching of maltreated gear wheels as part of the game, grasped the gear lever and gritted their teeth in both senses, and after a season's running, covering 1,500 or 2,000 miles, resigned themselves to the expense of an overhaul which usually included renewing most of the gear wheels. As engines became more flexible and capable of being throttled down, at least to some extent, the business became easier but nevertheless it remained a hazard. There is plenty of evidence to show that the principles of correct gear changing on the normal 'crash' box (the very name is revealing) were not understood, even by expert drivers, for a long while. Although a small minority of drivers discovered the art of 'double-declutching' quite early it did not become a generally practised procedure until the 1920s: and the great majority of drivers never mastered the art at all, but continued to regard a silent and jerk-free gear change as little short of a miracle. From the pages of Massac Buist* we learn that even Charles Rolls could be guilty of a rough gear change.

Therefore a car which could do most of its running on top gear had an immediate sales appeal though, in many instances, maximum speed and fuel consumption were allowed to suffer in the interest of top-gear flexibility. The matter was brought to the fore as early as 1905 when that skilled publicist S. F. Edge had one of his fine 40 h.p. 6-cylinder Napiers driven (by his cousin Cecil) from Brighton to Edinburgh using top gear only. This feat made a great impression on the public though the more knowledgeable were quick to point out that the car was so low geared that its maximum timed speed was only 46 m.p.h. (not an impressive speed for a car of 8 litres capacity), and that to achieve even this speed the engine was turning at some 2,300 r.p.m. This was considered hideously low geared in 1905.

Though the Napier may have been specially geared for the job the fact that it could travel from 5 to 45 m.p.h. on its top gear set other manufacturers on their toes, and for many years 'top gear only' runs from A to B, duly observed by the Automobile Club, were made by cars as diverse as the little twin-cylinder Phoenix and the magnificent 6-cylinder 'gearless' Sheffield-Simplex. The fact that these performances really only proved that a suitably geared clockwork mouse could climb the dome of St. Paul's was entirely lost on the buying public. A minimum of gear changing and a maximum of top-gear running were essential to success in the luxury car market, and the further fact that performances on any car could be immeasurably improved by judicious use of a well-planned gearbox (and the more speeds the better) mattered not at all.

Here, undoubtedly, the Rolls-Royce Company was at a disadvantage as it is obvious from letters and articles in the contemporary motoring press that the combination of 'direct drive third and overdrive fourth speeds' was not understood. If a potential buyer, at motor show or elsewhere, asked 'Will the Rolls-Royce climb so-and-so hill in top gear as the Napier does?', it was useless for the salesman to explain that the Silver Ghost's third gear

* *Rolls-Royce Memories*, by H. Massac Buist, privately published, 1926.

was the equivalent of another car's top gear, as this was quite beyond the understanding of the general public who were only concerned with a straight answer to a straight question. This influenced the company in their decision to abandon the 'sprinting gear' in favour of a conventional 3-speed box with the direct drive on the top gear in the usual way. Although many regretted the 3-speed box, and Rolls-Royce themselves were to have second thoughts after a certain chastening episode, the cars were now able to compete against all comers in top-gear-only runs.

The 3-speed Rolls-Royces of 1909 onwards had first-gear ratios of 7.8:1, 8.3:1 or 8.4:1 according to the type and weight of the body, the three ratios were fairly closely spaced and second gear was sufficiently low for the flexible Ghost engine to start the car on the level, or a moderate gradient, without much difficulty. For many years it was accepted practice amongst owners and chauffeurs to start away in second and to change into top at a walking pace. The awkward change, 'through the gate' from first to second or vice versa, was only necessary in emergency. Although the instruction manual advised using first gear for starting, tacit recognition was given to the fact that the 'through the gate' movement was held in dread by many by the following cautious instruction: 'Should there be any doubts about ascending a steep hill the car should be dropped on to the lowest gear at the *bottom of the hill* rather than the gear changed on the hill.' The italics are theirs.

On the Silver Ghost engine (and, indeed, on the Phantom I and early Phantom II) Royce retained the old-fashioned governor gear; but this was not, as in the early days, to prevent the engine racing when unloaded but was coupled to the throttle so as to keep the engine running at any desired speed, irrespective of load, from the slowest tick-over to half-open throttle. So beautifully was the governor mechanism made that setting its overriding control in any given notch would cause the engine to maintain the speed appropriate to that notch within very narrow limits even after years of use. This absolute certainty of function made the governor a valuable adjunct to foolproof smooth starting from rest, without using the throttle-pedal, and also permitted a special technique of gear changing to be used. Chauffeurs who were sent to the Rolls-Royce school were taught, for instance, to change from top to second not by acquiring sensitivity of ear, hand and foot, but by a purely mechanical system which could be learned by rote. A driver could set the governor lever to a particular point on its sector and then, when the speedometer indicated a certain speed, he could ease the clutch and move the gear lever secure in the knowledge that the engine and clutch shaft would automatically accelerate the precise amount needed to make a smooth and noiseless change. Drivers with the necessary natural skill preferred, perhaps, to keep the governor lever at minimum and to change gear by co-ordination of clutch and throttle-pedal in the usual way; but many private owners, and most paid drivers of the ex-coachman school, appreciated the leisurely but certain governor-controlled method, which could be used by the practised chauffeur to make 'clutchless' gear changes to the mystification of lesser mortals.

For the first few years of the century Napier could justly claim to be England's leading *marque:* part of this supremacy was founded on the tireless publicity, the racing successes and the forceful personality of Selwyn Edge, but it was no mere flash-in-the-pan success and

Edge could not have done what he did with poor material. Though it is easy enough now to deride some of Edge's more questionable assertions and activities there can be no doubt that he played a leading part in putting the English motor industry on its feet; in particular he provided the spur which encouraged Montagu Napier to produce some remarkably fine motor-cars. By 1909 Napier's position was being assailed, and their chief rivals were Rolls-Royce. For silent and vibrationless engines the newcomer had decidedly outstripped the old hand; in appearance, too, the Rolls-Royce scored, for the Napier engines were very long and to give reasonable body space on a reasonable wheelbase the Napier radiators had to be carried far forward of the front axles which gave the cars a sadly lumpish appearance. Top gear flexibility and speed remained Napier's trump cards, and in view of the continual criticism that top gear performance was bought at the expense of other desiderata Edge determined to prove the contrary.

This was done by taking a standard 65 h.p. Napier, slightly hotted up for the occasion, with 2.7:1 final drive ratio, on the usual R.A.C. observed top-gear-only run from London

Silver Ghost 1911–1912 inside the works at Derby.

to Edinburgh; a fuel consumption test was included, and to demonstrate that the car was no sluggard, a timed speed test was made at Brooklands after the car returned from Scotland. The results were impressive: fuel consumption worked out at 19.35 m.p.g. and the maximum speed at 76.42 m.p.h. This was a direct challenge to Claude Johnson who responded by asking the R.A.C. to stage a similar test with a 40/50 Rolls-Royce. This was done and the slightly smaller Rolls-Royce, on an axle ratio of 2.9:1, improved on the

Napier's performance by a respectable margin – fuel consumption, 24.32 m.p.g. and maximum speed 78.26 m.p.h. Sixty years later, this test was commemorated by an RAC-observed Silver Ghost run from London to Edinburgh. The official report stated that for the whole period the car (6051) ran smoothly and gave no trouble whatsoever.

The car with which this was done differed from standard in that cantilever rear suspension was fitted, the bonnet was tapered, the carburettor enlarged and compression ratio raised from 3.2:1 to 3.5:1; these modifications increased the output by about 16%. The London–Edinburgh type of car was then made available to the public and many connoisseurs consider it the best of all the Silver Ghost variants.

The driver of this London–Edinburgh car was E. W. Hives, later Lord Hives, who had joined Royce's team of specialists as a tester in 1908, though he had worked for C. S. Rolls and Co. for a short while in 1903. His name had first come before the public as a Trials driver in 1907 when he drove an Italian car called, in England, the New Junior. From 1908 onwards Lord Hives was closely concerned with the development of Rolls-Royce cars and engines. In 1946 he became managing director of the Company which he nursed through a most difficult period after the second German War. He died in 1965 at the age of 79.

Other triumphs followed the London–Edinburgh run; with a light single-seat body and higher geared back axle an otherwise standard 'L.-E.' type car covered the quarter mile at Brooklands at 101 m.p.h. This was in 1911, in which year also a Silver Ghost won the Empress of Germany's Cup in the Prince Henry Tour. The factory was enlarged, orders came in faster than they could be met, and although Royalty remained faithful to their Daimlers (officially at least; it had not escaped notice that King Edward VII favoured his Mercedes for private occasions and Queen Alexandra remained faithful to her 1906 Renault for nearly twenty years), quasi-Royal approval was given in 1911 when the Indian Government ordered eight Rolls-Royces for King George V and his suite to use at the Delhi Durbar.

The Silver Ghost had climbed to the top of the tree, but what of the men behind it? Here was a sadder tale of illness and death.

In addition to his motoring and business interests Charles Rolls had been a keen aeronaut since the beginning of the century; he had been an eager participant in those long-forgotten balloon races which were as much a part of the Edwardian scene as the Regatta at Henley, polo at Hurlingham or ice-cream at Gunter's. With the coming of heavier-than-air flight he transferred his allegiance to the new-fangled aeroplane which began to take pride of place in his affairs. Not that the fortunes of Rolls-Royce Ltd. were neglected but undoubtedly C. S. Rolls found less satisfaction and thrill in land-bound motors than formerly. In April 1910 he resigned his post as technical managing director of Rolls-Royce Ltd. and became merely technical adviser; but he was to fill this new post for only a short while and on 12 July 1910, whilst taking part in a landing-in-restricted-space contest at Bournemouth in his French-built Wright biplane, he crashed from 80 feet and died almost instantly.

This tragedy was not only a blow to Rolls' family and friends but to the nation. His death helped to harden military opinion against the aeroplane, and 'official' enthusiasm of some kind was essential if heavier-than-air flight was to become more than a pastime.

The aeronauts: Horace Short (with pipe), C. S. Rolls (at wheel) with Orville Wright beside him. Griffith Brewer and Wilbur Wright (facing camera) in the back seat, 1910.

Naturally enough his colleagues at Rolls-Royce Ltd. were shocked and grieved, but his death did not materially affect the company's progress. His enthusiasm, which had done so much for the industry in general and for Rolls-Royce in particular, had been almost entirely transferred to aviation and after he had helped to establish the Silver Ghost's supremacy he had played relatively little part in the business. Some of his enthusiasms may have been misplaced, such as his backing of the Hallé spring wheel and his advocacy of a rather cranky dietary reform movement, but he had nosed out some notable winners in his time and had made many friends in the process. It is true that his notorious parsimony did not pass unnoticed, but on the whole his friends were sufficiently glad to have his company to smile indulgently at his gift for remembering that he had to make a telephone call when it was his turn to buy the drinks.

Far more serious from the company's point of view was the collapse of Henry Royce's health in 1911; years of overwork and odds and ends of indigestible food snatched and gobbled abstractedly whilst working took effect at last and Royce was seriously ill.

Even marriage had had little effect on his appetite for work. Although we read of Mrs. Royce accompanying her husband on some of the test runs on the first cars it is clear that work absorbed him to such a degree that his wife saw little of him. There were no children, and although they remained on friendly terms the marriage virtually broke up before Royce's first illness. This does not mean that he was that most boring of human beings, a man with a one-track mind: he had a very wide range of interests but until physical failure forced a change upon him he forced himself at a pace which few could have stood. Even his hobby of fruit and rose growing was carried on when most people were sleeping, and his garden at Knutsford was almost entirely cultivated by the light of portable electric lamps ingeniously contrived for the purpose.

Claude Johnson felt great concern for his partner, not only because of his liking and respect but because he clearly saw that Rolls-Royce Ltd. might not survive the loss of its talented chief engineer. He also saw that if left to his own devices Royce would drive himself into an early grave; already during his convalescence at Overstrand in Norfolk he had shown signs of fretting for the factory so, almost by brute force, Johnson took him abroad. Most of the summer and autumn were spent driving about France, spending a week here and a fortnight there with, for Johnson, occasional hurried trips back to the factory. The winter was spent in Egypt, then inevitably recommended by English doctors when they did not know what else to do, but none of this journeying and resting did very much good. Royce's mind needed work, fretted without work, but his body could not stand the strain of work. In this state he returned to France.

Wandering about the South, without aim, they drove along the coast until chance brought them to the little-known bay and village of Le Canadel at the southernmost tip of the Riviera. Here they put up at the solitary hotel, and here Royce said to his companion 'I would like to build a house', whereupon according to Max Pemberton* Claude Johnson slipped away from the party and returned having bought the land saying 'We can begin to build whenever you like'.

In due time a villa, La Mimosa, was built high on the hill overlooking the bay with, significantly enough, a smaller villa below it for draughtsmen and assistants. A pattern for the future took shape in Johnson's mind; where Royce might choose to live his work must live near by for him to take up or relinquish as mood or health might dictate. Picked associates and helpers must be near at hand but, except on rare occasions, the chief designer of Rolls-Royce must never again be burdened with routine factory cares.

Broadly speaking this plan was followed for the rest of Royce's life. Certainly, while the villas were building, he returned to England (after another spell of illness) and took a house at Crowborough where he carried out tests and experiments with a modified version of the long-stroke Ghost engine. As winter set in he returned again to the hotel at Le Canadel (the villa being not yet ready) and here he collapsed again with the most serious illness yet. This was described as 'an intestinal disorder' and piecing together information from those who worked with him later on it seems certain that a malignant tumour had been diagnosed. Johnson once again came to the rescue, organising cars, ambulances, railways and attendants to bring his colleague back to England where he was immediately operated upon by Dr. Campbell Thompson.

The result of this severe illness and the radical operation was to leave Henry Royce a semi-invalid for the rest of his life. A skilled nurse, Miss Ethel Aubin, who had looked after him at Overstrand, took charge as soon as he left the nursing home and remained in constant but unobtrusive attendance for twenty years[†]. It is probably no exaggeration to say that she played a major part in extending his life by that amount.

As soon as he was well enough to travel they went to Le Canadel where the villa was now fit for occupation. Soon after, the little team of specialists joined him and the steady stream

*The Life of Sir Henry Royce, Bart., M.I.E.E., M.I.M.E., by Sir Max Pemberton, Selwyn & Blount, n.d.

of letters, directions, drawings and plans began to flow between the Riviera and the factory.

In his efficient unobtrusive way Claude Johnson smoothed away all difficulties and it is largely because of his genius for organisation that the 'Le Canadel Formula' was set up and worked so well. During the war the set-up was transferred to St. Margaret's Bay in Kent where a suitable house was found for Royce near to Johnson's own. After the war the pattern was repeated at West Wittering in Sussex during the summer months, most of the winters being spent at Le Canadel. But where Royce went his work went with him and though he lived in retirement for twenty years the volume and value of the work he inspired and directed are impressive by any standard.

6

The Great War and After

THE reader may well suppose the story to have been an unconscionable time a-reaching the point where the 40/50 Rolls-Royce was firmly established as 'the best car in the world' (this was, incidentally, a journalist's praise originally, and the company must be absolved from the charge of arrogance which has so often been levelled against it), but the story of the Silver Ghost *is* the story of Rolls-Royce to a great extent. Not only was the model in production for nineteen years, but the succeeding types, Phantoms I and II, were logical developments from it. More importantly the system laid down in the formative years of the Silver Ghost remains fundamentally unaltered and contains the secret of Rolls-Royce success.

The policy of continuing the one model and concentrating effort upon improving it freed Rolls-Royce Ltd. from the thraldom of producing a 'new' model every year; and the pattern which emerged in 1911–12 has, in effect, endured. From Derby to Le Canadel, Crowborough, St. Margaret's Bay or West Wittering, came design requirements, problems, suggestions, components and complete cars for trial and comment: to Derby went the answers, either in the form of letters, admirably clear and lucid, or drawings prepared by his personal staff under Royce's direction. This generally meant that the drawings were done again and again and again until Henry Royce was satisfied that the component to be produced from them could not be improved upon. He did not claim to be a draughtsman but he undoubtedly had the eye of an artist in the wider sense (indeed, he took to painting as a hobby). Johnson in particular, and Derby in general, might groan at the difficulty of getting working drawings from the design staff, and Royce's continual 'Rub out, alter, improve, refine' may at times have seemed carried to excess, but experience was to prove time and again that his insistence on working away until a thing *looked* right generally saved the company production time and money in the end. He possessed the rare gift of assessing the merits and shortcomings of mechanisms by eye alone.

As we have seen, the London–Edinburgh type was fitted with cantilever rear springs. By the time this was done the 'platform' rear suspension of the standard chassis had long been abandoned in favour of three-quarter-elliptic rear springing. Not, one suspects, because of any particular shortcomings in the 'platform' arrangement, but merely because the pundits of the motor world were beginning to consider it rather old-fashioned; it was, after all, a feature of the hansom cabs which were now, to the regret of many, in hasty retreat before the all-conquering motor.

Because the cantilever suspension, in a slightly different form, was to reappear on the

E. W. Hives and the 'streamlined' L.-E. Rolls-Royce 1701 at Brooklands, 1912.

'Continental' and standard Ghost models of 1913, it is as well to take a look at this type of suspension, the principal merit of which was that in a given length of wheel base it allowed the use of the longest possible springs which could therefore be made to oscillate more slowly than the conventional half- or three-quarter elliptic variety.

As it is known that R. L. Messervy, one of Royce's team, took a 38 h.p. 6-cylinder Lanchester to France for him to use and study, there can be little doubt about the source of the cantilever suspension. Henry Royce always kept his feet firmly on the ground, commercially speaking, and would have realised how the unorthodox appearance of the Lanchester must have deterred all but the connoisseurs of engineering who could appreciate its many fine qualities; but he must also have been impressed by the superb riding qualities given to the Lanchester by the exceptionally long, slow, and supple cantilever springs used both front and back. Without major alterations to the chassis it would not have been possible to adapt the Rolls-Royce to cantilever springing in front, nor were the Lanchester parallel-motion radius links copied, but the use of long, soft cantilever springs at the back enabled the Silver Ghosts of 1913 onwards to maintain high speeds over bad surfaces without risk to the car or undue discomfort to the passengers. Royce's pursuit of perfection is reflected in the many minor alterations made to the springs, anchorages, torque members and dampers.

The other major change to the 40/50's specification was the reversion to a 4-speed gearbox without, however, the overdrive fourth speed of the earlier period. The events which brought this about have often been described, and described moreover with an undercurrent of gibing at the company for suffering what Massac Buist (and all those who have copied him without acknowledgement) described as a 'disgraceful episode'. This refers to the occasion when, to the consternation of all, a Rolls-Royce baulked at a hill: it was as though a bishop had offered an improper suggestion to an elderly maiden lady of impregnable propriety in a first-class railway carriage.

True enough, the hill in question had a gradient of 1 in 4, a bad surface and was, moreover, some 2,000 feet above sea level; for the failure occurred during the 1912 Austrian Alpine Trial when James Radley, driving a London–Edinburgh Rolls-Royce, came to rest on the steepest section of the Katschberg and was obliged to dismount two of his passengers. The episode was chastening rather than 'disgraceful', and showed up a weakness in the Rolls-Royce testing procedure. The fact that similar cars had been proved on similar, or even steeper and rougher, gradients in England and Scotland had been thought sufficient. Only a short while before, Claude Johnson had taken a standard Silver Ghost, with six passengers, up Glendoe Hill. But this, though as steep as the Katschberg, was of lesser altitude and it was clear that when the rarefied atmosphere of the Alps was taken into account the lowest ratio of the three-speed gear simply was not low enough.

This was the starting point of the high-speed long-distance continental testing to which so many Rolls-Royces have since been subjected. Under Eric Platford's command a team of drivers took various cars to a number of Alpine passes to investigate the gradients, surfaces, angles of bends and barometric pressures and, of course, to determine the cars' reaction to these conditions. The immediate result was the evolution of the 'Continental' Rolls-Royce (usually miscalled the Alpine Eagle) which was a development from the London–Edinburgh and a basis for the standard model after the war.

The 4-speed gearbox developed for these conditions was arranged to provide a dreadnought low gear combined with three well-spaced higher ratios for normal use. Though many Rolls-Royce drivers in the 'twenties continued to use the 'start in third, change immediately into top and stay there' method of driving, the cars were now endowed with the type of close-ratio box which encourages the enterprising driver to display his mettle. Engine modifications included an increase in compression and altered cam contours. It has been stated that the cars specially prepared for the 1913 Alpine Trial were fitted with aluminium alloy pistons, but recent research has shown this to be incorrect: aluminium pistons were first fitted in 1925. The cantilever rear springing of the London–Edinburgh type was modified and improved for the Continental model, and Henry Royce devised a bumping machine which could simulate the effects of some thousands of miles of rough running in a few hours.

The 'Continental' engines developed approximately 70–75 b.h.p.; by contrast the output of the standard engines had risen from the 48 h.p. of 1906 to about 60 h.p. By modern standards these figures are not impressive and critics have ever been ready to say that Rolls-Royce sacrificed efficiency to silence. In the sense that motor-car design is always a matter of compromise there is a germ of truth in this, but seen in the context of the time Rolls-Royce were well abreast of their contemporaries; the specific output was about 5% more than that of the nearest comparable model of Napier and nearly 15% better than the contemporary 45 h.p. sleeve-valve Daimler. In the range of English cars intended for the 'carriage trade' it is probable that only the 38 h.p. Lanchester, which developed about 65 b.h.p. from an engine some 20% smaller, exceeded the Rolls-Royce in specific output.

Four Rolls-Royces competed in the 1913 Austrian Alpine Trial. Three were entered by the Company and driven by Hives, Friese and Sinclair, and the fourth was entered and driven by James Radley whose *débâcle* the previous year had been the catalyst. As the regulations required the bonnets to be sealed, thereby making carburettor flooding and induction pipe priming impossible, a cylinder priming device was hurriedly devised by Royce; so hurriedly, indeed, that George Clegg, who made up the device, recalled that the drawing given to him omitted to show any means for the little pump, mounted on the steering column, to draw its charge of petrol from the carburettor. As time was running out he committed the 'crime' of not working to drawing and improvised the necessary connection. Thanks to the priming device the three works' cars lost no marks through starting delays in the chilly dawn of Alpine altitudes, though on the second morning Hives lost one mark by stalling his engine on the way out of the *parc fermé*. Radley's car, which was not equipped with a primer, did incur a penalty of three marks for a late start.

The four Rolls-Royces completely dominated the Trial, not only by their speed, where speed was possible (Radley held a steady 70 m.p.h.* with ease on the run into Wiener Neustadt and lopped three minutes off his nearest competitor's time up the Loibi pass), but for their effortless performance. Though fast and powerful the Rolls-Royces showed themselves still to be luxury carriages in the grand manner. The team prize only eluded them because Sinclair's car was damaged by collision with a non-competing Minerva which left him to finish the last leg of the course with only his third speed in action: this in itself was a triumph.

At the time of this Austrian Alpine Trial those with ears to hear might discern the rattling of Teutonic sabres, and distant rumblings as the chariot of war was manœuvred into position, but these ominous portents were apparent only to the few and in the hey-day of the twentieth century the Rolls-Royce became firmly established as the 'Best Car in the World' and a symbol of British supremacy. The little-known Spanish Grand Prix of 1913, which was organised at the instigation of that ardent enthusiast King Alfonso XIII, was won by a Rolls-Royce driven by Don Carlos de Salamanca, the newly appointed Spanish Agent. He finished by a three-minute lead over a 60 h.p. Lorraine-Dietrich whilst Eric Platford, on a second Rolls-Royce*, had a twenty-eight-minute lead over the fourth finisher. This success opened the Spanish market, hitherto dominated by the French, to Rolls-Royce cars which were already selling well in France, with showrooms in the Champs Elysées, and in North America, despite 60% tariff with showrooms and repair depots in New York and Toronto, as well as in Austria, Italy, India and Australia.

In 1914, although the company decided that another official entry would savour of painting the lily, James Radley again entered for the Alpine Trial and again triumphed by being the only competitor in his class to lose no marks, despite competing, with an engine of 7,428 c.c., against a Benz of 8,496 c.c., a Graf und Stift of 8,490 c.c. and two other Benz

* The car Radley drove had a top speed of 82 m.p.h.

* These two cars were specially built for this event and were subsequently sold to customers in Spain.

of 10,100 c.c. Scarcely had the dust of the contest settled before the fog of war blotted such sports from the minds of the competitors.

*   *   *

When the war started it was natural enough to suppose that the demand for luxury cars would vanish, and the decision to make all Rolls-Royce chassis available as staff cars or ambulances was logical. The prodigious contribution the company made to the war effort in other directions was not envisaged at first. Although many people foresaw that motor transport would play a great part in a modern war, few saw how great that part would be. The European armies had made only tentative steps towards mechanisation and, characteristically, the English War Office had sedulously averted their eyes from the mechanical vehicle.

As early as 1898 the mountebank Pennington had demonstrated a fearsome motor quadricycle intended for military purposes to the War Office who had, understandably enough, declined to have anything to do with so palpably impractical a machine. The 'War Car' exhibited by Frederick Simms in 1902 had in it the germ of the armoured fighting vehicle but would undoubtedly have proved too feeble for serious use. Steam traction engines had been used during the Boer War and in 1906 the authorities unbent so far as to take half-hearted interest in the remarkable petrol-engined track-laying tractor designed and built by Ruston-Hornsby. Though intended merely for dragging cannon or wagons this advanced machine was the first successful 'caterpillar' vehicle, steered by its tracks, and its fully sprung 3-point track suspension system was not surpassed for more than thirty years. It performed admirably, but the military pundits were so overawed by the dangers of petrol on the field of battle (comparable, one might suppose, to being afraid of draughts whilst at sea in a hurricane), that they demanded its conversion to operate on paraffin. This was done, but the resultant power loss was so severe that the pundits were in the happy position of being able to declare the tractor under-powered and it was laid aside. Attempts were then made to adapt the track-vehicle principle to the ordinary steam traction engine, but the abortions born of this unhappy coition soon proved useless for cross-country work as the pitching over rough ground could deprive the fire-box crowns of water. The constant hazard of boiler explosion from this should have made the supposed dangers of petrol appear trifling.

August 1914, therefore, found the British Army with little mechanical transport beyond a number of soundly designed 'subsidy' motor-lorries, little different from their civilian counterparts and mostly useless on soft ground, and a sizeable fleet of steam traction engines and steam lorries operated by the 'Jam Stealers', or Army Service Corps, most of which did not survive the retreat from Mons. One of the lessons of the Great War was that the horse, mercifully, had had his day as a beast of martial burden and civilian cars, vans, lorries and 'buses were impressed in ever-growing numbers: even so, many thousands of horses, mules and camels worked and died in horrible conditions.

Armoured fighting vehicles, as such, did not exist at all, but as early as September 1914 the first standard Rolls-Royce chassis were being adapted to this service. Of all the types modified to this work as the war went on the Rolls-Royce was the only one to be wholly and conspicuously successful, if one excepts the Lanchesters which saw service in Russia towards the end of 1916. Most of the civilian vehicles which were converted into armoured cars proved, like the American Peerless lorries, too heavy for their power and consequently too slow and too easily baulked on heavy ground. For other kinds of work, however, it must be said that perfectly standard vehicles as diverse as the invincible Leyland or the ubiquitous Model T Ford, and the splendid Lancia, Crossley and Vauxhall R.F.C. Tenders, showed themselves capable of arduous service under terrible conditions. By 1918 nobody who had seen service could any longer dismiss the motor-car as a rich man's plaything.

Although Rolls-Royces won renown as staff cars, ambulances and tenders and, one may guess, also inspired envy in those relegated to humbler conveyances, it was the armoured cars (first used by the R.N.A.S.) which did so much to enhance their reputation. In France, Gallipoli, Palestine, Arabia, German West Africa, Libya and Russia* they were never known to fail except when knocked out by the enemy. Apart altogether from punctures caused by enemy bullets, the tyres were the only source of real trouble: as the cars were mostly working over rough roads or no roads and were carrying more than twice the weight they were designed for this is hardly surprising. Twin rear wheels were fitted, up to six spares were carried and, normally, speeds were kept down to about 20 m.p.h. to conserve the tyres, but the Silver Ghost in its fighting trim was still capable of well over 50 m.p.h. if necessary – a pace which made the laborious 16 m.p.h. gait of the Peerless very small beer.

Some trouble was experienced with hub-bearings because of the extra weight, and most of the armoured cars which went on to serve after the war in such places as Afghanistan, India and Shanghai were modified to overcome this slight difficulty. Apart from this virtually no mechanical failures were chalked up against the armoured cars and engine wear was incredibly slight even in those working in the desert without air-intake filters. A good deal of radiator boiling went on, particularly when the cars had to be driven with the armour-plate doors closed in front of the radiators, but the engines did not succumb to overheating, and no petrol starvation from vapour lock was suffered. A few of the armoured Rolls-Royces survived to fight again in the second German War on both sides.

Much of the success of T. E. Lawrence's work in the desert is attributable to his fleet of Rolls-Royces, but long before *Seven Pillars of Wisdom* had set the Bloomsbury dovecots a-flutter, their worth had been appreciated. A report in *The Times*, from W. T. Massey, in December 1916 said:

'I have motored in the desert . . . so perfect and reliable has the car supply service become that the cars move to a time-table . . . the armoured cars used in Egypt are all Rolls-Royces. Notwithstanding all the rough work they have done there has been no engine breakdown. The cars have run over thousands of miles of the roughest desert and the complete absence of engine trouble is a triumph for British workmanship.'

*At the end of the war, 321 Rolls-Royce cars were in service and in Red Cross hands: apart from two 20 h.p. models, one of which was 26357, they were all 40/50s.

Rolls-Royce army vehicles used in the Great War. (The Imperial War Museum)

As we are concerned primarily with the motor-cars this is no place for a survey of the Rolls-Royce aero engines. This subject would need a 'dam' great thick book' all to itself. But after 1915 the aero engine division of Rolls-Royce Ltd. far outgrew the parent motor-car division and, paradoxically, the divisions were indivisible, for it is doubtful whether the motor-cars could have survived on their own, without support from other activities between the wars. Also many aspects of aero engine design have influenced the development of engines for land vehicles, and much of the incomparable scientific and metallurgical knowledge garnered by the aero engine division of Rolls-Royce has been of service to motor-car manufacturers the world over.

In the beginning, naturally enough, aero engines derived from car engines and the Wright brothers first flew with, and subsequently fitted to their machines, a 4-cylinder-in-line engine clearly based upon automobile practice except that it was air-cooled (as, indeed, were quite a few American car engines at that time). Apart from this no attempt was made in the design to save weight except, as Dr. Lanchester observed, by 'cheeseparing': his suspicions were confirmed at the Rheims meeting in 1908 when a Wright biplane made a forced landing practically on top of him with a broken connecting rod dangling below a shattered crankcase.

Special designs were soon evolved; some like the V-8, direct-injection, Antoinette were extraordinarily advanced, but in all of them the balance between performance and reliability was very delicately poised. Cooling was a great problem; liquid cooling involved extra weight and direct air cooling of in-line engines, whether of single-row, V, X, or H formation, usually resulted in uneven temperatures between front and back cylinders with distortion and cracking. Undoubtedly the best-known and most successful of early aero engines was the ingenious Gnôme rotary which had its cylinders, like the spokes of a wheel,

Rolls-Royce army vehicle in mountainous territory during the Great War. (The Imperial War Museum)

revolving around a stationary hollow crankshaft, which served also as an induction pipe and fed the inflammable mixture to the combustion chambers via automatic valves in the piston crowns which, consequently, were kept cool by the incoming vapour. There were snags however. With the limits imposed by the engineering technique of the time the output of the largest version of pre-war Gnôme, which had fourteen cylinders double banked in sets of seven, was only about 150 b.h.p.; also the Gnôme was only to be lubricated by copious draughts of pure castor oil which it spewed unburnt from its exhaust stubs in such streams that the hapless pilot, in his exposed cockpit, absorbed sufficient of the nauseous stuff through clothes and skin to suffer the effect of having been liberally dosed by an old-fashioned nanny. The pilots' measure of speed, 'like a dose of salts', had unhappy connotations for many in the Kaiser's war.

It must be said that Claude Johnson's attempts to interest Royce in aero engines before the war had not met with much response, nor was there any real need to press the matter, but once circumstances forced his hand Royce threw himself into the project with energy, determination and skill enough for any ten fit and hearty men. The relatively short time spent in the development of the first engine from rough drawing to test-bench and its marked superiority over its contemporaries are the more astonishing when it is remembered that so much of the design lay in the hands of a frail man devoid of formal education and with no knowledge of science or mathematics beyond an uncanny instinct.

Late in 1914 it was decided that Rolls-Royce Ltd. should start making aero engines to the Renault specification, to be followed by others designed under direct Government auspices. Johnson was chiefly responsible for this move and, whether by design or not, it provided the spur needed to overcome Royce's strange reluctance to undertake aero engine design. He agreed to the plan as a temporary measure but, according to Harold Nockolds*, he was so offended by the engineering principles or lack of them, which he saw in the Renault design that he set about producing something worthy of the name of Rolls-Royce.

Design work, at first, was largely in the hands of Royce himself and A. G. Elliott, his chief assistant, who had formerly been with Napier and who became chief engineer in 1949. As time went on more specialists joined the design staff both at Derby and at St. Margaret's Bay or West Wittering. Mathematical and scientific problems, too, were submitted to outside experts and, later on, Royce's personal team was greatly strengthened by A. J. Rowledge. Soon the posts from Kent to Derbyshire were carrying a constant stream of letters, drawings and instructions which Johnson passed to the appropriate men at the works; principally to E. W. Hives as head of the Experimental Department. Royce's letters are revealing. He did not shine at communicating his ideas in speech, though when angered he could be direct and rough-tongued; indeed, to be blunt, his benign and rather sensitive face was not matched by any corresponding mildness of expression and his outbursts of profanity were startling in one so retiring by nature. The letters, however, as well as being direct and precise are unspoilt by any pomposity of language, and in a variety of ways they show that the writer had an extraordinarily wide range of interests and an analytical mind.

The instructions cover not only the basic design of the engine but the details of some 2,000 components and the varied and complex experiments needed to prove every detail before production started. All was subject to Royce's inflexible maxim 'There is no safe way of judging anything except by experiment'. Here the empirical engineer, Royce, is warmly supported by the scientific engineer, Lanchester, who wrote: 'It is probable that more scientific research and calculation has been bestowed on the aero engine than on any other mechanism, yet the final arbiter is the test-bench and the ultimate refinements are dictated by experience.'

The first complete 'Eagle' engine was tested in 1915 and at 1,800 r.p.m. developed 25 h.p. more than the 200 h.p. originally specified. Without any loss of reliability, or increase of cubic capacity (20.32 litres, 12-cylinder V-formation), the output was steadily increased. From 225 h.p. in 1915 the output rose to 266 h.p. by the following March, 284 h.p. by December 1916 and so by stages until, by February 1918, the engine designed for 200 h.p. was producing 360 h.p. at 2,000 r.p.m. The weight worked out at approximately 2.7 lb. per horsepower which would have been considered almost impossible by many engineers before the war. The dramatic development of the internal combustion engine is shown by comparing this with the Otto and Langen atmospheric gas engine of 1872 which developed only half a horsepower and weighed nearly a ton.

The principal merit of the 'Eagle' engine was its reliability; a feature which was shared

* *The Magic of a Name*, by Harold Nockolds, G. T. Foulis & Co. Ltd., n.d. (1938).

Rolls-Royce Tender at Akaba, 1916. (The Imperial War Museum)

by the other war-time engines, 'Hawk' and 'Falcon'. Rolls-Royce aero engines were often criticised for excessive complication, but the apparent complexity and duplication of parts was done to give the engines the greatest possible number of flying hours between overhauls and the greatest possible chance of flying home with, perhaps, half the ignition apparatus or the cooling system put out of action by enemy bullets. By the end of the war it was not uncommon for Rolls-Royce engines to fly 150 hours between overhauls, yet only eight years earlier it had been touch and go whether Bleriot's little engine would keep going at full power for the twenty minutes required to waft him across the English Channel.

The production problems connected with these engines were enormously and unnecessarily complicated by the Government. As early as 1916 Johnson warned that the policy of multiplying the number of establishments making complete engines, of whatever kind, was liable to collapse: he advocated limiting the central factories to six and making all the others into sub-contracting units each responsible for large scale production of a small number of components. It took two years to make this common-sense view prevail by which time the system *had* almost broken down.

Deliveries from Derby were, admittedly, often behind schedule and at one stage the President of the Air Board, Lord Londonderry, threatened that the Ministry of Munitions would take over the Derby factory and appoint a manager. The reason for the delays was clear; the company was called upon to produce new engines and to overhaul used ones in the same factory with the same staff. Johnson asked for permission to build a separate repair shop and recruit a special staff, but the Air Board refused until almost too late. Johnson then told the Board that his company could buy and equip a factory which could produce 2,000 'Eagles' at £2,400 apiece between June 1918 and February 1919, but the Air Board showed no interest.

Finally the situation threatened to get completely out of hand and, at the eleventh hour, the authorities took over the Clement-Talbot factory in Ladbroke Grove, London, and entrusted its management to Johnson as a repair depot for Rolls-Royce engines. It was also proposed to build 'Falcons' there but this did not materialise. A little later, in 1917, Johnson's sub-contracting scheme was grudgingly adopted.

The company may therefore be said to have fought most gallantly on land, in the air and against the most difficult opponent of all, official obstinacy. They scored handsomely on all these fronts and emerged from the bloody conflict ennobled but by no means comparably enriched.

*　　　*　　　*

One of the last instructions Hives gave to his experimental staff before turning his attention from cars to aero engines, was to dismantle a certain chassis and store the bits in an inspection pit: one of the first instructions he gave after the Armistice had been signed was to disinter these pieces, reassemble the chassis and refit a test body ready for use. The chassis in question was 49GB and the reason for the care taken to prevent it being commandeered by one of the Service Departments was that it embodied all the latest modifications made in the light of the Alpine Trials and it was now to be used as the basis for post-war production. Within a few days it was back on the road again and serving as 'shuttle' car between Derby and West Wittering.

Amongst the refinements which appeared on the post-war Ghosts was electric lighting and starting equipment, which had been occasionally fitted as an extra before the war: the new dynamos and starter motors were of Rolls-Royce design and make. Although electric lights had been fairly common from about 1910 onwards, full-scale dynamo-powered lighting and starting equipment had been comparatively rare on this side of the Atlantic; and the few manufacturers to adopt electric starting had mostly used American equipment. Lanchesters had been early in the field with a Delco 8/32 volt system on their 1912 25 h.p. and 38 h.p. models, followed soon after by Sheffield-Simplex with the U.S.L. flywheel dynamotor, but it seems fairly certain that credit must go to Cadillac as the first manufacturer to fit electric lighting and starting, as standard equipment, in 1912. Considering Royce's electrical engineering background it may seem a little odd that he was relatively late in the day, but it must be remembered that the Ghost engine, except when stone cold, would usually start on the switch in the most obliging fashion and, as usual, Royce would not standardise the electrical equipment until it had been rigorously tested, dismantled, redesigned, re-tested and finally brought as near perfection as possible.

Aluminium pistons were another innovation now standardised, and according to evidence in the 'Rolls-Royce Bible' (the bound volume of extracts from the correspondence

91

between the factory and Royce and his personal staff) the experiences with 49GB on test before the war were drawn upon to help solve problems of alloy piston design for the aero engines.

The lighter pistons were accompanied by lighter connecting rods, and power output was about 6% greater than the standard pre-war engine. A factor which contributed to the increase was the substitution of a non-trembling coil and jump-spark distributor for the trembler coil system formerly used for the battery ignition. In conjunction with the electric lighting and starting equipment (which ensured the batteries were always fully charged) this innovation made it a practical proposition to run continuously with both coil and magneto ignitions in action; before the advent of the dynamo lighting set it had been usual to conserve the batteries, for starting and emergency, by running on magneto only. In other words, from having duplicated ignition the Ghost now had dual ignition in the full sense, and with the two plugs per cylinder firing in unison better flame propagation and combustion were obtained. The manual control for 'Early or Late' firing (advance and retard in other manufacturers' language) moved over so wide a range that by flicking the lever to-and-fro it was possible to make the contact breaker points open and close and consequently the Rolls-Royce drivers' favourite trick of starting on the switch was still possible.

In common with most other manufacturers, therefore, the cars which Rolls-Royce exhibited at the first post-war Motor Show differed little outwardly from their predecessors, but in fact the company had not stood still and the first report in *The Motor* concerning the 'new' model credited it with a maximum speed of 78 m.p.h. with a fully equipped touring body, and spoke in glowing terms of the improved acceleration. Unfortunately road test reports at that time did not quote actual acceleration times or braking distances. A faint note of acerbity crept in, which would have been almost unthinkable before the war, and the journalist observed that the driving position was cramped and that he had been surprised to observe a certain amount of play in the transmission.

The student of early motoring publications will have noticed that at the beginning of the century nearly all reports on new makes or models were almost wholly adulatory. Unless some ill-conceived machine really was nasty beyond all description the motoring press scarcely ever sunk below 'modified rapture' in their descriptions, and a certain amount of experience of the style is needed before one can realise that a form of words like: – 'At certain speeds a trifling degree of trepidation could be felt and at the same time our auditory faculties were aware that the powerful engine was well in the collar', really meant that the whole machine shook like a jelly on springs and that the din was deafening. As time went on the expert writers began to be more truly critical in their approach, and the modern style of scientific road-test report, with its stereotyped formulae for assessing all aspects of performance, was gradually evolved. This was all to the good and Rolls-Royce were not the only cars to be subjected to more searching and knowledgeable scrutiny than they had formerly been given.

One of the points which the critics began to make was that the Silver Ghost had come to hold so pre-eminent a position before the war that comparison with other cars had been difficult as so few were really comparable. Now, however, many other firms were catching up or, in the opinion of some, overtaking the Rolls-Royce. On the English market the competition was not, at first, too severe. Napiers, though still a force to be reckoned with, had lost a lot of their early impetus and now definitely ranked behind their young rival; Daimlers still had a certain appeal to those who liked to ape Royalty and ride about, rather slowly, in stately, silent dignity laying behind them everywhere the nauseous blue smoke screen which Mr. Knight's ingenious double-sleeve-valve engine invariably emitted. Lanchester became more powerful competitors at this period with their fine new overhead camshaft 'forty' which was presented in conventional guise to overcome the sales resistance which the firm's unorthodox pre-war cars had engendered. From the Continent and, to a lesser extent, America, some newcomers in the luxury car bracket threatened Rolls-Royce supremacy.

Of these, the most influential was the new 'Boulogne' Hispano-Suiza which had appeared in 1919. In general specification and capacity it was comparable with the Silver Ghost, but the o.h.c. Hispano engine was undeniably much more up-to-date and efficient than the Rolls-Royce side-valve unit; and though not quite so quiet it was not lacking in refinement by any means. The Silver Ghost scored by having a 4-speed gearbox against the Hispano's 3-speed affair, but despite this those who contended that the Hispano could comfortably outstrip its rival over long distances were probably right. The reason for this superiority lay not in the maximum speed but in the better brakes of the Franco-Spanish-Swiss confection.

For a very long while the attitude of motor designers, particularly in England, towards 4-wheel brakes had been odd to say the least. Though most of them were prepared to admit that 4-wheel braking was logical, its advantages manifest, and the constructional difficulties not insuperable, there was general reluctance to do anything about it despite the wholly successful pre-war efforts by Argyll, Arrol-Johnston and a few more. Continental designers were much less hesitant in recognising that faster and heavier cars, and more and more of them, made better braking essential, and 4-wheel systems began to be standardised on the Continent soon after the war. It then became apparent, particularly on large and heavy cars, that moving the extra mechanism to work the extra pair of brakes entailed very heavy pedal pressures. Anybody who has driven, say, a large Panhard-Levassor of the early 'twenties will know that though the car can stop in a most impressive manner a strong right leg is needed. To overcome this difficulty various forms of 'servo' mechanism were evolved, and the vacuum system, which was based on railway practice, was in favour with some makers though it was disliked by many because of its tendency to be disconcertingly abrupt. Very much superior was the Hispano-Suiza's ingenious mechanical friction servo motor which in effect used the car's own momentum to apply the brakes.

Although criticism, published criticism that is, of Rolls-Royce cars continued to be enthusiastic there began to be implicit some hints to the effect that Rolls-Royce brakes no longer matched the standard set by the rest of the car. A report at the time of the 1922 Motor Show, for example, came out into the open about the inconvenience of the famous gear-lever which had to be un-latched from each separate notch for each change of speed (the blow was softened by the observation that it was hardly ever necessary to change gear), and dismissed the brakes rather coldly by saying that they were as good as 2-wheel brakes could be. The comment was fair. More outspoken complaints were made in private, and one influential motorist observed to Claude Johnson that on cars weighing more than two tons and capable of over 70 m.p.h. brakes on the back wheels only might land the incautious motorist in trouble: he got the reply that Mr. Royce was not being idle but that before Rolls-Royce fitted 4-wheel brakes they had to be sure that they were the best 4-wheel brakes possible.

By November 1923 Royce and his gang had experimented long enough and it was announced that the Ghost would now have 4-wheel brakes, though the innovation was, at first, called a six-brake system; this merely meant that the handbrake lever was direct-coupled to separate sets of brake shoes in the rear wheel drums in the usual modern manner. *The Autocar*, rather misleadingly, described the new brakes as being on the 'servo-hydraulic' system, but this was presumably just a misunderstanding on the reporter's part, as it soon became known that Rolls-Royce had adopted and refined the Hispano-Suiza type of frictional servo motor. However, some further difficulties arose and the 4-wheel brakes were not standardised until the following year; they were fitted, retrospectively and at the Company's expense, to cars ordered after the announcement in November 1923.

As the usual practice was (and still is) amongst motor manufacturers Rolls-Royce bought cars made by various of their rivals to see whether they could learn anything from them, and there are many references in 1921–3 to the Hispano-Suiza used by the design and experimental staffs. It was frequently driven by Hives who complained that the brakes were incurably fierce at low speeds though admirable otherwise. In the Rolls-Royce version this fault was eliminated and, proportionately, greater pedal pressure was needed at very low speeds than when travelling fast; this did away with the bugbear of jerky stopping and locked wheels which bedevilled so many servo systems. In outline, the mechanical servo depended upon a disc mounted on the side of the gearbox and rotated at very low speed by suitable gearing from the second-motion shaft. Pressure on the brake pedal was transmitted directly to the rear brake shoes by rods and cables in the usual way, but about 10% of the effort was diverted by suitable links to engage a friction clutch* with the rotating disc which then energised the front wheel brakes via cables and short rods, as well as assisting the pull on the rear brakes. The Rolls-Royce version of this mechanism was patented in 1925.

In common with all other points of Rolls-Royce design the mechanical servo and its appendages were continually refined and improved, but in essentials it remained unchanged during thirty years, though the front brakes were finally energised from the servo by hydraulic pressure. The company's reaction to those who began to call their brakes old-fashioned in the 'sixties was to point out that they would gladly change to a more modern system when it could be proved to be safer, more effective, longer-lived and quieter than their own.

* This single-plate form of servo clutch derives more from the Renault servo-system than from the Hispano-Suiza in which an expanding clutch was originally used.

As the specifications show many other small modifications were made to the Ghost's specification before it made its last bow in 1925, but the new braking system was the last major change and one which allowed the car which had first seen the light in 1906 to hold its own with honour to the end. Four-wheel brakes were standardised, without extra cost, during the last 18 months of production and many earlier models were brought back to the factory for alteration.

As the reader will have gathered, and may well have observed, contributors to the motor press used to slate Rolls-Royce for being 'old-fashioned' and 'dreary'. One well-known journal in particular, which has done so much to improve motor-journalism by being forthright in criticism, used to be singularly venomous in its comments. One article in this paper made passing reference to the Hispano-Suiza brakes and dragged in a typical sneer by remarking in parenthesis 'which Rolls-Royce pinched from them, remember'. The sneer was as malapropos as it was unintelligent, for it had nothing to do with the subject under review, and a moment's reflection would have shown the author that Rolls-Royce have never made any secret of the origin of their brake design, and any question of theft is absurd. The necessary licence arrangements were negotiated between the companies concerned and the appropriate royalties were paid during the life of the Hispano and Renault patents. But any stick is good enough to beat Rolls-Royce. By the time production stopped nearly 6,220 Silver Ghost chassis had been made in England, but by the end of 1925 the time had come for the most admired motor car of its period to give way to its successors.

7

The 'Baby Rolls', the New Phantom, and Springfield

❖

Since the first appearance of the Silver Ghost rumour had often credited Rolls-Royce Ltd. with being on the verge of introducing a new model, and without doubt several experimental cars were made and then, for one reason or another, abandoned, dismantled, the usable parts put into store, and the remainder scrapped. Rolls-Royce enthusiasts, naturally, deplore the dismemberment of these experiments, some of which, no doubt, would have been of great technical interest, but the company, after all, were in business to make saleable motor-cars and could not turn their factory into a mausoleum for abandoned experiments however interesting.

Rumour was particularly busy in the early 'twenties when tales were circulated about various prototypes including a 'baby' Rolls of about 16 h.p. Also there were speculations about a Rolls-Royce with epicyclic gearbox which probably did exist, and another with a swash-plate engine which was almost certainly a figment of journalistic imagination based upon the fact that the company did experiment with a swashplate aero engine at about that time. *The Motor* shot nearer the mark in September 1921 with an article headed 'A Mystery Car' which was illustrated by a couple of photographs, one showing a three-quarter-front view of a tourer with a Rolls-Royce-like radiator, partially obscured by a gentleman apparently overcome with drink or in a state of exhaustion from his efforts at the starting handle. The other picture showed half-elliptic rear springs and Michelin disc wheels, and the text of the piece said the taxation disc disclosed the rated h.p. as 20.1 (it seems odd that it did not also disclose the name of the maker); centrally placed gear and brake levers were remarked upon, and it was said that the engine had four cylinders though it was not disclosed how this became known if the car was as carefully guarded as most experimental models are.

Except for the number of cylinders these speculations were accurate enough, for a year later the company announced their new 20 h.p. model with a 6-cylinder pushrod-operated overhead-valve engine of 3 in. (76 mm) bore and $44^{1}/_{2}$-in. (114 mm) stroke. The cylinder head was detachable for the first time in Rolls-Royce practice and other new features were that the governor-controlled throttle was *not* fitted, but that the ignition had automatic advance-and-retard mechanism in addition to an overriding hand control. No magneto was originally fitted, and the most striking departure from normal English usage was, as *The*

Motor had said, that the gear and brake levers were centrally mounted: this arrangement was then thought very cheap and nasty. Compression ratio was 4.6:1 and 50 b.h.p. was claimed. From the capacity of 3,150 c.c. this represents about 16 h.p. per litre.

Not only was the gear change lever centrally mounted but the gearbox had only three forward speeds. Henry Royce had always contended that with a sufficient power to weight ratio and a flexible engine three speeds were enough. Even after the Alpine episode he had been in favour merely of lowering the bottom gear ratio and he had, apparently, been reluctant to pay heed to the advice of Johnson and Platford who favoured a 4-speed transmission. As most of his customers continued to use the Rolls-Royce as though it were a 2-speed car, at least until the advent of synchromesh, he was probably right, but he failed to appreciate the curious duality of outlook of the average British motorist who always prefers four speeds though generally reluctant to use them. Their attitude to the manufacturer is, in effect, 'I'll be damned if I'll use four gears, but I'll be doubly damned if I'll let you fob me off with any fewer'. Not until November 1925 did the Company bow to public opinion and fit the 20 h.p. model with an admirable four-speed gearbox which greatly improved its performance for those who were interested in such things, whilst the usual Rolls-Royce ability to trickle through traffic at a walking pace in top gear remained unimpaired.

The centrally placed gear and brake levers were universally condemned and the four-speed version of the Twenty reverted to the traditional right-hand control.

Myth and legend surrounded the name of Rolls-Royce from an early period. There are still plenty of people who will tell you in all seriousness that the cars are guaranteed for life, that the bonnets and all mechanical parts are sealed by the makers and that a broken seal will mean cancellation of the guarantee. They will also tell you at the drop of a hat that the Rolls-Royce mascot is made of solid silver and that a friend of a friend of theirs had an old Rolls and when he took it to the works for some slight attention (for the first time in forty years) they said it was the rarest model in existence and that they wanted it for their museum. Though reluctant to part with an old friend the owner at last yielded to their entreaties and in exchange he was given, absolutely free, the very latest and finest Rolls-Royce and a guarantee of free service for the rest of his life.

A slightly less credulous body of people firmly believed that the lower gears of the Rolls-Royce were for emergency use only. This is hardly surprising as road test reports invariably illustrated the renowned Rolls-Royce flexibility by saying that normally it was only necessary to use third and fourth speeds, and that the car could even be started from rest in the highest gear without protest from the engine. The famous top-gear-only runs of pre-war days were not forgotten, and so well had the work been done that many motorists believed it was not only possible (under favourable circumstances) to start in top gear but entirely proper to do so on all occasions. It was also thought that the only time it was necessary to change down was when some quite exceptional gradient threatened to bring even the Rolls-Royce to a standstill.

The Silver Ghost, particularly in closed form, had been thought of almost exclusively as the province of the paid driver, as it was, of course, contrary to the etiquette of the time for any but a liveried servant to be seen in command of a formal limousine or landaulet. Although open-bodied versions might often be conducted by their owners the chauffeur was usually still in evidence. The 20 h.p. model, however, was intended more as an owner-driver's car and the myth of 'You never need change gear on a Rolls' led to a certain amount of trouble. Quite a number of buyers were attracted to the new model solely because contemporary reports credited it with top gear flexibility equal to that of its larger relative, and some of these new owners insisted on making top-gear starts on every possible and impossible occasion. The maltreatment they were given, coupled with an inherent propensity for oil to reach the clutch from the back main bearing, caused a certain amount of clutch trouble on the Twenties, and a good many modifications had to be made.

In one instance known one of the authors, a woman motorist bought a 20 h.p. Rolls-Royce solely because of the top gear myth. Formerly she had never taken a car out on her own and her driving had been confined to occasional stretches of level country roads when she would take command and relegate her chauffeur to the back seat where he would grit his teeth and groan at the series of appalling crunches with which she would force her hapless Sunbeam on to its highest gear. Changing down while the car was in motion was quite beyond her, though in all other ways she drove quite skilfully. So a Rolls-Royce was bought, and because the Rolls-Royce would start in top gear that is what it was made to do; and, moreover, that is what it went on doing with singularly little protest for some twenty-five years. The experience of riding in that car and being baulked by traffic at the foot of the Star and Garter Hill at Petersham, then starting again on the rising gradient and immediately tackling the short pitch of 1 in 9, all on top gear, was enough to make one weep for fine machinery. Though it is now fashionable to sneer at the Twenty as a 'gutless wonder' its ability to survive maltreatment of this sort, and still remain exceptionally quiet and smooth running, showed that Rolls-Royce still had the magic touch. For this particular car was still in use in 1950 (having been re-bodied before the war), and though it may have consumed rather more than its quota of clutch plates the engine bearings and crankshaft had never needed attention.

The taunt that the Twenty was gutless must be put in perspective. On their first road test *The Motor* credited the car with a maximum speed of 62 m.p.h. but observed that road conditions had prevented the absolute maximum being reached. The slowest pace in top gear, without slipping the clutch, was 4 m.p.h., and top gear acceleration from 10 to 30 m.p.h. took $10^2/_3$ sec. Fifty miles an hour was the comfortable cruising pace, petrol consumption was 22 m.p.g. and a half mile rise of 1 in 7 was climbed at 23 m.p.h. in top gear.

Certainly this performance would be considered derisory today for a car of slightly over three litres capacity, but it must be remembered that in 1922 60 m.p.h. was to most motorists what 'the ton' is now, and the man who wanted to dash along then at 60 or 70 m.p.h. was expected to be content (as indeed he was) with the thunderous progress of a 3-litre Bentley or some similar stark and harsh-riding automobile. The contemporary English car nearest to the Twenty Rolls was the 'little' Lanchester of 21 h.p. which came out in 1923 in direct competition with its more famous rival. In outright performance the Lanchester was superior and, having four-wheel brakes, its stopping power was certainly better, but the most ardent Lanchester enthusiast must concede that the Rolls-Royce scores for lightness and delicacy of control, and for silence. The overhead-camshaft Lanchester engine was *quiet* where the pushrod o.h.v. Rolls-Royce was *silent*. The Lanchester's steering, though precise and pleasant, certainly needed the touch of a master's hand whereas the smaller Rolls-Royce could be driven without strain by a woman. When the Rolls-Royce was given its 4-speed gearbox it was also given 4-wheel brakes (optional at first) and these improvements redressed the balance.

It must also be remembered that although Rolls-Royce Ltd. imposed fairly strict control upon the coachbuilders as far as weight was concerned, there was nothing to be done about reducing the wind resistance encountered by the closed bodies of the time. Though motor bodies were lower than they had been before the war, fashion had not yet decreed that they should go to the opposite extreme and be so low that they can only be entered by assuming a fœtal posture. With reasonably proportioned tourer or two-seater bodies the Twenties were far from sluggish, but many buyers had them equipped with 7-seater limousine or landaulet bodies which were as upright as a Wee Free Minister and no more streamlined than the Tower of London.

The design requirements for the 20 h.p. engine had stipulated output of 50 b.h.p. coupled with good low-speed torque; the prototype engine had twin overhead camshafts which, had they been put into the production engines, might have removed the wearisome stigma of 'old fashioned' which the critics of Rolls-Royce were so fond of applying. As the sales branch wanted to put the car on the market by 1922 there was not time for the necessary development work to make the o.h.c. valve gear acceptably silent, hence the choice of push-rod o.h.v. The actual output of the original 20 h.p. engines was 53 b.h.p. at 3,000 r.p.m. with an m.e.p. of 84 at 500 r.p.m.

The critical speed of the engine was 3,300 r.p.m. which would have coincided with a top gear speed of 76 m.p.h. The then Chief Engineer of the Motor Car Division, H. S. Grylls, in a paper read before the Institution of Mechanical Engineers in 1963, observed of this critical speed and the various steps taken to raise it: 'Luck was with us for a time. A little below this critical speed the distributor ceased to function and the cam-wheel came adrift. Even this happened very rarely as the flywheel, at 3,100 r.p.m., had a resonance of its own whose thunderous noise dissuaded most drivers from seeking an Elysium further on.'

The 20 h.p. engine is of paramount importance in the history of Rolls-Royce because the overall dimensions of the unit, broadly speaking, were determined by the distance between the cylinder bore centres. This dimension was 4.150 in. which was decided upon to ensure plenty of cooling-water space and adequate intermediate bearings: the choice of 4.150 in. proved extremely happy, for this dimension remained unchanged for 37 years, at the end of which time $3\frac{3}{4}$ in. diameter pistons had been accommodated in the same centre-distance, and the 1922 output of 53 b.h.p. at 3,000 r.p.m. had risen to 215 b.h.p. at 4,200 r.p.m. Needless to say the 'magic' dimension of 4.150 in. was practically the only factor the 1959 engine had in common with that of 1922.

There was one feature of the Twenty which some critics thought retrograde, though paradoxically it was right in the fashion of the time. This was the adoption of half-elliptic rear springs and what is rather misleadingly called 'Hotchkiss drive'. From the beginning of the century all but the smallest and cheapest cars, no matter what the form of suspension or final-drive, were fitted with some kind of torque-reaction linkage which very often was made to do double duty by serving also as radius rods for the back axle. Many manufacturers, including Royce, had followed Renault practice with a triangulated torque arm pivoted at about mid-point of the chassis, but from about 1910 onwards many firms favoured the 'torque tube' which enclosed the propeller shaft, transmitted the torque to a ball-joint mounted, usually, at the back of the gearbox, and allowed the rearmost universal joint to be dispensed with. This excellent arrangement was not only to be found on the later Silver Ghosts but on cars as diverse as the lordly Delaunay-Belleville and the humble Model T Ford. A few firms such as Lagonda and Siddeley-Deasy copied Lanchester's parallel-motion linkwork which not only relieved the springs of all driving and braking torque, but allowed the axles to rise and fall vertically in relation to the frame instead of describing part of a circle; much of the virtue of the best modern independent suspension designs lies in the fact that, after sixty years, the importance of confining wheel movements to a truly vertical path is properly understood.

'Hotchkiss drive' merely meant that the springs were not hung on swinging shackles at both ends, as formerly, but were pivotally anchored at their leading ends; the rear axle, instead of being attached to the rear springs by trunnion bearings was now rigidly clamped to them so that driving and braking efforts were transmitted to the chassis through the main leaf of each back spring. It was, obviously, a rather crude arrangement which was at one time thought suitable only for very light, low-powered cars, but it became generally acceptable in the 'twenties (at one point in which the Hotchkiss people themselves abandoned it), and universal in the 'thirties; the advantages were that the system was cheap (of little importance to Rolls-Royce), weight was reduced, and a potential source of rattle was eliminated; this was probably the chief merit in Royce's estimation. The drawbacks were that the springs had to be made rather stiffer than would otherwise have been necessary, and under powerful acceleration or braking (particularly the latter) the distortion of the springs caused by the torque reaction had the effect of stiffening them still further which could, on some occasions, set up 'patter' or 'axle tramp'. However, even the critics who thought it odd of Royce to adopt the Hotchkiss drive admitted that the 20 h.p. model was completely free from these vices, and were full of praise for the way in which the back wheels clung to the road under all conditions.

*   *   *

Before considering the demise of the Silver Ghost and the birth of the New Phantom the American venture* must be considered, as it fits into the picture chronologically at this point.

* For detailed studies, see *Rolls-Royce: The Years of Endeavour*, by Ian Lloyd, Macmillan, 1978, and *The American Rolls-Royce*, by A. W. Soutter, Mowbray, 1976.

This venture has sometimes been described as one of Claude Johnson's few mistakes, but this seems less than just. In the first place the foundation of the American company was not entirely brought about by Johnson (though he was certainly keen on the project), and seen in the context of the time the development was sound and logical. Secondly the various events which ultimately forced Rolls-Royce of America Inc. into bankruptcy were entirely outside Johnson's control for the unanswerable reason that they did not take effect until some years after his death. During his lifetime the Springfield plant prospered satisfactorily if not outstandingly.

The American corporation was formed in November 1919, and the objects were twofold, the first, and more important obviously, being to increase American sales by circumventing the very high tariffs which are traditionally part of the American fiscal scene. The other object was to exploit the organisation set up towards the end of the war to make Rolls-Royce aero engines in various American factories. A number of Derby-trained men had been sent to supervise these affairs, and to train American fitters and supervisors in Rolls-Royce methods. Thanks to good will and adaptability on both sides the experiment had been an unqualified success although none of the American Rolls-Royce engines actually flew in battle as the Armistice intervened.

There was, therefore, a nucleus of Rolls-Royce-minded fitters and supervisors available as well as the original body of technicians from Derby whose number was ultimately augmented to fifty-three when the motor-car project got under way. A disused factory at Springfield, Massachusetts, was bought from the American Wire Wheel Company and equipped by the new corporation, which had capital in ordinary and preference shares to the value of £800,000. A majority of voting shares was held by the parent company, so that control of the American company was predominantly British; American interests were well represented on the Board, and the president, E. J. Belnap, was Canadian.

The American motoring picture in the 'twenties was almost completely filled by that remarkably endearing and versatile eccentricity, Henry Ford's Model T, which owed its success not to the fact that it was a good car in the engineering sense, but to the splendid value it gave for the money it cost, to its high power-to-weight ratio, to the foolproof nature of its controls, and to the nation-wide (indeed, almost world-wide) availability of cheap spare parts which could be fitted by unskilled labour. There was no point in cosseting a Model T, or repairing worn or broken parts, when it was possible for the owner to walk into any hardware store and ask for a 'valve for a Ford' or 'axle shaft for a Ford' secure in the knowledge that, as there was only one type of Ford, a dollar or so would buy the necessary piece of ironmongery to enable him to pursue his clamorous but purposeful progress. As John Steinbeck wrote*: 'Two generations of Americans knew more about the Ford coil than the clitoris, about the planetary system of gears than the solar system of stars. With the Model T, part of the concept of private property disappeared. Pliers ceased to be privately owned and a tyre pump belonged to the last man who had picked it up. Most of the babies of the period were conceived in Model T Fords and not a few were born in them.'

* *Cannery Row*, by John Steinbeck, William Heinemann Ltd., 1945.

Rolls-Royce Works at Springfield, Massachusetts.

There *were* other makes than Ford, many of them, and there were a number of firms, of limited output, who concentrated entirely upon the 'carriage trade' and made no attempt on the mass market, but a photograph taken in the Main Street of any typical American town of the 'twenties would show far more cars than were to be seen in any comparable European town, and would also suggest that at least 99% of them were Tin Lizzies.

The scope for the manufacturer of high-quality cars therefore was fairly limited in proportion to the total demand, and one of the obstacles to be overcome was that many of the customers who were prepared to spend $7,000 or more on a motor-car preferred to import one from Europe or England rather than buy a native product. This was not because the imported cars were necessarily better than the best American machines, but because the snob value of a foreign car attracted a certain type. This is the reason often put forward for the failure of the Springfield project, and though there is much truth in this it is not the whole truth, and 'The idiot who praises in enthusiastic tone, every century but this – every country but his own' was confined to what might be unkindly described as the lunatic fringe of Hollywood-America. That the attitude undoubtedly *did* exist is revealed in the American corporation's early advertisements which laid very great stress on the fact that the Springfield cars were to be mechanically identical to their English counterparts and were to be tested in exactly the same way at every stage of manufacture.

It was widely believed at one time that the first Springfield products were chassis imported from England complete and merely checked and tested at Springfield, but this is not so. From the beginning, early in 1920, very few imported components were used; the most vital being the crankshafts, almost all of which came from England during the whole span of the American venture.

Apart from the cranks, therefore, the first Springfield Silver Ghosts were American except for the wheels and some of the electrical equipment. Very soon, however, the English dual ignition system (Rolls-Royce coil and distributor, and Watford magneto) gave way for a short while to a combination of English R-R. coil and American Bosch magneto. This did not last long and by the end of 1920 the magnetos were dispensed with and American Bosch coil equipment substituted for the English components. American wire wheels followed soon after and by 1923 the R-R. dynamos and starter-motors had been replaced by Westinghouse units. Despite the advertisements, therefore, the Springfield cars soon ceased to be mechanically identical with their English counterparts.

Seen from the 1980s the oddest characteristic of the first Springfield Silver Ghosts was that all were built with right-hand steering and controls. No concession at all was made to the American rule of the road and it was not until late in 1923 that left-hand control was available as a modification, and 1924 before it was standardised. The left-hand-drive models were, of course, given central gear and brake levers and a 3-speed gearbox was substituted for the normal 4-speed affair. Though the United States had the greatest number of cars, relative to population, of any country in the world it is a measure of the comparative scarcity of traffic that right-hand-drive cars were still saleable so late. Even some of the native manufacturers were still building right-hand-drive models for home consumption, though Ford and most of the big producers had changed to left-hand-drive well before the 1914–1918 war.

In outward appearance the Springfield cars were indisputably Rolls-Royces and at the same time distinctively American. The open-bodied versions were higher in the scuttle and waist-line, and with less 'tumble-home' than their English counterparts, and there had long been a most distinctive cut to the folding tops of American touring bodies. To blend into the higher scuttle line the radiators were raised by packing on most of the early cars, and after 1924 the radiators were made an inch taller than the English variety. Bumpers fore and aft were commonplace in the States some years before they were general in England, and these, together with the cylindrical headlamps which were then fashionable, gave the Springfield Royces a markedly American air.

The specifications in Part II show the detail changes and range of chassis and engine numbers. On early examples the chassis numbers were allocated from the series currently used in England, and they are not always reliable as aids to dating; but the engine number provides a trustworthy guide. The first American chassis was delivered in February 1921 and in the succeeding ten years Springfield turned out 1,701 Silver Ghosts and 1,225 Phantom Is. An average of 294 cars a year may seem pretty small beer by comparison with the figure of 833,000 odd which must have been Ford's average output if the commonly accepted total of fifteen million Model Ts in eighteen years is correct, but it is quite an impressive total for a fairly small plant organised on a system which regarded skilled hand-fitting of practically every part essential.

Unlike the parent company, Rolls-Royce of America always advertised coachwork and supplied complete cars at the buyer's option. The Rolls-Royce Custom Coachwork, as it was called, was identified by small plaques and a number of body-builders supplied the bodies to R-R. specification. The best-known suppliers were Brewster and Co. and in 1926 they were bought up by Rolls-Royce of America: for the remaining five years of production nearly all the Springfield cars were Brewster bodied.

The 20 h.p. Rolls-Royce was never built at Springfield and not very many were imported, but by 1926 Springfield had followed Derby and started production of the New Phantom as the Silver Ghost's successor was known at first. Curiously, the first 66 Phantoms did not have the servo-assisted 4-wheel brakes (they were later recalled and modified), but from the start they were furnished with that most valuable adjunct, the centralised chassis lubricating system, which was not copied by Derby until nearly four years later.

The best year for Springfield was 1928 when nearly 400 PIs were produced, but in the following year the figure was halved although there was a slight increase in the number of English Rolls-Royces imported into the States (either through Springfield or by other agencies). It is this which supports the theory that it was preference for English-built cars which led to Springfield's decline, but a more valid reason is that by 1929 Derby had started supplying the Phantom II and Springfield continued with the Phantom I: not unnaturally, most customers who wanted a Rolls-Royce also wanted it to be the latest type.

The directors at Springfield must have been faced with a hard choice: sales had dropped since the announcement of the new model and it would have seemed logical to organise its manufacture at Springfield with the least possible delay. But the change from PI to PII was a more extensive and costly business than the change from Silver Ghost to Phantom I, which was not so much a new car as a re-engined version of the old one. It is just possible that a bold policy would have saved the day, but already the dead hand of the depression was throttling the business world and the following figures tell the rest of the sad story: 200 cars were made in 1929 but only 100 in 1930, in which year, significantly enough, the number of imported Rolls-Royces also declined sharply. In 1931 Springfield stopped production and during the next two or three years the Derby factory supplied 127 left-hand-drive chassis which were tested at Springfield and most fitted with Brewster bodies.

Service facilities continued, and in 1933 a few cars were assembled from surplus spare parts but by 1934 the corporation was in the receiver's hands. Repair and maintenance work continued and some business was done in Brewster cars which were assembled on Ford V-8 chassis. In August 1935 the factory closed and the experiment was at an end.

*　　　*　　　*

Claude Johnson died on 1 April 1926: he was only sixty-three which is no great age, and he who had virtually nursed Henry Royce back to life, and seen to it that the departmental chiefs such as Wormald, Hives and the rest took enough time off to avoid overstrain, had clearly been suffering from exhaustion and nervous fatigue for some while. He died, in fact, of overwork and it is probable that his ceaseless activity and worry during the war had started the decline. The country was very much in his debt, not only directly for his war efforts, important though they were, but for his work in making the organisation which has done more to enhance the reputation of British engineering than anything else in this century. Although he was popular with those who knew him it seems that his forthrightness in his battles with officialdom had made him *persona non grata* with the hierarchy and he died plain Mr. Johnson. However, when one reflects upon the cynically corrupt way in which Lloyd George's government sold honours after the war this was in itself almost a distinction.

It is unlikely that Rolls-Royce Ltd., and all the name means, would have come into existence without Claude Johnson and it is extremely doubtful whether it could have survived its early years without him. It has often been said that he had a genius for organisation and for once the word 'genius' is not misused. Plenty of men have a talent for organisation, but all too often their motive for developing and using it is one of self-aggrandisement. But Johnson's talent did amount to genius, for he was able to get things done without riding roughshod over those who differed from him, and although, like all sensible men, he was not without a proper measure of self-interest, the success of Rolls-Royce and the health and well-being of those who made the success possible meant more to him than the mere acquisition of money.

It is common knowledge that Johnson's organisation of Royce's way of life after 1911 possibly saved his life and certainly prolonged it; the unobtrusive way in which he so arranged affairs that Royce was freed from the day-to-day cares of the factory yet was still able to give the company the benefit of his skill prevented almost certain disaster. It is less common knowledge that Royce's illness was a blessing in disguise for the company: this may seem a harsh judgement but the plain fact was that Henry Royce was a perfectionist and there comes a time when perfectionists can be too expensive a luxury for any commercial concern. Left to himself Royce would have carried his efforts to make a perfect motor-car beyond the bounds of commercial reason. It was largely because of this that Johnson favoured the one-model policy, which provided the opportunity for the company to concentrate on a motor-car which Royce may not have considered perfect (what machine is?) but which, at least, was nearer perfection than its contemporaries. It was clear at the time that Royce was a trifle piqued by the decision to abandon, in particular, the 20 h.p. 4-cylinder model which was so popular, and Rolls-Royce enthusiasts may mourn that (relatively) so few of these entrancing vehicles were built; but there can be no doubt that the decision was sound from the business point of view.

So, too, was Johnson's decision that both for the preservation of his health and for the smooth functioning of the factory, it was essential to keep Royce away once the initial stages were over. Just as Royce's habit of suddenly diverting men from their proper tasks had been the despair of the foremen in the old Cooke Street days so were his rare visits to Derby apt to produce chaos, blue language and wholesale sackings. At bottom, Henry Royce was a kindly and courteous man; it was typical of him to add to his report on an electrical speed indicator the words '. . . and we ought to thank the winder for having produced such neat winding on this model', but his was not the temperament to fit happily into the hurly-burly of a large organisation. To have curbed him without hurting his feelings might have been beyond Johnson's powers, but the illness which forced his hand allowed the transition to semi-retirement to be made without any hurt pride or friction.

As head of the business side of the concern Johnson did not often intervene in technical matters, and when he did he applied the same robust common sense that he gave to commercial problems. It was largely because of his urging that the 4-speed gearbox was fitted to the Silver Ghosts after Radley's Alpine Trial failure. Though the solution Royce preferred, retaining the 3-speed box but providing a lower bottom gear, was sound enough on technical and constructional grounds, Johnson's preference for the 4-speed box was sounder commercially and showed that he understood the psychology of his customers. Similarly over the famous radiator: as real wages rose so this elegant component became more and more expensive as no form of die-stamping can produce so sharp-edged a structure, and a great deal of costly hand work must be lavished upon it. As far back as 1922 Royce wanted to abandon the Grecian shell for some more practical form, but Johnson knew that this was a matter over which sentiment must be allowed to outweigh economics, and that the famous shape was almost worth its weight in gold.

When Claude Johnson died the company's two new models, the 20 h.p. and the New Phantom, were firmly established, the system which kept the experimental work done by Royce and his staff going in harmony with the factory worked smoothly, and the Rolls-Royce car was equally recognised by short-sighted old ladies in Kensington and sharp-witted motor-minded boys in Birmingham. The American venture had not fallen on hard times and the financial success of the business is shown in these figures:

During the last years at Manchester (1905), the joint capital was £104,112 on which a profit of £5,390 was earned. At the end of the first year (1907) at Derby, with 5,325 square yards of floor space in use, the profit was £9,063. By 1913 the factory had grown to 29,838 square yards and the profit to £91,183. In the last full year of Johnson's management (1926–7) the issued capital stood at £813,852, the working area had grown to 66,758 square yards and the profit rose to £163,673. Johnson certainly left to his successors a going concern: for the first two years after his death his brother Basil S. Johnson was managing director, and for the next eighteen years the post was filled by Arthur Sidgreaves who had come to the company as export manager in 1920.

*   *   *

The New Phantom took over from the Silver Ghost in 1925, though the latter was not superseded at one blow but remained available as an alternative (at least in theory) for some while. There was, indeed, no great difference in the two cars except for the engines, and the new chassis followed the lines of the old, with engine and gearbox still as separate units (though a plate clutch replaced the cone type), torque tube transmission and cantilevered rear springs. The last Silver Ghosts had been given spirally cut gears instead of straight-toothed for the final drive bevels and this refinement, naturally, was found on the new model. Spiral-bevel gearing had been used by *Amédée Bollée Fils* as early as 1898 but it did not really come into its own for another twenty years as its advantages of silence and greater strength for a given size of tooth were offset by constructional difficulties. When these

Phantom I Sports. Chassis No. 16EX.

difficulties were overcome the spiral-bevel gearing quickly ousted the older form as it was inherently quieter and, as far as Rolls-Royce were concerned, their standards of silence could be attained with much less of the laborious hand finishing they had had to lavish on their straight-toothed gears; though, if necessary, the spiral bevels were still given a finishing touch with the polishing stone after being run for some hours under a stream of mildly abrasive liquid.

The new engine was of slightly smaller bore and considerably longer stroke than the old; the dimensions were 108×139.5 mm and the capacity 7,668 c.c. The major differences lay in the use of detachable cylinder heads and pushrod-operated overhead valves as on the Twenty. Except that the larger engine still had its cylinder blocks arranged as a pair of triplets (with one cylinder head common to both) it could be regarded as an enlarged version of the 'little' Rolls, and the combustion chambers and valve layout were very similar. The governor control for the throttle was retained, and the ignition advance was automatic (as on the last Ghosts), but it was deplored that the thermostatic control of cooling water flow introduced on the Ghosts in 1923–4 was not fitted, hand-controlled shutters being used instead. These were vertical in contrast to the horizontal louvres of the Twenty.

The Phantom I was the shortest-lived of all the Rolls-Royce models, and used to be the one least sought after by collectors. It was regarded by the enthusiasts for vintage cars as a transitional affair lacking in the effortless 'long stride', the period charm, and the historical interest of the Ghosts (the pre-war examples of which are particularly sought after), and not so exciting in appearance as its immediate successors; but it was enthusiastically received at the time. *The Autocar* reported in May 1925 that the much improved acceleration and maximum speed of approximately 80 m.p.h. had not been bought at the expense of the traditional Rolls-Royce silence and smoothness. As usual, the point was made that almost all the running could be done in top gear, and that normally the car could be started in third and slid immediately into top. That curiously archaic R-R. feature, the notched gear-lever gate which locked the lever in position, was damned with the faintest of praise: 'The gear-change, a point on which there has always been a controversy, is a little easier to handle than hitherto once one becomes accustomed to the locking mechanism . . .'. As the locking mechanism had been abolished from the 20 h.p. model without any dire consequences, and had been under fire so often, its retention on the Phantom is not easy to defend.

Braking, steering and suspension were said by *The Autocar* to be above reproach – particularly the suspension. The new design of shock absorber, which was readily adjusted to suit varying conditions, allowed fast cornering without roll. At least, thus said the report. But it seems that the reporter cannot have ridden in the back of the car, or if he did that he was a good sailor, for a valid criticism of the first Phantom Is was that, when driven fast, any back seat passengers slightly inclined to queasiness soon had reason to wish themselves elsewhere. This unpleasant shortcoming was largely overcome in the later models.

There are those who said that the steering of the Phantom I was its poorest feature, particularly by comparison with the Silver Ghost; this criticism probably stems from the fact that the arrival of the new model coincided with the general acceptance of 'balloon' tyres of larger section and lower working pressure than their straight-sided or beaded-edged predecessors. These relatively wide section tyres undoubtedly posed problems, and it will generally be found that nearly all cars of the period, not only Rolls-Royces, were less nimble and precise than their forerunners which ran on narrow high-pressure tyres.

Much of the connoisseurs' lack of enthusiasm for the Phantom I arose from the fact that it had a fairly ponderous 'feel' to it, whereas the Ghosts, particularly the pre-war ones, somehow contrived to give their drivers the impression of being smaller than they were which was a most pleasing attribute. By the time the Phantom I appeared most cars in the luxury class had become more than a little elephantine both in appearance and handling qualities: the new Rolls-Royce possessed these defects to some degree but it is only necessary to compare the handling of a Phantom I with, for instance, a 40/50 Napier (the last private car to be turned out by that famous firm), or a large Panhard or Mercedes of the time to realise that Rolls-Royce Ltd. were still well ahead of the field.

The maximum output of the New Phantom engine was not disclosed by the company, and the motoring journalists of the time do not seem to have bothered themselves with making approximate calculations. As with all Rolls-Royce engines the specific output was steadily increased during the life-span of the model, and the last innovation was an aluminium cylinder head which allowed a higher compression ratio with no loss of refinement. On the basis of the cars' performances the power ultimately developed may be calculated at about 90–100 b.h.p. The company's claimed maximum speed of 75 m.p.h. was, as always, on the modest side and for those who felt that this was too slow the output could be increased with no loss of reliability. In 1939 a thirteen-year-old Phantom I was supercharged for that most enterprising connoisseur of fine machinery, Mr. Douglas Fitzpatrick. No alteration was made to the engine bearings or crankshaft, nor did they give any trouble, though in blown form the car's comfortable cruising speed was raised from about 5 m.p.h. to 75 m.p.h., and its maximum pace was not very far short of the magic hundred.

8

More Phantoms, the Bentleys and the Wraith

———

T HE decade from 1929 to 1939 which started with the financial crisis and ended with Germany's second attempt to dominate the world was scarcely a happy one for the motor industry. A large number of motor firms were swept away by the great depression which is now seen to have been largely artificial and almost wholly avoidable; most of those who remained in business only did so by ruthlessly lowering their standards in order to cut prices to the bone. It happened also to be a period of stagnation in design when, for the first time, the advertising and sales men dominated the engineers instead of working in harmony with them. This combination of circumstances had disastrous results on car design in general and most of the bread-and-butter cars of the 'thirties were quite remarkably nasty. That Rolls-Royce not only survived, but prospered without any relaxation of standards, is due in part to their aero engine business but largely because of the traditions established by the founders.

During this period the Phantom II arrived, was developed and finally succeeded by the Phantom III. The 20 h.p. car grew up first into the 20/25, then became the 25/30 from which was developed the Wraith series which was continued after the war as the Silver Wraith. Finally, to the astonishment of the motor world Rolls-Royce Ltd. bought up the Bentley business when that company was forced into liquidation in 1931.

Opinions are fairly evenly divided on the Phantom II. That well-known Rolls-Royce fancier, David Scott-Moncrieff*, describes it as '. . . a magic carpet, wafting you silently . . .', to which another expert, John Bolster, who has also handled many Rolls-Royce cars of all periods, robustly retorts in his review of the book 'What arrant nonsense', adding '. . . an even rougher car than the Phantom II was the Isotta-Fraschini'. As always, the truth lies somewhere between the two extremes. To describe the Phantom II, as some critics have done, as 'a rough old lorry' betrays gross ignorance both of Phantom IIs and of lorries, but it is not unjust to say that it had lost some of the magic carpet quality of the earlier Silver Ghosts, and at high speeds some mechanical effort from the engine could be both heard and felt; but it must be remembered that the Phantom II was a very much faster car than the Ghost and usually carried much heavier coachwork. As the model developed, various

---

* *The Thoroughbred Motor Car, 1930–40*, by David Scott-Moncrieff, B. T. Batsford Ltd., 1963.

modifications to the bearings and engine mountings, together with a redesigned and heavier crankshaft, restored to the engine Rolls-Royce's traditional silkiness of operation.

A virtue the Phantom II inherited from its predecessors was that of longevity. Repair costs in terms of miles run were remarkably low and the petrol consumption of approximately 12 m.p.g. was far from unreasonable considering the car's size and performance.

Many of the chassis details were similar to those of the smaller model and represented a final departure from the Silver Ghost plan. Engine, clutch housing and gearbox were assembled in unit, the cantilever rear springs and torque tube gave way to long underslung semi-elliptics and 'Hotchkiss drive', whilst a valuable innovation, borrowed from Springfield practice, was the centralised chassis lubricating system which fed all the movable chassis parts, such as brake and clutch shafts, spring shackles and so forth, with oil from a reservoir by a suitable pedal-operated force pump. An ingenious arrangement of drip plugs proportioned the supply to the needs of the components receiving it. The system was not, at first, a 'one-shot' as with typical prudence the Derby engineers did not extend the system to the king-pins and other movable joints on the axles so as to avoid trouble with flexible piping. A single oil-nipple on the front axle and another on the back, together with one for each universal joint, and those on the spring gaiters, were the only points needing periodical attention with the oil-gun, otherwise the centralised system took care of everything in the most efficient and painless manner. This was a far cry indeed from the pre-war Silver Ghosts which, if maintained according to the manual, had some ninety-nine points for the driver to lubricate by hand once a week. On the later Phantom IIs the objections to flexible piping were overcome and the system became a full-scale 'one-shot', leaving only the propeller shaft universal joints in need of occasional attention with the oil-gun.

At a quick glance little difference could be found between the Phantom II and Phantom I engines: bore and stroke were the same at 108×139.5 mm and the two blocks of three cylinders shared a common aluminium head. But there were several unobtrusive changes; the combustion chambers and manifolds had been wholly redesigned and inlet and exhaust manifolds (the latter a 3-branch affair) were now on opposite sides of the engine. Magneto ignition served sparking plugs on the near side of the engine whilst the coil and distributor, as on the PI, looked after those on the off side.

As with all the Rolls-Royce models the modifications made to the Phantom II during its life span were designed not only to iron out imperfections but to improve performance. In September 1929, for example, *The Motor* carried out a road test of a short chassis model: the maximum speed was recorded as 'well above 80 m.p.h.', and the car accelerated from 10 m.p.h. to 52 m.p.h. in third gear in 17 seconds. In March 1934 a short chassis 'Continental'* was taken for test and returned a properly timed maximum speed of 90.2 m.p.h., accelerated from standstill to 60 m.p.h. in 23 seconds and knocked two seconds off

---

* Designed by H. I. F. Evernden who, with John Bletchley, was also responsible for the post-war 'Continental' Bentley.

its predecessor's time to reach 52 miles an hour in third speed; in which gear, incidentally, 68 m.p.h. was easily attainable. By the time this chassis was tested Rolls-Royce were fitting synchromesh mechanism to third and fourth gears and this improvement, together with a change in driving habits and increased traffic, made the 'start in third, change directly into top and stay there' technique less attractive. Nevertheless the traditional top-gear flexibility was still there and though the maximum speed of the last 'Continental' Phantom IIs was in the neighbourhood of 95 m.p.h., and their acceleration, handling and braking such as to put most contemporary sports cars to shame, they could still be driven in top gear at 5 m.p.h. without trace of jerk or snatch.

It has been said that the Phantom II, like the Hispano, was undergeared in order to keep this sort of top gear flexibility: this is hardly fair comment as the axle ratio of the 'Continental' was 3.4:1 which, in conjunction with 21 in. tyres can hardly be regarded as unduly low geared. True, the car had not the fascinating 'long-stride' of the pre-war Ghosts with their large diameter wheels and 2.9:1 axle ratio, but for a car weighing $2^1/_2$ tons, carrying spacious closed coachwork, a top gear range from walking pace to within sight of the century was not to be despised.

A point which is often proclaimed with joy by all those motor pundits who delight in decrying Rolls-Royce and all its works is that, early in the 'thirties, the company issued a mild warning against driving continuously at full throttle, particularly on the new *autostrada* and *autobahnen* which brought a new concept of high-speed motoring into being. This warning is interpreted as 'Rolls-Royce admit the Phantom II won't stand up to fast cruising' which is more than a little unjust. Engineers producing or operating machines as diverse as locomotives, mill-engines, marine-engines, and electric generating sets have always acted on the principle that normal 'full-speed' working should be a little below the ultimate possible maximum so as to have a reserve of power for emergencies. Signalling 'Full ahead' to a ship's engine room, for example, results in the engineer on duty setting his engines to run at about 10% to 15% below their maximum capacity; motor engineers originally thought on similar lines.

In the first days of motoring when engines ran unthrottled and the very limited power-to-weight ratio meant that they seldom could reach peak speed in top gear, designers of most of the larger cars generally relied upon an exhaust valve governor to limit over-revving in the lower gears, and the ungoverned engines found on small cars were saved from self-immolation by their sheer inefficiency. Later, with more efficient engines and throttle control the risks of overdriving were automatically guarded against by the continual checks imposed by road and traffic conditions. When the new roads made it possible for drivers to continue at full-throttle for miles on end a number of motorists discovered that the old engineering principle of always keeping a little in reserve had much to commend it, and it was typical of Rolls-Royce's honesty that they warned their customers accordingly.

The acidulous critics who were ready to pour scorn on the Phantom 11* because of this warning were usually equally ready to heap ecstatic praise upon the contemporary 38/250 Mercedes of comparable capacity and performance. In doing so they lost sight of the fact

112

that this Mercedes, though undeniably a most exciting, impressive and well-made motor-car, could only reach its maximum speeds and briskest acceleration by the help of a supercharger which came into action when the accelerator pedal was pressed hard down. This action resulted in impressive acceleration to the accompaniment of a hideous pig-like squealing which presumably appeals to those who share the Teutonic taste for arrogant self-assertion, but where Rolls-Royce contented themselves with a mildly phrased warning against overmuch bravura on fast roads, Mercedes issued a strict injunction not to run the engine at maximum output for more than twenty seconds at a time.

* * *

Rolls-Royce's purchase of the Bentley business came as a considerable surprise; at first sight nothing could seem less likely than the Company which put silence and refinement high on their list of priorities interesting itself in the 'Bentley boy' type of customer who, at that time, positively scorned comfort, liked noise and regarded the motorist who stopped to put up his hood in a heavy rainstorm as an effete fuddy-duddy fit only to pilot a Baby Austin at 25 m.p.h.

Times were changing, however, and although the hairy-chested continued (and will long continue, praise be) to enjoy the combination of rugged stamina, brute force and fine engineering which made the name of Bentley great in the 'twenties, the Bentley company themselves were moving in the direction of greater luxury, silence and passenger comfort, to be combined with speed of course, when the great depression engulfed them. The 3-litre Bentley had already given way to the $4\frac{1}{2}$-litre, the refinement and mechanical quietness of which was masked by the typical burbling, gobbling exhaust note. The $6\frac{1}{2}$-litre car was smoother and quieter still, but marred by poor road-holding and suspension; these short-comings were eradicated from the fabulous (but perhaps over-rated) 8-litre Bentley of which only about 100 were made before the financial collapse. And if Bentley were moving towards the luxury carriage market it must not be forgotten that Rolls-Royce had never despised speed.

Seen in this light, therefore, the liaison is less strange, but the threat of renewed competition from their old rival, Napier, was doubtless the deciding factor in Rolls-Royce's decision. Napier's last private car (production stopped in 1925) had been rated, like its rival, at 40/50 h.p.; it was propelled by a smooth running 6-cylinder overhead camshaft engine, with aluminium cylinder block, of remarkably advanced design and singularly disap-pointing performance. There was no smaller model to help keep the name before the public and declining sales, coupled with a great increase in their aero-engine business, decided the company to give up car production, temporarily at least. There must have been many occasions when nostalgia for their great past tempted Napiers to return to the fold: nevertheless it was a bold move, and one showing great faith in the Bentley reputation,

---

* Similar warnings were given in respect of the Phantom III, which was not supposed to be driven *continuously* at more than 75/80 m.p.h., and the smaller models.

1937 4¼-litre Bentley.

114

when the decision was taken to buy the assets of the Bentley company and start producing an 8-litre Bentley-Napier at a time when most manufacturers were drawing in their horns.

Negotiations between Napier, Bentley Motors Ltd., W. O. Bentley himself and the Receiver were almost complete, and plans for the new car were well advanced, when Rolls-Royce Ltd. stepped into the picture. All that was required was the approval of the Receiver's Court for the take-over and this was thought to be a mere formality. The barrister acting for Napiers put forward the proposed terms, but before the presiding judge could signify approval another man of law rose to announce that he was empowered by 'The British Equitable Trust' to offer a larger sum for the assets of the Bentley concern. Nonplussed, the Napier representative asked for time to consult his principals who would, he felt sure, increase their bid as the difference in prices offered was not large, but the judge announced that it was not his function to preside over an auction sale and that in the interests of the creditors the British Equitable Trust's offer must be accepted. W. O. Bentley recorded in his autobiography* that he, and the others, were astounded by this intervention and that more than a week passed before he learned that the British Equitable Trust were acting for Rolls-Royce Ltd.

One cannot view the failure of Bentley Motors Ltd. (and other individualistic motor firms) as anything but a tragedy, and W. O. Bentley himself was understandably somewhat embittered by the way in which financial manœuvres beyond his control had left his beloved company stranded when quite a modest extension of credit might have kept it afloat. Understandable, too, that he was distressed by the unexpected collapse of the Napier-Bentley plans which would, at least, have left him in command of design; but seen from the purely commercial point of view Rolls-Royce's intervention was prompted by sound common sense.

W. O. Bentley worked for Rolls-Royce between 1931 and 1935, but he had no direct influence on the design of the first Rolls-built Bentley cars although, indirectly, his reports on the handling characteristics of various chassis were of great value. In his autobiography he said 'My service agreement with Bentley Motors, Rolls-Royce told me, was still in force. I was not a free man to select my own future. I was, they made clear, part of the assets which they had purchased together with the office furniture, my medals, cups and trophies.' It is clear that he felt more than a little resentful towards Rolls-Royce Ltd., and also felt, at first, that he was merely being used as a glorified tester; but he soon came to feel warm admiration for the staff of the Design and Experimental Departments who were, he records, unwearied in their search for improvement and never complacent about their mistakes. In particular, he concluded that part of his book which deals with this period with an enthusiastic and obviously sincere appreciation of E. W. Hives both as a man and an engineer.

It is common, but incorrect, to regard the $3^1/_2$-litre Bentley of the early 'thirties as a 20/25 h.p. Rolls-Royce with a different radiator and a mildly hotted-up engine. The chassis

---

* *W. O. The Autobiography of W. O. Bentley*, Hutchinson & Co., Ltd., 1958. It should be noted, however, that the managing director of Bentley Motors had suggested a merger some four months previously to Rolls-Royce.

was, in fact, derived from an experimental 18 h.p. $2^3/_4$-litre Rolls-Royce which had been proposed as a sort of economy version of the 20/25, but which had been laid aside when it became clear that it would be very little cheaper to produce than the standard version. The handling qualities of this chassis were outstandingly good as Bentley reported after carrying out high-speed trials at Brooklands, whereupon rather disappointing experiments were conducted with a supercharged engine: disappointing, that is, because although the supercharged car was fast and docile a good deal of trouble was experienced with the crankshaft. Rather than redesign the engine to overcome this difficulty Hives decided that adequate performance and greater reliability could be had by modifying the 20/25 h.p. engine which had been introduced in 1929 to succeed the 20 h.p.

W. O. Bentley. Following Rolls-Royce's acquisition of Bentley Motors Ltd, W. O. worked for Rolls-Royce from 1931 to 1935.

This was done, and the modified 20/25 engine was allied to the chassis of the $2^3/_4$-litre Rolls-Royce early in 1933 to make the first $3^1/_2$-litre Bentley, or Rolls-Bentley as it was generally called. The engine modifications included increased compression, re-designed manifolds, and twin carburettors. Though there was necessarily some increase in mechanical noise by comparison with the standard engine, the Company's claim that this was 'the silent sports car' was wholly justified.

The principal difference between the 20/25 h.p. and 25/30 h.p. Rolls-Royce cars and their Bentley counterparts (the $3^1/_2$-litre and the $4^1/_2$-litre) is in the breathing. On the Rolls-Royce engines the manifolds and push-rods were on the same side of the engine which was not the best arrangement for unrestricted gas-flow: for the Bentley engines the induction manifold was put on the side of the engine opposite the push-rods, and this made it possible to redesign the cylinder head to provide better ports and make higher compression pressures possible. Also the Bentley engine had twin S.U. carburettors, and by choosing the best size of connecting passage between the two halves of the induction pipe ram-effect increased the power available in the middle range of speed at the expense of a slight loss in low-speed torque. Because of the importance of flexibility, and a reliable, slow, tick-over, the Rolls-Royce engines were not given dual carburettors until 1955. The buyer of a Bentley car in the 'thirties could be expected to use his gearbox and a slight loss of flexibility was of little consequence.

According to George Oliver, who has had much experience of the cars of the period, 'The driver of a 20/25 Rolls-Royce is aware of the engine, in the gears, as a smothered commotion whereas in the Bentley there is less fuss even though there is more noise. As far as passengers in a 20/25 are concerned, it is only at 50 m.p.h. or more in third, for example, that there is any suggestion of engine.' The output of the standard $3\frac{1}{2}$-litre Bentley engine was 105 b.h.p., and that of the $4\frac{1}{2}$-litre which supplanted it 126 b.h.p.

Probably because of the absence of the fascinating burbling boom that distinguished the true Bentley, the hairy-chested fraternity were apt to dismiss the $3\frac{1}{2}$-litre Bentley as another 'gutless wonder', but the chassis could carry a comfortable saloon body, quietly and smoothly, at speeds calculated to set the driver of a 'real' Bentley on his mettle, despite the help afforded by his lightweight open Van den Plas bodywork and thunderous near-open exhaust.

W. A. Robotham was chiefly responsible, under E. W. Hives, for the $3\frac{1}{2}$-litre Bentley, and much fame was earned for the model by E. R. Hall who was, at that time, racing M.G.s with conspicuous success. He took his Bentley with him to Italy in 1934 and used it as a practice car round the Mille Miglia course to save his M.G. for the race itself. He was so impressed by its performance on this difficult course that he asked the company to lift their usual ban on the use of their cars for racing so that he could compete in the Tourist Trophy. Rolls-Royce Ltd., as usual, made no objection provided the car was entered privately under Hall's name, and promised support and help in tuning the car for the race.

E. R. Hall driving the $4\frac{1}{4}$-litre Bentley into second place on handicap on the Ards Circuit at Belfast: in the two previous years, with a $3\frac{1}{2}$-litre Bentley, he had also come second on handicap, but achieved the highest average speed (78.4 m.p.h. and 80–81m.p.h.) in all three races.

By raising the compression ratio to 7.75:1, fitting larger inlet valves, and a straight-through exhaust system the output was raised to 130 b.h.p. which, with suitably altered axle gearing, gave the car a top speed of 110 m.p.h. By a curious coincidence the result was similar to that of 29 years earlier and Hall took second place. 'Ifs' and 'buts' have no place in motor race results, but there is little doubt that the need for two tyre changes, with 54-minutes lost struggling with a jammed wheel nut, robbed the Bentley of first place, as its speed of 78.4 m.p.h. was highest in the event.

In 1935 Hall tried again. To overcome the problem of excessive tyre wear larger wheels were fitted and the back axle ratio altered to suit; further tuning raised the engine output to an impressive 155 b.h.p. Despite this, Hall again had to be content with second place, being 73 seconds behind Dixon's Riley on handicap, but he again had the satisfaction of knowing that his average speed of 80.34 m.p.h. was the fastest in the race and enabled him to beat Lord Howe's 3.3-litre Bugatti by three minutes. The following year saw a repition of events for Hall's Bentley, now fitted with the new $4^{1}/_{2}$-litre engine, was again pipped by 26 seconds, on handicap, by Dodson and Dixon in the Riley. Hall drove the 478 miles single-handed and made the fastest time then recorded for the T.T. for all classes including supercharged cars. He was no less than nine minutes ahead of the Lagonda which was the nearest competitor in the same class. Though first place had always eluded him these remarkably consistent performances of Hall's proved that the Rolls-Royce formula for fast motoring lacked neither potency nor stamina.

The $4^{1}/_{2}$-litre engine fitted to the Bentley chassis from 1936 onwards allowed heavier and more commodious coachwork to be carried with no loss of performance, and the last pre-war refinements were the overdrive and, on the Mark V, the independent front suspension. Even the most captious critic is hard put to it to fault this car, particularly as body-design had by then emerged from the slough into which it had fallen during the early 'thirties when fashion decreed that all cars of sporting pretensions must have such elongated bonnets and high scuttle and waist lines that the hapless occupants peered through little windscreens scarcely higher than letter box slits.

In 1938 Walter Sleator commissioned a specially prepared chassis with the $4^{1}/_{4}$-litre engine and a streamlined body: he found the car capable of 112 m.p.h. without apparent effort, and that this was no mere flash in the pan was proved when George Eyston covered 114.7 miles in the hour at Brooklands in the same car. Emboldened by this success the company decided to make a modified version of this special car as a standard model, and with this effort the pre-war Bentley story ends on a sad note. The prototype was sent to France to be fitted with a body by Vanvooren of Paris which was to be a model for the production bodies to be made by Park Ward & Co. After being bodied the 'Corniche' Bentley was put through its 15,000 miles endurance test and returned to Dieppe just as war was declared. It was apparently destroyed by a German bomb before it could be shipped to England, and six years later the ignition key was returned to Robotham by the faithful R.A.C. Port Representative at Dieppe. It is sadder still that Paulin, the body designer, was shot by the Germans for his work in the Resistance movement.

*   *   *

Henry Royce died on 22 April 1933. Although he did not live to see the outcome of the Rolls-Royce–Bentley combination he played a part in the start of the project and during one of his rare visits to the London offices he had an interview with W. O. Bentley. He saw the Phantom II firmly established, and the engine of the popular 20 h.p. model enlarged into the 20/25 which gave that pleasant car a most satisfactory performance. Above all he saw the triumph of the Rolls-Royce 'R' engines in the Schneider Trophy contests of 1929 and 1931.

The 1931 race resulted in Britain's third consecutive win (the first having been in 1927 with a Napier-engined S.5 seaplane) and

T. S. Haldenby, joined Royce & Co. as apprentice in 1900 and worked on first cars 1903/4. General Manager R.-R. Ltd. 1946–1952.

entitled her to keep the Trophy in perpetuity. This win was a walk-over as the other contestants withdrew and it was only necessary for Flight-Lieutenant Boothman to fly the course on the day of the race to clinch the matter. This he did at 340.08 m.p.h. and two hours later Flight-Lieutenant Stainforth made a new world's speed record by making four runs of a 3-kilometre section at an average speed of 378.05 m.p.h. Later in the year, again using an 'R' engine, he achieved 407.5 m.p.h.

Although development of this engine was not Royce's last piece of work (for he and his personal staff were as active as ever until almost his last week), it was his last major undertaking and probably his greatest. When it is considered that the basis of the design was the 850 h.p. version of the Buzzard engine of 1927, the output from which was increased to 1,900 h.p. for the 1929 race and further enhanced to 2,300 h.p.* in its final form, the achievement is truly remarkable. The final power increase of 21% was accompanied by an increase in weight of only 6½% which was a triumph for the metallurgical staff at Derby. The whole great project was, necessarily, a team effort but Royce played the leading part with Hives, Elliott and Rowledge as his principal lieutenants.

For his work in the first German war Henry Royce was rewarded with the O.B.E. which, as Mark Twain observed of the Cross of the *Légion d'honneur*, was a distinction which few could escape. For his contribution to the Schneider Trophy success he was made a baronet in 1931, but Sir Frederick Henry Royce, Bart., O.B.E., M.I.M.E., remained – in his own estimation – Henry Royce, mechanic. And mechanic he was, *par excellence*,

---

* 2,783 b.h.p. was actually extracted during development.

** More recent evidence suggests that this may not in fact have been the case.

combining an uncanny aptitude for finding the best and making it better, with the eye of an artist and unwearying patience and attention to detail.

As with many other great craftsmen, such as John Harrison who made the first practical marine chronometer or George Stephenson (both of whom were practically illiterate), Royce's lack of formal education was offset by intuitive skill and an enquiring mind. His knowledge of mathematics was limited to the simplest arithmetic, he never used a slide rule and his own engineering drawings were no more than rough sketches, yet his contribution to modern engineering was considerable at the very lowest estimation, and he was never too proud to submit to others mathematical and scientific problems which were beyond his scope. He did not make the mistake of underrating his capacity, but his essential humility preserved him from the failing of so many self-made men who, like Henry Ford, became so high-flown with success as to believe themselves indispensable and infallible.

Perhaps the best tribute to Sir Henry Royce is found in the spirit which still pervades the Rolls-Royce organisation. Though his visits to the factory were rare, the most damning and potent criticism which can be made is still 'That would not do for Henry Royce'.

From the start of his semi-retirement onwards all the design work which went into improving the cars, and developing the new models, was the result of team-work so that it is impossible to say of any particular type that 'Royce did this', 'Hives did that', 'Clegg did the other'. Ideas were bandied to and fro across the table or through the post, rough sketches were worked up into finished drawings, rubbed out, altered and done again, components, testing devices, tools and complete cars were altered, rebuilt, modified or run to destruction by any one of a number of different men, but throughout this apparently complex procedure Royce remained very firmly the chief designer. This type of team-work can only develop satisfactorily if the head of the team is a strong enough personality to keep a firm guiding hand, but not so domineering as to reduce his colleagues to mere dogs-bodies. Designing by team-work in the Rolls-Royce way can produce the happiest results, as the post-war combination of Alec Issigonis and the B.M.C. design staff demonstrated, but all too often it degenerates into designing by committee which results in a body of men, mostly more concerned with finance than engineering, deciding which of a great variety of components, engines, body-pressings, gearboxes and so on, can most economically be combined to make a complete motor-car and then instructing their engineers to compose the motor-car accordingly. Though good motor-cars (or refrigerators, or washing machines) can be designed in this way the confection which emerges is all too often a curate's egg as it is nobody's business to see that the filler plug of Back Axle A, for example, will be completely inaccessible if the axle is used for Chassis B, or that the front suspension of Car C will lose its virtue on being married to Engine D.

Henry Royce's death was naturally a great blow to all his associates, but the Rolls-Royce method had been so carefully nurtured over the years that the work of constant revision and improvement continued unchecked. Soon after the chief designer's death the entwined initials RR on the radiators were enamelled in black instead of red. A legend which persists to this day says this is a sign of mourning for Sir Henry, but the real reason

Kneeling Spirit of Ecstasy optional on Rolls-Royce cars 1934–1939; standard on Silver Wraith and Silver Dawn 1946–1955.

is less romantic. The change was decided upon before Royce's death, because the red initials occasionally clashed with an owner's colour scheme, whereas black suits anything.

*　　　　*　　　　*

The first series Phantom III was announced in the autumn of 1935, and it was at once seen that the rumours, so often circulated, that Rolls-Royce had been experimenting with a Vee engine were not unfounded. Indeed, these experiments went back to the middle 'twenties, when an o.h.c. 6-cylinder, a straight eight, and a V-12 had all been produced experimentally during the search for the best engine to replace the Silver Ghost unit. The engine which finally emerged in 1935 was extremely advanced in design, materials and construction and obviously owed a lot to aero engine practice. The reason for adopting the Vee formation was the same as that which had influenced the choice of a V-8 for the abortive bonnetless cars of 1905, namely to save space; the new engine was so compact that it was possible to reduce the wheelbase by eight inches *vis à vis* the Phantom II whilst providing increased space for the bodywork.

It was considered that it was not practicable to coax any more power out of the big 6-cylinder engine without risking loss of refinement, and the straight-eight engines then so popular with some Continental and many American firms were inordinately long. The choice of a V-12, and not the more usual V-8, occasioned some surprise but was logical enough considering the company's long experience with V-12 aero engines.

Other factors which probably influenced the choice of a 12-cylinder engine were the need to keep abreast, or preferably ahead, of opposition from Cadillac, Packard and Hispano-Suiza, and Royce's expressed wish in one of his memoranda to the factory, which may be paraphrased as: 'I want a car which will run well with more things wrong than any other in existence'. According to the Secretary of the Phantom III Technical Society of America, this was written after another 'chastening episode' when some distinguished visitors to Le Canadel were being shown one of the latest Continental Phantom IIs. After showing various details of the car, Royce went to start the engine in order to give his guests a ride, but to his chagrin it refused duty. After some quick work by his assistants, accompanied one may confidently assume by some Roycean strong language, the car did start, but the fault was not fully cured and there was enough roughness of running to be apparent to a layman.

Some details of this story may be apocryphal but in essence it rings true, and the Phantom III engine was certainly endowed with the ability to 'come home on a piston ring and a prayer', as Ian Hallows puts it. The engine design was sometimes denigrated for being too complex, but the virtues of simplicity are sometimes overstated, as Sir Harry Ricardo pointed out in his famous book on high speed internal combustion engines. Considered purely as a piece of mechanical engineering it is very difficult to fault the Phantom III engine, but its very ability to keep going with no apparent loss of refinement but with gross faults putting as many as four cylinders out of action was a

122

mixed blessing. Such virtue in an aeroplane engine may save lives, but in a motor car may needlessly inflate the bills when the long-overdue attention is given.

With bore dimensions of 82.5 mm and stroke of 114 mm (it will be noticed how often this length of stroke crops up) the 7,340 c.c. capacity of the new engine was 328 c.c. less than that of the Phantom II; the output, however, was greater: 165 b.h.p. at 3,000 r.p.m. was given in 1937, subsequently developed to about 180 b.h.p. The cylinder blocks, angled at 60°, were of the skeleton type with 'wet' liners, and the cylinder heads were of aluminium alloy. Marine type connecting rods were paired, each sharing a common crank-pin of the six-throw shaft which ran in seven main bearings.

No longer was there a magneto, not even the purely stand-by affair found on the contemporary 20/25 h.p. car. As before, there were two sparking plugs to each cylinder but, as one coil and distributor would have been hard put to it to serve twenty-four plugs, there were two coils and two sets of distributor mechanism so contrived that plug 'A' in each cylinder was fired by one ignition set whilst its opposite number, plug 'B', was served by the other ignition circuit. The two ignitions were not quite simultaneous but were set with a miniscule time lag between 'A' and 'B' to allow good flame spread. As on the Phantom II engines a series of relief valves varied the pressure at which oil was supplied to various parts of the engine – 25–35 p.s.i. to the crankshaft, 10 p.s.i. to the valve gear, and about $1\frac{3}{4}$ p.s.i. to the timing gear and auxiliary drives. On the first Phantom IIIs a heat exchanger in the form of a small honeycomb radiator provided for quick warming of the oil and then kept it at the most suitable temperature. The most notable innovation was that the overhead valves were worked by pushrods from a single camshaft, in the conventional way, but the tappet-clearances were automatically kept correct by hydraulic rams.

These devices were usually referred to as hydraulic tappets which was rather misleading, as many people assumed from it that the valves were actually opened by hydraulic pressure. The object was to ensure silent working by doing away with the usual expansion gap in the tappet gear, and the idea was an old one having been devised by *Amedée Bollée fils*, as long ago as 1907. It has also been used by Cadillac and one or two other makers of fine cars. Unfortunately in the Phantom III the hydraulic mechanism was ultimately found to be a source of trouble for, unless the engine oils were changed, and the filters cleaned or renewed at the proper intervals (and human nature being what it is, sooner or later these things are always neglected), the small passage-ways serving the hydraulic plungers would become occluded with sludge, whereupon they could cease to function properly and set up excessive loads on the cams and tappet faces which suffered accordingly. Consequently the majority of Phantom IIIs have been modified at some time during their lives by the substitution of a different camshaft and normal tappet mechanism in place of the hydraulic devices. This has led to the assumption that the system was a failure: had the maintenance instructions always been scrupulously observed, or had modern lubricants been available then, it seems likely that the trouble would never have occurred, and it is significant that the current V-8 Rolls-Royce engines are furnished with very similar mechanism.

The chassis was an exceptionally deep and stiff structure with central cruciform

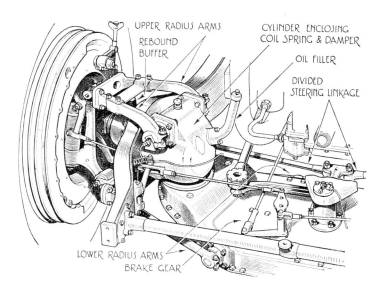

General Motors Corporation's independent front wheel suspension layout as refined by Rolls-Royce Ltd. for the Phantom III.

bracing. In the interest of good weight distribution, and to shorten the propeller shaft, the gearbox was not made integral with the clutch housing but was mounted amidships in the old-fashioned manner with a short jack-shaft to couple it to the clutch. Rear suspension by underslung semi-elliptic leaf springs, the servo braking system, and the hydraulic shock absorbers the resistance of which was increased as speed rose by a pump in the gearbox, and which could further be controlled by hand from a steering column control, were all as before. It was the front suspension which represented the sharpest break with previous Rolls-Royce practice.

Just as Royce and his design staff had taken a long hard look at various methods before adopting four-wheel brakes in the previous decade, various forms of independent front wheel suspension had been under review for some years before Rolls-Royce decided upon a modified form of the General Motors' system for the Phantom III chassis. As the diagram shows the coil springs are enclosed in tubular boxes, which were filled with oil and which also housed the telescopic hydraulic dampers. All the major parts therefore were protected from mud and stones, and were positively lubricated. It was found, however, that by enclosing the springs the pursuit of perfection had been carried too far. After a time – a very long time usually – the springs would develop a slight 'set' to one side, as any coil spring will, and it occasionally happened that this was sufficient to set up a disagreeable scraping noise as the spring rubbed lightly on the inside of the casing. On the post-war cars therefore the springs are exposed though otherwise the suspension has not been fundamentally altered.

As any motorist who was driving in the 'thirties knows, the improvement in riding comfort and road-holding which was afforded by the independent front wheel suspension systems, then being adopted by a few makers, was very great. Consequently the earlier arrangement of leaf springs and beam axle is derided by the *cognoscenti* who now write scathingly of 'cart springs', in ignorance of the facts that the majority of carts had no springs at all and that the virtue of i.f.s. lies less in the absence (in some systems) of leaf springs than in other factors. The motorist of even longer memory, however, knows that i.f.s. only restored the easy riding qualities possessed by the best cars of an earlier period before front wheel brakes had imposed on the much maligned leaf springs the additional duty of absorbing some or all of the braking torque reaction.

In other words, the use of ever-more-powerful brakes, and ever larger and heavier tyres, necessitated stiffer and stiffer front springs to absorb torque, and the riding and road-holding properties of many cars of the early 'thirties declined sharply by comparison with those of twenty or thirty years earlier. The merit of independent front wheel suspension lies less in the 'independence' (though, of course, the fact that each wheel is unaffected by the rise or fall of its opposite number is a great advantage), and hardly at all in the use of springs of different form from the conventional leaf variety, than in the emancipation of the spring from any duty but that of springing.

As early as 1901 Dr. Lanchester had demonstrated, with his first production model, that the desiderata for easy riding and good road holding are that the chassis shall be rigid and torsionally stiff, that the wheels shall be constrained by some suitable parallel-motion linkage to rise and fall only in a vertical plane in relation to the longitudinal line of the chassis, and that the springs shall be as supple as possible, shall be concerned only with springing and shall not be used as torque members. The introduction of independent suspension allowed these aims to be realised, with the important additional advantages of less unsprung weight and non-interference of any one wheel by the activities of its opposite number: the common form of 'wishbone linkage' is, in effect, Lanchester's parallel-motion radius and torque arms used transversely instead of longitudinally.

Both before and after Royce's death Rolls-Royce had studied the few cars with i.f.s. then on the market, notably the Lancia with the sliding pillar and enclosed coil spring system which had been used from 1922 onwards. The disadvantage of this arrangement was that it did not allow space enough for any but a fairly small diameter spring which, to carry a car of Rolls-Royce weight, would need to be unduly stiff. Hence the modification to Rolls-Royce requirements of the General Motors' system. The result was, and still is, admirable. The riding of the Phantom III was very much better than anything the company had done before and its ability to corner fast, even when carrying 7-seater limousine coachwork, put most of its contemporaries to shame.

The performance of the Phantom III was all that the discerning motorist of 1935 could wish. The maximum speed timed by *The Autocar* in October 1936 was scarcely greater, at 91.94 m.p.h., than that of the Continental PII, but this speed was reached in less than a quarter of a mile from a standing start and on a favourable bit of open road 96 m.p.h. was shown on the speedometer. Later types of PIll, if not too overbodied, were able to hold the magic hundred, and the 'overdrive' model could exceed this figure. Many years later the performance still seems impressive.

1935 3½-litre Bentley with 'top-hat'-type razor edge body by Freestone and Webb (chassis B76FB).

It was in acceleration and fast cornering that the new model scored over its predecessor. It could accelerate from standstill to 50 m.p.h. in 12.6 seconds, and from rest to 70 m.p.h. in 24.4 seconds. The gearbox was furnished with synchromesh on second, third and top speeds and, though owners of the contemporary 20/25 or 25/30 models might not agree, this was, perhaps, the sweetest gearbox ever fitted to a production car. The gear lever was still on the driver's right-hand side but had been moved back beside the seat (together with the brake lever) so that it was not only in the most convenient position for effortless use but the old Rolls-Royce hazard of getting the gear lever up one trouser leg when entering from the off side was finally abolished. Effortless was the correct adjective to describe the steering too, for although it was not unduly low-geared (three turns, lock to lock), it was astonishingly light (except at very low speeds) for so big a car. Indeed, in common with other really fine cars the machine 'felt' much smaller than it really was, and the driver of a Phantom III could confidently undertake a 400-mile non-stop journey, or a whole day of traffic crawling in the most crowded city, without feeling tired. This was in vivid contrast to most other large cars of the period.

The Phantom III can be criticised for being too complicated and costly to keep in perfect order. The Silver Ghost and, to a slightly lesser extent the Phantoms I and II and the smaller cars, were so fantastically long-lived and economical that the cost of maintenance of the PIII seems high by comparison. But this must be set in its proper

1938 4¼-litre Bentley B37LE. An unusual body by James Young with sedanca front, hard-top rear and patent parallel opening doors.

perspective: it will nearly always be found in cases where so disastrously expensive a rebuild is necessary that at some time in the car's life the maker's instructions concerning engine oil renewals and filter cleaning have been neglected. As already noted, the hydraulic tappet mechanism was apt to suffer from sludge blocking the oil-ways, and similar (but more expensive) mishaps could overtake the crankshaft and big ends if dirty oil was allowed to accumulate and gradually solidify in the oil-ways. These considerations apply to all engines, of course, but stripping a Phantom III engine was undeniably an expensive business and was often postponed too long. Obviously the present-day owner faced with a major overhaul is also faced with the prospect of labour charges many times greater than those which obtained when the cars were new.

During the war the majority of Phantom IIIs went into hibernation; in many instances without the elementary precaution being taken of draining out the old oil and filling up with fresh before putting the car away. After the war when motoring started again, but petrol rationing made big cars unsuitable for private use, many of these stored PIIIs were bought by hire-car operators who had a better petrol allowance than private owners; the life of a 'hackney carriage' is notoriously hard and it is small wonder that some of the survivors, which found their way back into private hands, cost their enthusiastic owners hours of toil and much hard-earned cash in making good the effect of years of neglect and misuse. Seen in the context of its own period, therefore, the Phantom III was not unduly expensive to run provided it was cared for properly.

The most captious critic is obliged to admit that a Phantom III in good fettle provides all that can be wished for in a large luxury motor-car. The comfort, silence and road-holding together with really impressive acceleration and maximum speed made a combination of virtues which few cars of the time could equal. As far as the English manufacturers were concerned there really was nothing to touch it: Lanchester* and Napier had both disappeared, and though Daimler continued to cater for the 'carriage folk' the contemporary large Daimler, the straight-eight of 1935 onwards, was a very sluggish performer by comparison and as heavy and exhausting to drive in traffic, despite its semi-automatic transmission, as the Rolls-Royce was light and easy. Though superb motor-cars in the $4^1/_2$ to 5 litre group continued to be produced by such firms as Hotchkiss, Lancia, Alfa Romeo, etc., the Continent had little to offer in the PIII class. The 7.7 litre Grosse Mercedes was probably nearest to it and was perhaps slightly better in outright performance, but like the straight-eight Daimler it was an unpleasant car for the chauffeur as the steering contrived to be both low-geared and heavy at the same time, whilst their oldest rivals, and the doyen of the motor trade, Panhard et Levassor had sunk to the depths with that curious aberration the Panhard Panoramique.

It was left to the Americans to produce a foeman worthy of Rolls-Royce's steel, and some of the large American cars of the late 'thirties, such as the Packards and Cadillacs, equalled the PIII in silence and refinement. In some aspects of constructional techniques they may well have been more advanced whilst, as always, the Americans led the way with creature comforts like interior heaters, wireless sets, step lights and so forth. The chassis design lagged behind, however, and though the ride was very soft the average American car of the time could not compare with the Rolls-Royce for stability and roadworthiness.

The revised versions of the 'little Rolls' came out alongside their big brothers; that is, the 20/25 appeared at about the same time as the Phantom II, and the 25/30 together with the $4^1/_2$-litre Bentley made their bows shortly after the Phantom III. On each occasion, as usual in R-R. practice, the old model continued in production alongside the new for some while. With the engine stroke remaining at 114 mm the bore was increased from 76.2 mm to 82.6, and finally to 89 mm. The specific output was nearly doubled between 1925 and 1935, though the increase in capacity only amounted to some 1,100 c.c.

These alterations removed the stigma of 'gutless wonder' from the smaller Rolls-Royce, and where the original Twenty had been good for little more than 60 m.p.h. the 20/25 was capable of 75 m.p.h. and the 25/30 could top the eighty mark comfortably and show acceleration figures up to 65 m.p.h. very little less impressive than those of the PIII.

Changes in specification marched with those of the bigger models and refinements like the automatically variable hydraulic shock absorbers, the 'ride control', the centralised chassis lubrication and synchromesh were all added in due time. Though the smaller

---

* 'The Lanchester Company did not survive the depression of 1931 as their Bank would not continue their overdraft: they were bought up by Daimler whose overdraft was so big the Bank dared not call it in. The Lanchesters of 1931–1954 were therefore small Daimlers in disguise and had nothing in common with the designs of Frederick and George Lanchester.

engines never boasted dual ignition in the full sense the 20/25s were fitted with that most valuable adjunct, a stand-by magneto (which could be coupled up in 30 seconds), so that an exhausted battery or burnt-out coil did not leave the car stranded.

In one respect the smaller chassis lagged behind the larger as i.f.s. was not fitted until 1938. This, the final transformation of the old Twenty, took place in time for the 1939 season but the new model – the Wraith – hardly had time to come into its own, and the Wraith story belongs more to the post-war period. Undoubtedly, though, the transformation made the smaller Rolls-Royce a most enviable possession. In addition to the new suspension the chassis was completely revised and became virtually a scaled-down Phantom III, and notable for being welded instead of riveted. The engine had little but cylinder dimensions and general lay-out in common with the 25/30 from which it derived. The manifolding had been redesigned, the valves were very much larger, and a great deal of work had been put into the design of the crankshaft, big-end bearings and the engine mountings to ensure the least possible awareness of mechanism at any speed.

Some Rolls-Royce enthusiasts found the handling of the Wraith less agreeable than its predecessor, though most owners and the contemporary press reports were enthusiastic. The reason probably is that, in common with the contemporary 'over drive' Bentley, larger section tyres than those formerly used were fitted and this necessitated having lower-geared steering. Many experienced motorists of that time preferred the more direct steering of the 'Vintage' car, even if it were heavier, and feared that this step might presage the sort of light, spongy and imprecise handling then often found on large American cars.

Unfortunately those who were able to buy a Wraith new in 1939 did not have much time to enjoy it before the Germans loosed upon the world such evil that the Germany of 1914 seems mild and benign by comparison, and the Franco-Prussian War, with the siege of Paris which so shocked the world in 1870, appears as a harmless bout of fisticuffs between schoolboys.

9

Post-War Developments – the First Twenty-Five Years

THE story of Rolls-Royce's contribution to the survival of England, and to the ultimate victory of the Allies, in the late war is too big to tell here. The most biased of anti-English observers are obliged to admit that Britain's decision to fight on alone after France was conquered, and the triumph of the Battle of Britain, preserved a great part of mankind from being made subject to the most depraved and debased manifestation of humanity's evil nature which the world has known since the days of Genghis Khan. And if Britain gave the world a breathing space by fighting the Battle of Britain, it was largely the Rolls-Royce engines of the Hurricanes and Spitfires which made that fight possible. Also, the success this country has had as an exporter of aircraft engines since the war has been almost entirely because of the Rolls-Royce effort, in the first place, and all those who are ever ready to decry private enterprise would do well to reflect that it was firms like Rolls-Royce which kept us alive economically in the dark decade after the war.

We are concerned with the motor-cars, not with economics or the aero-engine business, and the chief effect of the great expansion of this branch during and after the war was that when the time came for the motor-car division to emerge from its cocoon the original Derby factory could no longer accommodate it. Consequently since 1946 car production has been at the firm's factory in Crewe only 34 miles south of the original Cooke Street works.

An acute observer of the social scene in the early post-war world would have been justified in thinking there would be no place in the new world which was emerging for the Savile Row suit, the hand-made watch or the Rolls-Royce motor-car. The rise in real wages, it appeared, would make such luxuries economically impossible, changed social attitudes would make them undesirable, and technical developments would make them unnecessary.

What is necessary at this point is to take a look at what is meant by 'hand-made'. Unfortunately the term conjures up a vision of the proud but impoverished cottage craftsman laboriously fashioning superbly proportioned tables and chairs from massive baulks of oak with chisel and adze, or the simple village blacksmith making his wares with an accuracy of eye and dexterity of hand unmatched by the most elaborate machinery. This is all a trifle misleading, particularly as it is always seen through a haze of sentiment

The Crewe factory in 1939.

King George VI and the Queen on a visit to the factory in Crewe in 1940.

Sedanca de ville by Hooper, on Silver Wraith WTA62, for Nubar Gulbenkian. Not a successful design.

which obscures the fact that down the ages the village craftsman has (quite rightly) been ready enough to throw away his adze as soon as he could afford the new-fangled plane, or to install a power-saw and shaper as soon as electricity reached his village.

So it has been with the craft of making motor-cars. As the craft has grown into a huge industry more and more new tools, machines and automatic devices have been developed to simplify and cheapen the task. This means, in simple terms, that the skill of the fitter who stood all day scraping big-end bearings to be a perfect fit on a crankshaft, is now replaced by the greater skill of the craftsman who designs and makes a machine to bore a great quantity of bearings so accurately in the first instance that the gentleman with the hand scraper can devote his talents to some less humdrum task.

This does not mean, however, that the business of 'hand-finishing' is completely abolished. No matter how accurately and truly mechanical components may be fashioned by ingenious automatic machinery, there are still very few objects which, in the final analysis, cannot be made still better if the last touch, the last polish and the last adjustment are made by sentient human beings. As the machines improve the gap narrows and there is less and less 'finishing' for the human hand to perform and the human eye to check. But the gap is still there. Fortunately for the world at large there are still those who want the best that can be got, whether a watch by Vacheron et Constantin or a motor-car by Rolls-Royce. The fact that, increasingly, they may want these things for the wrong reasons is neither here nor there, and as Somerset Maugham observed: 'If you refuse to accept anything but the best you very often get it.'

Rolls-Royce Ltd. have never been backward in using machine tools and in this sense their motor-cars, like all others, have always been machine made. The chief differences now between a Rolls-Royce and a mass-produced motor-car lie less in the methods of construction than in the painstaking testing, inspection and tuning. Where the ordinary manufacturer is happy to use his supine and unprotesting customers as unpaid test drivers to discover the teething troubles of each new model (which, even then, may remain uncorrected), Rolls-Royce test procedures, not only of completed chassis but of individual components, are more rigorous than they were sixty years ago. So much so that it is less remarkable that a Rolls-Royce or Bentley car costs so much than that it costs so little, particularly when the rise in real wages is taken into account.

This rise is well illustrated by the cost of the Rolls-Royce radiator which is still hand made, as no way has yet been found of making so sharp-edged a structure by any die-stamping process.

Mechanical aids to testing are used as much as possible. Mention has already been made of the 'bump machine' which was devised before the first world war but many ingenious (and sometimes horrific) appliances have been added since then. Some of these are not concerned with testing so much as with 'running in' complete units like rear axles or steering assemblies. Before being built into a chassis, for instance, steering gears and their associated linkages are run in under load on a special machine until the force needed to turn the mechanism from lock to lock does not vary by more than a couple of ounces from the figure specified by the design department. This has been in use for many years, but of more recent origin, and less pacific intent, is a terrifying engine of Spanish Inquisitorial ingenuity which tests the power-assisted steering of the current cars. This consists of 8-inch high concrete kerb stones held in place by springs a suitable distance from each front wheel, and a mechanical arm which flings the steering wheel from lock to lock for thirty hours on end so that at each movement the front wheels have to shoulder the concrete blocks aside a set distance against the resistance of the springs. When this has been done the castor and camber angles, and the toe-in, are measured, and if they are not within the very narrow limits specified in the drawings the steering assembly will be rejected.

All newly designed chassis, or components (which will be mounted on a special chassis for the purpose) have to endure 300 hours on a singularly diabolical instrument of torture which simulates the effect of driving the complete car, loaded with $^3/_4$ ton of ballast, at 50 m.p.h. along a road with slightly rounded humps of concrete, 6 in. high, so staggered at four-foot intervals that near- and off-side wheels take the blows alternately. Every so often production models are also put through this test, and one in every twenty frames is taken to the Production Experimental Department, cut into sections, torn asunder or bent and twisted into weird shapes to make sure that all the welded joints or attachment points are well above the tolerance factor.

Since the Cooke Street days it has been Rolls-Royce practice to have a test piece left on forged components such as crankshafts or connecting rods, and when each part has been through the various processes of machining, grinding, polishing and balancing the test piece is sent to the laboratory for analysis. The results of the analysis are recorded in the history sheet of the chassis for which the component is destined. A test piece is also included in each forging for removal and testing before machining is begun.

Not only are the individual parts of each component meticulously inspected during manufacture, but each complete unit is given a run on a test-rig before being passed to the chassis assembly shop. Such things as oil-pumps, water-pumps, shock-absorbers and so on are subjected to loads they will seldom be called upon to bear during service, and the precise details of each test are passed to the history file of the chassis for which the parts are intended.

It may be seen therefore that when an engine is assembled on the Rolls-Royce method, with the raw material being analysed before and after processing and each part from the crankshaft down to individual bolts being assessed several times, the finished article must be pretty good. Any part, either in the rough or finished, found to be sub-standard results not only in the rejection of that particular thing but in the return of the batch from which it came for re-processing.

Each engine is given a run on the test bench, burning coal gas and with fresh oil being pumped continually through the system. The first 30 minutes are at idling speed, then follow 30 minutes at nominal revolutions as a preparation for four to five hours at cruising revolutions. From each batch of engines in the process of assembly, one is selected at random and is given a twenty-four hour run on petrol, during which full power curves are taken. It is then stripped down to the last washer and every part is examined. Should any component show signs of wear, stress or heat, the remainder of this batch of engines is removed from production and every single one is checked. As if this were not enough, engines are occasionally taken at random by the Production Experimental Department and run to destruction under load. This takes a very long time but when the engine ultimately stops an exhaustive post-mortem is held to discover what has failed and why.

All this is but a preliminary to the tests the completed cars go through during the stages after the engine has been installed and allied to the transmission which, like all the other units, has been similarly proved beforehand. All systems on the car-transmission and gearbox with its different ratios and so on are tested on a roller test rig for the road equivalent of forty miles before the start of a series of test runs on the road, after any one of which the examiner may order the removal, and further adjustmentor rejection, of any part.

When the car has survived all these tests it is again tested on the road. These tests are partly aimed at detecting and dealing with any source (or potential source) of squeak, groan or rattle from the coachwork, but the fine tuning and adjusting of the mechanical parts still continues.

Le Mans, 1949: a night stop for the Hay/Wilson Bentley placed sixth (73.5 m.p.h.).

In all, each car spends from two to three weeks, and covers some 150 miles, in the final stages between leaving the assembly shop and passing to the sales department. The antepenultimate process is a return to the paint shop where the complete car is 'flatted', resprayed, repolished and passed through the drying oven to remove any minute blemishes caused during the final road test, which is a very tough affair indeed. The penultimate business is a thorough spring clean inside and out by a team of sharp-eyed women cleaners, then comes the final check by the quality engineers and, at last, perfect in every detail and groomed like a guardsman, the car is ready for sale.

*   *   *

The demand for motor-cars in the first few years after the war was prodigious. Returning servicemen with gratuities in their pockets, and all those whose lives had been disrupted by war (which meant, practically, the entire British nation) wanted to return to normal as quickly as possible and returning to normal included restoring to individuals the liberty to travel where, when and as they pleased which had been the motorcar's great gift to mankind. Demand far exceeded supply. Petrol was still strictly rationed and although the majority of folk saw no sense in continuing a restriction now that men's lives were no longer endangered in bringing fuel from overseas, the law-abiding habits of the English were then still so deeply ingrained that few ordinary citizens augmented their meagre rations by

At Arnage, 1950: the H. S. F. Hay/H. Hunter Bentley goes through the Esses. They finished 14th at 78.6 m.p.h.

135

buying petrol on the 'black market' where supplies were, apparently, limitless and the price not inordinately dear. The official fuel allowance was biased in favour of small cars and took no cognisance of vehicles rated at more than 20 h.p., under the old R.A.C. formula, consequently the majority of cars in the Rolls-Royce class remained in hibernation or were bought by hire-car operators.

Every pre-war small or medium-powered car which could run, or even stagger, was eagerly snapped up, prices soared, spare parts and tyres were virtually unobtainable and when the motor-car factories resumed production, in the face of innumerable difficulties, the situation soon became Gilbertian, and those who were able to buy a new car (after, perhaps, a two years' wait) had no difficulty in selling it the following day as 'second-hand' at two or three times its official list price. Even if the car were kept for a year, over-driven, wholly neglected and practically run to death, there were still plenty of people ready to pay a good deal more than its original price for it.

Because of the urgency the manufacturers naturally did what they could to get things moving, and the easiest way to do so was by continuing where they had left off in 1939. Therefore the first new cars to emerge in 1946–7 differed from those of 1939 only in minor external features and in being made with much less care from shoddier materials. It was not until 1948 that the first really new models began to be seen, and it took another five or six years to slough off the effects of over-demand, stagnation of design, and shortage of decent materials.

The 4¼-litre Bentley of E. R. Hall/T. G. Clarke at Mulsanne, 1950. They came eighth at an average speed of 82.9 m.p.h.

As far as their motor-car business was concerned Rolls-Royce's situation was particularly difficult. If they were to make motor-cars again there could be no lowering of their standards, yet on the face of it there could be little demand in Great Britain for a machine of Rolls-Royce size, quality and price. Although Rolls-Royce exports had always been large in proportion to their total output it would have taken a bold man to place overmuch reliance on foreign trade in 1946.

One of the stumbling blocks to motor-car exports had been the horse-power tax first levied in 1919 at the rate of £1 per horse-power; the horse-power being reckoned by a formula devised in 1906 and soon outdated. This formula was based on the number of cylinders and their diameter, the piston stroke and other relevant factors were ignored, and its effect was to encourage the development of high-speed small capacity engines of the least possible cylinder bore and the longest possible stroke; precisely the type of engine that is least suited to most foreign markets, where rough roads and long distances called for large 'lazy', fairly slow-running, flexible engines able to pull well at low speeds. Between 1920 and 1939 English manufacturers were often lambasted for their failure to export and traditional British markets like New Zealand, Malaya, India and Australia succumbed swiftly and completely to the Americans whose motor-cars were much better suited to the conditions.

In vain did the motor trade point out that a thriving export trade depends in the first instance on a flourishing home trade, and that the horse-power tax limited the home trade almost entirely to a type of motor-car unsaleable overseas. With typical obscurantism successive Governments responded merely by varying the rate of the tax according to their need to attract votes.

By 1947, with all British foreign investments liquidated to pay for the war, it was apparent even to the Treasury that some of the obstacles confronting exporters must be removed, and with shrill exhortations to the motor trade to export or die (which the manufacturers knew already as supplies of raw material were linked to export figures) the Labour Government did what no other Government had had the sense to do and at last removed the absurd horse-power tax and replaced it with a flat rate of £10 per car per year. Needless to say the £10 has grown enormously and to make sure that nobody should get away with anything the taxes on petrol are now not only very high, but are increased to even greater amounts at frequent intervals.

Nevertheless the new taxation system was a great help to the car manufacturers. It should have been of even greater service to makers of large, powerful cars than to the run-of-the-mill manufacturers, but other factors had to be taken into account. These were the purchase tax, personal income taxes, and what may be called a moral attitude.

The purchase tax was levied on a great range of goods during the war. Like many other burdens of the time it was necessary, and as with other special taxes imposed in other wars the Government promised that it should be only a war-time measure. There were, presumably, those naïve enough to believe in this, but in those who have read a little history it occasioned no surprise that the promise was dishonoured and, twenty years later, this modern version of the sumptuary law was clearly a permanent feature of the scene. It bore hardest on the makers of so-called luxuries, and though the rates were varied with such bewildering frequency that business-men did not know whether they were coming or going it added between £1,000 and £2,000 to the cost of a Rolls-Royce or Bentley car according to the bodywork.

During the war the Government had to raise enormous sums of money: they were also very properly concerned to prevent any repetition of the blatant profiteering of the earlier war, consequently the income tax and surtax were raised to such swingeing levels that no honest man, who paid his taxes, could afford to buy and run a new Rolls-Royce out of income. These tax rates have been reduced since then but for a considerable time after the war a man needed to earn nearly £100,000 in order to have £5,000 to spend. There were not many such people and this seemed to be another nail in Rolls-Royce's coffin.

When the dust of the war settled a little and the country was ready to relax (which it richly deserved to do) a series of financial crises, material shortages and the moral attitudinising of the Government all combined to prevent it. In understandable reaction from the rigours of war, a Socialist Government was voted into power in 1945. Their efforts to accelerate the nation's natural trend towards social reform were sincere, well meaning, generally beneficial but frequently muddle-headed. Their efforts to deal with the financial crises were as unsuccessful as they were inept. Worst of all the undeniable good they did was stultified by the bitterness and rancour of their attempts to engender class warfare and to prove that only the manual worker was worthy of a place in the sun. The pure doctrine: 'Of a little, take a little that the rest may have a little' became distorted to a creed which held that appreciation of the good things of life, and desire for them, were attributes only of the 'idle rich', and that if a man were rich he must be a capitalist, and that all capitalists were wicked men concerned only to grind the faces of the workers in the dust. This attitude did not make for the sort of climate in which Rolls-Royce, and firms like them, could easily sell their wares.

By a natural corollary the belief that all degrees of private wealth were evil was matched by the cult of austerity for austerity's sake, and many of the restrictions and deprivations necessary in war were continued as acts of policy in peace. The 'black market' flourished as it never had during the war and crime increased, whilst honest law-abiding citizens were made to feel almost guilty of treason if they quarrelled with the dictum of a member of the Government who proclaimed that processed mousetrap cheese was equal to the finest Stilton.

For much of this unhappy time the country's financial affairs were in the hands of an upright, dedicated and donnish theorist to whom austerity was second nature. Whilst his vegetarian principles, his taste for asceticism, and his failing health obliged him to nibble raw carrots and drink fruit juice he could see no reason why lesser men should yearn for rump steak and claret; and whilst he was insulated from the realities of commerce and from any real knowledge of the common man by possession of a large private fortune he could see no reason to modify the policy which was short-sightedly aimed at crushing luxury trades out of existence.

It was, therefore, courageous of Rolls-Royce Ltd. to return to the motor-car business in

1946–7, but fortunately the management (in particular men like Lord Hives and Dr. Llewellyn Smith, the head of the re-formed car division, and W. A. Rowbotham, Chief Engineer) realised, if the Government did not, that though the country was all in favour of greater social justice the natural tendency to want a bit extra for oneself cannot be suppressed by decree. Though no one can quarrel with the theoretical advantage of dividing the National Cake equally there will always be those, praise be, who have no compunction about saying they cannot stomach that nauseating confection and that they are ready to trade their slices for a ton of plain bread and butter or an ounce of caviare. The natural tendency of man to need an incentive and to want a bit of frivolity could not be suppressed and was, indeed, even to be found in the Socialist hierarchy. In his capacity as part-owner of a fleet of Rolls-Royce hire cars the writer was delighted to discover that one of his most appreciative regular clients was none other than one of the more notorious Socialist members, a formidable orator and demagogue who never tired of denouncing the 'idle rich' and all their works and possessions.

Two new developments marked Rolls-Royce's return to car making. First was a new design of engine, and second was the beginning of the policy of supplying complete motor-cars with standardised bodywork made to the company's specification and finished in their own workshops.

The engine change was, in fact, a reversion to Royce's original layout, in that the inlet valves were push-rod operated in the cylinder head whilst the exhaust ports were commanded by normal side valves. As we have seen this layout (nowadays known as the 'F-head') had been common enough at the beginning of the century, and though it had never entirely vanished from view, it had become rare enough to excite considerable comment when Rolls-Royce returned to it. Technical opinion seemed to be that though the arrangement was admirable in allowing the use of large valves and unimpeded gas passages, the combustion chamber shape would prevent the use of high compression pressures. Here, practice does not seem to have marched with theory as the compression ratio of the F-head engine was raised from 6.4:1 to 8:1 during its ten-year life.

In 1903–4 Henry Royce had adopted the F-head merely because he was following the practice of the time, but the return to it was dictated by the constant search for more power. Between 1922 and 1938 the successive stages of development of the 20 h.p., 20/25 h.p., and 25/30 h.p. engines had called for the use of ever larger and larger valves, and with each increase in valve diameter, naturally enough, the 'land' or bridge of metal between the valves grew smaller and smaller until, in 1938, the foundry reported that they could not guarantee adequate cooling water spaces if the valves were enlarged any more. Short of abandoning the 4.150 inch dimension on which the engine was based the choice lay between overhead camshafts (to save push-rod space) or the F-head. In the interest of silence the latter was chosen.

The F-head engine, therefore, was born in 1938 though it did not reach the public until after the war. Cylinder block and crankcase upper half were integrally cast in iron as experiments going back to the early 'thirties had proved this best for making a quiet engine. By making the big-ends narrower and the crank-webs thicker (a change made possible by the use of nitrided shafts, first used in 1933, and lead-bronze bearings) the critical speed of the crankshaft was finally raised to 5,400 r.p.m., or not far short of twice the critical speed of the 1922 engine.

By adding or removing a cylinder to either end of the basic 6-cylinder design it was possible to make a 4-cylinder unit or a straight-eight using the same major components for all three types, which was, again, a reversion to 1904 practice. Although the war prevented the sale of these engines a number of them achieved prodigious mileages in staff cars and lorries. One of the straight-eights, indeed, found its way into a Bentley chassis and gave great pleasure to those fortunate enough to use it.

The F-head engine used in the first post-war cars – the Silver Wraith and the Mark VI Bentley – also differed from the pre-war engines in a number of details. Prominent amongst the new features was the use of belt-drive for the water pump and dynamo which many of the old guard reviled as cheap and nasty. It was no more than a logical change made possible by the great improvement in transmission belting materials. On pre-war Rolls-Royce and Bentley engines the water pumps and dynamos had been driven from the timing gears, and to suit the lay-out of the auxiliaries this had necessitated a five-gear train in the timing-gear case. The business of keeping a train of five toothed wheels silent under the conditions of constantly varying speed and load of a car engine is formidable indeed. The usual expedient of using a chain drive for the camshaft and auxiliaries was not acceptable to Rolls-Royce, for however quiet and efficient this system may be when new, nobody has yet

A. J. Rowledge, 1876–1957. Joined R.-R. from Napier, as Chief Assistant to F. H. Royce, in 1921. Chief of Design Staff until 1933. Chief Consultant to the Company until his retirement in 1945.

succeeded in making a chain which does not stretch with use: a slack chain may rattle no matter how ingenious the tensioning devices and it will inevitably cause a slight lag in the valve timing. When the 25/30 h.p. engine was redesigned for the Wraith in 1937–8 repositioning the auxiliaries allowed the train to be reduced to three gears, and by allowing the water pump and dynamo to be driven from the fan belt a further reduction to two gears was made on the post-war engines.

A less noticeable innovation was that the upper parts of the cylinder bores were chromium plated. The design department aimed to give the new cars a 'life' of 100,000 miles between major overhauls and this was to be one of the ways of doing so. The experiment was not wholly successful; by 1950 many of the cars had covered 90,000 miles or so without trouble, but in some customers' hands bore wear set in at about 40,000 miles and increased very quickly as the 0.0015 inch thick chromium lining wore through. Many successive short runs and idling in town traffic were probably at the root of this trouble. The chromium-plated bores were given up and short liners of 30% chrome content were used instead with complete success.

Some of the early post-war engines also suffered from big-end failures caused by dirt which had not been trapped in the by-pass filter. The combination of nitrided shafts and lead-bronze bearings is almost everlasting if fed with good clean oil but proved to be less tolerant of dirt than pre-war materials. Full-flow oil filters got over this difficulty; but although the failures were not numerous they gave scope for complaints that even Rolls-Royce had fallen prey to post-war shoddiness and poor finish.

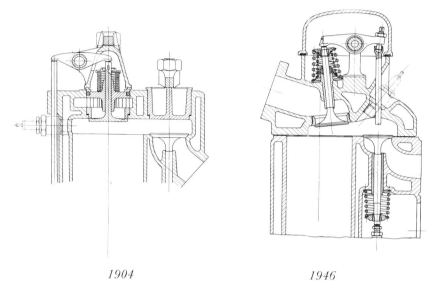

1904   1946

Inlet-over-exhaust valves.

The Silver Wraith car had a single downdraught Stromberg carburettor, and the Bentley model twin S.U.s and a higher lift camshaft. Otherwise the engines were identical, and as the demands for more speed, better acceleration and more luxurious coachwork continued the design staff were hard put to it to keep pace. Increasing the compression ratio to 7:1 was tried without much success; a small increase in power being accompanied by an intolerable increase in roughness. By taking the bold step of doing away with the water spaces between the cylinders it was possible to increase the bores to $3^5/_8$ inches in diameter, and although a great deal of work had to be done to design suitable pistons which would run without risk of seizure, the change was most successful. The bigger bore engine would stand 7:1 compression ratio and yet was smoother than its predecessor.

The increase of 7% in engine capacity was accompanied by an increase of considerably more than 7% in performance. In fact the maximum power went up from approximately 135 b.h.p. to 150 b.h.p. from the Bentley version of the engine; the 'softer' single-carburettor Rolls-Royce engine produced less, naturally, but had slightly better torque at low speeds. The available power was enough to give the 1951 'Continental' Bentley a top speed approaching 120 mph. There had been criticism of the earlier Silver Wraiths and

Bentleys that they were under-powered and sluggish by comparison with some of the top-rank American and Continental cars, and though there had not really been much substance in these complaints, as the differences in overall performance were only fractional, the added zest given by the bigger engine satisfied all but the most implacable.

For a time that is, because, inevitably, more power and torque were soon called for. New body shapes, improved road-holding, better tyres and the general trend of public opinion called for more and more speed and acceleration. Also, as always, the complete cars put on weight, not because of any fundamental changes but because every increase in the creature comforts which the customer is entitled to expect, every improved heating system, air conditioning, electric window-lift and similar convenience added its quota.

In 1955, therefore, the final metamorphosis of the 6-cylinder engine took place when the cylinder bores were increased to $3^3/_4$ inches to give a capacity of 4.9 litres. This was the limit, as any further increase in bore size would have been accompanied by a disastrous increase in the amount of foundry scrap. It was not the limit of the engine's development, however, as further modifications to the crankshaft, cylinder head and manifolding between 1955 and 1959 raised the output from about 162 b.h.p. to 178 b.h.p. from the twin-carburettor engine used for the Bentley chassis. The compression ratio by this time was 8:1 and the inlet valves no less than 2.150in. in diameter. With a direct-injection fuel system, similar engines supplied for military purposes gave 215 b.h.p., but Rolls-Royce Ltd. did not consider fuel injection systems suitable for private car work where simplicity is still a valuable adjunct. By racing- or sports-car standards the figures may not be all that impressive, but it must be remembered that the astonishing specific output of racing engines is often bought at the expense of reliability and flexibility.

So much, then, for the engines of the post-war cars up to 1959. In essentials the chassis design of the early post-war cars differed little from that of the 1939 Wraiths and Bentleys and efforts were, at first concentrated on simplification which was essential not only to keep pace with rising costs, but to make the cars acceptable in foreign markets where running repairs and adjustments might have to be carried out by ordinary garage staffs who had not been specifically trained in Rolls-Royce methods. The brake servo system, for instance, was redesigned not to improve the performance but solely to make it easier to adjust. Otherwise the main chassis and transmission parts were unaltered in principle though the paramount need to economise meant saying farewell to some of the traditional details and methods of construction. It is natural to mourn, for instance, the typical Rolls-Royce bolted assemblies with their rows of minute studs and nuts, like fine stitching, or the perfection of the riveting where riveting was appropriately used; in the post-war cars more and more welded joints have usurped the bolts and rivets though this trend had started well before the war. The visual effect may not be so pleasing, but the client may be sure that Rolls-Royce have never adopted a new technique merely because it is new or merely because it is cheaper than the old. By careful tests it must first be proved to be better.

Another change much regretted by the *cognoscenti* (as with the pre-war Wraiths) was the substitution of ordinary bolt-on wheels in place of the splendid Dunlop centre-lock hubs. The reason for the change was twofold: tyres had improved so much that quick-change wheel devices were not so necessary as formerly, and the majority of the new race of motorists (which included a new race of Rolls-Royce owners) were not enthusiasts in the old sense but were men (or women) who could not be bothered to learn how to work the centre-lock hub and its special removing tool. On the rare occasions when a roadside puncture afflicted them, there they were, cotched, as Lem Putt puts it, and a change had to be made to the conventional system.

The post-war plans did not include a large model. The Phantom III was discontinued and no successor appeared at first. The first post-war Bentley model, the Mark VI, was the same in all its major elements as the Silver Wraith with the all-important difference that, for the first time, the company offered a complete car with standardised Rolls-Royce-designed steel bodywork. Bentley chassis for completion by outside coach-builders continued to be supplied of course, and a step in this direction had been taken in 1939 when Park Ward (now an R-R subsidiary) had made a standardised body for Rolls-Royce or Bentley chassis at the rate of ten a week.

The decision to make so radical a change was influenced by the need to export. Whilst Rolls-Royce and Bentley cars were bodied entirely by various specialist firms, none of whom made more than a handful of bodies precisely the same, it was uneconomic for any of these firms to set up the costly plant to make steel body pressings, but the traditional coachbuilt body, with its ash frame and aluminium panels, was unsuited to a great many foreign markets. Consequently Rolls-Royce Ltd. set up their own plant to finish pressed steel bodies, made to their specification by the Pressed Steel Co., and this entailed also setting up all the ancillary workshops needed to deal with the furnishings, woodwork, upholstery and paintwork.

Naturally enough, you cannot please all the people all the time and to the murmurs of the technical pundits who complained, as usual, that Rolls-Royces were old fashioned, were added howls of protest from the old guard to the effect that even Rolls-Royce were clearly going to the dogs. Who, they asked, would buy a tin Rolls-Royce? Might as well have a Ford and be done with it.

In a very short time, however, it was easily seen that the pressed steel Bentley bodies were as elegantly proportioned, as highly finished, and as comfortably furnished as anything the traditional coachbuilders of the past had done; with the added virtues of immunity from rot and greater rigidity.

Though damp-rot, dry-rot, white ants or termites might hold no terrors, what about the demon rust? Most very early motor bodies had wooden panels, and aluminium became general for good quality work from about 1902; nevertheless a great number of early cars had sheet iron, or steel, body panels, mudguards, bonnets and so forth, yet many a seventy-year-old car has stood abandoned for years in barn or field and suffered surprisingly little from rusting. By contrast it is commonplace today for body panels to start rusting through in three years or even less. It is very rare, too, for a modern mass-produced car not to need a new silencer and exhaust pipe after two or three years' use, but the majority of the pre-1905 motor cars which make the annual pilgrimage from London to Brighton will be found to be still coughing their corrosive exhaust fumes down their original pipes and silencers.

A.W.M. Couper Mark VI Bentley; winner of the Grand Prix d' Honneur du Concours de Confort,
Monte Carlo Rally, 1952.

The use of lighter gauge metal today does not wholly account for the much more rapid decay.

It would be pleasant to be able to say that the Rolls-Royce–Bentley steel bodies were immune from rusting, but despite every care, and the use of the most up-to-date rust-proofing methods before painting, even they succumbed. In an article after the War on the comparative costs, pleasures, and pains of buying and running a new car in the £50 to £1,250 class, or a ten- to fifteen-year-old Rolls-Royce or Bentley, Maurice Wiggin wrote that 'of course' some signs of rusting must be expected in the steel bodies. The 'of course' was a sad indictment but a true one, and one clue to the then prevalent shortcoming of modern cars lay in the use of low-grade sheet steel largely reconstituted from scrap.

When Rolls-Royce started making cars again, and for some years after, supplies of sheet steel were rigidly controlled and all those who wanted it had to take what they could get, and there is no doubt that even Rolls-Royce had to put up with some pretty low-grade stuff which would start to rust where paint wore thin or was chipped no matter how elaborately it was 'rust-proofed'. The investigations of W. Howgrave-Graham into early ironwork conclusively showed that pure iron is practically immune from any but the lightest surface rusting, but that deeply corroded objects, on analysis, always showed a high proportion of impurities. Rolls-Royce Ltd. got over this hurdle, partly because the quality of the raw material improved again (though it was still far short of pre-war standards) and partly by the use of ever more elaborate rust-proofing methods, including immersion and spray-phosphating and a new deep-dip for water soluble primer which flowed into every nook and cranny of the bodyshell before the first of its many coats of paint were applied. As on the coachbuilt bodies, the door panels and boot-lids were still made of aluminium and so presented no problem.

The new body-building policy soon showed that the expense was justified and exports rose steadily. The 'standard steel' bodied car was also sold on the home market and the prophets of doom were soon seen to have been wrong, for although coachbuilders* continued to supply special bodies, individually or in small batches, for Rolls-Royce and Bentley chassis it was clear that the standardised product was more acceptable in modern conditions. To an individualist this may be regrettable, but the regret is tempered by the reflection that Rolls-Royce are always happy to modify seats, upholstery, interior fittings and controls to individual customers' needs; provided, that is, the alterations asked for do not conflict with their standards of safety. Rolls-Royce cars, as such, continued on the traditional lines a little longer than their Bentley counterparts and it was not until 1949 that a Rolls-Royce car was offered with standard coachwork. This was called the Silver Dawn and was, at first, for export only.

If a dozen different people are asked to give their views on a motor-car body at least half a dozen conflicting opinions will be put forward. Beauty is indeed in the eye of the beholder, but on the whole Rolls-Royce body design has been given high* marks on aesthetic grounds and adverse criticism has been confined to various details.

Rolls-Royce Ltd. always made the scuttle frames and dash-boards for their chassis and thereby dictated the height and curvature of the scuttle, and, to some extent, the waist line. This meant that the harmonious relationship between the commanding radiator and the bonnet and scuttle was not impaired by some freakish whim of the coachbuilder (or buyer); this was in marked contrast to many early cars on which there was no unity at all between the engine room and the carriage portion. Rolls-Royce's insistence on fixing the scuttle height meant that within the limitations of the different radiator heights (a small difference this) and steering column angles which they offered, the coachbuilder could not depart from the seating position which gave the driver the best possible command of his controls and an excellent view of the road. Apart from a few chassis which have been re-bodied by amateurs or 'unofficial' body-builders, Rolls-Royces have never been marred by the fashion of the 'thirties when so many large cars had the radiator, bonnet, scuttle and waist lines raised to an absurd height (to make the roof line appear lower) so that the hapless driver's eye level was but little above the top of a never-ending bonnet and his view of the road immediately ahead was completely obscured.

Modern cars are infinitely better in this respect, and standard Rolls-Royce bodies contrived by some magic to combine an impeccable forward view with an apparently old-

* Only H. J. Mulliner Park Ward, now owned by Rolls-Royce, still coachbuilds the company's cars.

fashioned, but very comfortable, high, commanding driving position. There were those who complained that the Rolls-Royce bodies did not afford the backseat passengers as much head and leg room as they were entitled to expect in so large and expensive a motor-car. There was something in this, and those of an age to remember them may sigh for the spacious days when a six-foot man could step up into his closed car without stooping or removing his hat. The writer sighs with them, for one of his favourite motor-cars, a 1909 Renault landaulet, was 8 feet 6 inches long in the wheelbase and 8 feet 9 inches high, but the seats of the Rolls-Royce were designed by a man who knows his anatomy and, once ensconced, the passenger was not conscious of any lack of space. The designers had reached a masterly compromise between a sleek shape for high-speed travelling, and interior spaciousness.

Lack of luggage space was another complaint, and the Rolls-Royce or Bentley boot was not big by some standards, but the Rolls-Royce designers have always been realists and it will not have escaped their notice that the prodigious luggage boots of most post-war cars either entailed an ungainly amount of overhang or encroached on the passengers' leg-room. Rolls-Royce did not subscribe to the notion that the rear-seat travellers must be cramped all the year round in order that the occasional piece of holiday baggage should travel in luxury.

Too small a rear window was another complaint, but as with all else this is a matter of compromise. The back window of the standard Rolls-Royce or Bentley was undeniably a good deal smaller than current fashion dictated, but the vast glazed area of most modern cars' rear aspects was felt to be larger than used to be necessary for safety, and many motorists in sunny countries have been obliged to furnish their mobile greenhouses with venetian blinds in order to preserve their passengers from heat stroke. The driver of a Rolls-Royce found no difficulty in reversing; the position of the seat in relation to the steering wheel made it easy to swivel round enough to get a good view through a rear window which was more than adequate; and the sort of people who liked the kind of motor-car Rolls-Royce built did not then take kindly to being exposed to view like so many goldfish in a bowl.

The 'old-fashioned' dash-board came in for a good deal of criticism too and here, one feels, the critics were on better ground. The 'dash-board' is in fact no longer a dash-board at all. What happened was this: the dash-boards of early cars were exactly comparable with those of horse-drawn vehicles; they kept a little draught off the driver's feet and made a suitable mount for such instruments as there were, each contained in its sturdy, waterproof brass case. From about 1908 onwards a scuttle or cowl was mounted over the dash-board so as to provide better weather protection and the windscreen, if fitted, instead of being mounted vertically on top of the dash-board was moved back and attached to the rearward edge of the scuttle, thereby protecting the occupants' faces much more effectively. The instruments and switches continued to be screwed to the dash-board and it was soon found that they were now obscured from view unless the driver ducked his head to peer under the projecting scuttle. The next move consequently was to fix a suitably shaped plank below the rearward edge of the scuttle and to mount the instruments on that. This new-fangled instrument board or 'fascia panel' was still misleadingly called the dash-board, though the dashboard proper had now become the bulkhead between the engine room and the passenger compartment. Whilst most cars were furnished with open bodies the instrument board was generally just a plain oak or mahogany panel, varnished against the weather, and suitably pierced to accommodate the instruments, but many makes of car were fitted with metal dash-boards varying from the plain black-painted sheet iron of the Model T Ford to the beautifully burnished and 'snailed' aluminium of the Bugatti.

On closed bodies it was feasible to veneer the dash, and other interior woodwork, with some more interesting and decorative wood. French coachwork, in particular, during the 'twenties was often adorned with bird's eye maple or amboyna, both of which looked very well as the small 'figure' of these woods makes a good surround for instrument dials. Rolls-Royce achieved a particularly handsome dash-board at this time, with all the dials symmetrically mounted on a matt-black, glass covered, oval panel mounted in the middle of the wooden surround.

In English coachbuilding circles walnut became fashionable in the late 'twenties and it has remained in fashion ever since: not alas, the small-figured burr walnut of the early eighteenth century but the rather flamboyant large-figured Circassian walnut so often seen (with the graining artificially enhanced with the air-pencil) on cocktail and wireless cabinets. Just as a large-patterned cretonne does not suit a small room, so this large-figured timber is ill-suited as a background and surround for dials and switches. As executed by Rolls-Royce the woodwork is magnificent. By suitable cutting of the veneers the panels, dash-board, door-cappings, garnish rails etc. present exquisitely matched mirror-image patterns of graining in the best cabinet-making tradition. All the woodwork is sprayed with acrylic lacquer, hand polished, rubbed down, re-sprayed and re-polished again and again until a deep lustre is reached which no piano-polisher could emulate. But the writer finds himself, for once, in agreement with the anti-Rolls-Royce brigade in thinking that a glossy wood-veneered instrument board is incongruous in a modern motor-car (some matt surface, preferably dark, being much more suitable), and that of all fine timbers Circassian walnut is the least suitable. He is probably in a minority of one in that last opinion, and as long as the customers want walnut wood Rolls-Royce will doubtless continue to supply it and to do it rather better than anyone else. In recent years, however, Rolls-Royce have reverted to burr walnut.

The next innovation was automatic transmission and this, like the steel bodies, first appeared on the Bentley car; the slightly more conservative who preferred the Rolls-Royce (though the difference now was only one of appearance and minor detail) were still, in 1952, a little wary of this innovation. In 1952, then, the R-type Bentley was offered, for export only at first, with fully automatic transmission; a year later it was available on the home market and at the end of 1953 the Rolls-Royce Silver Dawn followed suit. When Emile Levassor first devised the combination of petrol engine foot-controlled friction clutch, and sliding pinion change-speed mechanism he said of it *'c'est brutal mais ça marche'*. The brutality was hideously apparent and it is remarkable that the arrangement continued to march unaltered in principle in the majority of the world's motor-cars for some eighty years. A great number of alternative and far less brutal systems were devised quite soon after

M. Levassor had uttered his memorable words and many of them, such as the ingenious De Dion-Bouton system of constant-mesh gears brought into action by expanding clutches, were both technically and commercially successful.

As more and more manufacturers after 1900 copied the Panhard et Levassor layout, the combination of foot-controlled clutch and sliding-pinion gearbox came to predominate though it was widely condemned. Sales resistance more than technical difficulties hampered the spread of other, simpler, methods of control and such interesting inventions as the Barber progressively variable automatic gearbox, or the Lentz hydraulic transmission, fell by the wayside, and firms like Adams and Lanchester were obliged to disguise their admirably simple controls.

In America the motorist's objection to gear changing was particularly marked, and many early American cars were fitted with epicyclic gears which, being always in mesh, could not be crashed, and which were brought into action by contracting brakes on the drums containing the gear trains so that, as on the De Dion system, each speed had, in effect, its own clutch brought into action by the same movement which selected the speed. These methods did away with the bugbear of simultaneously moving a clutch pedal and a gear lever and, particularly as refined by Henry Ford on the Model T, they greatly simplified the driver's task. Without a lot of extra complication and weight it was difficult to provide for more than two forward speeds by epicyclic gearing and the ease of control was stultified by the awkwardness of the large gap between low gear and high. Dr. Lanchester overcame this difficulty with his compound epicyclic gear which he patented in 1898, but this solution of the problem was ignored by other manufacturers for thirty years.

The big step towards fully automatic transmission was taken in 1930 when Daimler combined the Föttinger 'fluid flywheel', or hydraulic coupling, with the Wilson pre-selective 'self-change' gearbox, which was a modernised 4-speed version of Lanchester's pre-selective 3-speed compound epicyclic gearbox of 1900. Although the 'self-change' gears could not be crashed and the fluid flywheel allowed the car to start gently from rest merely by accelerating the engine, the users soon learnt that the combination did not do away with the need for skill; proper co-ordination of the gear change pedal and the accelerator was essential if jerky changes were to be avoided.

There was no technical reason why the Daimler transmission should not have been made fully automatic from the start, with the changes of ratio related to engine speed and load and brought about by pneumatic, hydraulic or electro-magnetic servo mechanism. The motor world was still so dominated by the three-pedal convention that this was not done, and it was left to the Americans to take the next logical step.

The majority of automatic transmission systems now in use depend upon a multi-train compound epicyclic gearbox derived from Lanchester–Wilson–Daimler sources and the necessary clutch action between engine and transmission is usually taken care of by a modern version of the fluid flywheel or hydraulic coupling, though many firms prefer a form of mechanical torque converter which allows some progressive variation of ratio to supplement the positive gear trains.

The first Rolls-Royce automatic gearbox, like their original i.f.s., was based upon the

1951 Grand Prix d'Endurance, Le Mans: H. S. F. Hay's Bentley coming out of the corner after the Dunlop Bridge. (Klementaskis Studio)

General Motors design and was of the hydraulic coupling and 4-speed epicyclic variety, with hydraulic servo devices to control the speed changes. Following their usual practice the design staff made a long study of all the systems available, took the one they considered best and set about improving it. Many modifications were made after 1952 in their search to find ways of making a good mechanism even better and longer lived, and the result was very good indeed. It had the demerit that on a 'kick-down' change into third at about 60 m.p.h. there was some snatch (which could be avoided if the over-riding hand control was used) and in an article in *Autocar* Ronald Barker wrote: 'No one at Crewe, incidentally, is under the illusion that this transmission is completely smooth, but it has the overwhelming asset of transmitting full engine braking in the overrun through any of the four gears. Where a compromise has to be biased towards smoothness or controllability (and thus safety), the latter wins.

Automatic transmission removes the greatest single drawback from the internal-combustion-engined vehicle and it is astonishing that the motorists of the world put up with Emile Levassor's brutal system for so long. Once a driver grows used to a good automatic gearbox he never wants to return to the old hand and foot method. When automatic transmission became a reality the enthusiasts tended to sneer at it. It would take all the fun out of driving, they said, and by abolishing the need for skill would make for letting a lot of bad drivers loose on the road. It was also argued that the 'little man in the cog-box', being dependent on engine speed for his instructions, might elect to change up just when some traffic condition called for a lower gear and a quick spurt. Thus, they said, the little man would be a positive menace and a *real* motorist would always prefer to swap his own cogs.

There are still a few enthusiasts who advance these arguments but it is fair to say they quickly change their tune when they drive a good 'automatic'.

Good is the operative word. Some systems do not give the driver sufficient option to hold the lower ratios when necessary, and many of the earlier three-stage varieties suffer, like all three-speed transmissions, from too wide a gap between ratios. A good automatic box in which these shortcomings are avoided certainly does not take the fun out of driving, and the Rolls-Royce version was decidedly good. The care which went into making it was almost unbelievable and the gearbox shop was almost a holy place, as clean as the finest watch factory, with airtight glass cabinets to protect finished components from the atmosphere pending assembly. The machining, honing and polishing of the moving parts of the oil-control valve box (the 'brains' of the outfit) nearly went beyond watchmaking techniques and the final polishing was done not with jeweller's rouge, which was found too coarse, but with fine-ground oat husks.

The first series Silver Cloud, with automatic transmission and its Bentley

1951 Grand Prix d'Endurance, Le Mans: H. S. F. Hay's Bentley coming out of the Tertre Rouge preceded by the Stoop/Wilson Frazer-Nash and an Aston Martin. (Klementaskis Studio)

Grand Prix driver at the helm: Tony Brooks enjoying a bit of 'cross-armed stuff' in the wet. (Silver Cloud III).
(Klementaskis Studio)

counterpart, represent the final development of the 6-cylinder engine. The design and experimental departments felt no further development was possible and the need to get more power from an equally compact engine dictated another return to the Vee formation. In its final form the 6-cylinder engine certainly showed its paces by contrast with its ancestor of 1922, and in 1958 a standard saloon Rolls-Royce was timed by *The Autocar* at an average maximum speed of 106 m.p.h. (the mean of several runs in two directions); it could reach 100 m.p.h. in 50 seconds, and the practical limit of the original Twenty, 60 m.p.h., in 13 seconds.

Some mention must be made of the rarest of post-war Rolls-Royce types, the Phantom IV. This was a special long-chassis state car of which only eighteen were made 'for Royalty and Heads of State'. No two are exactly alike, and detailed particulars were not commonly disclosed at the time they were built. The most unusual feature for a Rolls-Royce car was a straight-eight engine. This was a 'civilian' version of the B-range straight-eight military engine which had been produced in quantity since the war. As these Royal cars were of considerable size the length of the engine was of small consequence, and considered as a processional carriage the Phantom IV, aesthetically, represented a remarkably successful blend of eighteenth-century splendour with functional twentieth-century engineering.

*   *   *

The V-8 engines used in Rolls-Royce and Bentley cars from 1962 onwards pack about 1$^1/_2$-litres greater capacity into rather less length than the 6-cylinder-in-line engine, and the specific output is calculated now to be at least 50% greater. The capacity is actually 6,750 cc. against 4,887 and the compression ratio is normally 9:1.

As with the abortive 'Legalimit' engine the two banks of cylinders form a 90° angle, but otherwise all is changed. The most significant difference is that the cylinder blocks are of aluminium-silicon alloy with 'wet' liners of cast iron. When the engine was being designed it is believed the company investigated the modern technique of very thin casting in iron and discovered it would be possible for cylinder blocks to be made of iron which would weigh no more than those of aluminium. Iron being inherently less resonant made this an attractive proposition, but, at that time, the foundry technique to produce such castings was exclusive to America, so Rolls-Royce decided upon the aluminium blocks in accordance with their usual policy.

Overhead valves, push-rod operated, in the V-engine posed a problem as the expansion of the aluminium blocks necessitated large expansion gaps in the valve gear; consequently there has been a reversion to Phantom III practice and the tappet clearances are automatically maintained by hydraulic plungers. Rolls-Royce are confident that the new design, together with modern lubricants and filters, has overcome the snags found on their earlier engines. As the specification shows, a rather unusual firing order has been adopted with the object of reducing crankshaft oscillation as far as possible. As usual, a torsional damper is also fitted.

Endowed with this engine the Silver Clouds II and III, and the comparable Bentleys, had speed and acceleration to suit the most exacting driver, and sure-footed stability to match anything but an outright racing car. The maximum speed was near to 120 m.p.h. and *The Motor* road test of August 1963 recorded 117 m.p.h. as the mean figure for properly timed runs in different directions. From standstill to 100 miles an hour took only 34.2 seconds against the 50 seconds of the previous model, and 60 m.p.h. was reached in a mere 10 seconds. Under full-power conditions the gear changes took place at 25 m.p.h., 40 m.p.h., and 72 m.p.h., whilst use of the manual control, or a kick-down on the accelerator, imposed a change down to third speed at any pace up to 65 m.p.h. if necessary. With this performance went petrol consumption of 12 m.p.g.

Rolls-Royce refuse to disclose the power output of their engines whilst they are still being produced and blandly state that it is 'adequate'. This infuriates their critics who complain of arrogance. Arrogant it may be, but what superb arrogance and in the light of the performance figures how justifiable.

Cornering, road-holding, visibility, suspension, lightness and precision of steering were good and that peculiar Rolls-Royce-like attribute, first observed on the Silver Ghost, of making a large car 'feel' small in terms of manœuvrability was still delightfully apparent. It is still a supremely safe car which brought out the best in every driver and inspired confidence from the start. The road-holding was markedly better than that of the first post-war cars.

At the same time that they introduced the Silver Cloud II Rolls-Royce Ltd. went back to the policy of making two basic R-R. models, and after a lapse of twenty years a Phantom (V) was offered to ordinary customers. The engine, transmission and other major parts differed but little from the Silver Cloud, but the chassis was lengthened by twenty-one inches and the necessary rigidity was maintained by a massive tubular member. The long chassis could carry coachwork of almost Edwardian spaciousness, but the weight distribution was so carefully planned that the big car had maximum speed and handling characteristics very similar to those of the smaller model.

It was very gratifying to see Great Britain back again in the narrow field of the 'travelling carriage' or 'state coach' type of vehicle, and in the Phantom V, Rolls-Royce and the body-builders really excelled themselves: the car had a dignified grandeur of appearance which quite belied its performance yet it had also an elegant beauty of line seldom seen in so large a machine. The interior was quietly opulent without being ostentatious. An obvious rival for the favours of the bigger big-business men, sheiks, oil potentates and other potential buyers of the Phantom V was the new large Mercedes 600 – *Der Grosse Mercedes* – which was powered by a V-8 engine of slightly larger capacity than that of the Rolls-Royce. The maximum speed claimed for the Mercedes was almost 10 m.p.h. faster, and the other performance figures are believed to be closely comparable. The premier German motor works has seldom produced a bad car and never a dull one, and this effort on the grand scale contained many advanced technical features, but the most avid admirer could scarcely claim that it was beautiful. It was imposing, no doubt, in a heavily Teutonic, almost Wagnerian, way, monolithic rather than magnificent, and that eminent connoisseur L. H. Pomeroy described it as: 'Impressive rather than elegant in appearance and with plush fittings of Edwardian opulence which would have delighted Cleo de Mérode'.

Ordinary motor-cars have improved so much since the war that extraordinary ones like Rolls-Royces need to be superb to keep ahead; eagle-eyed and knowledgeable critics are ready to pounce on any shortcoming and though inverted snobbery and bias are at the root of some complaints the criticism, on the whole, is well-informed and objective.

'Old fashioned' is the cry most often heard, and the one most easy to answer by observing that Rolls-Royces are old fashioned in exactly the same way that the lever escapement to be found controlling nearly every modern watch is old fashioned. Rolls-Royce design has always been based on the use of well-tried principles.

The drum brakes and the rear suspension by half elliptic leaf springs and a rigid axle were two details in particular which began to come in for adverse comment. 'Why not disc brakes?' asked the pundits, to which Rolls-Royce replied that when disc brakes became as efficient, long-lived and *quiet* as their drum brakes they would use them. No particular magic attaches to disc brakes (nor are they all that new for they were used in 1903) and their supreme virtue of comparative freedom from 'fade' is counterbalanced by the short life of the brake pads. These are easily replaced it is true, but the job still entails putting the car off the road for a while, and Rolls-Royce were undoubtedly right at that time to stick to their well-tried braking system.

Rolls-Royce Phantom V and Silver Ghost, both owned by Jack Barclay.

The Motor road test of the Silver Cloud III reported on some degree of fade after several stops in quick succession. This prompted an enthusiast to write 'It looks as though it is time R-R. threw away their drum brakes, doesn't it?' But a good look at the figures shows that the pedal pressure needed had only risen by 8 lb. at the end of the test, and after twenty stops in succession at one-minute intervals, from about 55 m.p.h., the pressure needed was no greater than at the tenth stop: $^1/_2$G deceleration was still achieved with a mere 50 lb. pedal pressure.

It is diverting to discover that a similar test conducted a few weeks later on a car with disc brakes (but of less than half the weight of the Rolls-Royce), revealed that pedal pressure rose 15 lb. against 8 lb. for the R-R., and that descending a 600-foot test hill under control of the brakes induced so much fade that the pedal pressure needed for a $^1/_2$G stop from only 30 m.p.h. had risen by another 30 lb. A further article in *Motor* then disclosed that the Rolls-Royce tested had some slight fault in the brake adjustment which accounted for the fade. A further test by *Motor*'s staff confirmed Rolls-Royce's claim that the brakes were virtually fade-free. It seemed the Rolls-Royce braking system was still not outmoded.

The criticism levelled at the rear suspension invoked the usual reference to 'cart springs'. The ease with which the Silver Cloud III rode over varying surfaces was admirable, and from the point of view of passenger comfort the sternest critic cannot find much to complain about. The ability to corner quickly but safely also merited praise, but perhaps the critics had a case in one respect, for it was apparent that the 'Hotchkiss Drive' had reached the limit of development. Although the cars were fitted with radius arms which partially relieved the springs of torque it was possible to make the back axle judder under

154

Rolls – from the statue at Monmouth by Goscomb John.

hard acceleration. The next stage of development, as we shall see, involved a completely new rear suspension and other fundamental changes.

Enthusiasts also regretted that the 'ride control' of the 'thirties, which allowed progressive stiffening of the damper action from minimum to maximum, had been replaced by an electric device which could only be switched from hard to soft, or vice versa. The reason for this apparently retrograde step was that the company found over the years that many owners or drivers never used the ride control, but left it permanently set in one position, with the result that it gave trouble when, after long neglect, someone did try to use it. It is indeed a pity that so elegant a device had to be scrapped but the system which replaced it was more foolproof.

Much the same sort of reasoning lay behind the abolition of that most agreeable Rolls-Royce refinement, the centralised chassis lubricating system. This admirable device was replaced by ordinary oil-gun points, twenty-one of them, which were designed to need attention only once in every 12,000 miles. This was a usefully long interval, but the departure of the 'one-shot' was a sad blow to the older generation of Rolls-Royce fanciers. Unfortunately most post-war owners are not enthusiasts in the old sense, and as many of the cars which came in for repair showed evident signs that people just could not be bothered to press the 'one-shot' pedal from time to time there was nothing to be done but

Grand Touring par excellence: Silver Cloud III takes Route Nationale to the sun, 1963.

scrap it. It is also true that the 'one-shot' could fail in part without the driver being aware of it. That is, the supply to some part might become stopped or reduced, or a 'drip-plug' might grow too large with use and so allow too much oil to pass at one point thereby diminishing the feed to some more distant part. These defects were rare and only manifested themselves after long use; many a pre-war Rolls-Royce with 200,000 miles or more to its credit still has its 'one-shot' working as well as the day it left the factory.

Many of the criticisms, in fact, came from the older motorists and a valid point they make is that the Silver Cloud was a noisier car than the Silver Ghost of fifty-five years earlier. So it was, at least from the point of hearing of the man in the street. For the occupants the car was blissfully quiet; under very hard acceleration some power roar could be heard but at all other times there was no more than a faint hum. There was very little wind noise as the body had been carefully designed to avoid it, and it was true that at 50–60 m.p.h. those who sat in the front seats could hear the dash-board clock ticking. And it was not a very loud clock.

From the outside, however, there was some mechanical noise to be heard. Not very much, but the uncanny impression the Silver Ghost gave of being drawn along by an invisible thread was no more. It could hardly be otherwise when it is considered that the power output of the Silver Cloud's engine was at least five times greater than that of the Ghost.

It would be possible to go on for ever advancing arguments for and against various details of design, not only of Rolls-Royces but of other cars. Engineering design, of motor-cars in particular, must always be a matter of compromise and whilst individuals retain their individuality something to please one and to displease another will inevitably be found. It is a good thing for the motor industry that there are so many professional or amateur critics ready to praise or denounce their brain children. Rolls-Royce Ltd. were undoubtedly right to be as proud of the Silver Cloud as they were of the Silver Ghost, and perhaps the fairest summing up which can be given is to say there is equally no doubt that Henry Royce himself would have been proud of it.

10

Shadows and Spirits

———•◦•———

WHETHER Sir Henry Royce would also have been as proud of the Silver Cloud's successors, the Silver Shadow, the Corniche, the Bentley counterparts and the lordly Phantoms V and VI is rather less certain, though it is fair to assume he would have given top marks for effort to all those on whom his mantle has fallen. This does not reflect any discredit on the design and execution of the motor cars but reflects the great social and technological changes since his death. Many of these changes were apparent in the cars and would inevitably distress and baffle a man who rose by his own efforts from poverty to relative prosperity in the last three decades of Queen Victoria's reign.

Undoubtedly the event which would most have distressed Royce and his contemporaries was the bankruptcy of Rolls-Royce Limited. The company had been synonymous with reliability, impregnable stability and quality for so long that its financial collapse in 1970 came as a devastating shock. A shock which was the greater because it came so soon after glowing accounts had reached the public of the company's record order for a new breed of aero engine which in part rested on the technical achievement of developing a new material, carbon fibre. Nobody, it seemed, could say Rolls-Royce were lacking either in commercial enterprise or engineering inventiveness. Yet scarcely had the city editors, financial experts and government spokesmen finished polishing their panegyrics than they were uttering Cassandra-like cries of Woe! and claiming that they had foreseen disaster from the beginning. To the British public, particularly to those of middle age or more, it was as though it had been revealed that Queen Victoria had run Windsor Castle as a bawdy house with Prince Albert as her pimp. How could Rolls-Royce 'go bust' they asked?

The answers are complex and lie beyond the scope of this book*. In the past it may be safely assumed that the motor car business sometimes drew support, directly or indirectly, from the aero engine business. It is doubtful, for example, whether the unsupported car business could have stood the expense of honouring the promise made in 1924 to call back all new Silver Ghosts sold after the autumn motor show and to fit front brakes to them without charge. Various setbacks had prevented the new 4-wheel brake system attaining the desired standard by the time of the show, but having announced the innovation Rolls-Royce felt obliged to modify all the cars sold between October 1924 and mid-1925. The expense was considerable as the modification involved not only fitting the actual front

* See *The Engines were Rolls-Royce*, by R. W. Harker, Collier Macmillan, 1979.

158

brakes, servo and appurtenances, but entailed also supplying and fitting new front wheels, axles and springs. Indirect support is difficult to define but is exemplified, for example, in the design of the Phantom III engine which clearly owed much to the aero-engine division. Such interdependence may obviously save money all round by preventing overlapping, but may also be used to conceal weaknesses in one division by off-setting development costs on to a stronger branch. It was very fortunate at the time of the collapse that the motor car division was so clearly prosperous, able to sell more cars than it could make: there was no question but that it had to be saved.

In the event all was saved and after some months of uneasy continuation under the Official Receiver the government stepped in and took the aero engine and ancillary business under state control whilst the motor car business was reconstituted as a wholly separate, privately owned, limited company, to the great relief of motor car enthusiasts the world over. It was touch and go, however, as it seemed for a time that that mysterious animal the money market would not cough up enough to meet the Receiver's price, and there were fears that the Rolls-Royce car business would pass into continental or even Japanese ownership: which most certainly would not have pleased Sir Henry.

Engineers often complain, usually with good reason, that they are not sufficiently represented on the boards of manufacturing companies, and that the accountants and financial experts who predominate do not sufficiently understand engineering problems. It could be that the balance was tilted a little too far in favour of the engineers in the period immediately before the collapse of Rolls-Royce. There may have been insufficiently strict control of development costs, and it seems that the financial managers became too much infected with the engineers' optimism over the carbon fibre development. If this is so they are scarcely to be blamed as the Labour government of the day urged on the project in every way they could short of outright nationalisation. The Minister of Technology was particularly active, fully justified his nickname of 'Whizzy-Wedgie', and publicly took great credit upon himself for the part he had played in securing the much-vaunted order from the Lockheed Corporation, which, it was claimed, was not only bound to enhance the glowing reputation of Rolls-Royce but to restore Great Britain's ever-ailing trade balance. Although there were other factors in the equation it was the terms of this contract which precipitated the crisis when technical problems supervened and the carbon fibre compressor fan blades had to be scrapped in favour of expensive titanium. If it is fair to say the officials of the company should have been more cautious, it is equally fair to observe that the Minister did not display the sort of grandmotherly prudence generally expected of a British government.

Perhaps the affair was salutary in the long run. Some dead wood may have been lopped from the tree, better financial management will be on the watch to avoid similar difficulties in the future and the R.B. Two-Eleven engine, the epicentre of the storm, despite some teething troubles with the titanium fan discs, *did* usher in a new era of jet engine quietness. As a Conservative government was in power by the time the crash came, and negotiated the state take-over to save the company, the affair also provided the former Minister of Technology with an opportunity to do a smart about turn to forget the lavish praise he heaped upon the company (and himself) when all was well, to denounce the inefficiency of capitalism which, alone, could make such mistakes and to sneer at the Conservative government for applying his favourite panacea of nationalisation. This at least provided some light relief in a situation which most people found tragic. Ultimately, however, ordinary stockholders received a total payment of 64.5p.

All of which takes us a long way from the motor-cars, but one of the most striking developments since the bankruptcy has been that the motor car division has done more business and enjoyed greater prosperity than ever before. No doubt this is purely fortuitous,

Mounting Silver Spur body onto running gear; Crewe factory, early 1980s.

but when (December 1973) *Motor* magazine published a list showing the average delivery times for all the principal makes of motor car this showed the 'waiting time' for a Rolls-Royce Corniche was no less than ten years. In a sense the figure is fictitious as it must be based upon the known rate of production and the known list of orders, but even if the production were doubled and half the potential customers withdrew their orders it would still be remarkable for a concern which had been in such danger.

One of the remarkable things is the way in which the company has adapted itself to changed circumstances. Rolls-Royce car buyers are very different now from what they were in Royce's day, and even then the day of the Tailor-made motor car was practically done. It is noteworthy, for example, that in the years immediately following his death the

160

Rolls-Royce carburettors, ignition coils, distributors and many other incidentals gave place to proprietary components, most of which were specially finished to Rolls-Royce specification, but which, nevertheless, were unashamedly 'bought-out'. Many of the customers of the 'thirties and 'forties deplored these innovations and there is little doubt Sir Henry would also have deplored them, although he would have been businessman enough to see why these and other changes had to be made.

When the Silver Ghost was establishing its reputation for reliability, economy and other virtues, Sir Henry and his colleagues were undeniably right to assume that no bought-out carburettors and many other vital parts could compare with those of their own design and make, but even before the first world war the company bought many items from specialists on the common-sense grounds that it was both technically and economically right to do so. They never attempted, for example, to make their own suspension springs, as Lanchester did in the 'twenties, and from the start they relied upon outside firms for chassis frames 'in the rough' and for cylinder castings. To extend the practice of buying-out in the 'thirties and subsequently was logical, and those who shook their heads at the sight of a Stromberg carburettor or a Lucas coil on a Rolls-Royce engine were closing their minds to hard economic facts. In some particulars the company insisted, as it still does, on making certain parts, not of their design, under licence in order to be sure of keeping the quality control under their supervision, even though this is a more expensive procedure than buying from the original manufacturer. The automatic gearbox is a case in point. As W. A. Robotham related in *Silver Ghosts and Silver Dawn*, when he and his colleagues agreed the time had come to fit automatic transmission it was also agreed that the General Motors 'Hydramatic' was the best available system, but it was thought unwise to rely on a foreign supplier for such a vital component particularly as the makers might find it necessary to lower their standards, leaving Rolls-Royce with no option but to find an alternative or accept something of lesser quality. It speaks volumes, incidentally, for Rolls-Royce's reputation in America that Mr. Robotham had little difficulty in persuading General Motors to grant a manufacturing licence, although the money involved was a mere flea-bite to so powerful an organisation. When the licence was first negotiated Rolls-Royce's annual requirement for gearboxes scarcely equalled General Motors' daily production.

During the time when Royce was the final arbiter on all details of design, and for some years after his death, quite a number of those who bought Rolls-Royces still had the fundamental knowledge of motor engineering which had been almost essential in the early days. The knowledge may not have been deep, but when they opened the bonnet of a Rolls-Royce they were able to recognise the essential components and expected to see, for example, a Rolls-Royce carburettor even though most of them would have been hard put to it to explain the subtle differences between a Rolls-Royce, a Zenith Triple Diffuser, a Claudel-Hobson or a Stromberg. It still made commercial sense, therefore, for Royce to insist on retaining certain home-made components even after bought-out ones of equal merit were obtainable more cheaply.

During the 1930s cars became much cheaper and more widely used, with a corresponding increase in service stations to cater for the new types of motorist. These neither knew nor cared what make of carburettor was fitted to their 'Family Fug-Box Four', and the discrimination of the Rolls-Royce class of buyer began to be focused more upon performance, appearance and convenience than upon niceties of mechanism. The old ritual of opening the bonnet and 'tickling' the carburettor before starting a cold engine was no longer required, and the appearance and cleanliness of the machinery were no longer matters of pride to the enthusiastic owner. There were indignant snorts of protest from the old guard when the Rolls-Royce radiator spout and filler cap became dummies, surmounting a 'shell' covering the real header tank, with the actual place for pouring in the water only accessible, as on any 'cheap' car, by opening the bonnet. By the time the second world war was over a new generation of Rolls-Royce buyers arrived who did not even realise the dummy was a dummy as they had cut their motoring teeth exclusively on cars on which the visible 'radiator' was no more than a hollow mockery, or ornamental flourish, executed in thin sheet iron decorated with chromium plated grilles and curlicues which reached the depths of ornate vulgarity in the 1950s, against which the classic simplicity of the Rolls-Royce 'radiator' stood proudly, even if its close friends knew it to be false. Though the traditionalists might deplore the changes and say that all the pressed tinware makes it more difficult to get at the machinery, the designers may justly reply that a well-designed modern cooling system so seldom needs replenishment that there is no point in a functional exposed filler cap, and that the false fronts of modern cars at least act as stone guards.

The new sort of post-war customer was exemplified by the writer's partner in a car-hire business who suffered a puncture when driving one of the firm's Phantom III's on his private occasions. In his efforts to change the wheel he completely ruined the delicate splines of the hub-locking device, as he was not mechanically minded enough to see how it functioned and was too impatient to look in the instruction book. Because of customers such as this, and because modern tyres so seldom puncture, Rolls-Royce were quite right to give up the elegantly designed, beautifully made and very expensive centre-lock wheels in favour of ordinary five-stud, bolt-on, pressed steel affairs in spite of the indignation of a diminishing band of purists. It is fair to assume Sir Henry Royce would have authorised the change, but it is doubtful whether he would have allowed the stylists to fit the new style wheels with snap-on nave plates fashioned to resemble the old-style centre-lock hub nuts. One feels he would have condemned this deceit.

It may also seem pettifogging to grumble about the uncouth dip-stick as the post-war cars have electric repeater oil-level indicators on the dashboards, and the modern Rolls-Royce owner is unlikely ever to see the tape-worm which is merely provided so that the mechanic may check the electric gauge when the car is serviced. Nevertheless the dip-stick would certainly have offended Sir Henry's mechanical susceptibilities; he would have agreed that the owner need never see it but he would surely have insisted that even the lowliest apprentice mechanic was entitled to find something less unseemly emerging from the entrails of a Rolls-Royce.

Sir Henry would then have been up against harsher realities of cost than those which existed when he was the final arbiter. Even before the first world war Royce's perfectionism often clashed with financial reality, and the ill-health which kept him away from the factory after 1910 made it possible to circumvent some of the expensive detail alterations which his refining zeal might have led him to insist upon had he been in daily attendance. If this was true before 1914 how much more true since the last war. Between the conflicting interests of what is best from the engineering standpoint and the demands of the customer, who is often swayed by fashion which, in turn, is too often dictated by stylistic whims in direct opposition to engineering logic, the modern car designer has a hard enough job. With the cash box rattling in his ears as well his task becomes almost impossible, and in this connection it must be remembered that although the name of Rolls-Royce may be great their production figures are puny by comparison with the giants. The Ford Company could shrug off a mistake of Edsel-like proportions which would sink Rolls-Royce without trace. It is surely better that there should still be Rolls-Royce cars, even though the old guard may wince at some of their details, rather than that they should be priced out of existence by too-rigid adherence to the sorts of minor refinements which were possible in Sir Henry's day.

With all the knowledge which has been garnered, and despite all the new materials, machine tools and processes which have been developed it is paradoxically far more difficult to design and make motor cars (and many other things) profitably now than at the beginning of the century; and it has been well observed that the job of building the Crystal Palace, which covered eighteen acres and was erected in twenty-two weeks, would probably take several years today. Returning to Rolls-Royce ignition coils illustrates the point if we consider how the job was done at Cooke Street, where the coils were wound by Miss Florrie Austin on a home-made machine which had been simply and cheaply grafted on to the base of an old Singer treadle sewing machine. Miss Austin treadled happily away and handed the coils to the electrician who fitted the tremblers, tested the circuits and passed the finished assemblies to the carpenter who cased them neatly in polished mahogany boxes. The coil winding did not occupy all Miss Austin's time, and she also engraved the Rolls-Royce insignia on hub-caps, control-lever plates, switches and so forth on a very old Taylor, Taylor and Hobson pantograph machine; as a pleasant change from coil winding and engraving she cut the slots for the valve-stem cotters on a simple double-head milling machine bought second-hand from the Two-Speed Gear Company of Salford. In between whiles Miss Austin brewed tea and, one may suppose, exchanged badinage with her workmates: for her toil she was paid the going rate of about twenty-seven shillings a week.

Whilst not defending the poor rates of pay current in the Cooke Street days one cannot but regret the passing of such a cosy way of doing things. Florrie Austin's modern counterpart would be paid probably nearly fifty times as much, which is fair enough, but what trades' union today would allow its members to use a treadle-driven machine? Some much more complex and expensive device would be needed, and if a present-day Florrie were asked to perform all her predecessor's tasks there would be instantaneous strikes by the Hub Cap Engravers Union, the Incorporated Sodality of Valve Stem Slotters and the Confederated Sorority of Tea Infusers. The modern motor manufacturer has little choice but to buy his ignition coils from an outside supplier, and to pray that *their* production will not be strike-bound.

Although a few individualists, such as Frederick Lanchester and Leslie Hounsfield (the designer of the Trojan utility car), contrived to swim against the tide, motor car design has always been a matter of compromise in which fashion has played a large part. Fashion and common sense are rarely compatible and the Silver Shadow, the basic design of which dated back to 1955, and the modern Corniche models developed from it, conform to fashion in being lower than Silver Cloud types and in looking broader and squatter. It would have been folly for the company not to have conformed for, as we have seen, it was beginning to be complained that the Silver Cloud, in which traces of the old dignified 'perpendicular' style could be seen, was out of date. Indeed, it was very difficult to set an acceptably low modern body on the traditional chassis. Nevertheless, the fashionable shape makes less sense than the older ones whether it is executed by Rolls-Royce or anybody else. Motor cars are intended to carry people, and people obstinately persist in being people-shaped and people-sized. Consequently, they are best carried in a rectilinear box on wheels, but attempts to soften the outlines and reduce wind resistance by curving the shape result in a loss of interior space as the people have to be brought nearer the centre of a fish-shaped conveyance if they are to have enough head room to sit comfortably.

In order to free the body designer from the restraints of the chassis the fundamental step was taken with the design of the Silver Shadow and its successors to follow modern practice by having a 'unitary' or integral body-frame structure. Like so much in motor history the idea was not new, and like all engineering compromises it has drawbacks as well as advantages. The great benefit of cheaper production does not really apply at Rolls-Royce levels but the reduction in overall height and weight for a structure of given rigidity and capacity is attractive. The disadvantage of greater susceptibility to rust because of exposure of the stiffened, load-bearing, floor structure to the corrosive and abrasive spray thrown up by ever-wider and faster-turning tyres is one which causes serious deterioration unless very thorough rust-proofing processes are used, and no expense is spared on the current models of Rolls-Royce and Bentley to keep the dreaded 'tin-worm' at bay.

With the new unitary construction came a new suspension system with both back and front wheels independently sprung, and with an ingenious automatic levelling mechanism, hydraulically powered by an engine-driven pump. The new suspension system was warmly praised on the whole when it first appeared, though there were reservations about the amount of roll, or a kind of lurching movement felt by the back seat passengers when steering lock was put on at speed. Modifications to the anti-roll bars and other details improved matters without affecting the general handling qualities which allow a modern Rolls-Royce to be hustled through corners very quickly and safely.

The integral construction of the Silver Shadow allowed the roof line to be put four inches lower than that of the Silver Cloud. Though really of negligible benefit this was an essential part of keeping abreast of fashion, and one of the distinguishing marks of the average Rolls-Royce owner nowadays is that he is apt to be very much younger than was once the case. Consequently he is not only very conscious of fashion but not so set in his ways and stiff in his joints as to find the lower-built cars inconvenient. The principal disadvantage of integral construction is that it makes it almost impossible to achieve the degree of freedom from road noise which the Rolls-Royce class of customer is entitled to expect. In order to get the best possible compromise between permissible 'shake' (inevitable in so long a structure) and insulation from road noises, Harry Grylls, Chief Engineer, and the design team used metallic mounting devices for the suspension which were known properly as 'Vibrashock' mounts and more familiarly as 'panscrubbers'. Though not as good at insulating sound as rubber block mountings they were less liable to deteriorate with age, but there was no denying that road noise *was* more obtrusive on the first Silver Shadows than on their predecessors. Further modifications closed the gap.

Modern cars, particularly the large American ones, are so quiet in general that a Rolls-Royce has to try twice as hard as its rivals to stay in the place the Silver Ghost carved for itself. As noted in connection with the Silver Cloud the modern generation of Rolls-Royce V-eight engines are not so quiet at tickover speeds as a properly tuned Silver Ghost but they are impressively quiet at speed; and it must be remembered that a Shadow or Corniche can go nearly twice as fast as a standard Ghost. Wind noise, which was scarcely a problem in the Ghostly era, is commendably unobtrusive unless the windows are opened, and there is no noticeable exhaust boom or intake roar at full power. These good points make what road noise there is more obvious, and considering the difference between 1965 and 1979 models in this respect it is also obvious that the 'minor modification department' had been working overtime. The business is not helped by the fact that the fashion for low, squat motor cars means having ever-smaller wheels, which must rotate more times in a mile than bigger ones, carrying ever-wider tyres and causing ever-more tyre roar. The compensating advantage of better adhesion is sometimes overstated, and the recent increases in tyre width underline the difficulties facing a motor car designer who has to balance so many conflicting requirements. The matter sets aesthetic as well as engineering problems as the small fat wheels of modern cars make it difficult for the body designer to achieve harmonious proportions; but as fewer and fewer people remember the excellent balance of line which could be achieved when wheel diameters were greater and tyres were narrower it is pointless to cavil.

The new style of construction allowed the Silver Shadow to be five inches shorter, three inches narrower and four inches lower than the Silver Cloud with no sacrifice of interior space. Indeed, a small increase was claimed, but the advantage was more apparent than real as the subtle changes of interior curves, angles and juxtaposition of parts result in the rear seat occupants feeling less adequately catered for than in a Cloud, even if the tape measure tells them they have more room. Judgement, even expert judgement, is often swayed by what it expects to find and as the name Rolls-Royce had always been synonymous with spacious luxury the *Motor* road test report of a Silver Shadow, in November 1968, had two photographs of the rear compartment, with occupant or occupants, captioned: 'The well-shaped seats will take one or two in great luxury and three in comfort'. The picture of the three abreast gives the lie to the alleged comfort as the man in the middle could not get both shoulders against the back-rest; he had to sit cater-cornerwise so that his right shoulder overlapped the left shoulder of the girl beside him. She was grinning happily, perhaps at his discomfiture, but he looked understandably sour and personal experience of 150 miles as pig-in-the-middle inclines one to share his gloom, particularly as the combination of a long spine and the too hasty traverse of a hump-backed bridge brought the writer's head into intimate contact with that lowered roof. There was, in fact, $36\frac{1}{2}$ inches from compressed seat cushion to roof, which is not over-generous.

More leg space could be given to the back seat passengers if the front seats were less opulently thick, and here one cannot blame the designers for their attempts some years ago to introduce thinner (but no less luxurious) seat-backs provoked adverse comment. Rolls-Royce buyers still want great fat, opulent, seats just as, apparently, they still want plenty of high-gloss, acrylic-lacquered, burr walnut trimmings, which look even more incongruous to a motor car interior than they did in the past. On the other side of the picture it must be said that those front seats can be adjusted electrically to suit every size, shape and idiosyncrasy of the human frame and the walnut veneers are as carefully matched and beautifully finished as ever they were.

Though one may disagree with *Motor*'s dictum that the leg room in the back of the Shadow was 'tremendous' the point was made, and it is valid, that a modern Rolls-Royce is much more likely to be driven by its owner than was the case years ago. Consequently it is essential to give the occupants of the front seats the utmost possible space and comfort with an unobstructed view and sensibly placed controls which are light to handle. This has certainly been done, but in an ideal world the design of any car which purports to be a four or five seater ought to be based on the assumption that all the occupants will be of full size and equally entitled to fair shares of space, seating-comfort, freedom from bumps, heat, ventilation, view and any other goodies that are going. To treat the back seat passengers as second-class citizens is just as indefensible as was the bad old practice of cramping the chauffeur's quarters in large cars in order to benefit the gentry in the rear compartment.

No matter what reservations there may be about the rear compartment of the Silver Shadow the designers gave the occupants of the front seats no cause for complaint. This is particularly true of the driver who has a chair capable of almost endless variations of adjustment, a commanding view of the road and well-placed controls of finger-tip lightness. There are those, indeed, who said the steering was too light and consequently a trifle 'dead', and it is interesting to find that this criticism came almost exclusively from older drivers, particularly those acquainted with pre-war Rolls-Royces, whilst those with only fairly recent experience noticed nothing except the light precision of the steering. Whether he had to cover four or five hundred miles as quickly as possible, or to battle inch by inch in the worst city traffic, the driver was cosseted and kept from irritation and fatigue in the most exemplary fashion. Here, the Shadow and its Bentley counterpart showed to advantage over their American rivals which seemed a trifle unwieldy by comparison. Also, splendid though they were as pieces of advanced production engineering, the big American cars gave the impression that their designers were not only concerned to insulate their drivers from unpleasantness but to isolate them from reality to an extent which could be dangerous.

The trifling reductions in width and length of the Silver Shadow *vis-à-vis* the Silver Cloud helped the impression, so often noticed in Rolls-Royces of all ages, that it was not really a big car; and it is wonderfully manoeuvrable in traffic as an American test report noted. The lowering of the roof-line, wind-screen height and seating position brought no advantage as the higher the car the better as any truck driver or veteran car owner knows. The boon of being able to look over the roofs of the minis and other automotive detritus as it scuttles about the city streets is as great as the joy of looking over the hedges and round the bends on narrow country lanes. It is an odd manifestation of inverted snobbery that the 'new' generation of Rolls-Royce buyers no longer find the dignified 'presence' of the older models acceptable, but would yet be horrified if the Company were to abolish the dummy 'Grecian' radiator though it is no longer defensible either functionally or aesthetically.

The specifications of the Silver Shadow and its derivatives and successors reveal that after forty years' faithful service the mechanically power-assisted drum brakes were supplanted by a hydraulic disc system which the most captious critics were unable to fault. Except, that is, that one test by *Motor* magazine revealed that the hand-brake failed to hold the car on a one in three gradient. Before Sir Henry Royce could start turning in his grave it became apparent that this was a freak result which was not, apparently, duplicated.

The new footbrake system was probably the most elaborate ever fitted to a motor car. Power assistance is provided from hydraulic 'accumulators' in which pressure is maintained at about 1,500 p.s.i. by a pump driven from the camshaft. The effort from the accumulator is channelled into two separate circuits to the brake cylinders as a guard against failure or leaks in any one part. In addition to actuating these duplicated powered circuits, the pedal also operates a conventional master cylinder which is coupled through a deceleration-sensitive pressure-limiting valve directly to the rear wheel brakes. This arrangement not only adds a strong piece of string to the belt and braces of the duplicated powered system but puts 'feel' into the pedal so that the driver knows what is happening. Of the total braking effort when the pedal is pressed the first circuit from the hydraulic accumulators provides 46%, and the second circuit gives 31% whilst the master cylinder circuit adds the final 23%. Total failure of the foot-brake is almost impossible.

As noted, some critics complained of the power steering, and as Rolls-Royce have such a strong following in the United States it is worth quoting the opinion given in *Road & Track* whose reporters wrote in August 1969:

> 'One doesn't expect a Rolls to take kindly to sporty driving and the Shadow holds no surprises. It rolls a lot (current ones, with larger front anti-roll bar and a rear one added, roll less), and this fact coupled with the very dead power steering – General Motors by the way – really discourage one from proceeding with anything but dignity.'

It is not improper to interpolate here that dignity is relative, and acceleration from standstill to 60 m.p.h. in eleven seconds with a true maximum speed of 114 m.p.h. quite lift the car out of the funeral carriage class. The *Road & Track* report continues:

> 'The handling is predictable, however, with no tendency at all for the tail to slide, and we found the independent rear suspension to help keep the rear wheels on the road when negotiating tight turns up our favourite hill.

Braking is very good indeed, as it should be with so elaborate and expensive a system . . . no tendency for the rear wheels to lock up in panic braking on dry pavement. Fade resistance is also satisfactory. The handbrake is less happy, however . . . a trace of squeal is occasionally heard from the discs despite R-R's clever use of a spring-steel band set into the disc's periphery.

What, then, does the Silver Shadow offer when compared to other luxury, prestige sedans such as, for instance, a Lincoln or Cadillac at less than half the price or a Mercedes 6.3 at two-thirds? Well, there's the traditional R-R finish and materials, every bit as good now as they were in the past though a bit anachronistic now. Pin striping, leather, and burr walnut do have their appeal. In performance and handling characteristics

Soldering Rolls-Royce radiator shell header tank; Crewe factory, early 1980s.

it is so close to the Lincoln and Cadillac (at least under American conditions) that the difference is negligible, although it is certainly more manœuvrable in traffic than those cars . . . It does stop better than the Americans too. It cannot be driven in the sporting manner as the Mercedes can, nor is its ride that much better to compensate for the fact.

The conclusion, then, is that the Rolls has to justify itself on psychological grounds. It is most likely a durable thing – the whole car is warranted for 50,000 miles and will satisfy the buyer who is attracted to it in the first place. But it also demonstrates that a small manufacturer is hard-pressed these days to match the standards set forth by the giant auto-makers – American or otherwise – and that Rolls-Royce can no longer be considered the completely magical motoring experience it once had the reputation for.'

This is a very fair assessment bearing in mind that *Road & Track*, like the English journal *Motor Sport*, caters particularly for the sporting fraternity. It is also fair to add that in the years since the report was written the brakes of American cars have improved and the suspension and handling of the Rolls-Royce have been refined, whilst it must also be remembered that the Rolls-Royce matches Lincoln or Cadillac performance with a smaller engine.

The car which *Road & Track* tested had the then-latest 3-speed automatic gearbox with an hydraulic torque-converter in place of the 4-speed box with an hydraulic coupling (or fluid flywheel as it used to be called when the English Daimler company first adopted it over sixty years ago), which was retained on those cars made for sale in England for four years after the more modern transmission was fitted to the export models. All now have the torque-converter type, which provides some progressive variation of ratio between fixed points on the low and intermediate speeds. This amply compensates for the loss of the fixed ratio third speed of the earlier type.

Professional critics in England had looked askance at the 4-speed box for some time as there was an awkwardly wide gap between the ratios of second and third speeds. Also, although it was possible for the automatic devices to fulfill the functions of a well-trained chauffeur, who was supposed to drive, change gear, accelerate and slow down so that his passengers were unaware of alterations of direction or velocity, really imperceptible changes sometimes needed co-operation from the driver by judicious use of the selector over-ride, or by 'gentling' the throttle pedal. Under certain full-power conditions some changes, particularly by the 'kickdown', qualified the older-type 'hydramatic' transmission for its nickname of the 'jerkomatic'.

It was not merely the English preference for four speeds (even badly spaced ones) which kept the Rolls-Royce designers faithful to the old hydramatic box. They were reluctant to lose the very agreeable third speed – the ratio of which suited the car well under so many conditions of narrow country roads, or traffic-choked towns, where cars in Great Britain spend so much of their time. They thought the torque converter three speed transmission might occasionally seem fussy, but it has been so much refined, both by General Motors and by Rolls-Royce that this objection no longer applies.

The gearbox is a beautiful piece of machinery and with the Rolls-Royce addition of electric power-assistance for the selector control it is fairly complex and expensive. Its gear changing methods are usually described as 'almost imperceptible' or 'practically free from any noticeable jerk'. No doubt the Rolls-Royce design staff are following their usual practice of refining the existing mechanism whilst also looking at alternatives such as, perhaps, the Perbury progressively-variable mechanism which bears a remarkable resemblance to the Hayes gearbox fitted to a few Austin cars in 1935, which, in its turn, bore a family likeness to something Amédée Bollée, senior, patented in 1898. It is ironical that the only modern type of automatic motor car transmission which is *absolutely* free from jerking when changing ratios, and which is progressively variable over its complete range is the ingenious arrangement of Vee-belts and expanding pulleys used so successfully on the DAF cars. One can scarcely conceive of a belt-driven Rolls-Royce, however.

Nor could many people conceive of Messrs. Rolls-Royce engaging in the truck business, but in fact after the Second World War many thousands of military lorries, scout cars, tenders and other components of what used to be called the Waggon Train were propelled by Rolls-Royce engines originally designed for civilian use.

These were the 'B' range engines, made in the firm's Shrewsbury plant, and they admirably fulfilled the army's need for tough, long-lasting engines which combined reliability with low servicing costs, and the greatest possible degree of interchangeability of components amongst motors of similar design but differing power.

Rolls-Royce fulfilled the last requirement by going back to the practice of 1904–07 and offering the 'B' engines as four-, six- or eight-cylinder units, all of in-line formation and all of the same bore and stroke with the same dimensions of valves and valve-ports. Therefore, pistons, piston-rings, connecting-rods, valves, springs, rockers, guides and other items were common to all. The engines also had the 'F-head' or inlet-over-exhaust valve arrangement, similar to that of the two-, three-, four- and six-cylinder models of seventy years ago.

Durability and reliability being the prime considerations, the power produced by these 'B' engines was relatively modest at about 40 b.h.p. per litre of swept volume capacity, and in order that they could run on low-octane fuel, unleaded if need be, the compression ratio was also modest at 7.8 to 1.

As well as meeting all the war department's requirements so well that no major design changes were called for in a quarter of a century, the engines also qualified for private car use because, given adequate silencers and suitable engine mountings, they came up to Rolls-Royce standards of quietness and refinement. Therefore, as stated in Chapter Nine, the eight-cylinder version was used in the Phantom IV long-wheelbase 'state' cars, of which only eighteen were made (the later Phantom V and Phantom VI models use special versions of the standard V-eight engines), and from 1964 to 1968 Rolls-Royce Limited took the unprecedented step of supplying engines to an 'outside' firm for private car use.

The firm in question was the British Motor Corporation, now BL, which was then in the throes of making sense of its amalgamation of the Austin and Morris companies, which included *their* offshoots of Wolseley, Riley and a rag-bag of assorted goodies – or baddies. The rag-bag included the English Van den Plas concern which had started life as a small Belgian body-making business, and had risen to fame in the 1920s when it became the principal supplier of stark but handsome and feather light sports-tourer bodies to the old Bentley company.

As so often happens when a 'conglomerate' acquires a famous name it seems that the British Motor Corporation were at a loss to know what to do with Van den Plas, and as their mass-production methods left less and less scope for the 'bespoke' body builder the Van den Plas label was increasingly used as a snob name for superior versions of standard models. Just as a different radiator grille and some leather upholstery could transform a Morris or Austin into a Wolseley, so the further addition of differently shaped boot or trunk panels, lamps, and other items, together with a gold coach-line and some walnut wood, would transmogrify the Wolseley into a Van den Plas.

The motor car chosen for the Rolls-Royce engine was fundamentally the 3-litre Austin A-110 'Sheerline' (unkindly known as the sheer-slime) which could also be had dressed up as a Wolseley 6-110. In the specially bodied and equipped Van den Plas version it was known as the Van den Plas Princess, or Princess R to indicate the most superior version with the Rolls-Royce engine. The engine in question was the 6-cylinder 'B' type of 3.9 litres, with 2 SU carburettors which developed 175 b.h.p. (gross) at 4,800 r.p.m. This was married to a Model 8 Borg-Warner automatic gearbox.

Prices fluctuated during the four-year life of the Princess R, but in round figures it cost £850 more than the Wolseley version and £930 above the Austin. The car was handsome, roomy, comfortable and dignified without looking old-fashioned. With or without the Rolls-Royce engine it came to be associated with the sorts of government officials and Very

Important Persons who were not quite important enough to qualify for a Rolls-Royce proper. As such it attracted the disapprobation of some critics who complained that the steering linkage consisted of rubber rods attached to rubber couplings: one went so far as to say the rubber was of that degree of tenuous elasticity usually associated with attempts to control the population explosion. It was also said nobody would pay nearly a thousand pounds over the odds just for the privilege of having a Rolls-Royce engine; but the complaints of soggy steering were exaggerated and some seven thousand 'nobodies' proved the prophets wrong. Moreover they appeared to value their Princess R's highly.

*   *   *

In the first twenty-five years or so of Rolls-Royce history it was much easier to judge their motor cars than it is today. The superiority of a Rolls-Royce over most of its contemporaries was so obvious as to need no close examination, but a small number of rival makes were sufficiently like the Rolls-Royce in general specification, performance and, above all, price as to make direct comparison possible. At different times Napier, Daimler, Lanchester, Delaunay-Belleville, Sheffield-Simplex, Pierce and a few more were directly comparable and it is generally possible to show that although individual characteristics of these or other cars might be superior to those of the Rolls-Royce the total score of virtues put Rolls-Royce at the head of the league. Now that no car is comparable for price, the business is much more difficult, and the concept of the 'Best Car in the World' which was always pretty silly, is sillier still now that so many quantity-produced cars have so many virtues that there are numerous 'best cars' from which the customer may choose the one which best suits him. *Motor's* Road Test Report of the Silver Shadow I stated the case:

'No one seriously disputed the superiority of the early Silver Ghosts . . . the margin of success was too big for argument . . . Sixty-odd years later, judgement of the latest Rolls-Royce is a much more difficult business since reliable and sensible transport is no longer a preserve of the very rich. Nor is excellence any more within the grasp of wealthy customers only (though the search for it may bring a manufacturer to the verge of bankruptcy) for nowadays cheap, mass-produced cars are often outstandingly good in certain aspects of their design. A car with less engine and transmission noise than a big American automatic, for example, is a very quiet car indeed; anyone who succeeds in suppressing road noise better than in a Peugeot 404 or wind noise more effectively than in a Saab is doing well, as is the designer who succeeds in making a big car steer and handle better than a Jensen FF or ride more smoothly on rough roads than a Citroen DS. These are the alpha plus standards by which the Silver Shadow must be assessed . . .

Overall we rate the car very highly because although it scores an alpha plus for only a few of its traits and no more than a beta for one or two – it clocks up a big total of solid alphas in all others in a way that few cars can rival.'

Engine balancing; Crewe factory, early 1980s.

All this is irrefutable, although *Motor*'s statement elsewhere in the piece, 'More than any other manufacturer, Rolls-Royce showed that, for the rich at least, the motor car could be a practical and reliable form of transport rather than the joke that most people felt it to be', is nonsense and most unjust to those manufacturers such as De Dion Bouton, Olds, Renault and others who made reliable transportation for the middle class a reality before the Silver Ghost was born: and had *Motor*'s staff writer forgotten the Ghost's august contemporary – the Model T Ford?

Shakespeare's Dogberry may well have thought comparisons are odorous, but we need not regard them as odious and it was fortunately possible to make a direct comparison, over very similar roads, between a Silver Shadow I and a Mercedes 600. Although the Mercedes was then considerably cheaper (the gap later closed) the two cars were intended for the same sort of buyer and were sufficiently alike in specification as to make the comparison useful. Chauvinism and a lifetime's admiration for Rolls-Royce must be overcome to allow the admission that the Mercedes equalled the Rolls-Royce in many respects and excelled it in some. Both had, and have, so many good points it would be absurd to describe one as 'better' than the other.

The design and dimensions of the Mercedes allowed the back seat passengers more space and a more comfortable ride, but from the driver's and front passenger's point of view the balance tilted in favour of the Rolls-Royce, particularly for town work and on those winding country roads on which fast travelling was impossible. Here, the impression of compact manœuvrability of the English car showed to advantage. The hydraulic servants who wait upon the occupants of the Mercedes, by opening the windows, tilting the seats, closing the sliding roof and so on, went about their duties in complete silence; but if they were to go on strike they would be more difficult and expensive to coax back into business than the electric slaves who fulfil similar functions for Rolls-Royce with a certain amount of subdued clicking and whirring.

In outright speed and acceleration the Mercedes carried the day. The margin was small and it is a matter of personal choice how much value to put upon an extra five miles an hour or on the one or two seconds gained in accelerating from 50 to 80 m.p.h. As nearly all cars can now go faster than can safely be allowed on most roads, these questions are academic and it is the safe handling which becomes of greater importance. On the score of braking most critics gave Rolls-Royce the palm, whilst on matters of cornering, road-holding and so forth the experts will argue for ever. The Mercedes inspired confidence from the start but it is significant that most Rolls-Royce owners like the way the car handles better and better as the miles accumulate on the odometer. Both cars had rather too much walnut rather too highly polished, and the German car had that rather aggressive appearance, often characteristic of Mercedes cars of any period, which many people dislike. It is possible to pick individual details or fitments of either car which are superior to those of their rivals. Therefore, there was little to choose between them and the lower price ought to have made the Mercedes the better seller; but the reverse is true and the Silver Shadow was a commercial triumph for the Rolls-Royce Company whilst its German counterpart was a relative disappointment for Daimler-Benz A.G.

173

What was true of the Silver Shadow and its Bentley counterpart is equally true of their successors. The engines are fundamentally unaltered from the type first produced in 1959, but as the present cars weigh slightly more than their immediate predecessors, and the engines have to provide power for more complex air-conditioning plants and other ancillaries, as well as complying with emission-control regulations, and yet have slightly better performance, it is fair to assume the output has been steadily increased.

It always infuriates Rolls-Royce critics that for many years past the Company have refused to disclose the brake horsepower developed by their engines and have contented themselves with saying it is 'adequate', which is manifestly true. The reasons for what is often seen as arrogance are firstly that some firms in the past have made inflated claims which have led to public distrust, and secondly that there are so many different ways of calculating horsepower that the term is almost meaningless to the layman and is therefore best avoided. When it is considered that the little Citroen, which the French credit with two of their 'steam horses' (C.V. – *cheval vapeur)*, would have been rated at seven horsepower under the old British R.A.C./Treasury formula and develops the power of some 17 German (DIN) horses or nearly 20 American (SAE) nags, it can be seen why Rolls-Royce fight shy of the whole business. When it is further considered that an actual horse-type horse can briefly exert some ten horsepower as defined by James Watt one cannot but agree with them.

Those who complain that Rolls-Royce are arrogant in this respect are also given to disparaging the V-eight engine as 'typically American'. Quite why this should attract a sneer is very hard to understand. Rolls-Royce made no secret of their long-standing policy of taking the best they could find and trying to make it better, and the widespread use of V-eight automobile engines in the United States fully entitles American motor engineers to claim the excellence in designing and making them which no unbiased observer should dispute. Indeed, to be pedantic, the modern American V-eight engines are only American because of their widespread use in the U.S., and their descent may be directly traced from the 1910 De Dion-Bouton which was copied and much improved by Cadillac in 1914/15. It might even be called a three-nation effort as the chief draughtsman who laid out the design for Cadillac was an Englishman named D. McCall White who had formerly been with Napier.

With the usual processes of improvement and refinement applied to them there is little doubt that the present generation of Rolls-Royce engines will be able to hold their own for some years to come. Unless, that is, the present fuel crisis grows even worse and forces the company to put fuel economy higher on the list of desirable attributes. This may well happen. For an engine of $6^3/_4$ litres capacity able to propel a large car weighing between two and three tons at more than 110 m.p.h. the Rolls-Royce unit is not extravagant, as it burns petrol at beween 10 and 18 miles to the imperial gallon, but there are signs that consumption on this scale will not be acceptable much longer.

It is not easy to see how matters could be materially improved by modifications to the present engines, as there is not much room left in their design to improve their thermal efficiency. Something could doubtless be done to improve fuel economy, without

Attaching gearbox to engine; Crewe factory, early 1980s.

increasing noxious exhaust emissions beyond existing limits, by a number of expedients such as variable-lift valves or the use of the 'stratified charge' system, used by Frederick Lanchester on gas engines eighty-five years ago, as well as by further experiments with combustion chamber forms and, possibly, by a suitable direct-injection fuel system in place of a carburettor. All these expedients would only make marginal improvements and a more radical approach may be needed.

Until the present 'energy crisis', as it is rather emotively called, in the industrialised countries suddenly made many people aware (as a number had seen for some time) that all natural materials and resources are finite, and that the rate of consumption in recent years has been criminally irresponsible, motor engineers everywhere had been looking at alternatives to the conventional reciprocating internal combustion engine because of the urgent need to reduce toxic exhaust emissions. Rolls-Royce and other manufacturers who had to meet the U.S. regulations (those of other countries being slightly less onerous), found that the modifications their existing engines needed added some weight, quite a lot of cost and reduced efficiency.

'Cleaner' alternatives which were looked at included the steam car which, to the delight of enthusiasts who have never given up hope in the last eighty years, almost looked as though it might stage a comeback, and the Stirling engine which, though often mis-spelled 'sterling', is no more than our boyhood's friend the hot-air engine invented by the Rev. Patrick Stirling in 1818. Though the steady-state combustion processes of both these types of engine make for cleaner exhaust fumes the fuel shortage has highlighted their drawbacks. The poor thermal efficiency of the steam engine puts it out of court, as tests in San Francisco in 1972 seemed to confirm. A 50-seater steam bus tested in the city consumed furnace oil at the rate of between 0.74 and 0.86 m.p.g., against one of the city's standard 50-seaters which covered an average of 4.5 miles per gallon of diesel oil. This particular steam bus was admittedly poorly designed, but even if its thermal efficiency were trebled the gap would still be wide. In its original hot-air form the Stirling engine was also abysmally inefficient thermally as air is almost the worst possible conductor of heat. Using the best possible gaseous conductor, hydrogen, the latest form of Stirling engine developed experimentally for automotive work is much better able to compete, but the engineering and safety problems associated with using hydrogen under high pressure are formidable.

Applying wood veneer; Crewe factory, early 1980s.

176

Of all the alternatives to the reciprocating petrol engine proposed in recent years the only one to have made real headway is the Wankel rotary. It is known that the Rolls-Royce Company (before the bankruptcy and subsequent total separation of the car division) took a great interest in the Wankel, and made some important contributions to it. As more car manufacturers, including General Motors, develop Wankel-engined prototypes, and relatively large numbers of passenger cars have been produced commercially in Germany and Japan, it may be that a Wankel-engined Rolls-Royce is a possibility; but it is unlikely to be seen in the near future.

On the present showing the all-important factors of reliability and longevity are not yet proven to Rolls-Royce standards. They are well on the way, but the probability of permanent shortage and certainty of increased cost of petroleum products put another hurdle in the Wankel's path. It is, as yet, a thirsty creature and as the fuel consumption of an internal combustion engine is dependent, amongst other factors, upon the shape of the combustion chambers it is very difficult to see how the best possible shape can be arrived at in a machine the combustion chambers of which constantly change shape as the rotors revolve. Also, the promised advantages of less weight and size by comparison with piston engines of comparable power have not yet been realised. In the present state of the art Wankel engines have poorer torque characteristics at low speeds, and those who make much of their vibrationless running appear to forget that the defeat of the vibration bogey was amply demonstrated over seventy years ago when Rolls-Royce balanced a half-crown piece on edge on the radiator cap of a Silver Ghost without stopping its 'crude up-and-down action', as a Wankel enthusiast recently described the working of a conventional motor engine.

It seems most unlikely therefore that the next generation of Rolls-Royces will be Wankel-powered, whilst a steam or hot-air R-R appears improbable enough to belong to the world of fantasy; but, if present developments take their logical course, an electric Rolls-Royce is a distinct possibility by the end of the century.

In the present state of affairs it might seem rash to suppose that there will be any Rolls-Royces at all in twenty-five years' time, but if human ingenuity is once again able to triumph over the results of human folly to prevent the collapse of civilisation people will still want motor cars, probably on a reduced scale, and there is no reason to suppose that seekers after good quality products will be entirely extinct.

Returning from a pessimist's view of a gloomy future to the gloomy present, the current series of Rolls-Royce cars, as the specifications show, do not differ fundamentally from the Silver Shadow and Bentley T models. Indeed, the Corniche cars are modernised versions of the original two-door Silver Shadow. The Corniche standard saloon or convertible bodies, particularly the latter, are really very handsome in anybody's language. Purists might object that that dummy radiator is really indefensible now, but how right Claude Johnson was all those years ago to insist that it was indispensable. Every attempt so far made by designers of special bodies to find an alternative has been disastrous, but the Rolls-Royce design team have contrived to blend the severe perpendicular shape into the curved outline of the complete car remarkably happily, and the sales figures prove that the mock-Grecian portico* still attracts the money-bees better than the dummy honeycomb of the Mercedes rival.

Praise for the general standards of finish and comfort, and particularly for the great range of adjustment available for the front seats, is universal. A supple young motor journalist who stands 6 feet 5 inches was as loud in his approbation of the driving comfort as a stoutish sexuagenarian who barely tops 5 feet 6 inches. The Rolls-Royce body design department is certainly free from the Procrustean tendencies of so many designers who put the roof so near the seat cushion that a tallish man has to slouch uncomfortably in order to see out, whilst at the same time they put the pedals so far above the floor that small women cannot keep their heels on the floor whilst working the clutch.

The question asked by the *Road & Track* reporter in 1969 is still valid and not easy to answer. What is there about a Rolls-Royce which justifies its price being so much higher than that of cars of comparable quality, comfort, quietness and performance? At least one answer is that Rolls-Royce products are still good value for money.

As the report said, a Rolls-Royce is 'a durable thing', which would certainly not be denied by those who took part in, or witnessed, the 1973 re-enactment of the 1913 Alpine Trial. The sight of a gaggle of Silver Ghosts, their ages ranging from fifty to sixty-five years, storming Alpine passes with a vigour which belied their years, and on more than one occasion outstripping the film crew in their Range Rover, was memorable. Typical of the cars entered was the Hon. Alan Clark's 1923 Ghost which had passed through the usual cycle of private limousine, hire car, station taxi, hearse, truck, abandonment and rehabilitation, during which it had covered some quarter-million miles, but was still able to average more than 50 miles an hour over nearly five hundred miles of poor roads for a fuel consumption of between 12 and 14 m.p.g. Because of their different methods of construction, and far higher maximum speeds, it is unlikely that the present generation will last quite so well; but they seem able to outlast their contemporaries by a large margin, and the guides to the Royal Mews can always be assured of gasps of astonishment when they tell tourists the age of four of the Queen's Rolls-Royce 'state' cars.

This durability means that a ten to fifteen-year-old Rolls-Royce will give not only faithful service but also a great deal of pleasure. For it is undeniably part of Rolls-Royce's rather indefinable charm that most of their owners do grow very much attached to them. There is no doubt that a number of those who buy new Rolls-Royce or Bentley models do so for the wrong reasons of snobbery or ostentation, but the majority of those who are content with one which has reached an age at which most of its contemporaries have long since been relegated to the scrap yard do not have to worry about first cost. It is enough for them that 'the quality remains after the price is forgotten'.

* It takes one man one day to make a Rolls-Royce radiator, followed by five hours' polishing. The radiator is made entirely by hand and eye, without measuring instruments, and the craftsman then engraves his initials on the back.

Rolls-Royce armoured car (Wedding Bells II) owned by the Tank Museum, Bovingdon.

*　　　*　　　*

One striking development since the 1960s has been a remarkable growth of interest in the older cars*. At first, impecunious students used them as cheap (and often clapped-out) transport, and the early efforts of clubs such as the 20-Ghost Club, the Rolls-Royce Enthusiasts' Club, the Rolls-Royce section of the Vintage Sports-Car Club and the Midland Rolls-Royce Club in Britain, and the Rolls-Royce Owners' Clubs of America and of Australia, to encourage the preservation, restoration and use of the older cars were not at first welcomed by the company. As time went on, however, it began to be clear that the use and exhibition in first-class condition of cars that were many decades old was excellent publicity for Rolls-Royce, and ultimately a great deal of help was given to the clubs and their activities.

The club movement had begun on quite a small scale with picnics, meetings at historic houses and the occasional *concours d'élégance*. In 1961, the 20-Ghost Club created a

---

* However, a 1906 Rolls-Royce with a modernised four-seater sports body took part in the run from London to Brighton in 1927 organised by the *Daily Sketch* and *Sunday Graphic* for cars over 21 years old. Since 1929, the age limit has been fixed as the end of 1904, so that the 10 h.p. car 20154 would appear to be the only Rolls-Royce eligible for the London to Brighton Veteran Car event, although 20162 and 20163 have taken part, through acceptance by the Veteran Car Club dating committee of their having been under construction in 1904.

precedent by running a tour: this was of England only, and lasted three days, but it was successful enough to be followed up in 1962 by a tour through France to Monaco, where the prizes were presented by H.S.H. Princess Grace. Other tours by the same club in following years included one to Holland, Germany and Denmark and another to the châteaux of the Loire Valley. Then the Rolls-Royce Enthusiasts' Club, which was growing rapidly in numbers, embarked on tours to Vichy and to the Bordeaux vineyards, and has, since then, arranged tours too numerous to list.

The writer took part in all these early tours and found as much enthusiasm on the Continent for the old cars as in Britain. Misunderstandings sometimes took place: at Versailles, the authorities thought the 20-Ghost Club wished to hold a seance; in Monaco, an elderly French lady was heard to explain to her companion that a rally of old London taxi-cabs was taking place. But generous hospitality was offered everywhere by civic authorities, motor clubs, local Rolls-Royce agents and petrol companies.

In 1962, however, a visit to Britain by members of the RR Owners' Club of America had led to the organisation by the British clubs of a very large meeting at Blenheim Palace in Oxfordshire at which more than 550 Rolls-Royce and Bentley motor cars were exhibited. Two further very large meetings were held (at Goodwood) for American visits, in later years, on one of which the American-owned cars were brought to England on the last voyage of the *Queen Elizabeth*. Later, a party of British-owned cars went to the United States on one of the maiden voyages of the *QE II*. In 1973, the sixtieth anniversary of the Austrian Alpine Trials was marked by a tour of the original course organised by the RREC. H.M. The Queen's Silver Jubilee was celebrated in 1977 by an RREC meeting at Windsor and Ascot which raised over £30,000 for charity, and a combined road and air exhibition held at Duxford in 1979 raised nearly £14,000 for the Sir Henry Royce Memorial Foundation: a similar event took place in 1984.

An appeal had been launched in November 1977 to establish this Foundation. Its objects were as follows:

1   To honour the life and works of Sir Henry Royce and his distinguished colleagues, who created the name and legend of Rolls-Royce and contributed so much to the defence of the free world.
2   To preserve the vast collection of historical, experimental and technical records – the archives of Rolls-Royce – which were in danger of dispersal, destruction or entombment.
3   To create a permanent home for the archives and for appropriate artefacts and memorabilia, for the pleasure, interest and instruction of Rolls-Royce enthusiasts the world over.
4   To encourage the pursuit of excellence in engineering as exemplified by Sir Henry, especially among young people.
5   To provide an eventual permanent repository for appropriate items at present in private ownership.

The Foundation is a registered (U.K.) charity and carries on its operations at the Hunt House, Paulerspury, in Northamptonshire, where the archives are now properly housed. There is also a display illustrating the history of Rolls-Royce; the offices of the Rolls-Royce Enthusiasts' Club rented from the Foundation; much personal memorabilia of Sir Henry Royce; a room devoted to Rolls-Royce in America and the Springfield car; a library, lecture room and fully equipped workshop; histories of over 50,000 Rolls-Royce and Bentley cars; and examples of many Rolls-Royce engines. Much of the fund-raising and conversion of the existing building was carried out by RREC members and sections.

Another major event organised by the RREC was the club's Silver Jubilee event in 1982, marking also the seventy-fifth anniversary of the Silver Ghost and the sixtieth anniversary of the Twenty. The celebrations included a Scottish tour, following the most interesting parts of the 1907 Scottish Reliability Trial route.

*   *   *

Continuous development* of existing Rolls-Royce models and the introduction of new models has continued over the years. The Silver Shadow, for example, had first a four-speed automatic gearbox and then a three-speed one. (The writer preferred the 'kickdown' on the earlier box, which seemed to him to give better acceleration than the later one.) The Camargue and the Shadow II had a much improved air-conditioning system which obviated the internal misting that had sometimes happened in damp, humid weather with the earlier models (a much earlier solution had been an interior wiper, working when required with the external wipers – an example was fitted to the writer's PIII). Then, new coachwork was introduced for the Silver Spirit, Silver Spur and Bentley Mulsanne, to be followed by turbo-supercharging on a small number of Mulsannes, which resulted in an increase of top speed from 119 m.p.h. to 135 m.p.h and better acceleration: with a 2.7:1 axle ratio, a 5% improvement in fuel consumption was achieved.

When the writer was carrying out research in 1961 for the first edition of this book, he was forbidden to consult any records for post-1939 cars. Fortunately, this prohibition was later relaxed, and it may be that this was a small step towards the infinitely greater disclosure that now exists. Thirty years ago, for example, who would have foreseen advertisements stating that tests carried out on the latest models included slamming the door of a Silver Spirit 100,000 times to ensure that it would always close with a subdued clunk (or even the use of the word 'clunk')? Or to be told (in a mixture of imperial and metric units) that impact tests involved five Silver Spirits being crashed at 30 mph. into a 100-tonne block of metal and then a 2000 lb block of concrete being rammed at 20 m.p.h. into the back of the cars?

The company is proud of its current air-conditioning system, and with good reason. This system, which costs as much to make as a complete mass-produced car, is the only one in service anywhere to be separately controlled at both knee and head height: it can change

* There were 2,000 separate improvements to the V-eight engine between 1959 and 1982.

the air in the car three times a minute, and could run from the Arctic Circle to the Equator without adjustment. Even in minor details (as in the story of the golf tees), the company 'thinks of everything'. Perhaps recalling the mythical story of the owner who took his car in for service because the ashtrays were full, automatic emptying has been installed for the ashtrays on the current models.

*　　　*　　　*

Rolls-Royce Motors Limited, which had been set up as a public company after the collapse of Rolls-Royce Limited in 1971, remained independent and successful for some years, but in August 1980 merged with Vickers, the armaments company whose lack of profitability ten years earlier had seen the Prudential Assurance Company make financial history by leading a shareholders' revolt and forcing the board to appoint its own nominee as managing director. The results of the first two years of the merger were encouraging, but the outset of the depression affected sales of new cars and prices of second-hand ones. Costs of depreciation therefore rose, and at one time quite large discounts were offered by agents on new models. Production in 1982 was 2,494 cars, compared with 2,440 in 1981, and in 1983 the company's U.K. dealer network was cut by 20 per cent; and considerable redundancies (including those of about 40 senior managers) took place between 1981 and 1983. However, the weakness of the pound against the dollar (which therefore reduced the dollar price of current models) gave encouragement that the 1983 production target of 2,400 to 2,500 cars would be reached, with exports planned to rise from 60 per cent to 70 per cent. In fact, only 1,454 cars were produced in 1983, and due to a five-week strike during the year production was insufficient to meet demand.

The writer hopes he will be allowed to end this part on a personal note. He has owned several Rolls-Royce motor cars and has driven most other models. As he has owned no other type of car and has only once ever driven one, he has not, as had his late co-author, the ability to make comparisons with other quality cars, but only to judge between different Rolls-Royce models. In an ideal world, he would select a sedanca-de-ville Phantom III and a drophead Corniche for his transport.

11

New Cars for The Eighties and The Bentley Phenomenon

———◆◆◆———

NINETEEN-EIGHTY was a defining year for Rolls-Royce Motors Ltd.: it put the uncertainties of the 'seventies behind it and within days of the merger with Vickers it had announced the launch of three new models to replace the Silver Shadow Project SY cars, which had been in production since 1965. In fact, these cars were not completely new, but unlike in the story of *The Emperor's New Clothes*, the long wheelbase Silver Spur, the standard Silver Spirit and the Bentley Mulsanne really did wear impressive new coachwork. All three were also technologically up-to-date, but it was technology that had been previously used on earlier models.

Designated Project SZ, they have the same drive train as the Silver Shadow II and basically the same big V8 engine first used to power the Silver Cloud II in 1959. To the surprise of many, and contrary to initial press comments, neither inheritance would prove to be a drawback. Public and press alike soon accepted the new cars, partly because performance was as usual 'more than adequate', but also because the sleek new style with a one-third increase in glass area and immaculate interior appointments cleverly melded modern concepts into traditional design. There was some initial criticism, but Rolls-Royce's chief stylist Fritz Feller, and a design team that included Graham Hull, his successor, would eventually receive acclaim from both press and public. The new Silver Spirit, although only three inches longer and two inches wider than the Silver Shadow II, ingenuously deceives the eye to appear comparatively larger. Martin Bennett, writing about the first Silver Spirits in his book *Rolls-Royce and Bentley – The History of the Cars*, attributed this to more angular styling, a lower waistline and an extra inch on the wheelbase. Others see them as lower and longer, or wider and more rounded, but almost everyone now accepts them as visually striking and handsome cars.

This was not so in the months following the launch. Several motoring journalists were less than complimentary and the public was constantly reminded that the running gear on the new cars was almost identical to that of the cars that they were replacing (i.e. the Silver Shadow II, the long wheelbase Silver Wraith II and the Bentley T2). In a harsh judgement, Rolls-Royce was said to be under-capitalised and cutting costs, and they were slated for not producing a new engine. This appraisal was partially untrue: cost is a factor in every production decision, but Rolls-Royce was not at the time under-capitalised and profits were healthy. More prosaically, the reasons behind the company's planning decisions were to some extent influenced by a long-standing policy of continuous evolution. There were, of course, many other considerations – not least, the limitations of a small design team already over-stretched by the need to meet new, far-reaching North American legislation on emissions and safety.

These limitations, plus the fact that Rolls-Royce did not have the required economies of scale to simultaneously design a new body and a new engine, affected many board decisions. Development choices were largely dictated by prudence, and the necessity to fully realise the value of investments in recent design features that had been tested and proven on earlier models. Amongst these, and of equal importance were Project Gamma 1971–1995 (the Corniche), Project Delta 1975–1987 (the Camargue) and the Silver Shadow SY series that had also been continuously modernised and updated. All these improvements were incorporated into the development of the Silver Spirit and later SZ cars and the series continued to evolve throughout its life. The success of this policy may be judged by the fact that Silver Spirit-based cars remained in production for twenty years – five years longer than originally planned.

One of the most important early developments on Silver Spirit-based cars from 1980 concerned the handling characteristics and ride. The ride in SY cars was soft by modern standards and it was accepted that the new SZ cars should have a slightly firmer ride to reduce roll on corners and accommodate modern road conditions and potential increases in speed. In a fine illustration of what could be achieved by adapting the best features of several earlier models a rear suspension system[*], (introduced on the Corniche convertible and Camargue in March 1979) was married to front suspension improvements and rack-and-pinion steering carried over from the 1977 Silver Shadow II. The former improved stability and kept the car's attitude to the road constant regardless of load distribution, while the latter improved feedback and roadholding.

The use of Hydraulics System Mineral Oil (HSMO) was another major change previously introduced and tested on the Corniche and Camargue. Derived from mineral sources, HSMO has important advantages over the previously used synthetic brake fluid. (Because seals made from natural rubber deteriorate when exposed to mineral oils, motor manufacturers used synthetic brake fluid in hydraulic systems.) From 1980 on, by adopting improved seals made from materials compatible with mineral oils Rolls-Royce was able to use the far less corrosive HSMO and benefit from its superior lubricating and vibration damping qualities.

Whatever the antecedents of the new cars, these technical and design advances had brought them bang-up-to-date and the sales figures were initially very good. At the same time, the marketing department, although completely orientated toward the promotion of Rolls-Royce, was becoming more aware of Bentley. The giant that had lain dormant for many years was stirring, and despite a standardisation policy that had merged Rolls-Royce

---

[*]The Rolls-Royce self-levelling system works by automatically adjusting oil levels in rear suspension struts connected via columns of hydraulic fluid to gas springs and a self-levelling system.

6¾ litre V8 engine.

and Bentley to the point where there were few differences apart from radiators and badges, Bentley, the marque with the sporting heritage retained a strong and partisan following. There were still Bentley enthusiasts who had not been put off by a decline that began in 1955 with the introduction of the almost identical Silver Cloud and Bentley S and continued through 1978 when Rolls-Royce was the name cast on to the rocker covers of the Bentley T2. At about the same time, with the instruments on the Bentley fascia carrying entwined R's and the chassis number embossed on a Rolls-Royce nameplate, the demise of Bentley seemed imminent. Indeed, in a design first, the 1980 Silver Spirit and Bentley Mulsanne even have carefully matched pressings that enable identical bonnets to be married to the different radiator shapes.

These measures cut production costs, though the savings could only have been marginal at best, and the Bentley marque was at its nadir when 'Mulsanne', the name proposed by Graham Hull, caught the public's imagination. Evocative of Bentley's Le Mans racing triumphs, this memorable designation started the winged B emblem on the road back from obscurity. Thereafter, the change in fortunes was rapid, and Bentley's meagre 3 per cent of total sales had grown to over 66 per cent by the end of the 'nineties. More significantly, the marque had regained a distinct identity and a new presence: the days when Sir David Plastow had considered dropping the name altogether were long past. At this stage it is interesting to note that, although more actively promoted and successful than their predecessors, the 1980 Mulsanne and 1981 Mulsanne L were still little more than copies of the Silver Spirit and Silver Spur. The real breakthrough for Bentley did not come until the launch of the Mulsanne Turbo and Mulsanne Turbo l.w.b. at the 1982 Geneva Motor Show. Erroneously hailed by the press as the return of the famous Blower Bentleys, they are, even by today's standards, blisteringly fast. They are also extremely complicated and refined examples of Rolls-Royce's engineering skills, for they generate substantial extra power without increasing revs or stressing a 6.75-litre engine that copes effortlessly with the boost of a Garrett AirResearch turbocharger. Luxury and dignity were not, however, sacrificed at the altar of performance and those who bought this innovative and exciting new Bentley were still privileged to enjoy all the traditional Rolls-Royce virtues. Highly polished walnut veneers, soft blemish-free leather and carpets of pure wool (as always) pamper drivers and passengers in the Mulsanne Turbo. Naturally, signs indicating the extra power are discreet and turbo badges on the boot and front wing flanks are the only features distinguishing the Mulsanne Turbo from the more mundane Mulsanne.

Much faster, The Mulsanne Turbo nonetheless has the same suspension settings as the non-turbocharged Silver Spirit and Mulsanne and credence has to be given to press reports suggesting that, despite changes in 1980, the suspension was too soft for a car capable of 135 m.p.h. Whether or not this was accepted by Rolls-Royce is not known, but their answer, the magnificent Turbo R and Turbo RL[*] were launched in 1985 with dramatically improved handling. Performance also began moving up the scale and an estimated 298 b.h.p. using the Solex 4A1 carburettor was increased to 330 b.h.p. from 1986 using Bosch fuel injection. By 1995, it was 385 b.h.p. and for many enthusiasts the Turbo R now encapsulated the Bentley ethos of power and speed. Selling in unprecedented numbers, this model set the marque squarely on a road that would eventually lead to Bentley dominating Rolls-Royce production.

Of course, turbocharging was not the only factor affecting the relative positions of the two marques. The inbuilt preferences of motorists were probably about even and handling improvements normally adopted across the range were equally beneficial on the slower, non-turbocharged models. Non-turbocharged Rolls-Royces were probably more popular than identical non-turbocharged Bentleys, but turbocharging definitely improved the fortunes of Bentley. This fact is, perhaps, best illustrated by the fate of the 1980 non-turbocharged Bentley Mulsanne and the non-turbocharged Mulsanne S that replaced it in 1987–8. From 1980 to 1992, production of these two Rolls-Royce copies and their long wheelbase equivalents totalled 1,499 – a respectable total, but a long way below the apex of 5,494 genuinely different Bentley Turbo R and RL models produced from 1985 to 1996. These figures alone would surely justify reinstating the Bentley marque as a separate and distinct entity.

So far, Rolls-Royce, even under the aegis of a huge international engineering conglomerate, had disdained selling on cost. Unfortunately, even traditional Rolls-Royce customers no longer believed that talking about money was vulgar. Rival manufacturers

---

[*] Long wheelbase version of the Turbo R.

The Turbo R had a sporting image.

were now offering them cars of comparable performance and luxury for less money. And further down the scale, quite ordinary family cars were being loaded with many of the extras that had once been the prerogative of the rich. A bargain basement Rolls-Royce or Bentley would be unthinkable, but by 1984 sales were declining and something had to be done. That year Rolls-Royce quietly broke with tradition and made cost-cutting a promotional virtue. The Bentley Eight, selling for nearly £6,000 less than the Mulsanne and more than £12,000 less than the Mulsanne Turbo, was launched. A beautiful and luxurious motor car that seemed to gain more in panache than it lost in trim, it was aimed at potential customers who might not otherwise have considered a Bentley to be within their price range. Distinguished by a distinctive wire mesh grill, stiffened front suspension and barely noticeable reductions in interior trim, it was the most popular non-turbocharged Bentley to date. During a nine-year production run that ended in 1992, 1,734 Eights were sold and it was ultimately more successful than either the Mulsanne (1980–87), or the Mulsanne S (1988–92).

By now, Bentley sales figures were getting closer to Rolls-Royce and nine new saloons bearing the flying B emblem emerged from the Crewe factory during the 'eighties. Over the same timespan, there were only three new saloons to carry forward the Spirit of Ecstasy.

Burr walnut is the most familiar veneer used at Crewe; it has a distinctive pattern that is produced over the years by a fungus that affects the root ball, which is more valuable than the tree.

However, the Silver Spirit, the Silver Spur, and the Silver Spur Limousine Rolls-Royce were still ahead in terms of total numbers produced – 14,466 as against 9,247 Bentley's. Additionally, and apart from new launches, the Phantom VI limousine and three Rolls-Royce two-door models: the Camargue, the Corniche and the Corniche II were all in production during at least part of the 'eighties. These models added to the numeric advantage of Rolls-Royce by 2,752, though the difference was marginally offset by 30 two-door cars badged as Bentley Corniches, plus two Mulsanne L Limousines built during the same period. Of course, the latter two, as remnants of the earlier policy, were copies of their Rolls-Royce equivalents.

From 1986, in another move that turned out to be advantageous to Bentley, the name Corniche became exclusive to the Rolls-Royce convertible and the Bentley Corniche became the Bentley Continental. Like Mulsanne, this too was an inspired choice of name conjuring misty memories of huge Bentleys sweeping imperiously across Europe on the almost deserted roads of the early 'fifties. This name change also boosted sales and a further 430 were built until the model was dropped in 1995, three years after the introduction of the Continental R and the Continental Turbo in 1992.

Amongst the cars being built during and overlapping the period 1980 to 1990, the Phantom VI, the Corniche and Corniche II, the Camargue and the Continental must

It takes 13 days to produce a set of veneers and each unique veneer is marked with the chassis number of the car for which it was produced so that it can be traced back to the tree from which it came.

surely bear four of the most evocative and enduring names in automotive history. The earliest of these, the Phantom VI, launched in 1968 and produced in limited numbers until 1990, is essentially the same as the Phantom V, and as such, it is also the final link with traditional post-war coachbuilding techniques. As if wishing to go back to another era in motor car construction, a massive chassis, almost 20 feet between bumpers, was adopted for the Phantom V and retained for the Phantom VI. This gave the design team scope to go for the ultimate in coachwork styles and allow even the tallest and most rotund passengers the luxury of spacious shoulder and leg-room. There was, however, no such luxury for the driver separated by a central division in a compartment that was, considering the size of the car, quite cramped. Designed for a chauffeur rather than an owner, the firm, straight-backed driver's seat was also obviously less than comfortable for anyone above average height. To the author, it seems as if vestiges of the prejudice that had moved Rolls-Royce to limit the supply of the Phantom IV to royalty and heads of state survived to discomfort chauffeurs well into the 'eighties.

In contrast, the Corniche, Rolls-Royce's most successful convertible, is very much a car for those who love to drive. As beautiful and exclusive as the scenic Riviera route after which it is named, it has the same SY/SZ floor pan as the last Corniche saloon built for the 1981 model year. More surprisingly (or maybe not, considering the purity of line and form), the exterior design remained unchanged throughout a life span that extended to the Corniche IV and Corniche S models of 1995. Despite this, nothing about the car is dated, the thoroughbred lines are timeless, and as in the Camargue, all major production modifications were applied in advance of their use on the standard saloons.

Like the Corniche, the Camargue also bears a name linked to Provence[*] and the South of France, and as with the cars, so the places they are named after are very different in character. In the Camargue the open beauty, sea and sunshine of the Route Corniche is replaced by mists that drift across and veil vast expanses of inland marsh. It is a remote place famous for black bulls and flamingos – and a very rare and select car built by Rolls-Royce from 1975 to 1986. In this instance, 'select' and 'rare' really are the operative words because, despite its long production, run, only 526 Camargues were ever sold. Sales averaging less than one a week hardly suggest profitability, and it has been said that the prestige gained from building such an exclusive car compensated for any financial loss. This may or may not be true, and some motor industry experts believe that the model was profitable. Either way, the Camargue's 1975 launch price of £29,250 meant that it was double the price of a Silver Shadow and half as much again as a Corniche. Much of the background to this car remains a mystery, but for this sum a privileged few acquired a two-door coachbuilt car designed by Pininfarina with what many say is the finest interior of any Rolls-Royce ever built. As far as exterior appearances go there are to this day mixed reactions; some do not like the suggestion of bulk imparted by Pininfarina's flat surfaces, and many have said that it would look far better with the more moulded Bentley radiator.

[*] La Villa Mimosa at Le Canadel in the South of France was Sir Henry Royce's winter home and design centre during the last twenty years of his life.

In retrospect, some ultra-critical appraisal may be seen as inevitable: not only was the Camargue incredibly expensive, it was also the first post-war Rolls-Royce to be designed by an outsider and the first to be built using metric measurements. What was the Rolls-Royce design team supposed to think of it? By all accounts not nearly as much as the mainly American buyers for whom it was specifically designed. Nonetheless, it remains an unusual and imposing example of Rolls-Royce excellence that is sought after by enthusiasts throughout the world.

12

The Final Decade and The End of an Era

———◆———

Firstт seen by the public at the 1989 Frankfurt Motor Show, the 1990 Silver Spirit II, Silver Spur II saloons and the Corniche III convertible were outwardly similar to the cars that they were replacing. There were, however, significant interior changes and all the saloons featured a new Automatic Ride Control system. This was not specified for the Corniche III convertible and when it was eventually fitted two years later, the Corniche III became the Corniche IV. No doubt someone, somewhere in the company hierarchy had a sound reason, but on the *face of it*, this was a puzzling reversal of previous practice in which coachbuilt cars almost invariably received new technology in advance of other models. In a further anomaly, the new Bentleys did not receive the series two tag given to Rolls-Royces. They did, however, get all the improvements including the new Rolls-Royce Automatic Ride Control, which was the most significant change.

The fruit of four years' intensive development by the experimental department at Crewe, the new Automatic Ride Control eliminated the main drawbacks of post-1965 self-levelling systems and an older Ride Control system that had been in use since the 'thirties. Utilising the latest electronic technology, the new system collects data from vertical and lateral accelerometers monitoring acceleration, deceleration, road surface conditions and steering changes. This data is then transmitted via external transducers and switches to a microprocessor control unit, where it is continuously compared with programmed threshold values for each switching control. As a result, because suspension values are adjusted within milliseconds, the ride can move imperceptibly from soft to firm and vice versa. At the time, Rolls-Royce claimed, 'Passengers will be completely unaware of the changes even when cornering at speed.' Press reports agreed that this was quite true and it would also be true to say that neither passengers or drivers could fail to be aware of other highly visible, ergonomic and cosmetic changes to the cabin and instrument layouts.

Individually they were modest, but they combined to create an aesthetically pleasing and modern design that also preserved traditional Rolls-Royce values. The new dash-board had controls and switches repositioned more conveniently, and a new warning module was installed directly in the driver's field of vision to give data on vital systems and fluid levels when activated by a switch. Performance and safety were improved by a new K-Motronic engine management system, a remote anti-theft alarm, an automatic brake release electronically linked to the gear selector, and new alloy wheels with stainless steel trims (Bentleys kept their own alloy wheel designs). As always, smooth, silent operation was a prime directive, but this time, by installing a ten-speaker 100-watt audio system, Rolls-Royce designers also offered the option of almost concert-hall sound quality. Two additional outlets in the dash-board allowed more precise tuning of the split-level air conditioning, a single-action window lift was fitted to the driver's door and heated front seats with electrically operated lumbar support added to comfort. Other cosmetic interior changes included a leather-covered steering wheel and new wood veneers: plus new boxwood inlays exclusive to Rolls-Royce models.

The new decade also marked the end of an era for the venerable Phantom VI; a Silver Cloud-based limousine that is a direct descendent of the Phantom V launched in 1959. Periodically updated from 1978 onward, these are the most expensive, the biggest and the most luxurious of all Rolls-Royces, but only 23 have been built since 1980 and the last two were delivered in 1991. The penultimate model was a limousine purchased by George Moore C.B.E. who was handed the keys by Rolls-Royce Motor Cars Chairman and Chief Executive Peter Ward at a ceremony held in the Berkeley Square, London showrooms of Jack Barclay Ltd. Offers of several million pounds for the final Phantom VI, a landaulette built specifically for retention by the company, were refused despite the onset of a recession. The company held on and resisted the temptation to sell, but when the market for Rolls-Royces slumped to a third of 1990 levels it weakened, and in 1992, the very last Phantom VI was sold to the Sultan of Brunei for a huge, but undisclosed sum.

The time when such an individual car could be a viable commercial proposition was past. A replacement was out of the question but a special Mulliner Park Ward-finished Silver Spur II, launched at the Frankfurt Motor Show in September 1991, became the best choice for those who still sought the ultimate in comfort and luxury until surpassed by the Touring Limousine in 1992. Visually a great improvement on earlier stretched Silver Spur limousines, which had 36 or 42 inches added to the centre section, the Touring Limousine retained the classic six-window configuration with a more modest 24 inches added aft of the rear doors.

Until mid-1994, the Touring Limousine was built at the scaled-down Mulliner Park Ward factory in Willesden, London, where modifications to a Silver Spur II bodyshell, minus rear doors and roof, were carried out. In the main, this involved adding length to the floor pan, fitting a new roof 2 inches higher than standard and fitting rear doors with no cutaways for wheel arches. Standard Silver Spur II front doors, fitted with taller window frames to fit the higher profile, were then added before sending the assembled bodyshell to Crewe. At Crewe, the bodies were mounted on their front and rear subframes and the wiring was completed before they were sent back to Hythe Road, Willesden for painting, interior trimming and finishing. Later, the last three operations were also switched to Crewe, and by

1994 all the expensive shunting back and forth between London and Crewe was brought to an end by the closure of the London operation. It was a sad day when the last 40 craftsmen finally left the Willesden premises that had played such a large part in the Rolls-Royce story.

Sales were declining, the company was not doing as well as they had done in the 'eighties and an output of 3,567 cars for the 1989 model year slipped to 3,071 for 1990. From that point they plunged into the abyss. Only 305 Rolls-Royces and 497 Bentleys were produced for the 1992 model year – 2,198 below the completely unsustainable break-even point of 3,000 cars per year. The painful solution was a drastic rationalisation that entailed lay-offs, redundancies, early retirements and a streamlining of working practices that resulted in a more realistic break-even figure of 1,300–1,400 cars per year. Consequently, there was a partial recovery during the next few years. Profitability was restored, and by 1999 sales had climbed back up to 2,358, but this was the peak. Despite the valiant efforts of a slimmer and fitter workforce who were maintaining the highest quality standards, overall sales for the ten-year period 1990–2000 were disappointing. (Of a total of 1,991 cars built for the model year 2000, 1,458 were Bentley's.)

Apportioning success or failure to a worldwide recession or to either marque is not possible, but company finances were clearly helped by the comparatively strong demand for several Bentley models. During the three most difficult years (January 1990 through to the end of 1992, when the break-even point was still 3,000 cars a year), production of all models totalled only 6,762, of which 2,512 were Silver Spirit IIs and Silver Spur IIs introduced in 1990. By comparison, the Bentley Eight, which had been in production since 1984, and the Turbo R and the Turbo RL, introduced in 1985, did better and achieved sales of 2,862. Add in the Bentley Continental and the Mulsanne S, introduced in 1986 and 1988 respectively, and Bentley's figures increase to 3,651. The total production figure for all Rolls-Royces during the same period was 3,111.

Another characteristic of the Bentley revival during the 'nineties which makes chronicling their development difficult was the plethora of models being built simultaneously. By the 1992 model year the number of different Bentleys in production was 8, with 10 in 1995 and 1999, 11 in 1998 and never less than 7 in the intervening years up to 2000. During the same period, Rolls-Royce typically built only four or five different models in any one year, apart from 1995, when there were seven.

The Bentley Brooklands in s.w.b. and l.w.b. form were fine examples of the marque's burgeoning success and 1,531 were sold from 1993 to 1997. Conceived as a replacement for the Mulsanne S, the specification was similar to the last example of this model. Exceptions include: a four-speed automatic transmission selector in hand-stitched leather located on the centre console, a radiator shell painted in the body colour, no chrome moulding along the centre line of the bonnet, and a new front air dam with integral fog lamps. Power on later models was increased to 300 b.h.p. by a light pressure turbocharger[*] that helped extend the life of the model into the 1998 model year and add 191 to the above production total.

At this stage, due to their influence on the power configuration of Bentley Continental coupés in production throughout the nineties, it is worth mentioning the Bentley Turbo

[*] Also included in the Brooklands R and Brooklands Mulliner specifications.

and Turbo RL, which were produced alongside the Brooklands until 1996. Launched in 1985, they continuously sold in substantial numbers until they were renamed as the Turbo R s.w.b. and the Turbo R l.w.b. in 1997. The latter two designations were used only for the 1997 model year, during which 480 l.w.b. and 8 s.w.b. cars were built. These were followed in 1998 and 1999 by the Turbo RT s.w.b. (only 2 cars built), the Turbo RT l.w.b. (250 cars) and the Turbo RT Mulliner (56 cars). Prior to this, the Turbo S and the Continental S produced in limited numbers for the 1995 model year were high-performance niche models that matched the world's fastest production cars without sacrificing luxury. On the Turbo S, the faithful 6.75-litre turbocharged engine gained revised induction features, liquid-cooled intercooler, and a new engine management system that utilised Formula 1 technology to provided an 0 to 60 m.p.h. time of less than 5.8 seconds. In the 1995 model year 39 Continental Ss also had this 385 b.h.p. engine and it became standard in the Continental R from 1996.

Launched at the Geneva Motor Show in March 1991, the Bentley Continental R, another model enhanced by developments perfected on the Turbo R in the late 'eighties and early 'nineties, was mistakenly described as the 'first new Bentley since 1952'. It is, in fact, the first Bentley since 1963 that does not share a body style with Rolls-Royce. Similar in appearance to 'Project 90' a (full-size fibreglass mock-up built six years earlier for the 1985 Geneva Show), it is an absolutely stunning two-door coupé. An instant hit with the press and public, it is remembered as one of the few cars to inspire a spontaneous round of applause when first unveiled. Conceived as a response to the number of people attempting to place orders for a 'Project 90'-type car, it is actually based on the 'Project 90' design which influenced the company's decision on how to proceed. Previous ideas about using a two-door version of a standard saloon body were quickly dropped, and by 1986 a design team, aided by John Heffernan and Ken Greenly of International Automotive Design, had started styling the aerodynamic 2 + 2 coupé body of the Continental R.

Although it was always planned that production of the new coupe should be entirely Crewe-based, Heffernan and Greenly worked on the design in a studio adjacent to the Mulliner Park Ward works in London. Departures from tradition, such as doors cut into the roof and the use of composite polymers for the integrated bumper system, were incorporated into the design and it became the first automatic Bentley in which the gear selector was mounted on the centre console. Interior changes were, however, limited and early drawings indicating a radically different interior were, in the event, modified. With the exception of the centre console, which was extended back into the rear compartment, the layout of the instruments and controls was similar to that of the Turbo R. Initially, the 15-inch wheels that had been used on all Rolls-Royce and Bentley cars since 1955 were increased to 16 inches and fitted with low-profile tyres, but later models had 17-inch wheels. Powered by the same engine as the Turbo R, the Continental R was capable of 0–60 m.p.h. in 6.6 seconds and a top speed regulated to 145 m.p.h. by turbo boost.

The Continental R set new parameters of style and performance, and together with the Continental R Mulliner, the Continental R Le Mans, the Continental T, and the

Continental T Mulliner it was still being produced for the 2001 model year. Later models, the Continental SC, Continental SC Mulliner and a Millennium model were withdrawn in 2000 after a much shorter lifespan. In the latter group, the 1998 model year Continental SC has the distinction of being the first new Bentley following the takeover by Volkswagen. However, when judged by performance, the most important of these models is the 1996–2001 Continental T, a direct derivative of the Continental R. With a 4-inch shorter wheelbase, special 18-inch alloy wheels and wide ultralow-profile tyres, it has a more powerful and aggressive stance than the Continental R. It also has a strikingly retro interior with a turned aluminium fascia, straight-grained waistrails and a distinctive red starter button reminiscent of the days when W.O. Bentley's original company built racing cars. Up front, a stainless steel grill, another throwback to the racing Bentleys of the 'twenties, adds to an overall impression of latent power. But the real clues to this car's character stem from an engineering triumph that was the cumulative result of skills unique to Rolls-Royce.

The engineers from Crewe had, at last, realised the full potential of the big V8 that had powered all Rolls-Royces and Bentleys since the 'fifties. In doing so, they had created a massive 420 b.h.p. beast that could switch from a gentle cruise to a terrifying power surge quicker than a driver could draw breath. Development was ongoing, and by 1998, although this was now the most powerful Bentley ever, it was even more impressive in other areas. Rival manufacturers also made powerful motor cars: the Ferrari Marenello can raise an extra 60 b.h.p., the Chrysler Viper 30 b.h.p., but neither has anywhere near the torque of the Continental R. This Bentley is all about effortless torque – a massive 650 lb./ft. of it at just 2200 r.p.m. To put this in perspective, the 1998 McLaren F1 had only 427 lb./ft. and there was not a car in the 1997 British Grand Prix that got even close to the Bentley's 650 lb./ft. Mind you, none of them had to haul two or three people, plus 2500 kg. of metal, wood, leather, glass and sundry luxuries from 0 to 170 m.p.h.

Using the same engine and drive train as the 1996 Bentley Continental T, the 1998 Turbo RT and Turbo RT Mulliner are almost as powerful. Under the bonnet, a remapped Zytec engine-management system and a Garrett T2 turbocharger boosts the naturally aspirated output of the big 6.75 V8 from 246 b.h.p. to 400 b.h.p. at 4,000 r.p.m. Impressive figures, which put these cars on a par with the 408 b.h.p. of the Mercedes S600, but take into account the Turbo RT's torque of 590 lb./ ft. at between 2000 and 3450 r.p.m. and the big Merc's 427 lb./ ft. starts to look puny. Straight-line performance is outstanding: 0–60 m.p.h. in 6.7 seconds, 0–100 m.p.h. in 16.9 seconds and on up to a 152 m.p.h. top-speed. Fair figures for a lightweight sports car, but add to the equation the inertia of 2,476 kg. and you begin to get some idea of the power of this motorway leviathan. An indefinable air of grandeur, with individually specified luxuries such as two television sets, a champagne cooler and, as always, enough Wilton, leather, and wood to furnish a palace, puts this car beyond comparison. It is like no other, but any plebeian concern with running costs injects instant doses of reality: up to one gallon every 5.1 mile. That is, in fact, the figure achieved during performance testing, but under normal conditions, with accelerator pedal pressure limited by corners, tight bends and prudence, about 14 m.p.g. is more likely. Computer-controlled suspension helps disguise the age of the chassis, and although the anti-lock brakes do not fade as on the previous model, the dive when stopping quickly could easily send passengers' drinks sliding on to the carpet. The unusually flexible chassis and high tyre walls also induce pronounced roll on corners and despite excellent traction control, which stops things getting too far out of shape, the experience is decidedly unsettling for everyone bar the driver. Like so many of the most outstanding Bentleys, this high-performance saloon is a glorious folly for immoderately rich enthusiasts unconcerned with the practicalities of public roads and speed limits.

To say that the far fewer number of different Rolls-Royce models launched in parallel with the ultra-fast Bentley models were more practical would not be true. Cost and the display of wealth implied by ownership of such cars bars any such definition, but just as Bentleys can be seen as slightly raffish, Rolls-Royces seem to personify the more traditional values that make them the choice of more conservative owners. Any implication that they are staid would, however, be misplaced. The 1995 Flying Spur and the new series III Silver Spirit and Silver Spur, launched in 1994, had more than 70 engineering changes, representing the company's biggest ever investment in a new model. The Flying Spur, powered by a re-badged Bentley Turbo R engine, was the first turbocharged, and the fastest ever Rolls-Royce – and, the series III Silver Spirit and Silver Spur had re-designed cylinder heads and manifolding that substantially increased power.

These latest versions of the now ageing Silver Spirit design were also engineered to meet worldwide emission standards through to 2000. Perhaps this, together with the announcement that an engine developed in conjunction with BMW would power the next generation of Rolls-Royces misled motoring journalists, but for whatever reason, speculation about the imminent launch of a completely new model range was incorrect. Silver Spirit-based cars had not yet reached the end of their allocated span and although the numerical suffix was dropped, the Silver Spirit and Silver Spur launched in 1996 were, without doubt, updated versions of the 1994 series III models. For the Silver Spirit, this was the final upgrade and the last six were built for the 1997 model year. Thereafter, Rolls-Royce bowed to market demands and ruled that long wheelbase would be standard on all cars. This, and the fitting of a low-pressure turbocharger in the same year gave the Silver Spur an extra two years of life and it continued in production until 2000. This left the Silver Dawn, an entry-level Silver Spirit-based car launched in 1995, as the only non-turbocharged Rolls-Royce. In 1998, despite respectable sales figures that had averaged almost 60 a year, this model, which had been introduced to woo North American customers away from cheaper rival makes, was also discontinued.

The same period also saw the introduction (in 1996) of the Rolls-Royce Park Ward Limousine, offered as an alternative to the Touring Limousine which continued until the 1997 model year. This move clearly illustrates the company's intention to continue exploiting the prestige attached to the Mulliner and Park Ward names despite the closure of the Willesden factory in 1994. To do this they had to transfer some existing employees and engage new craftsmen and specialist technicians at Crewe. The value of this strategy was proven by the late 'nineties, and with almost 50 per cent of limousine customers

Continental SC.

specifying individually commissioned cars, the company were increasingly distinguishing between the two marques by using the Mulliner suffix for Bentleys and the Park Ward prefix for Rolls-Royces.

Whether the closure of Willesden and its integration into Crewe was part of an efficiency drive, or part of a planned transition from a builder of motor cars to a builder of motor car bodies became a moot point when Vickers, the parent company, announced that engine-building at Crewe would cease in October 1996. At or about the same time, further disruption was caused by the announcement that Cosworth, another famous Vickers engineering company, would take over the building of the Rolls-Royce V8, the engine that had for so long symbolised the excellence and superiority of Rolls-Royce engineering skills.

In the event, this extremely unpopular decision was not allowed to stand for very long and the building of Rolls-Royce engines was returned to its rightful home in Crewe soon after the Volkswagen–BMW takeover debacle that finally reached its conclusion in August 1998. After the acrimonious, litigious and protracted disputes between Vickers PLC (Rolls-Royce's parent company), Rolls-Royce PLC, BMW, and Volkswagen, this was a relief for all concerned. Later a very much shortened (but still interminably long) version of the resultant four-way resolution was made public. In even more abridged form, the bald facts are – Volkswagen agree to pay Vickers PLC $795 million for Rolls-Royce Motor Cars and retain British management. Volkswagen also agree to acquire Cosworth from Vickers PLC for an additional $200 million. It then becomes clear that at some stage during the

2001 Bentley Continental T, personal commission storage/luggage.

2001 Bentley Continental T, personal commission interior.

The hides of 15 cows, each one specially selected and providing about 46 sq. ft. of leather, are needed to trim one Bentley.

negotiations, BMW have acquired the Rolls-Royce name and logo from Rolls-Royce PLC for $68 million. Eventually, they agree to allow Volkswagen to continue using the name and logo through to December 31 2002. Volkswagen retain all rights to the Bentley name and will continue building the Rolls-Royce Silver Seraph alongside the Bentley Arnage at the Rolls-Royce factory in Crewe until December 31 2002. At this time Rolls-Royce production will revert to BMW, who say that they intend building 1,500 Rolls-Royce cars per year at a new factory near Goodwood. Unable to keep his promise to continue producing both marques at Crewe, Graham Morris, the Chief Executive of Rolls-Royce Motor Cars resigns. Volkswagen state that they intend to continue building 10,000 Bentleys a year at the Crewe factory. BMW state that they have applied for planning permission to build a multi-million pound underground factory on the Goodwood Estate in England. They also say that their first Rolls-Royce customer will take delivery of a car produced in this factory on 1 January 2003.

For the sake of clarity it should be stressed that, rather than trying to prevent a sale to a foreign buyer, Rolls-Royce PLC had been attempting to influence the choice of buyers in favour of BMW, its existing aero engine business partner. The two companies had co-operated well in the past and in 1994 BMW had agreed to supply and assist in the development of powertrains for a new line of Rolls-Royces. In the event, despite the lack of design input from Rolls-Royce and an incredible amount of confusion and dithering, the agreement stood. In 1998, before the dust stirred up by the most muddled sale of the

Only Connolly A-grade leather is used at Crewe and every hide is pre-tensioned and checked for quality and imperfections on delivery.

century had even begun to settle, the BMW-powered Silver Seraph was launched. Initially the result of a bold £200 million investment by parent company Vickers, this was the first new Rolls-Royce since the 1980 Silver Spirit. Much more than a revamp of an existing model, the Silver Seraph really is an entirely new car, but whether it will ever be fully accepted as a Rolls-Royce was still as uncertain in November 2000 as it had been on the day when it was first announced. Will customers previously willing to pay a huge premium for a very special and unique motor car accept the loss of an engine designed and built by Rolls-Royce engineers and seen as the heart and soul of the Rolls-Royce motor car?

Today, with Teutonic honesty, the men from Munich no longer cast the Rolls-Royce name into an engine that is standard on BMWs that sell for a fraction of the cost of a Rolls-Royce. We too have to accept the facts: Volkswagen now build Bentleys, and BMW will build Rolls-Royces from 1 January 2003. The position regarding new Bentleys is clear; although owned by Volkswagen, they will be built in the existing Crewe factory by the same people who built them in the past. But the Silver Seraph poses awkward questions. Can a car built in a Rolls-Royce factory owned by Volkswagen and powered by an off-the-shelf BMW engine with the same automatic ZF 5-speed adaptive unit used on big BMW's be a genuine Rolls-Royce? Also, will the next Rolls-Royce, which is to be built in a new Rolls-

Royce/BMW factory by a newly recruited workforce, generate the traditional pride and enthusiasm that has always been an essential part of Rolls-Royce ownership? More importantly, and quite understandably, have Volkswagen concerned themselves with the long-term promotion and success of a car bearing the name of the company destined to be their closest rival? The latter is a question that will be answered when the Silver Seraph production figures for 2001 are released. These are expected to show Rolls-Royce models – i.e. the Silver Seraph, the New Corniche, and the Park Ward to be about 3 per cent of total production.

It has been said that an estimated £45 million was saved by not developing a new engine, but those who believed that the Silver Seraph would cost less than its predecessors were disappointed. The new model is considerably more expensive than the one it has replaced. This is probably because, as Rolls-Royce say, the £45 million plus a great deal more was invested in a facility to build bodyshells. Clearly a forward-looking decision, this broke the company's 50-year dependence on outside suppliers of bodyshells and facilitated future Bentley production. It was certainly not a short-term measure meant to reduce the cost of the last few Rolls-Royces to be built in a factory where the once familiar Grecian temple radiator and Spirit of Ecstasy mascot are now a rare sight. By late 2001, only an occasional Silver Seraph and negligible numbers of Corniche Convertibles and Park Ward Limousines were emerging from the factory; of these, only the Park Ward with its individually customer-specified interior was in any way unique to Rolls-Royce.

As has often been the case with other models, the Bentley Arnage and the Rolls-Royce

As if solving a jigsaw puzzle, the coach trimmers 'nest' the knives on the hide in the optimum configuration to achieve 60 per cent usage.

Silver Seraph share the same bodyshell, but for the first time since Rolls-Royce acquired the Bentley marque in 1931 they have different engines. Although also BMW-powered, the Bentley Arnage, and later models, the Arnage Birkin and Arnage Green Label, have a V8 4398 c.c. 350 b.h.p. engine that develops 413 lb./ft. of torque at 5500 r.p.m – a slightly more powerful unit than the larger V12 5379 c.c. 322 b.h.p. engine that develops 361 lb./ft. of torque at 3900 r.p.m. on the Silver Seraph. In production at the same time, Bentley Continental Coupes and Bentley Azure Convertibles are still powered by the 'old' 6.75-litre turbocharged V8 Rolls-Royce engine. Later, in September 1999, in a move that marked a clear separation from their Munich-based rival, Volkswagen launched the Bentley Arnage Red Label, a new four-door saloon also powered by the 6.75-litre Rolls-Royce engine. Many will now see the use of this engine as the closest connection to the history and tradition of Bentley motor cars and the people who built them.

It is, however, a connection that was strengthened by the world debut of the Bentley Arnage T at the North American International Auto Show in Detroit on 7 January 2002. Powered by a totally redesigned version of the long-serving 6.75-litre V8 engine, the Arnage T is the result of a three-year project to re-engineer the 1998 Arnage saloon and create the first model in the Bentley Series Two Arnage family*. Interestingly, the genesis of this new engine goes back to Bentley's decision in 1998 to offer the Arnage with the older 6.75-litre engine as an alternative to the BMW derived 4.4-litre engine offered at launch. The response from Bentley customers was so overwhelming that very soon the larger engine powered every new Arnage.

There could be no clearer indication of the enduring demand for the fabled turbocharged aluminium V8 that first appeared in the Mulsanne Turbo in 1982. Nonetheless, by the late 'nineties this engine was starting to show its age and with ever-increasing demands being put upon it by emissions legislators, and a clientele expecting nothing but the best, it was evident that it would need either re-engineering or replacing. Bentley's engineers chose the former option and retained the basic structure while carrying out extensive modifications to create a new engine for the 21st century. The result is a power plant, producing 450 b.h.p. at 4,100 r.p.m. and 645 lb./ft. of torque at 3,250 r.p.m., that can propel the Arnage T from 0–60 m.p.h. in 5.5 seconds and on to a top speed of 168 m.p.h.

The most obvious change is the fitting of two Garrett T3 turbochargers to replace the single T4 used until now. The advantages of a twin turbo layout are many, but producing extra power while reducing emissions are two of the most important. The use of two small turbochargers instead of one big one effectively reduces inertia and response times across a wider rev range. This in turn gives a more immediate throttle response and speeds up delivery of the torque beloved of Bentley drivers. The use of twin turbochargers also expedites the fitting of close-coupled catalytic converters close to the exhaust manifold. Located thus, in a position not possible on a Vee-formation engine using a single

---

* Volkswagen say that it will be joined later in 2002 by two other models, successors to the Arnage Red Label and Arnage Long Wheelbase.

Imposing reception area at the Crewe factory, only 34 miles south of the original Cooke Street works.

turbocharger, the catalytic converters dramatically cut emissions by taking less time to reach normal operating temperatures.

Turbochargers aside, the single most important external change is the adoption of the Bosch Motronic ME 7 engine management system[*] which further reduces emissions and improves response times. Crucially, it also facilitates the replacement of the Arnage's traction control with the latest Bosch ESP 5.7 stability system to dramatically enhance active safety. Using individual sensors, the system monitors all relevant issues such as wheel speed, steering angle, yaw, pitch and throttle opening and continually feeds the information back to a central control unit that sets certain parameters within which the car is judged to be safe and under control. The moment one of these parameters is breached, the ESP will use whatever combination of throttle and individual brake control is required to re-establish stability. This contrasts starkly with a standard traction-control system, which merely cuts the power when a loss of traction is detected.

There are, of course, many other changes, but the out-going unit's greatest strength – a tidal wave of torque at very low engine speeds – has been enhanced. To achieve this and

[*] The engine management system also enables an electronic 'fly by wire' throttle, which is essential to the working of the ESP stability system.

Engineers at the Crewe works assembling the distinctive Bentley radiator.

its emissions targets required a total re-evaluation of most of the major engine components at the most fundamental level. It was also decided to raise the maximum permissible engine speed from 4,500 to 5,000 r.p.m.; this was not to accommodate a higher power peak, which remains at 4,100 r.p.m., but to allow better use of the gearbox and the new gearing. To this end the GM 4L80-E four-speed automatic gearbox and the internal gear ratios used in the Arnage Red Label have been retained, but the back axle ratio has been lowered to further exploit the immense torque and facilitate more relaxed running at speed. By raising the final drive ratio from 2.69:1 to 2.92:1 the Arnage T adds 36.78 m.p.h. for every 1,000 r.p.m. in top gear. This means that at the UK's motorway speed limit of 70 m.p.h., the engine is ticking over at just 1900 r.p.m.

The Arnage T powertrain has been tested in simulations at ambient temperatures from -40 to +50°C and at altitudes from −100 to +4000 metres. One particularly punishing new test involves running an engine at maximum effort on the bench for 500 hours, punctuated only by thermal shock cycling. This means that once the engine is at its absolute maximum temperature, it is flushed through with ice-cold coolant to induce a maximum gradient of heat loss before heating back to maximum temperature again. This naturally expands and contracts all the castings in the engine, taxing joint faces, gaskets, bolts and numerous other fittings to an extent that would be almost impossible to replicate in the real world.

One of the most important design strategies for the Arnage T involved adding further rigidity to the body while avoiding any significant increase in weight. A concept based on an automotive engineering principle that states '–all things being equal, the stiffer the structure of a car can be made, the better its handling and ride is likely to be'. However, if the increase in rigidity is accompanied by a commensurate increase in weight, any advantage can be entirely negated. To improve the Arnage T's rigidity, Bentley's engineers used finite element analysis and computer modelling to define first what was theoretically possible, then adapted it to see what was practically possible. Adding a brace inside the wheel arches, strengthening the sills, inserting an extra bow in the roof and reinforcing the front bulkhead, together with the use of adhesive bonding materials around the door frames and stronger mounts for the steering column were based on this research. The result is a dramatic improvement in the dynamic stiffness of the finished body from a first mode of 41 hz. to 45 hz., for a weight increase of just 15.6 kg.

Bentley's main aims, realised in the transformation of the Series Two Arnage chassis, were twofold. first there was a general improvement of both ride and handling across the entire model range. But for the new Arnage T, the most sporting Bentley saloon in history, the Bentley engineers also had a separate strategy. Their intention was to make the Arnage T handle better than any other Bentley while retaining the primary ride comfort that is synonymous with the marque. This work on improving the suspension began in early 1999, using modelling software and bespoke Bentley programmes to put the car through simulated manoeuvres on the computer and assess the effects on ride, roll, pitch and yaw characteristics when different spring, damper and bush rates were used. The results were then built into prototype cars and proved, not only on Volkswagen's test facilities, but also on the Nurburgring race track, the Pyrenees, Finland, the Alps and, of course, normal public roads in the UK.

As a result of these tests, the basic architecture of the suspension, which already featured an optimal double wishbone layout at each corner, was retained, but every other aspect of the suspension was examined to create and refine the chassis. Changes to the handling balance were made, but the most fundamental change is the introduction of a rear anti-roll bar and the stiffening of the front anti-roll bar to increase roll control while allowing greater scope to adjust spring and damper settings to suit the differing needs of the model range. In the case of the Arnage T, an indication of the sporting characteristics of the chassis can be gained by comparing it to the Arnage Red Label Chassis, which has 43 per cent less roll stiffness.

An all-new aerodynamics department was established at Crewe in 1999 and one of its first jobs was to go through the Arnage from end to end to enhance its aerodynamic performance. Consequently the most notable aerodynamic change on the Arnage T is an integrated boot spoiler that improves stability at high speeds and matches aerodynamic performance to the weight distribution of the car at all speeds. The brakes of the Arnage were also updated in 1999 and with massive ventilated discs at each corner no further modifications were needed for the Arnage T or the other Series Two Arnage models.

The major enhancement in passive safety for the Series Two Arnage is the incorporation of side thorax airbags for both front and rear seat passengers, and the installation of full-length side air curtains. Thanks to the excellent structural nature of the Arnage (it is capable of passing Federal side impact tests without airbags) it was possible to apply the new airbag systems to the existing structure rather than starting from scratch. The side airbags have been packaged into the outboard sides of the front and rear seats rather than in the doors so that wherever the seat is positioned, the airbags will always be located where they can offer maximum safety to the cars' occupants.

The decision to fire the airbags is taken within 10 milliseconds (0.01 sec) of impact and 20 milliseconds (0.02 sec) later, the airbag system will be fully deployed. The side curtains are deployed simultaneously from the cantrail and A-pillar. The new side airbags and curtains join an already strong arsenal of passive safety features, including two front airbags, front seat belt pre-tensioners and four channel ABS.

Bentley design chief Dirk van Braeckel has avoided major exterior design changes in favour of subtle enhancements. One of the least visible but most significant of these is the use of the famed Black Label badge, reserved only for the most sporting Bentleys and otherwise used only on the Continental T. Also, there is a new front bumper with a lower air dam, which reduces lift and provides a more solid appearance. Front fog lamps have been incorporated into the bumper and there are larger openings to provide extra air to the charge coolers and brakes. The intakes in the bumper are now covered by the same laser-cut matrix that is used for the radiator grille. Thicker sills have been designed for the sides of the car and all the chrome on the sides, front and rear has been removed, though the chrome used for the glass and door frame areas has been retained. If specified, the new three-piece, split rim, five-spoke 19-in alloy wheels add an additional degree of purpose to

Arnage T at speed.

the car's profile. Like the front bumper, the rear bumper has been restyled to arc around the large diameter twin tail-pipes. Parking Distance Control (PDC) sensors are incorporated into both front and rear bumpers. Also at the rear, the integrated spoiler previously mentioned provides further visual evidence of the Arnage T's performance potential.

The interior of the Arnage T has also received attention, most notably the wide range of enhancements to the seats. Bentley is one of just a few manufacturers left in the world who design and manufacture their seats entirely in-house, and has spent two years building CAD-profiles of the best seats on the market against which to benchmark its own products. The result: seats that offer both more comfort and support, while providing distinctive looks that come from the combination of a diamond pattern using perforated Connolly hide and contrasting stitching (they also carry an embroidered Bentley motif). The door covers carry the same distinctive diamond pattern as the seats, while extensive knurling is used for the sill buttons, door handles, organ stop ventilation controls and lighting switch. The Arnage T cabin also features a bespoke steering wheel and gear selector, a 'Sport' mode button for the transmission and a distinctive black 'Engine Start' button. There are new grab handles in both the front and rear, and the roof lining is made from perforated hide. To give the interior a more distinctive sporting look, engine-turned aluminium is used for both the instrument surround and the waist rails in the doors and the stain on the wood in the cabin has been darkened.

If, as would appear to be the case, the Arnage T is typical of the type of car to be produced under the aegis of Volkswagen, Bentley's core focus is now on the production of

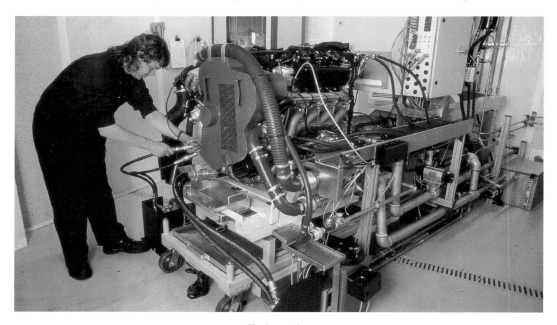

Engine testing.

208

Dirk van Braeckel, Director of Design.

high-performance Grand Touring cars. But pointers to their determined effort to preserve a reputation for the ultimate in luxury can also be seen in the appointments of the next two models in the Series Two Arnage range. Scheduled to make their sales debuts in the summer of 2002 as successors to the Arnage Red Label and Arnage long-wheelbase the marginally slower but ultra-refined Arnage R and Arnage RL must surely put Bentley, at least temporarily, at the pinnacle of the luxury car market. Perhaps, even more significantly, an investment of around £10 million in the creation of a State Limousine to be presented as a gift to Her Majesty the Queen to celebrate her Golden Jubilee poses a direct and serious threat to the historic supremacy of Rolls-Royce in this sector of the market. Bentley Motors has been entirely responsible for the design, styling, chassis and commissioning of the car. Conceived and worked on by a Bentley-led consortium of British Motor Industry manufacturers and suppliers, the car has been assembled in a dedicated area of Bentley's Personal Commissioning Department. Throughout the world this hugely imposing car is seen as the highest endorsement of Bentley's ability to create the

*The Golden Jubilee of Her Majesty Queen Elizabeth II in 2002.

ultimate in opulence and luxury. And as such, despite being unique in every respect and most definitely not a customised version of any other model, it is also the most striking example of the company's ability to personalise and tailor existing models to the requirements of individual customers.

While the car will be the first State Bentley, the tradition of Crewe-designed and -built State Limousines dates back over half a century to 6 July 1950, when a new Rolls-Royce Phantom IV was delivered to Princess Elizabeth and the Duke of Edinburgh. Since then four other Rolls-Royce limousines have been presented – two Phantom Vs and two Phantom VIs – the most recent in 1987. Fundamentally different to these earlier Rolls-Royces, the new Bentley bears no relationship in appearance or physical proportions to any other Bentley product. Designed with continual reference to and input from the Queen, the Duke of Edinburgh, and of course, the Head Chauffeur, it is largely the work of Bentley design director Dirk van Braeckel and exterior stylist Crispin Marshfield. In May 2000, when the Queen and the Duke of Edinburgh were presented with the design, it was immediately approved with requests for only minimal changes.

Although the idea that the Queen should be offered a new State Limousine for her Golden Jubilee came from within Bentley Motors, it must have been inspired by the occasion of her Silver Jubilee in 1977, when the UK Society of Motor Manufacturers and Traders presented her with a Rolls-Royce Phantom VI State Limousine, a car, which, after covering over 125,000 miles in 25 years, remains her first choice of transport on State occasions. Hopefully, from June 2002, it will be retired gracefully into the reserve ranks of a Royal fleet that still retains the later (1987) Phantom VI and two Phantom Vs, dating

Clay model of the State Limousine, front three-quarters.

Clay model of the State Limousine, rear three-quarters.

from 1960 and 1961. Now rarely seen, these cars are steeped in history and tradition, and in keeping with tradition, the new car is painted in Royal Claret below the waistrail and black above, with a red coachstripe along each side. Rear seats are upholstered in West of England cloth, while all remaining upholstery is light grey Connolly hide. The carpets are pale Baroda blue with a royal blue foot rug fitted in the rear, while the front cabin area carries a dark blue theme throughout. At the time of writing the mechanical specification of the car was not known, but Bentley have said that it has been designed to accept an environmentally friendly Low Pressure Gas (LPG) fuel system. It will, of course, also enjoy all the benefits of monocoque construction, compared to the body on chassis configuration of previous state limousines. This more space-efficient design, while enabling a lower roofline and preserving the requisite interior height, also locates the entire transmission tunnel beneath the flat cabin floor. Another key design innovation features rear doors that are hinged at the back and open through nearly 90 degrees, allowing the Queen to face her audience and enjoy an unimpeded exit by standing up straight before stepping down to the ground. The doors themselves, actually cut into the cantrail and hinged at the back, also have considerably wider apertures than previously seen on Royal cars. The interior of the rear compartment is configured for two principal occupants, typically the Queen and the Duke of Edinburgh, while two rear-facing occasional folding chairs are fitted for additional passengers. Removable, opaque panels over the backlight on the rear of the car allows occupants to choose between normal levels of privacy, or having the covers removed to provide the best possible view into the car with the D and E pillars carefully sited so that

Clay model of the State Limousine, side view.

the Queen is clearly visible between them.

Just as a Bentley State Limousine is a break with tradition, Team Bentley's triumphant reappearance at the Le Mans 24-hour race in 2001 is an equally momentous return to another much older tradition. Tony Gott, Chief Executive of Bentley Motors, commenting on the Bentley race car said: 'It is the noisiest, most uncomfortable, cramped and arguably most impractical Bentley ever made. The Bentley EXP Speed 8 drinks fuel at a rate that makes the most thirsty four-by-four sports utility seem like it's on an economy run; it has no airbags, cup-holders or satellite navigation and it'll never sell.' So what? To Bentley aficionados these are mere details. The EXP Speed 8 was designed specifically for the 2001 Le Mans 24-hour race, an event so important to Bentley that it could be said to be part of their DNA. In the event, the EXP Speed 8, driven by Andy Wallace, crossed the line in third place, beaten only by the two all-conquering Audi R8s that have dominated Le Mans in recent years. For Bentley it was a return to their roots:, the success of a car that W.O. Bentley himself would have been proud of in a race which they won in 1924 and again in 1927, 1928, 1929 and 1930.

For Rolls-Royce, the future is even more uncertain and less clearly mapped out than that of Bentley. In 2000, BMW unveiled plans to build Rolls-Royce cars in a factory to be built on a greenfield site at Goodwood. By April 2001, the awkwardly named Project Rolls-Royce was beginning to take on form and substance and they had a Rolls-Royce design team beavering away in a former Barclays Bank Building overlooking Hyde Park Corner in London. Subsequently, drawings of a new Rolls-Royce to be launched on 31 January 2003 were leaked to the press and computer-simulated pictures of what appears to be a mix of Silver Cloud, Silver Shadow and Silver Seraph appeared in the *Daily Mail* and *The Autocar*. Since then, for whatever reason, there has been very little information about the new car, and by the spring of 2001, problems with planning permissions meant that construction of the new factory had not begun. However, in January 2002 construction of the vast multi-million pound, purpose-built underground plant was well underway and details of a new Rolls-Royce for 2003 was eagerly awaited throughout the world.

Prototype Bentley EXP Speed 8 Le Mans Racing Car.

213

PART TWO

'Doctors and others connected with the medical profession have, after trying the leading makes, declared the Rolls-Royce to be the only petrol car that they could bring up to a patient's house and drive away, without the possibility of disturbing the patient.'

1905 Catalogue

Rolls-Royce and Bentley Specifications

In the outline specifications of Rolls-Royce and Bentley models that follow, an indication is given of general mechanical features and of major design changes. Details of chassis series and numbers quoted have been taken with permission from Rolls-Royce records.

THE ROYCE CARS
1904

ENGINE

GENERAL Two cylinders (cast iron), $3^3/_4 \times 5$, 1,800 c.c. approx. (about 12 b.h.p. at 1,000 r.p.m.). Compression ratio 3·4:1 approx.

VALVES Overhead inlet, side exhaust. One camshaft for inlet valves on one side of engine, and one for exhaust valves on other side.

One of the first three Royce 2-cylinder cars circa *1904.*

CRANKCASE Aluminium alloy (16% zinc). Main bearings in lower half, with hand hole cover in side for big end inspection.

CRANKSHAFT Carried in two phosphor-bronze bearings.

CAMSHAFT Driven by spur wheels.

1904 Royce 4-seater car.

LUBRICATION Total loss, supplied from cast aluminium tank on dash, pressurised from exhaust system with adjustable sight drip-feeds to regulate supply for cruising. Supplementary hand pump for high-speed work augmenting drip-feeds. Stand-pipe and drain plug provided in each crank chamber compartment for draining off to the correct level.

IGNITION Carpentier high-speed trembler coil and 24 mm spark plug for each cylinder (adaptor provided for 18 mm plugs). Low-tension commutator with wipe-type contacts. Timing gear drive enclosed. Two accumulators coupled to coil and commutator through a two-way switch.

COOLING SYSTEM Top and bottom tanks connected by vertical tubes threaded through and soldered to thin horizontal gill plates. No fan on first engine (15196): five-bladed fan on second engine, with variable angle of incidence of blades for experimental purposes. Gear type water pump driven by half-speed shaft through flexible coupling.

CARBURETTOR French Longuemare type for first and second cars. Third car, Royce-designed carburettor of float feed spray type, fitted with an automatic air valve.

ENGINE CONTROL Centrifugal governor valve mounted in inlet pipe. Hand throttle and mixture control.

TRANSMISSION

GEARBOX Three forward speeds and reverse. Single selector, gears in line ahead on quadrant change. Ratchet-type freewheel at end of layshaft of gearbox in second car.

CLUTCH Internal cone type, lined with leather, connected to gearbox by universal joint.

FINAL DRIVE Fully floating live axle, bevel drive with spur-type differential gears.

BRAKES

Footbrake at rear end of gearbox, acting on differential. Handbrake internal expanding type operating on rear wheels.

SUSPENSION

Semi-elliptic springs front and rear.

WHEELS

Artillery pattern with wooden spokes.

CHASSIS DETAILS

Tyres 810 × 90
Weight 12 cwt.

Speeds in gears, m.p.h.	1	2	3
	$7\frac{1}{2}$	17	30

NUMBER PRODUCED

Three. None now exists, but the second Royce engine and gearbox are in Manchester.

10 H.P. 2-CYLINDER CAR
1904–1906

ENGINE

GENERAL Two cylinders (cast iron). $3^3/_4 \times 5$ ($3^{15}/_{16} \times 5$ for later cars), 1,800 c.c.

VALVES Overhead inlet valves, and side exhaust valves.

CRANKCASE Cast aluminium with crankshaft bearings in bottom half. Inspection doors to examine connecting rods.

CRANKSHAFT Nickel-steel forging with three phosphor-bronze bushed bearings.

CAMSHAFT Driven by enclosed spur wheels.

LUBRICATION Main bearings oiled by ring and splash, and crankpins by centrifugal force

Rolls-Royce 10 h.p. 2-cylinder car; 2-seater body, 1905.

219

1905 10 h.p. 2-cylinder 2-seater car: now in the Science Museum, London.

1905 10 h.p. 2-cylinder 4-seater car.

and splash. Pump on dash driven by spring wire belt forces oil to sight feed lubricators at 4 lb./in². Supplementary hand pump for high-speed work. Sight feed lubricators on dash regulated by conical screws on top to give necessary feed to bearings. 1 gal. oil reservoir at bottom of crankcase has overflow tap to check level.

IGNITION High tension, with two independent sets of accumulators and R-R induction coil with double trembler. Commutator is fitted on crankshaft.

COOLING SYSTEM Radiator made of vertical thin solid-drawn brass tubes, with horizontal brass plates for cooling surface. Belt-driven fan and gear-type circulating pump.

CARBURETTOR Float feed spray type with automatic air valve.

ENGINE CONTROL Centrifugal governor maintains set engine speed but can be overridden by accelerator pedal.

PETROL SYSTEM 6 gal. capacity tank.

TRANSMISSION

GEARBOX Three forward speeds and reverse, with direct drive on third. Sliding-gear type of box. Intermediate neutral notches between each forward speed on gear-lever quadrant.

CLUTCH Internal cone type, leather lined. Connected to gearbox by universal joint.

PROPELLER SHAFT Universal joint at front end and flexible coupling of square type at rear end. Torque rod employed.

FINAL DRIVE Fully floating live axle, bevel drive, with spur-type differential gears. Differential box carried on plain bearings.

BRAKES

Footbrake acting on drum just behind gearbox. Handbrake internal expanding type operating on rear wheels.

SUSPENSION

Semi-elliptic springs front and rear.

STEERING

Hard steel worm, working in phosphor-bronze.

WHEELS
Artillery pattern with wooden spokes. Front wheels on hardened steel sleeves and bronze bushes, rear wheels on ball bearings.

LIGHTING
Oil.

CHASSIS DETAILS

Wheelbase 75 in.

Track 48 in.

Width of frame 36 in.

Tyres 810×90

Weight without tyres $10^3/_4$ cwt.

Speeds in gears, mph.	1	2	3
Low gear ratio	11	19	32
Medium gear ratio	13	22	36
High gear ratio	14	$23\frac{1}{2}$	$39\frac{1}{2}$

CHASSIS NUMBERS
20150, 20152–20163, 20165–7.

NUMBER PRODUCED
Sixteen. Only known survivors are 20154, 20162, 20163.

15 H.P. 3-CYLINDER CAR
1905

ENGINE

GENERAL Three cylinders (cast iron) as separate castings. 4 × 5, 3,000 cc. VALVES Overhead inlet valves and side exhaust valves.

CRANKCASE Cast aluminium, with crankshaft bearings in bottom half. Inspection doors to examine connecting rods.

CRANKSHAFT Nickel steel forging, with four phosphor-bronze bushed bearings.

CAMSHAFT Driven by enclosed spur wheels.

LUBRICATION Main bearings oiled by ring and splash, and crankpins by centrifugal force

15 h.p. 3-cylinder car: double brougham body, 1905.

and splash. Pump on dash driven by spring wire belt forces oil to sight feed lubricators at 4 lb./in^2. Supplementary hand pump for high-speed work. Sight feed lubricators on dash regulated by conical screws on top to give necessary feed to bearings. 1 gal. oil reservoir at bottom of crankcase with overflow tap to check level.

IGNITION High tension, with two independent sets of 40 A.hr. accumulators coupled to coil and dashboard-mounted commutator by two-way switch. Single coil and trembler.

COOLING SYSTEM Radiator made of vertical thin solid-drawn brass tubes, with horizontal brass plates for cooling surface. Belt-driven fan and gear-type circulating pump.

CARBURETTOR Float feed spray type with automatic air valve.

ENGINE CONTROL Centrifugal governor maintains set engine speed but can be overridden by accelerator pedal.

TRANSMISSION

GEARBOX Three forward speeds and reverse, with direct drive on third.

CLUTCH Internal cone type, leather lined. Connected to gearbox by universal joint.

PROPELLER SHAFT Universal joint at front end and flexible coupling of square type at rear end. Torque rod employed.

FINAL DRIVE Fully floating live axle, bevel drive, with spur-type differential gears. Differential box carried on plain bearings.

BRAKES

Footbrake acting on drum just behind gearbox. Handbrake internal expanding type operating on rear wheels.

SUSPENSION

Semi-elliptic springs front and rear. Platform rear springs on some cars.

STEERING

Hard steel worm, working in phosphor-bronze. Nut sector, with end play in worm taken up by adjustable ball thrust bearing, and backlash between teeth of worm and sector by eccentric bushes on worm shaft.

WHEELS

Artillery pattern, with wooden spokes. Front and rear wheels on ball bearings.

LIGHTING
Oil.

CHASSIS DETAILS

Wheelbase 103 in.
Width offrame 36 in.
Tyres 810 × 90
Weight without tyres 13 cwt.

Speeds in gears, mph.	1	2	3
Low gear ratio	$11^1/_2$	$19^1/_2$	32
Medium gear ratio	13	22	$36^1/_2$
High gear ratio	14	$23^1/_2$	$39^1/_2$

CHASSIS NUMBERS
23924, 24272, 24273, 26330–2.

NUMBER PRODUCED
Six. Only known survivor is 26330.

1905 15 h.p. 3-cylinder car.

20 H.P. 4-CYLINDER CAR
1905–1906

ENGINE

GENERAL Four cylinders (cast iron) in two groups of two. 4×5 (first one built was $3^3/_4 \times 5$), 4,000 c.c.

VALVES Overhead inlet valves, with detachable cages, and side exhaust valves.

CRANKCASE Cast aluminium, with crankshaft bearings in bottom half. Inspection doors to examine connecting rods.

CRANKSHAFT Nickel-steel forging, with five phosphor-bronze bushed bearings.

CAMSHAFT Driven by enclosed spur wheels.

A production model Heavy 20 open tourer of 1905. Note the 3-speed gearbox control and the dished steering wheel.

LUBRICATION Main bearings oiled by ring and splash, and crankpins by centrifugal force and splash. Pump on dash driven by spring wire belt forces oil to sight feed lubricators at 4 lb/in^2. Supplementary hand pump for high-speed work and for priming main bearings when starting from cold. Sight feed lubricators on dash regulated by conical screws on top to give necessary feed to bearings. $^1/_2$ gal. oil reservoir at bottom of crankcase with overflow tap to check level.

IGNITION High tension, with two independent sets of 40 A.hr. accumulators coupled to coil and dash-board mounted commutator by two-way switch. Single coil and trembler. A magneto was a selected later fitting on only a few from new.

COOLING SYSTEM Radiator made of vertical thin solid-drawn brass tubes, with horizontal brass plates for cooling surface. Belt-driven fan and gear-type circulating pump.

CARBURETTOR Float feed spray type with automatic air valve, Rolls-Royce design.

ENGINE CONTROL Centrifugal governor maintains set engine speed but can be overridden by accelerator pedal.

TRANSMISSION
GEARBOX Prototype (24263) and heavy models, three forward speeds and reverse. From 40500 heavies had a 4-speed box. Light model, four forward speeds and reverse, with direct drive on third and overdrive on top.

CLUTCH Internal cone type, leather lined. Connected to gearbox by universal joint.

BRAKES
Footbrake acting on drum just behind gearbox. Handbrake internal expanding type operating on rear wheels.

SUSPENSION
Semi-elliptic springs and platform rear suspension.

STEERING
Hard steel worm working in phosphor-bronze nut. Light model had sector, with end play in worm taken up by adjustable ball thrust bearing, and backlash between teeth of worm and sector by eccentric bushes on worm shaft.

WHEELS
Artillery pattern with wooden spokes. On light model, front and rear mounted on ball bearings. On heavy model, front on hardened steel sleeves and bronze bushes, rear on ball bearings.

LIGHTING
Oil.

CHASSIS DETAILS						Light				Heavy			
Wheelbase						106 in.				114 in.			
Track						52 in.				56 in.			
Overall length						141 in.				155 in.			
Width of frame						$33^{1}/_{2}$ in.				36 in.			
Tyres, front						810×90				870×90			
Tyres, rear						810×100				880×120			
Weight without tyres						$13^{1}/_{2}$ cwt.				15 cwt.			
Speeds in gears, m.p.h.	*Ratio*	1	2	3	4		*Ratio*	1	2	3	4		
Low gear ratio	—	—	—	—	—		1:3·6	10	$16^{1}/_{2}$	$28^{1}/_{2}$	$35^{1}/_{2}$		
Medium gear ratio	1:3·0	13	$21^{1}/_{2}$	$31^{1}/_{2}$	$44^{1}/_{2}$		1:3.25	11	$18^{1}/_{2}$	$31^{1}/_{2}$	38		
High gear ratio	1:2·6	15	24	36	50		1:3·0	13	22	38	47		
TT no. 4	1:2·4	16	$26^{1}/_{2}$	39	52		—	—	—	—	—		

CHASSIS NUMBERS

24263, 24264 1905

23926, 26350, 26350B–4, 26356–9, 40500–11, 40519–33 1905–06

NUMBER PRODUCED

Forty. Only three known survivors: 26350, 40509, 40520.

30 H.P. 6-CYLINDER CAR
1905–1906

30 h.p. 6-cylinder car: Pullman body by Barker, 1906.

ENGINE

GENERAL Six cylinders (cast iron) in three groups of two. 4 × 5, 6,000 c.c.

VALVES Overhead inlet valves, with detachable cages, and side exhaust valves.

CRANKCASE Cast aluminium, with crankshaft bearings in bottom half. Inspection doors to examine connecting rods. From 60500, crankshaft in after crankcase.

CRANKSHAFT Nickel-steel forging, with seven phosphor-bronze bushed bearings.

CAMSHAFT Driven by enclosed spur wheels.

LUBRICATION Main bearings oiled by ring and splash, and crankpins by centrifugal force and splash. Pump on dash driven by spring wire belt forces oil to sight feed lubricators at

229

30 h.p. 6-cylinder car: Roi des Belges body by Rippon Bros.

4 lb./in². Supplementary hand pump for high speed work and for priming main bearings when starting from cold. Sight feed lubricators on dash regulated by conical screws on top to give necessary feed to bearings. 1 gal. oil reservoir at bottom of crankscrews with overflow tap to check level.

IGNITION High tension, with two independent sets of 40 A.hr. accumulators coupled to coil and dashboard-mounted commutator by two-way switch. Single coil and trembler. A magneto was later fitted in addition.

COOLING SYSTEM Radiator made of vertical thin solid-drawn brass tubes, with horizontal brass plates for cooling surface. Belt-driven fan and gear-type circulating pump.

CARBURETTOR Float feed spray type with automatic air valve, Rolls-Royce design and manufacture.

ENGINE CONTROL Centrifugal governor maintains set engine speed but can be overridden by accelerator pedal.

TRANSMISSION
GEARBOX Four forward speeds and reverse, with direct drive on third and overdrive on top. Early cars were 3-speed. Fitted with ball bearings throughout.

CLUTCH Internal cone type, leather lined. Connected to gearbox by universal joint.

FINAL DRIVE Differential box carried on ball bearings.

BRAKES
Footbrake acting on drum just behind gearbox. Handbrake internal expanding type operating on rear wheels.

SUSPENSION
Semi-elliptic springs and platform rear suspension.

STEERING
Hard steel worm, working on phosphor-bronze sector, adjustable for wear.

WHEELS
Artillery pattern, with wooden spokes. Wheels on hardened steel sleeves and bronze bushes, later converted to ball bearings.

LIGHTING
Oil side and tail lights, acetylene head lights.

30 h.p. 6-cylinder car: 7-seater Limousine by Rippon Bros.

CHASSIS DETAILS

	Short	Long
Wheelbase	112 in.	118 in.
Track	56 in.	56 in.
Overall length	157 in.	158³/₄ in.
Width of frame	36 in.	36 in.
Tyres, front	870 × 90	880 × 120
rear	880 × 120	895 × 135
Weight without tyres	17 cwt.	17¹/₂ cwt.

CHASSIS NUMBERS

23927, 24274, 24275   1905
26355, 26370–5   1905–06
60500–11, 60524–38   1906

NUMBER PRODUCED

Thirty-seven. Only known survivor is 26355.

V-8 LEGALIMIT AND INVISIBLE ENGINE MODELS

1905–1906

ENGINE

GENERAL Eight cylinders, in four groups of two forming 90° V. $3^1/_3 \times 3^1/_4$, 3,500 c.c.

VALVES Inlet and exhaust valves interchangeable.

CRANKCASE Cast aluminium in two halves jointed horizontally, with upper half carrying crankshaft bearings.

CRANKSHAFT Hollow, supported by three main bearings. White-metalled connecting rod big-end bearings.

V-8 invisible engine model; motor landau, 1906.

V-8 invisible engine model; tourer, 1906.

LUBRICATION Oil supplied to bearings at 15 lb./in.^{2} by gear pump driven off crankshaft.

IGNITION Each set of four plugs with own coil and trembler but a common (double) distributor.

COOLING SYSTEM Radiator made of horizontal thin solid-drawn brass tubes with vertical brass plates. Fan mounted at front end of crankshaft.

ENGINE CONTROL Centrifugal governor maintains set engine speed but can be overridden by accelerator pedal.

TRANSMISSION

GEARBOX Three speeds and reverse, with direct drive on third. Ball bearings throughout.

CLUTCH Internal cone type, leather lined. Connected to gearbox by universal joint.

FINAL DRIVE Differential box carried on ball bearings.

V-8 Legalimit, 1906.

BRAKES
Footbrake acting on drum just behind gearbox. Handbrake internal expanding type operating on rear wheels.

SUSPENSION
Semi-elliptic springs.

STEERING
Hard steel worm, working in phosphor-bronze. Nut sector, with end play in worm taken up by adjustable ball thrust bearing, and backlash between teeth of worm and sector by eccentric bushes on worm shaft.

WHEELS
Artillery pattern, with wooden spokes. Rear, mounted on ball bearings; front, hardened steel sleeves and bronze bushes.

CHASSIS DETAILS

	Invisible Engine	Legalimit
Wheelbase	90 in.	106 in.
Track	52 in.	52 in.
Width of frame	37½ in.	33½ in.

Tyres: front		820×120			810×90	
rear		810×120			810×100	
Weight		—			20 cwt.	
Speeds in gears, m.p.h.	1	2	3	1	2	3
Low gear ratio	9	15	$21^{1}/_{2}$	8	$13^{1}/_{2}$	$21^{1}/_{2}$
High gear ratio	11	18	26	$9^{1}/_{2}$	16	26

CHASSIS NUMBERS
Legalimit, 40518, Invisible Engine, 80500 (only numbers recorded).

NUMBER PRODUCED
Three and parts of a fourth. It is not known that any survives.

THE BRITISH SILVER GHOST
1907–1925

ENGINE

GENERAL Six cylinders in two groups of three. $4^{1}/_{2} \times 4^{1}/_{2}$, 7,036 c.c. (1909, $4^{1}/_{2} \times 4^{3}/_{4}$, 7,428 c.c.—1100 series). Cast iron pistons (1914, aluminium alloy for L—E Alpine models; 1919, aluminium alloy standard—J series). Non-detachable cylinder heads. Engine attached to chassis frame by compensated suspension to prevent transmission of road shocks to engine casing.

VALVES Side valves, operated by single camshaft through rocking-levers carrying friction roller lying between valve spindle and cam. Interchangeable inlet and exhaust valves. Tappets, valve-guides and springs not enclosed.

CRANKCASE Cast aluminium, with upper half carrying crankcase bearings and lower half being detachable.

6-cylinder Rolls-Royce Colonial, 1914. The Colonial Silver Ghost was introduced in late 1912, at first with a 3-speed gearbox but soon with a 4-speed type, higher radiator (22in. against 20in.) and greater ground clearance.

1907 Silver Ghost, touring body by Barker.

Silver Ghost, late 1908 Landaulette.

Silver Ghost: two-seater tourer by Barker, 1910/12.

CRANKSHAFT Hollow, supported by bearing between each crank (1911, vibration damper flywheel fitted to forward end, the earliest few being mounted externally, as were some fitted retrospectively—mid 1500 series).

LUBRICATION Oil supplied by gear-type pump driven by extension to distributor spindle. Pressure capable of regulation from 1 lb. to 10 lb./in^2 (1 lb. To 20 lb./in^2 in later cars). Oil delivered under pressure to crankshaft, big ends and gudgeon pins (1908, extra supply of oil provided for cylinder walls when engine working with throttle more than two-thirds open, controlled by valve interconnected with throttle-opening mechanism). Oil capacity 8 pints, with 11 pints in reserve tank.

IGNITION Two independent systems, with separate set of plugs for each system. One system high tension with trembler coil and accumulators coupled to coil and comutator (1919, non-trembler coil on front of dash replaces trembler coil—J. series; 1921–2, coil on platform extension from distributor tower—P series); other system high-tension magneto driven through gears from crankshaft. Simms Bosch magneto (1909, Bosch D6—1100; 1912, Bosch ZR6—last half of 200 series; 1913, Watford C6—A series; 1919, Watford E.6—J series; 1923, Watford E.O.6—late P series). On/off switch on dash for magneto ignition; three-way battery switch for 'off' and either one of the two accumulators (1910, four-position ignition switch on steering column for 'off'; magneto; battery; and magneto and battery together—1400 series).

COOLING SYSTEM Centrifugal water pump driven from crankshaft through spur gears, and belt-driven fan. Radiator of vertical thin solid-drawn copper tubes, with horizontal copper plates for cooling surface (1921, thermostat in cooling system—O series).

1907 Silver Ghost Limousine: the 'Pearl of the East' by Cockshoot.

Silver Ghost open tourer.

CARBURETTOR Two-jet type with dash control and automatic air valve (1910, mixture control on steering column quadrant—1400 series). Water-heated throttle valve (late 1923, exhaust heated). Priming cup (1919, pressure priming—J series; 1921, primer replaced by starting carburettor—P series).

ENGINE CONTROL Centrifugal governor maintaining engine speed set by hand lever on steering wheel, but can be overridden by accelerator pedal.

STARTER Standard fitting from 1919—J series. Starter motor drives layshaft of gearbox by chain through jaw clutch. Epicyclic reduction gears on motor and gearbox.

PETROL SYSTEM Gravity feed, assisted by exhaust pressure, from tank under front seat (1909, pressure feed, by air pump driven off gearbox, from tank at rear—1100 series; 1919, pump worked off distributor drive—J series). Late 1924, Autovac.

TRANSMISSION

GEARBOX Four speeds, with direct drive on third (1909, three speeds—1100 series; 1913–14, four speeds, with direct drive on top—2400 series for Colonial cars, later B series for standard chassis).

CLUTCH Cone type.

PROPELLER SHAFT Open shaft and radius rods (1911, enclosed in torque tube—1700 series).

FINAL DRIVE Ratios 22:65 or 26:55 (1910, 22:65 or 24:65—1400 series; 1912, 18:52—1900 series; 1912, 16:52 or 17:52—2100 series; 1919, 16:52—J series; 1921, 15:52—later O series; 1923, 15:52 or 14:52 for cars over 50 cwt. gross weight—R series).

BRAKES

Footbrake external contracting type acting on propeller shaft, handbrake internal expanding type in brake drums on rear hub (1913, footbrake also internal expanding type, concentric with handbrake in rear brake drums—A series: 1924, front brake system operated by mechanical servo—S series).

SUSPENSION

Semi-elliptic front springs and platform rear spring suspension (1908, three-quarter elliptic rear springs—60581; 1911, London–Edinburgh model and early replicas had cantilever rear springs sliding in trunnions attached to be undersurface of the back axle casing while later L–E type cars had cantilever springs mounted over the axle; late 1912, cantilevers standard). 1908, friction type shock absorbers—900 series (1913, rear shock absorbers discontinued—2300 series; 1921, Hartford friction type—P series).

Silver Ghost open-drive Limousine.

STEERING
Worm and nut.

WHEELS
Normally, artillery pattern with wooden spokes (1909, double-spoked wire wheels available but wooden artillery wheels normal; 1911, triple-spoked wire wheels available but wooden artillery wheels more usual; 1913, wire wheels prevail but wooden artillery wheels available until 1921—end of P series).

LIGHTING
By acetylene lamps (1914, complete electric lighting by dynamo and C.A.V. system available as an optional extra; 1919, electric lighting as standard—J series).

CHASSIS DETAILS

	1907		1914	1923	
	Short	*Long*		*Short*	*Long*
Overall length	180 in.	187$\frac{1}{4}$ in.	190$\frac{1}{4}$ in.	190$\frac{1}{4}$ in.	196$\frac{3}{4}$ in.
Width of frame	36 in.	36 in.	36 in.	36 in.	36 in.
Wheelbase	135$\frac{1}{2}$ in.	143$\frac{1}{2}$ in.	143$\frac{1}{2}$ in.	144 in.	150$\frac{1}{2}$ in.
Track	56 in.	56 in.	56 in.	56 in.	56 in.
Front tyres	875 × 105	880 × 120	895 × 135	33 × 5	33 × 5
Rear tyres	880 × 120	895 × 135	895 × 135	33 × 5	33 × 5
Weight	18$\frac{1}{2}$ cwt.	19$\frac{1}{2}$ cwt.	25$\frac{1}{2}$ cwt.		
	(without tyres)		(with tyres)		

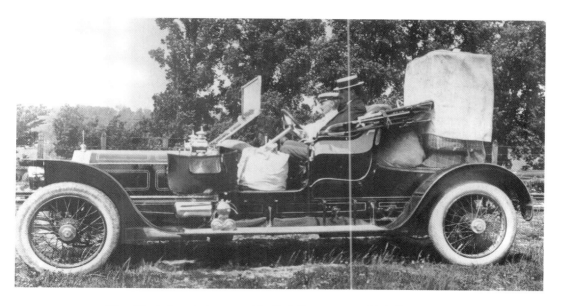

Silver Ghost: 2-seater tourer used by C. S. R. to transport his balloon, 1908.

SERIES AND CHASSIS NUMBERS

		60539–60592	1907
		60700–60799	1907–08
		919–1015	1908–09
		1100–1199	1909–10
		1200–1399	1910
		1400–1499	1910–11
		1500–1799	1911
		1800–1999	1912
		2000–2699	1912–13
A	Series	1CA–20CA; 1NA–59NA	1913–14
		1MA–30MA	1914
B	Series	32MA–56MA; 1AB–67AB; 1EB–25EB	1914
C	Series	26EB–60EB; 1RB–68RB; 1PB–4PB	1914
D	Series	5PB–65PB; 1YB–62YB	1914
E	Series	63YB–66YB; 1UB–67UB; 1LB–23LB	1914
F	Series	24LB–68LB; 1GB–48GB; 1TB–29TB	1914–15
G	Series	30TB–37GB, 55TB; 1BD–32BD; 1AD–32AD; 1ED–34ED	1915
		1RD–21RD	1915–16
H	Series	22RD–35RD; 1CB–37CB; 18PD–30PD; 1AC–28AC	1916–17
J	Series	1PP–36PP; 1LW–48LW	1919
		1TW–81TW; 1CW–CW	1920

K	Series	98CW–102CW; 1FW–121FW; 1BW–136BW	1920
L	Series	138BW–165BW; 1AE–141AE; 1EE–85EE	1920
M	Series	86EE–141EE; 1RE–81RE; 1PE–81PE; 1YE–36YE	1920
N	Series	37YE–81YE; 1UE–81UE; 1LE–81LE; 1GE–81GE; 1TE–81TE;	1920
		1CE–67CE	1921
O	Series	68CE–107CE; 1NE–108NE; 1AG–182AG; 1LG–198LG;	
		1MG–213MG; 1JG–76JG; 1UG–35UG	1921
P	Series	36UG–97UG; 1SG–91SG; 1TG–94TG; 1KG–43KG; 1PG–44PG;	
		1RG–43RG; 1YG–81YG; 1ZG–81ZG; 1HG–102HG	1922
R	Series	1LK–100LK; 1NK–100NK; 1PK–63PK	1923
S	Series	1EM–135EM; 1LM–71LM	1924
T	Series	1RM–103RM; 1TM–85TM	1924
U	Series	1AU–141AU	1924
		1EU–127EU	1925

Note – In order to give an indication of the period of the year in which certain chassis series were produced, the company has provided the following final test dates: 750 July 1908, 1000 June 1909; 1500 January 1911; 2000 July 1912; 2500 June 1913; 2699 October 1913.

NUMBER PRODUCED
6,173

Note – Of the series above, 508 chassis were omitted, but 140 were duplicated, the second chassis being given the suffix E (for Extra). The number 13 was only used in CA and MA series. Some chassis numbers in the following series were allocated to Springfield-built Silver Ghosts (see list on p. 249).

CE, NE; AG; LG; MG; JG; UG; SG; TG; KG.

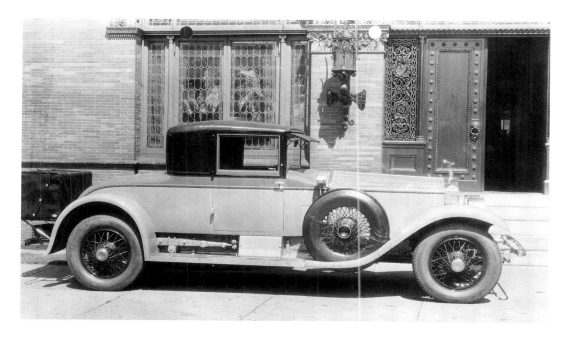

Springfield Silver Ghost: Willoughby coupé on chassis No. S214ML, 1926.

Springfield Silver Ghost: 1926 Berwick Saloon.

245

THE SPRINGFIELD SILVER GHOST
1921–1926

ENGINE

GENERAL Six cylinders in two groups of three. $4^{1}/_{2} \times 4^{3}/_{4}$, 7,428 c.c. Aluminium alloy pistons. Non-detachable cylinder heads. Engine attached to chassis frame by compensated suspension to prevent road shocks being transmitted to the engine casing.

VALVES Side Valves, operated by single camshaft through rocking-levers carrying friction roller lying between valve spindles and cam. Interchangeable inlet and exhaust valves. Tappets, valve-guides and springs not enclosed until 1925—S101MK.

CRANKCASE Cast aluminium, with upper half carrying crankshaft bearings and lower half being detachable.

Springfield Silver Ghost Limousine.

246

Springfield Silver Ghost: chassis No. S249PL, 1926.

CRANKSHAFT Hollow, supported by bearing between each crank. Vibration damper flywheel fitted to forward end.

LUBRICATION Oil supplied by gear-type pump driven by extension to distributor spindle. Pressure capable of regulation from 1 lb. To 10 lb./in^2. Oil delivered under pressure to crankshaft, big ends and gudgeon pins. Extra supply of oil provided for cylinder walls when engine is working with throttle more than two-thirds open, controlled by a valve interconnected with throttle-operating mechanism. Oil capacity 8 pints.

IGNITION Two independent systems, with separate set of plugs for each system. One system is high tension with non-trembler coil: the other system is high-tension magneto driven through gears from crankshaft. Right-hand drive models use Watford magneto (S102CE) and then American Bosch magnetos (33AG); 1922, American Bosch single-battery ignition and Bosch horizontal coil—S45UG; 1924, 6 V. system—S201KF (except for S248KF–S259KF); 1925, American Bosch double battery ignition—S101MK.

COOLING SYSTEM Radiator is made of vertical thin solid-drawn copper tubes, with horizontal copper plates for cooling surface. The fan is belt-driven and the centrifugal water pump is driven from crankshaft through spur gears. (1925, horizontal shutters; 1926, vertical shutters—S326RL). Water capacity, 9 gal.

CARBURETTOR Two-jet type with automatic air valve. Mixture control on steering column quadrant. Water-heated throttle valve (1925, exhaust-heated—S201PX). Starting carburettor.

ENGINE CONTROL Centrifugal governor maintains engine speed set by hand lever on steering column, but can be overridden by accelerator pedal.

STARTER 1921, Starter motor drives layshaft of gearbox by chain through electro-magnetically operated jaw clutch. Epicyclic reduction gears on motor and gearbox (1922, Bijur starter—S98JG: 1924, Westinghouse starter—S201KF).

PETROL SYSTEM Pressure feed, by air pump driven off distributor, and auxiliary hand pump. 21 gal. tank at rear.

TRANSMISSION

GEARBOX Four speeds, with direct drive on top (1925, left-hand drive, three speeds and centre gear change—S101MK).

CLUTCH Cone type.

PROPELLER SHAFT Enclosed in torque tube.

Springfield Silver Ghost Cabriolet.

FINAL DRIVE Ratio 1:3.25 (1922, 1:3.47—2UG, 5UG, 48UG, 73UG, 1922, 1:3.72—119TG, 124TG, 128TG, 5BG onwards).

BRAKES
Footbrake internal expanding type, concentric with handbrake in rear brake drums.

SUSPENSION
Semi-elliptic front springs and cantilever rear springs. 1925, torque reaction dampers—S401MF.

STEERING
Worm and nut. 1925, left drive—S101MK.

WHEELS
Wire wheels. 1922, American wire wheels—40TG.

LIGHTING
1921, Lucas dynamo, belt-driven from gearbox—102CE; 1922, Bijur dynamo—63LG, 1924, Westinghouse dynamo—201KF; 1925, larger dynamo—S101MK.

CHASSIS DETAILS

	Short	Long
Overall length	190¼ in.	196¾ in.
Wheelbase	144 in.	150½ in.
Width of frame	36 in.	36 in.
Track	56 in.	56 in.
Tyres, front	33 × 5	33 × 5
rear	895 × 135	895 × 135

CHASSIS NUMBERS
102CE–107CE; 112NE–123NE; 7AG, 11AG, 15AG, 19AG, 22AG, 26AG, 30AG, 33AG, 36AG, 39AG, 42AG, 45AG, 51AG, 53AG, 57AG, 60AG, 63AG, 66AG, 69AG; 4LG, 7LG, 14LG, 16LG, 19LG, 22LG, 27LG, 30LG, 35LG, 39LG, 43LG, 46LG, 50LG, 53LG, 58LG, 63LG, 67LG, 72LG, 75LG, 79LG, 83LG, 87LG, 90LG, 94LG, 97LG, 100LG, 105LG, 108LG, 111LG, 114LG, 119LG, 123LG; 5MG, 9MG, 14MG, 19MG, 24MG, 28MG, 33MG, 39MG, 42MG, 46MG, 50MG, 55MG, 59MG, 63MG, 68MG, 73MG, 77MG, 82MG, 85MG, 89MG, 95MG, 99MG, 103MG, 108MG, 112MG, 117MG, 120MG, 125MG, 131MG, 136MG, 140MG, 143MG; 4JG, 9JG, 15JG, 21JG, 26JG, 30JG, 35JG, 39JG, 44JG, 49JG, 55JG, 58JG, 59JG, 63JG, 69JG, 74JG, 78JG, 82JG, 87JG, 93JG, 96JG, 98JG, 103JG, 107JG, 112JG, 116JG, 122JG, 128JG, 133JG, 142JG, 147JG, 151JG, 155JG; 2UG, 5UG   1921

8UG, 12UG, 15UG, 18UG, 21UG, 24UG, 27UG, 30UG, 33UG, 36UG, 39UG, 42UG, 45UG, 48UG, 51UG, 53UG, 56UG, 59UG, 62UG, 65UG, 66UG, 68UG, 70UG, 73UG, 76UG, 80UG, 83UG, 86UG, 90UG, 93UG, 96UG; 5SG, 9SG, 14SG, 19SG, 23SG, 28SG, 34SG, 39SG, 43SG, 47SG, 51SG, 55SG, 59SG, 63SG, 68SG, 74SG, 78SG, 82SG, 85SG, 89SG, 94SG, 99SG, 103SG, 108SG, 112SG, 116SG, 120SG, 124SG, 128SG, 132SG, 136SG, 140SG; 4TG, 7TG, 10TG, 18TG, 22TG, 26TG, 30TG, 34TG, 36TG, 40TG, 45TG, 49TG, 53TG, 58TG, 63TG, 67TG, 71TG, 75TG, 79TG, 83TG, 87TG, 91TG, 95TG, 99TG, 105TG, 109TG, 114TG, 119TG, 124TG, 128TG, 133TG; 5BG, 11BG, 16BG, 17BG, 21BG, 22BG, 25BG, 30BG, 35BG, 39BG, 43BG, 44BG, 49BG, 55BG, 60BG, 64BG, 68BG, 74BFG, 80BG, 85BG, 89BG, 95BG, 101BG, 106BG, 111BG, 115BG, 121BG, 126BG, 132BG, 139BG, 145BFG, 150BG, 154BG, 159BG, 164BF,

254BG, 263BG, 275BG; 276KG–364KG	1922
365KG–400KG; 301XH; 326HH–450HH; 51JH–175JG	1923
176KG–300KF; 302LF–400LF; 401MF–450MF	1924
S51LK–S100LK; S100MK–S200MK; S201PK–S300PK; S301–S400RK; S401FK–S408FK	1925
S109ML–S225ML; S226PL–S325PL; S326RL–S403RL	1926

Note – Remaining chassis numbers in the following series (that is, those numbers not listed above) were used for British-built Silver Ghosts:

  CE; NE; AG; LG; MG; JG; UG; SG; TG; 1KG–43KG.

  The number 13 was not used in any series.

NUMBER PRODUCED
1,701

TWENTY
1922–1929

ENGINE

GENERAL Six cylinders, monobloc with detachable cast iron head. $3 \times 4^1/_2$, 3,127 c.c. (21.6 h.p. R.A.C.). Unit construction with gearbox, mounted in U-shaped sub-frame attached to chassis at three points. Compression ratio 4.6:1. Firing order 142635.

VALVES Overhead, operated by push rods. Tappet clearance cold 0.004 in., inlet and exhaust.

CRANKCASE In two parts, the upper half carrying the crankshaft.

CRANKSHAFT Carried in seven bearings with slipper drive vibration damper at front end.

CAMSHAFT Carried in seven bearings.

LUBRICATION Gear type pump delivers oil at full pressure to crankshaft bearings, big ends and gudgeon pins. Relief valve lowers pressure for timing wheel case and overhead valve gear. Oil capacity 10 pints.

IGNITION Coil (1923, stand-by magneto available—60-H-1; 1924, stand-by magneto as standard—GH58). Semi-automatic timing advance; hand lever controls first 35° of advance and governor in distributor takes care of remaining 35°. 12 V. system, 50 A.hr. battery, six sparking plugs. Distributor gap 0.017–0.021 in., magneto gap 0.014 in., plug gap 0.025 in.

COOLING SYSTEM By pump driven through a flexible disc coupling, and by belt-driven fan. Cellular pattern radiator. Horizontal enamelled shutters on most models (1923; nickel silver shutters available—GA12; 1928, vertical shutters—GFN71; 1929, radiator $1^1/_2$ in. higher—GLN22). Water capacity $3^3/_4$ gal.

CARBURETTOR Two-jet type with dash-board control and automatic air valve (1928, mixture control on steering column quadrant—GFN71). Starting carburettor.

ENGINE CONTROL No governor fitted. Hand throttle on steering column in addition to pedal.

20 h.p. 6-cylinder car: fixed head coupé by Caffyns, 1927.

20 h.p. 6-cylinder 2-seater car: open tourer by Hooper, 1926.

20 h.p. 6-cylinder car: Sedanca by Hooper, 1927.

20 h.p. 6-cylinder car: Sedanca by Binder of Paris, 1929.

STARTER Bijur pinion type, with switch operated by pedal.

PETROL SYSTEM 14 gal. fuel tank at rear, feeding carburettor by autovac; dial gauge alongside filler (1928, 2 gal. reserve—GXL42).

TRANSMISSION

GEARBOX In unit with engine. Three speed, with centre-mounted gear lever and handbrake (1924, handbrake to driver's side of gear lever—GAK32; 1925, four speed, right-hand brake and gear lever—GPK1). Oil capacity 2 pints.

CLUTCH Single dry-plate type.

PROPELLER SHAFT Open shaft, with enclosed oil-retaining joints.

FINAL DRIVE Spiral bevel drive, fully floating rear axle. Final drive ratio, 4.6:1 or 4.4:1. Oil capacity 2 pints.

BRAKES

Internal expanding type, foot- and hand-brake of same diameter, side by side, and operating on same drum on rear wheels (1925, four-wheel brakes available, internal expanding, servo operated—GPK1).

CHASSIS LUBRICATION

By oil gun (1929, partial centralised system—GVO11).

1926 Rolls-Royce Twenty, 21 h.p. type open tourer by Barker.

SUSPENSION
Semi-elliptic springs front and rear, fitted with frictional dampers (1926, hydraulic front dampers—GMJ1; 1928, hydraulic rear dampers—GYL1).

STEERING
Worm and nut.

WHEELS
23 in. straight sided (1927, 21 in. well base—GMJ1; 1928, 20 in. well base—GFN71).

Twenty: 3/4 coupé by Salmons on chassis No. GMJ15, 1927.

CHASSIS DETAILS

Overall length 178 in.

Wheelbase 129 in.

Track 54 in. (56 in. for later models).

Tyres $32 \times 4^{1}/_{2}$ (straight side), recommended pressures 45 lb./in.^{2} (1927, $5^{1}/_{4} \times 21$ (well-base), recommended pressures 35 lb./in.^{2} front, 40–45 lb./in.^{2} rear—GMJ1; 1928, 600 $\times$ 20 (well-base), recommended pressures 35 lb./in/^{2} front, 30 lb./in.^{2} rear—GFN71).

Turning circle R.H. 42 ft., L.H. 40 ft.

Ground clearance 8 in.

Weight: chassis (with tyres, battery, fuel, oil and water but excluding spare wheel, lamps and other accessories) 2,305 lb., increasing to 2,635 lb. for later models.

SERIES AND CHASSIS NUMBERS

A, B, C, D, E:	40-G-1–50-G-0; 50-S-1–60-S-0; 60-H-1–70-H-0;	
	70-A-1–80-A-0; 80-K-1–90-K-0; GA1-81; GF1-81;	
	GH1–81; GAK1–81; GMK1–81; GRK1–84;	
	GDK1–81; GLK1–81; GNK1–94	1922–25
F:	GPK1–81; GSK1–81	1925–26
G:	GCK1–81; GOK1–81; GZK1–41	1926
H:	GZK42–81; GUK1–81; GYK1–92	1926
J:	GMJ1–81; GHJ1–81; GAJ1–41	1926–27
K:	GAJ42–81; GRJ1–81; GUJ1–81	1927
L:	GXL1–82; GYL1–81; GWL1–41	1928
M:	GBM1–81; GKM1–82; GTM1–40	1928
NA:	GFN1–82; GLN1–21	1928–9
NB:	GLN22–87; GEN1–41	1929
OA (1–50):	GEN42–82; GVO1–10	1929
OA (51–130):	GVO11–81; GXO3; GXO4, GX06, GXO8	1929

Note – Number 13 as not used in any series.

NUMBER PRODUCED

2,940

THE BRITISH NEW PHANTOM
(PHANTOM I)
1925–1929

ENGINE

GENERAL Six cylinders in two groups of three. $4^{1}/_{4} \times 5^{1}/_{2}$, 7,668 c.c. (43.3 h.p. R.A.C.). Engine attached to main frame by three-point suspension, with friction torque reaction dampers fitted between either side of crankcase and frame. (1928, flexible engine suspension—1WR). One-piece detachable cast-iron cylinder head, all twelve plugs on near side (1928, aluminium cylinder head, six plugs on each side— 1CL). Gearbox as separate unit. Aluminium pistons. Firing order 142635. Compression ratio 4.:1 (1928, 4.2:1—1CL).

VALVES Overhead, pushrod operated. Inlet and exhaust valves interchangeable. Tappet clearance cold 0.003 in., inlet and exhaust (1928, 0.006 in.—1CL).

CRANKCASE Aluminium alloy, in two halves, with crankshaft bearings in upper half.

CRANKSHAFT Carried in seven bearings, with slipper flywheel at front end, including damped spring drive to timing gears (1928, stiffer crankshaft—1AL).

LUBRICATION Gear-type oil pump maintains oil at full pressure to crankshaft bearings, connecting rods and gudgeon pins, relief valve lowers pressure to timing wheel case and overhead valve gear. Extra supply for cylinder walls when throttle more than two-thirds open. Oil capacity 12 pints.

IGNITION Independent coil and magneto systems, both normally used simultaneously. Automatic advance and retard, and hand control. 12 V. system, 75–80 A.hr. battery (1929, battery in frame—1KR). Distributor gap 0.017–0.021 in., magneto gap 0.014 in., plug gap 0.025 in.

COOLING SYSTEM Centrifugal pump and belt-driven fan. Round tube honeycomb radiator, with hand-operated vertical shutters. Temperature gauge on dash-board (1926, some had radiator 1 in. higher—110NC–122NC, 1LC–131LC, 1SC–7SC; 1929, higher radiator standard—1KR). Water capacity 7 gal.

CARBURETTOR Two-jet type (adjustable by mixture control lever on steering wheel) with

Phantom I: tourer on chassis No. 99EF, 1927.

Phantom I: open tourer by Windovers.

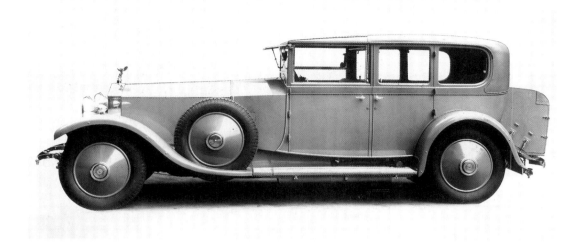

Phantom I: Pullman Limousine de Ville by Barker on chassis No. 95WR, 1928.

automatic air valve. Exhaust heated induction pipe. Starting carburettor.

ENGINE CONTROL Centrifugal governor can be adjusted to maintain any constant speed of engine. Can be overridden by accelerator pedal.

STARTER Drives layshaft of gearbox by chain through jaw clutch. Epicyclic reduction gears on motor and gearbox.

PETROL SYSTEM 18 gal. tank at rear (20 gal. To special order). Autovac. Gauge on tank (1927, 3 gal. reserve—1EF; Hobson hydrostatic petrol gauge on late models).

TRANSMISSION

GEARBOX Four speed. Separate unit from engine, three-point suspension. Oil capacity 8 pints.

CLUTCH Single dry-plate type (1926, light clutch—31NC).

PROPELLER SHAFT Enclosed in two-part tapered torque tube. Universal joint of ring type enclosed in oil-tight steel sphere with projecting arms mounted on heavy brackets suspended to a tubular cross-member of the frame. A bronze sphere, forming the front end of the torque tube, surrounds the steel sphere.

FINAL DRIVE Spiral bevel gears and spur type differential. Fully floating rear axle. Oil capacity 8 pints. Final drive ratio 3.47:1 (1927, 3.25:1 optional—1UF).

258

Phantom I Pullman Limousine.

BRAKES
Internal expanding type. Four-wheel brakes, independent rear brakes operated by hand lever. Friction type servo mounted on gearbox and driven by final shaft to supply 75% of power required to operate brakes (1929, side by side rear brakes—1KR).

CHASSIS LUBRICATION
By oil-gun.

SUSPENSION
Semi-elliptic front springs, cantilever rear springs. Adjustable friction type shock absorbers (1926, front hydraulic shock absorbers—31NC; 1927, rear hydraulic shock absorbers—1RF).

STEERING
Worm and nut.

WHEELS
Wire wheels but steel artillery wheels also available.

CHASSIS DETAILS

	Normal	Long chassis
Overall length	$190^{1/4}$ in.	$196^{3/4}$ in.
Wheelbase	$143^{1/4}$ in.	$150^{1/2}$ in.
Track, front	57in.	$58^{1/2}$ in.
rear	56 in.	$57^{1/2}$ in.

259

1925 Phantom I open tourer by Maythorn.

Width of frame	36 in.	36 in.

Tyres 33×5 (straight side) recommended pressures 55 lb./in.^{2} front, 60 lb./in.^{2} rear; 700 × 21 (well-base), recommended pressures 40 lb./in.^{2} front, 35 lb./in.^{2} rear.

Turning circle, R.H.	53 ft.	55 ft.
L.H.	46 ft.	48 ft.

Ground clearance 8 in.

Weight: Chassis (with tyres, battery, fuel, oil and water but excluding spare wheel, lamps and other accessories) 4,000 lb. Approx.

SERIES AND CHASSIS NUMBERS

Series V:	1MC–122MC, 145MC, 155MC; 1RC–125RC; 1HC–122HC;	
	1LC–132LC; 1SC–7SC	1925–26
X:	8SC–121SC; 1DC–87DC	1926
Y:	88DC–121DC; 1TC–70TC	1926
A2A:	7ITC–121TC; 1YC–50YC	1926
A2B:	51YC–123YC; INC–30NC	1926
B2:	3INC–131NC	1926–27
C2A:	1EF–101EF	1927
C2B:	1LF–102LF	1927
D2A:	1RD–101RF	1927
D2B:	1UF–101UF	1927
E2A:	1EH–102EH	1928
E2B:	1FH–101FH	1928
F2A:	1AL–101AL	1928

F2B:	1CL–103CL	1928–29
G2A:	1WR–101WR	1928
G2B:	102WR–132WR: 1KR–71KR	1928–29
H2:	72KR–132KR; 1OR–91OR	1929

Note – Number 13 was not used in any series.

NUMBER PRODUCED
2,212

Phantom I Sports by Barker 16 EX.

THE SPRINGFIELD NEW PHANTOM (PHANTOM I)

1926–1931

Springfield Phantom I: Speedster phaeton by Brewster on chassis No. S185FR, 1928/29.

ENGINE

GENERAL Six cylinders in two groups of three. $4^{1}/_{4} \times 5^{1}/_{2}$, 7,668 c.c. Engine attached to main frame by three-point suspension, with friction torque reaction dampers fitted between each side of crankcase and frame (1930, modified engine mounting—S101PR). One piece detachable cast-iron cylinder head, all twelve plugs on near side (1928, aluminium cylinder head, six plugs on each side—S101FR). Gearbox as separate unit. Aluminium pistons. firing order 142635. Compression ratio 4.0:1 (1927, 4.2:1—S361FM).

VALVES Overhead, pushrod operated. Inlet and exhaust valves interchangeable. Tappet clearance cold 0.006 in. inlet and exhaust (1928, 0.007 in.—S101FR).

CRANKCASE Aluminium alloy in two halves, with crankshaft bearings in upper half.

CRANKSHAFT Carried in seven bearings, with slipper flywheel at forward end, including damped spring drive to timing gears.

Springfield Phantom I: Sedanca de Ville, 1927.

LUBRICATION Gear-type oil pump maintains oil at full pressure to crankshaft bearings, connecting rods and gudgeon pins. Relief valve lowers pressure to timing wheel case and overhead valve gear. Extra supply for cylinder walls when throttle more than two-thirds open (1928, extra oil coupled to carburettor level—S201FP). Oil capacity 12 pints.

IGNITION Twin coil and twin distributor, with separate sets of plugs. 6V. Automatic advance and retard, and manual control. Distributor gap 0.018–0.020 in., plug gap 0.030 in. Westinghouse generator (1927; Rolls-Royce generator—S216RM–S300RM and S391FM onwards).

COOLING SYSTEM Centrifugal pump and belt-driven fan. Round tube honeycomb radiator, with hand-operated shutters (1929, thermostatically controlled shutters—S201KR). Water capacity 8 gal.

CARBURETTOR Two-jet type (adjustable by mixture control lever on steering column quadrant) with automatic air valve. Exhaust-heated induction pipe (some modified later to water heating). Starting carburettor.

ENGINE CONTROL Centrifugal governor can be adjusted to maintain any constant speed of engine. Can be overridden by accelerator pedal.

STARTER Drivers layshaft of gearbox by chain through jaw clutch. Epicyclic reduction gears on motor and gearbox.

PETROL SYSTEM 18 gal. Tank at rear. Autovac. Hydrostatic petrol gauge.

TRANSMISSION
GEARBOX Three speeds. Separate unit from engine, three-point suspension. Centre gear lever, 1927, second gear ratio changed—S101PM. Oil capacity 8 pints.

CLUTCH Single dry-plate type.

PROPELLER SHAFT Enclosed in two-part tapered torque tube. Universal joint of ring type enclosed in oil-tight steel sphere with projecting arms mounted on heavy brackets suspended to a tubular cross-member of the frame. A bronze sphere, forming the front end of the torque tube, surrounds the steel sphere.

FINAL DRIVE Spiral bevel gears and spur type differential. Fully floating rear axle. Oil capacity 1 gal. Ratio 3.72:1.

BRAKES
Internal expanding type. Four-wheel brakes and independent rear brakes operated by hand lever. Friction type servo gear mounted on gearbox and driven by final shaft to supply 75% of power required to operate brakes.

CHASSIS LUBRICATION
Centralised lubrication system (1928, modified one-shot system to pivots and steering tube—S101FR; 1931, aluminium fittings on one-shot system—S101PR).

SUSPENSION
Semi-elliptic front springs; cantilever rear springs. Adjustable friction-type shock absorbers (1927, R-R. front shock absorbers—S251RM; 1928, R.R. rear shock absorbers—S301KP; 1928, front axle control dampers—S101FR).

STEERING
Worm and nut.

WHEELS
21 in. wire wheels (1928, 20 in. wheels—S301KP).

CHASSIS DETAILS

	Normal	Long chassis
Overall length	190¼ in.	196¾ in.
Wheelbase	143½ in.*	146½ in.
Track, front	57 in.	58½ in.
rear	56 in.	57½ in.
Width of frame	36 in.	36 in.

Tyres 700×21 (1928, 700×20—S302KP) recommended pressure, 40 lb./in.^{2} front, 35 lb./in.^{2} rear.

Castor angle 2°, *camber* 1°, *toe-in* ⅛ in.–¾ in.

Turning circle R.H.	53 ft.	55 ft.
L.H.	46 ft.	48 ft.

Ground clearance 8 in.

Weight: chassis (with tyres, battery, fuel, oil and water but excluding spare wheel, lamps and other accessories) 4,000 lb. approx.

CHASSIS NUMBERS

S400FL–S465FL	1926
S66PM–S200PM; S201RM–S300RM; S301FM–S401FM	1927
S101RP–S200RP; S201FP–S300FP; S301KP–S400KP	1928
S101FR–S200FR	1928–29
S200KR–S300KR; S301LR–S400LR	1929
S401MR–S500MR	1930
S101PR–S241PR	1930–31

NUMBER PRODUCED
1,225

* 1928, all chassis 146½ in.—S301KP

20/25 H.P.
1929–1936

ENGINE

GENERAL Six cylinders, monobloc with detachable head. $3^{1}/_{4} \times 4^{1}/_{2}$, 3,699 c.c. (25.3 h.p. R.A.C.). Unit construction with gearbox mounted in sub-frame attached to chassis at three points. (1930, flexible engine suspension—GLR55; 1932, diamond engine mounting—GBT22; 1935, flexible engine mounting—GAF52). Compression ratio 4.6:1 (1930, 5.25:1—GLR55; 1932, 5.75:1—GKT22). Firing order 142635.

VALVES Overhead, operated by pushrods (1932, heavy exhaust valves—GKT22). Tappet clearance cold 0.004 in., inlet and exhaust.

CRANKSHAFT Carried in seven bearings with slipper drive vibration damper at front end. (1932, vibration damper changed to low-inertia spring drive type—GKT22). 1933, nitralloy crankshaft—GLZ28.

CAMSHAFT Carried in seven bearings. 1932, high lift cams—GKT22.

LUBRICATION Gear-type pump delivers oil at full pressure to crankshaft bearings, big ends and gudgeon pins. Relief valve lowers pressure for timing wheel case and overhead valve gear.

IGNITION Independent coil and stand by magneto systems, used separately. 12V. system, 50 A.hr. battery (1932, two-rate charging system—GBT22; 1933, three-rate charging system—GWX22; 1935, voltage controlled dynamo—GAF32). Distributor gap 0.017—s0.021 in., magneto gap 0.014 in., plug gap 0.020–0.025in.

COOLING SYSTEM By centrifugal pump and belt-driven fan. Hand-controlled shutters, with red light on dash to indicate 90°C (1932, thermostatically controlled radiator shutters and flip-flap bonnet shutters—GBT22). 1931, anti-splash radiator cap—GFT1. 1932, radiator 4 in. deeper—GBT22. 1932, overhanging bonnet—GKT22; 1933, Marston-type radiator—GGA22. 1932, *Staybrite* radiator shell and shutters—GBT22. Water capacity $3^{3}/_{4}$ gal.

CARBURETTOR Two-jet type with steering column control and automatic air valve (1934, single-jet expanding type with control on dash-board—GYD25).

266

20/25 h.p. tourer by Windovers on chassis No. GLR9, 1930.

20/25 h.p. open touring car.

1932 20/25 h.p. drophead coupé by Park Ward.

1930 20/25 h.p. Barker tourer.

ENGINE CONTROL Hand throttle on steering wheel.

PETROL SYSTEM Autovac. 14 gal. tank at rear of chassis. (1932, 18 gal. tank—GAU58). 1930 single level tank—GGP1; 1931, reserve petrol supply—GFT1; 1932, remote control reserve—GBT22. Hobson hydrostatic fuel gauge (1932, electric gauge—GAU58).

TRANSMISSION
GEARBOX Four speeds (1932 synchromesh on third and top—GKT22; 1933, silent second gear—GLZ52; 1936, isolated gear lever—GBK22). Gear ratios 3.73:1, 2.33:1, 1.49:1, 1:1. Oil capacity 2 pints (1932, $4^{1}/_{2}$ pints—GKT22).

CLUTCH Single dry-plate type (1936, Borg and Beck—GTK42).

PROPELLER SHAFT Open shaft with enclosed oil-retaining universal joints (1934, needle bearing propeller shaft—GKC22).

FINAL DRIVE Spiral bevel drive, fully floating rear axle (1936, hypoid rear axle—GTK42). Ratio 4.55:1. Oil capacity 2 pints.

BRAKES
Internal expanding, servo assisted on all four wheels, independent handbrake operating on rear wheels (1933, cast-iron rear brake drums—GEX1; 1933, cast-iron front brake drums—GLZ52).

CHASSIS LUBRICATION
Partial centralised system, and oil gun (1932, complete centralised system—GBT22).

20/25 h.p. Sedanca de Ville.

SUSPENSION
Semi-elliptic springs, front and rear (1932, split piston hydraulic shock absorbers—GBT22; 1934; controllable hydraulic dampers, superimposed manual control–GYD25).

STEERING
Worm and nut (1936, Marles cam and roller—GTK42).

JACKING SYSTEM
1934 D.W.S. permanent screw jacks fitted front single and rear pair—GKC22.

WHEELS
Well-base wire type, 19 in.

CHASSIS DETAILS
Wheelbase 129 in. (1930, 132 in.—GLR1).
Track 56 in.
Tyres 600 × 19, recommended pressures 35 lb./in.^{2}
Turning circle R.H. 47$^1/_2$ ft., L.H. 42 ft.
Ground clearance 8 in.
Weight: chassis (complete with tyres, battery, petrol, oil and water but excluding lamps and other accessories) 2,653 lb., increasing to 2,915 lb. For later models.

20/25 h.p. four-door saloon.

SERIES AND CHASSIS NUMBERS

Series O:	GXO11–111	1929–30
P:	GGP1–81; GDP1–81; GWP1–41	1930
R (1–25):	GLR1–25	1930
R(26–200):	GLR26–82; GSR1–81; GTR1–41	1930
S:	GNS1–81; GOS1–81; GPS1–41	1930–31
TA:	GFT1–81; GBT1–21	1931–32
TB (101–180):	GBT22–82; GKT1–21	1931–32
TB (181–200):	GKT22–41	1932
U:	GAU1–81; GMU1–21	1932
V:	GMU22–81; GZU1–41	1932
W:	GHW1–81; GRW1–81; GAW1–41	1932–33
X:	GEX1–81; GWX1–81; GDX1–41	1933
Y:	GSY1–101	1933
Z:	GLZ1–81; GTZ1–81; GYZ1–41	1933
A2:	GBA1–81; GGA1–81; GHA1–41	1933
B2:	GXB1–81; GUB1–81; GLB1–41	1934
C2:	GNC1–81; GRC1–81; GKC1–41	1934
D2:	GED1–81; GMD1–81; GYD1–69	1934
E2:	GAE1–81; GWE1–83; GFE1–41	1934
F2:	GAF1–81; GSF1–81; GRF1–41	1934–35

G2:	GLG1–81; GPG1–81; GHG1–41	1935
H2:	GYH1–81; GOH1–81; GEH1–41	1935
J2:	GBJ1–81; GLJ1–81; GCJ1–41	1935
K2:	GXK1–81; GBK1–81; GTK1–63	1936

Note – Number 13 was not used in any series.

NUMBER PRODUCED
3,823

ROAD TESTS

	The Autocar 29 May 1931	*The Motor* 18 December 1934	*The Autocar* 7 June 1935
Time speed over ¼ mile	67.66 m.p.h.	74 m.p.h.	76.27 m.p.h.
0–50 through gears	—	20 sec.	21 sec.
0–60 through gears	—	—	$31^{2}/_{5}$ sec.
Petrol consumption	18 m.p.g.	14 m.p.g.	15–17 m.p.g.
Minimum speed in top	—	3 m.p.h.	—

1929 20/25 h.p. Limousine de Ville by Thrupp & Maberly.

PHANTOM II

1929–1935

1931 Rolls-Royce Phantom II 6-cylinder Continental.

ENGINE

GENERAL Six cylinders, in two groups of three. $4^{1}/_{4} \times 5^{1}/_{2}$, 7,688 c.c (43.3 h.p. R.A.C.). One piece detachable aluminium cylinder head. Engine and gearbox in one unit. (1931, diamond engine mounting—62JS; 1935, flexible engine mounting–101TA). Compression ratio 4.75:1 (1931, 5:1—82JS; 1933, 5.25:1—2MY). Firing order 142635.

VALVES Overhead, operated by pushrods (1933, heavy exhaust valves—2MY). Tappet clearance cold 0.003 in., inlet and exhaust.

CRANKSHAFT Carried in seven bearings with slipper drive vibration damper at front end, 1930, vibration damper changed to low-inertia spring drive type.

CAMSHAFT (1933, high-lift cams—102MY; 1935, low-lift camshaft—101TA).

LUBRICATION Gear-type oil pump maintains oil at full pressure to crankshaft bearings, connecting rods and gudgeon pins, relief valve lowers pressure to timing wheel case and

272

Phantom II Limousine.

overhead valve gear. (1931, extra cylinder lubrication for starting—1JS; 1931, *Auto-Kleen* oil filter—62JS.) Oil capacity 16 pints.

IGNITION Independent coil and magneto systems, both normally used simultaneously. Automatic advance and retard, and hand control. Two sparking plugs per cylinder. 12 V. system, 72 A.hr. battery. 1930, new type coil—69GN; 1931, two-rate charge for summer and winter—1JS; 1934, constant voltage dynamo—157RY. Distributor gap 0.017–0.020 in., magneto gap 0.014 in., plug gap 0.025 in.

COOLING SYSTEM Centrifugal pump and belt-driven fan. Manually operated radiator shutters (1931, thermostatically controlled shutters, *Staybrite* radiator shell, single-point radiator suspension and pressure radiator cap—1JS; 1931, flip-flap bonnet shutters—62JS; 1933, overhanging bonnet—46MS). Water capacity 6¾ gal.

CARBURETTOR Two-jet type, adjustable by mixture control on steering column quadrant. With automatic air valve (1931, starting carburettor and extra oil supply interconnected and operated by hand lever on dash-board—1JS; 1933, single-jet semi-expanding type—102MY; 1935, large choke carburettor—101TA). Water-heated induction pipe (1930, exhaust-heated—120GN).

ENGINE CONTROL Centrifugal governor can be adjusted to maintain any constant speed of engine. Can be overridden by pedal (1933, governor deleted—102MY).

1929 Phantom II Cabriolet by Thrupp & Maberly.

1934 Phantom II fixed head coupé by Gurney Nutting.

Phantom II.

STARTER Sequence starter operated by dash-board switch. Starting pinion is fully engaged with teeth on engine flywheel before full power is fed to the turning motor.

PETROL SYSTEM Autovac with engine-driven vacuum pump. Hobson hydrostatic fuel gauge on instrument board. 20 gal. tank (1930, 3 gal. reserve—178GY; 1931, remote control reserve—1JS; 1933, 28 gal. tank and electric petrol gauge—14py).

TRANSMISSION

GEARBOX Unit construction with engine. Four speed (1933, synchromesh fourth and third—46MS; 1933, silent second gear—65MW; 1935, synchromesh second gear—101TA). Gear ratios 3.31:1, 1.98:1, 1.33:1, 1:1 (Continental, 3.49:1).

CLUTCH Single dry-plate type.

PROPELLER SHAFT Open type, with enclosed oil-retaining universal joints.

FINAL DRIVE Hypoid bevel gears, fully floating rear axle. Rear axle ratio 11:41 (1930, 12:41 available—GN68; 1934, 12:41 standard—136SK; first Continentals to 158MS had 11:41 ratio, but 2MY–62UK had 12:41). Oil capacity 2 pints.

BRAKES

Internal expanding type. Four-wheel brakes, independent rear brakes operated by hand lever. Friction type servo mounted on gearbox and driven by final shaft to supply 75% of power required to operate brakes. (1933, cast-iron brake drums—2MY).

SUSPENSION

Semi-elliptic springing front and rear (1933, controllable hydraulic dampers, centrifugally

Phantom II Limousine by Arthur Mulliner.

controlled pump increasing damper loading as road speed increases: super-imposed manual control on steering column quadrant—160PY; 1931, split piston shock absorbers—62JS; 1933, new shock dampers—65MW). Continental models had stiffer five-plate type front and rear springs, auxiliary Hartford front and rear shock dampers on early models and Hartford (André) Telecontrol shock damper to later models (1933, extra shock absorbers only when specified—162PY).

CHASSIS LUBRICATION
Partial centralised system, and oil gun (1931 complete centralised system—1JS).

JACKING SYSTEM
D.W.S. permanent screw jacks fitted front (single) and rear (pair).

STEERING
Worm and nut. Continental chassis fitted with low rake steering column.

WHEELS
Wire type with well-base rims. 21 in. (1930, 20 in.—169GN; 1933, 19 in.—2MY; late Continentals, 17 in.).

Phantom II: tourer by Barker on chassis No. 105MW, 1933.

CHASSIS DETAILS

	Short chassis (also Continental)	Long chassis
Overall length	200 in.	206 in.
Wheelbase	144 in.	150 in.
Track, front	58½ in. (58 ¾ in.—102MY)	
rear	58½ in. (60 in.—1JS; 60¼ in.—102MY)	

Tyres 7.00 × 21 (1930, 7.00 × 20—169GN; 1933, 7.00 × 19–2MY; 7.00 × 17 late Continentals).

Turning circle, R.H.	54 ft. 10 in.	55 ft. 10 in
L.H.	48 ft. 8 in.	50 ft. 6 in.

Ground clearance, 8 in.

Weight: chassis (complete with tyres, battery, petrol, oil and water, but excluding lamps and other accessories), 3,810 lb. approx. (1934, Continental with two up, 5,712 lb.).

SERIES AND CHASSIS NUMBERS

Series J2:	1WJ–133WJ; 1XJ–71XJ	1929–30
KS:	72XJ–204XJ; 1GN–68GN	1929–30
L2:	69GN–202GN; 1GY–68GY	1930
M2:	69GY–205GY; 1GX–68GX	1930
N2 (1–50):	1JS–61JS; 201AJS–276AJS*	1931
NS (51–88):	62JS–84JS: 2MS–44MS; 277AJS–303AJS*	1931–32
	201AMS–224AMS*	1932–34
N2 (89–150):	46MS–170MS	1933
O2 (10–50):	2MY–100MY	1933

*LH steering.

Phantom II, body by Arthur Mulliner Ltd.

O2 (51–150):	102MY–190MY; 3MW–107MW	1933
P2:	2PY–206PY	1933–34
R2:	3RY–211RY	1934
S2:	2SK–196SK	1934
T2:	1TA–201TA	1934–35
U2:	2UK–84UK	1935

Note – Most chassis in MS, MY, PY, SK and UK series were allotted even numbers and most in the MW, RY and TA series were allotted odd numbers.
Number 13, 113, and 213 were not used in any series.

NUMBER PRODUCED
1,672 (Continental 280)

ROAD TESTS
The Autocar, 4 August 1933 (Continental chassis):
    0–70 through gears   28 sec.
    0–60 $19^3/_5$ sec.
    0–50 $14^2/_5$ sec.
    Timed speed over $^1/_2$ mile 92.31 m.p.h.
    Fuel consumption 10–14 m.p.g.
The Motor, 20 March 1934 (Continental chassis):
    0–60 through gears 23 sec.
    Top speed 90.2 m.p.h.
    Fuel consumption 10–12 m.p.g.

BENTLEY 3 ½ LITRE

1933–1936

Bentley 3½-litre drophead coupé with body by Barker and dicky seat, 1935.

ENGINE

GENERAL Six cylinders cast in one block. $3\frac{1}{4} \times 4\frac{1}{2}$, 3,669 c.c. (25.3 h.p. R.A.C.). Detachable cylinder head. Engine and gearbox in one unit, suspended at four points with torsional flexibility (1935, rubber rear engine mounting—B2DG). Compression ratio 6.5:1. Firing order 142635. Aluminium alloy pistons of split skirt type (1935, Aerolite pistons—B2EF).

VALVES Overhead, operated by pushrods. Tappet clearance cold 0.004 in. inlet, 0.006 in. exhaust.

CRANKCASE Aluminium.

CRANKSHAFT Runs in seven white-metal lined bearings. Friction driven flywheel to damp out crankshaft vibration. Connecting rods have white-metal lined big-end bearings and floating for small ends.

Bentley 3½-litre, body by the Carlton Carriage Co., 1935.

CAMSHAFT Carried in seven plain bearings, driven by helical gears.

LUBRICATION Pressure feed to all crankshaft and connecting rod bearings. Positive supply to hollow valve rocker shaft from which valve rockers, pushrods and tappets are lubricated (1935, extra cylinder lubrication—B189DK). Oil capacity $1^3/_4$ gal.

IGNITION Coil and distributor, with automatic and hand control of timing. 50 A.hr. battery. Plug gap 0.020 in.

COOLING SYSTEM Centrifugal pump and belt-driven fan. Thermostatically controlled radiator shutters. 1933, centre point radiator mounting—B33AE.

CARBURETTOR Two S.U.'s. Mixture control at top of steering wheel.

PETROL SYSTEM Dual electric pumps. 18 gal. tank at rear, with 2 gal. reserve controlled by tap on dash-board.

TRANSMISSION
GEARBOX Four forward speeds and reverse, with synchromesh on third and fourth. Right-hand control lever (1935, isolated gear lever—B2FB). Ratios 2.76:1, 1.73:1, 1.24:1, 1:1. Oil capacity $4^1/_2$ pints.

CLUTCH Single dry-plate type.

Bentley 3½-litre, Park Ward body designed by Everden, 1933.

PROPELLER SHAFT Open type, with universal joints (1935, propeller shaft damper—B2DG).

FINAL DRIVE Hypoid gears with bevel differential, full-floating type. Rear axle ratio 10:41 or 11:43. Oil capacity 2 pints.

BRAKES
Internal expanding, operated by mechanical servo. Independent handbrake operating on rear shoes.

CHASSIS LUBRICATION
Centralised system supplied by pedal operated pump mounted on dash-board. Oil capacity 2 pints.

SUSPENSION
Semi-elliptic front and rear (1934, hydraulic shock absorbers automatically controlled by governing device which adjusts loading of dampers to most road speeds but can be overridden by lever at bottom of steering wheel—B1CW).

STEERING
Worm and nut.

JACKING SYSTEM
Separate jacks used.

WHEELS
18 in. detachable wire wheels (1935, Dunlop—B2DG; 1935, Rudge–Whitworth—B2EF). Right- and left-hand threaded hub caps.

CHASSIS DETAILS
Wheelbase 126 in.
Track 56 in.
Overall length 174 in.
Overall width 69 in.
Tyres 5.5 × 18
Ground clearance 6 in.
Turning circle, R.H. 42 ft., L.H. 40 ft. 8 in.
Weight: chassis (with tyres, battery, fuel, oil and water but excluding spare wheel, lamps and other accessories) 2,550 lb. approx.

CHASSIS NUMBERS

B1AE–B203AE	1933–34
B2AH–B198AH; B1BL–B201BL; B2BN–B99BN; B2CR–B200CR	1934
B1CW–B203CW	1934–35
B2DG–B200DG; B1DK–B199DK; B2EF–B200EF; B1EJ–B203EJ; B2FB–B200FB	1935
B1FC–B161FC, B175FC, B185FC, B187GC, B191FC, B201FC, B205FC, B207FC, B209FC, B211FC, B215FC, B217FC, B219FC	1935–36

Note – AE, BL, CW, DK, EJ and FC were odd numbers and AH, CR, DG, EF and FB were even numbers: BN was numbered consecutively. Number 13 was not used in any series.

NUMBER PRODUCED
1,191

25/30 H.P.
1936–1938

25/30 h.p. Park Ward saloon.

ENGINE

GENERAL Six cylinders, monobloc with detachable head. $3^1/_2 \times 4^1/_2$, 4,257 c.c. (29.4 h.p. R.A.C.). Unit construction with gearbox, 1937, deturbulated cylinder head—GRP1. Compression ratio 6:1. Firing order 142635.

VALVES Overhead, operated by pushrods. Tappet clearance cold 0.004–0.006 in. inlet and exhaust.

CRANKCASE In two parts, the upper half carrying the crankshaft.

CRANKSHAFT Carried in seven bearings with low inertia spring drive vibration damper at front end.

CAMSHAFT Carried in seven bearings.

LUBRICATION Gear-type pump delivers oil at full pressure to crankshaft bearings, big ends and gudgeon pins. Relief valve lowers pressure for timing wheel case and over-head valve gear. Oil capacity 14 pints.

283

1936 25/30 h.p. drophead Sedanca coupé by Salmons.

25/30 h.p. 4-door saloon.

25/30 h.p. drophead coupé.

IGNITION Battery and coil, with automatic and manual controls. 12 V. system, 60 A.hr. battery. Six sparking plugs, with standby coil. Distributor gap 0.015–0.018 in., plug gap 0.025 in.

COOLING SYSTEM Centrifugal pump and belt-driven fan. Thermostatically controlled radiator shutters. 1936, improved radiator—GAN1. Water capacity $3^{3}/_{4}$ gal.

CARBURETTOR Stromberg downdraught type, with accelerator pump.

STARTER Bijur pinion type. Motor operates through small planetary reduction gear.

PETROL SYSTEM 18 gal. tank at rear of chassis. Twin S.U. electric pumps on bulkhead.

TRANSMISSION
GEARBOX Four speeds. Synchromesh for third and fourth gears. Oil capacity $4^{1}/_{2}$ pints. Gear ratios 3.1:1, 1.98:1, 1.32:1, 1:1.

CLUTCH Borg and Beck single dry plate.

PROPELLER SHAFT Open shaft, with enclosed needle roller bearings (1936, damper reinstated—GXM72).

FINAL DRIVE Hypoid gears, fully floating rear axle. Ratio 4.55:1. Oil capacity 2 pints.

25/30 h.p. Sedanca de Ville.

BRAKES
Internal expanding, servo operated, on all four wheels, independent handbrake operating on rear wheels.

CHASSIS LUBRICATION
Complete centralised system operated by pedal.

SUSPENSION
Semi-elliptic springs front and rear. Hydraulic shock dampers automatically controlled by hydraulic governing device which adjusts loading of dampers to most road speeds but can be overridden by lever on top of steering wheel.

STEERING
Marles cam and roller.

JACKING SYSTEM
D.W.S. permanent screw jacks fitted front (single) and rear (pair).

WHEELS
Detachable well-base wire wheels, 19 in. rims.

CHASSIS DETAILS
Wheelbase 132 in.
Track $56^5/_{16}$ in.
Tyres 600×19 recommended pressures 35 lb./in.^{2} front and rear.

Turning circle R.H. 47¹/₂ ft., L.H. 42 ft.

Ground clearance 7¹/₂ in.

Weight chassis (with tyres, battery, fuel, oil and water but excluding spare wheel, lamps and other accessories) 2,930 lb. Approx.

SERIES AND CHASSIS NUMBERS

Series L2:	GUL1–82; GTL1–81; GHL1–41	1936–37
M2:	GRM1–81; GXM1–81; GGM1–41	1936–37
N2:	GAN1–81; GWN1–81; GUN1–41	1936–37
O2:	GRO1–81; GHO1–81; GMO1–41	1937
P2:	GRP1–81; GMP1–81; GLP1–41	1937
R2:	GAR1–81; GGR1–81; GZR1–41	1937–38

Note – Number 13 was not used in any series.

NUMBER PRODUCED
1,201

25/30 h.p. saloon.

287

PHANTOM III

1936–1939

1939 Phantom III Coupé Cabriolet by Park Ward.

ENGINE

GENERAL Twelve cylinders in two rows of six forming 60° V. $3^{1}/_{4} \times 4^{1}/_{2}$, 7,340 c.c. (50.7 h.p. R.A.C.). Engine attached to main frame by mounting torsionally insulated by rubber. One-piece detachable heads (1938, four-port heads—3DL2). Gearbox as separate unit. Firing order (A offside; B near bank), A1, B6, A4, B3, A2, B5, A6, B1, A3, B4, A5, B2. Compression ratio 6:1.

VALVES Overhead, pushrod operated from single camshaft mounted in V of crankcase. Double valve springs (1938, single valve springs—3DL2). Hydraulically operated tappets (1938, solid tappets—3DL2). Tappet clearance cold 0.015 in., inlet and exhaust (hydraulic tappets); 0.010 in., inlet and exhaust (solid tappets and conversions from hydraulic tappets).

CRANKCASE Aluminium alloy, with cast-iron 'wet' liners.

CRANKSHAFT Seven bearings with vibration damper at front end (1938, Hall's metal big ends—3DL47).

CAMSHAFT Carried in eight plain bearings.

288

1939 Phantom III Sedanca de Ville by Park Ward.

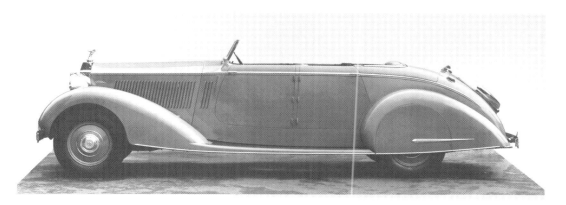

1939 Phantom III tourer by Park Ward.

Phantom III saloon by H. J. Mulliner.

1936 Phantom III Sedanca de Ville by Park Ward 37EX.

Phantom III.

1937 Phantom III Sedanca de Ville by Hooper.

LUBRICATION By gear pump driven by engine. Oil from pressure side of pump passes through filter and heat exchanger and then enters relief valve determining three different pressures obtained by spring-loaded release valves arranged in series: crankshaft and connecting rod bearings at 25 lb. to 35 lb./in.^{2}, overhead valve rocker shafts at 10 lb./in/^{2}, timing wheels at $1^3/_4$ lb./in.^{2} (1938, heat exchanger deleted—3DL4). Oil capacity 22 pints.

IGNITION Dual battery ignition through two independent coils, twin contact breakers in each distributor, with two sparking plugs for each cylinder. Timing is controlled automatically by a centrifugal governor incorporated in each distributor with overriding hand lever control on steering column quadrant. 12 V. constant voltage dynamo, 64 A.hr. battery. Distributor gap 0.030 in., plug gap 0.025 in.

COOLING SYSTEM Centrifugal pump and belt-driven fan. Thermostatically controlled radiator shutters. Water capacity $5^3/_4$ gal.

CARBURETTOR Down-draught double-choke model of plain tube type, with accelerator pump and economiser jet. Air cleaner fitted to air intake.

ENGINE CONTROL Hand throttle on steering column quadrant.

STARTER Starting pinion is engaged before electrical power is applied (1938, modified starter—3DL44).

PETROL SYSTEM 33 gal. Tank at rear of chassis, electrically operated duplex pumps (1936, petrol filter on second cross-member—3AX35; 1937, petrol pump in frame—3CM35). No reserve, but warning light on dash-board indicates when 4 gal. left.

1936 Rolls-Royce Phantom III V 12-cylinder.

TRANSMISSION

GEARBOX Four speed, synchromesh on all gears except first and reverse. Separate unit from engine, mounted on frame cross-members by rubber insulated feet. Ratios 3:1, 1.98: 1.32:1, 1:1. (1938, overdrive—3DL172). Oil capacity 8 pints.

CLUTCH Single dry plate totally enclosed in a two-part casing bolted to crankcase (1937, long clutch plate—3CM79).

PROPELLER SHAFT Open shaft with enclosed oil retaining universal joints and needle-type roller bearings.

FINAL DRIVE Hypoid bevel gears, fully floating rear axle (1937, rubber mounted rear axle—3CM35). Ratio 4.25:1. Oil capacity 2 pints.

BRAKES

Internal expanding, operated from servo-motor driven by transmission and mounted on side of gearbox, on all four wheels. Independent handbrake operating on rear wheels.

CHASSIS LUBRICATION

Centralised system operated by foot pedal.

SUSPENSION

Independent front suspension of wishbone type with helical springs in oil-filled casing also containing controllable hydraulic dampers. Rear suspension semi-elliptic springs, with torsional stabiliser and automatic lubrication. Shock dampers at front and rear

1936 Rolls-Royce Phantom III V 12-cylinder.

automatically controlled by hydraulic governing device which adjusts loading of dampers to most road speeds but can be overridden by lever at bottom of steering wheel.

STEERING
Marles cam and roller.

JACKING SYSTEM
Built-in hydraulic jacks fitted to front suspension and rear axle operated independently or together by hand pump under front passenger's seat. Hydraulic fluid reservoir on bulkhead.

WHEELS
Wire type, with 18 in. well-base rims.

CHASSIS DETAILS
Overall length 191 in.
Overall width 77 in.
Wheelbase 142 in.
Track front 60$^1/_2$ in., *rear* 62$^1/_2$ in.
Tyres 7.00 × 18, 7.50 × 18 to special order. Recommended pressures 35 lb./in.^{2}.
Weight chassis only (excluding spare wheels, lamps and other accessories), 4,050 lb.
Turning circle 48 ft.
Ground clearance 7$^1/_2$ in.

SERIES AND CHASSIS NUMBERS
Series A: 3AZ20–238; 3AX1–201   1936
    B: 3BU2–200; 3BT1–203   1937
    C: 3CP2–200; 3CM1–203   1937–38
    D: 3DL2–200; 3DH1–9   1938–39

AZ, BU, CP and DL were even numbers only (except for 3AZ43, 3AZ47); AX, BT, CM and DH were odd numbers only (except for 3AX34, 3AX36, 3CM108, 3CM112). Numbers 13 and 113 were not used in any series.

NUMBER PRODUCED
710

ROAD TESTS
The Autocar 2 October 1936
    Fuel consumption 10 m.p.g.
    Max. speed over $^1/_4$ mile 91.84 m.p.h.
    From rest to 30 through gears   5.5 sec.
                        50   12.6 sec.
                        60   16.8 sec.
                        70   24.4 sec.
    Acceleration, sec.

Gear	10–30	20–40	30–50
4	7.4	7.7	82.
3	5.7	6.3	6.6
2	4.2	5.0	—

Note – The first PIIIs were fitted with four Claudel carburettors.

BENTLEY 4¼ LITRE

1936–1939

Bentley 4½-litre saloon.

ENGINE

GENERAL Six cylinders cast in one block. $3^{1}/_{2} \times 4^{1}/_{2}$, 4,257 c.c. (29.4 h.p. R.A.C.). Detachable cylinder head (1937, deturbulated head—B1KU). Engine and gearbox in one unit, suspended at four points with torsional flexibility. Compression ratio 6.8:1 (1937, 6.4:1—B101KU). Firing order 142635. Aluminium alloy pistons of split-skirt type.

VALVES Overhead valves operated by pushrods. Tappet clearance cold, exhaust 0.006 in., inlet 0.004 in. (1939, 0.010 in.—B2MR).

CRANKCASE Aluminium.

CRANKSHAFT Runs in seven bearings with aluminium-alloy bearing metal. Friction-driven flywheel to damp out crankshaft vibration. Connecting rods have aluminium-alloy big-end bearings and bronze bushes for small ends.

CAMSHAFT Carried in seven plain bearings and driven by single helical gears.

LUBRICATION Pressure feed to all crankshaft and connecting rod bearings. Positive supply to hollow valve-rocker shaft, from which valve rockers, pushrods and tappets are lubricated. Oil capacity 14 pints.

IGNITION Battery, coil and distributor, with automatic and hand control of timing. 12 V. system, with automatic regulation of dynamo output by vibrator control. 60 A.hr. battery. Plug gap 0.020 in., distributor gap 0.018 in.

COOLING SYSTEM Centrifugal pump and belt-driven fan. Thermostatically controlled radiator shutters (1939, thermostat and dummy shutters—B2MR). Water capacity 3 gal.

CARBURETTOR Two S.U.s. Mixture control on steering wheel.

PETROL SYSTEM Feed from 18 gal. Tank at rear of chassis by electrically operated duplex pump. 2 gal. reserve, brought into operation by change-over tap on dash-board.

TRANSMISSION
GEARBOX Four forward speeds and reverse, with synchromesh on third and fourth. In one unit with engine. Right-hand control lever. Ratios 2.76:1, 1.73:1, 1.24:1, 1:1 (1939 2.38:1, 1.49:1, 1:1, 0.85:1—B2Mr). Oil capacity 4 pints.

CLUTCH Borg and Beck single-plate dry type.

PROPELLER SHAFT Open type, with needle-type universal joints.

FINAL DRIVE Hypoid gears with bevel differential, full-floating type. Rear axle ratio 10:41 (1939, 10:43—B2MR).

BRAKES
Internal expanding, operated by mechanical servo. Independent handbrake operating on rear wheels.

CHASSIS LUBRICATION
Centralised chassis lubrication system supplied by pedal-operated pump mounted on dash-board.

SUSPENSION
Semi-elliptic springs front and rear. Hydraulic shock dampers automatically controlled by hydraulic governing device which adjusts loading of dampers to most road speeds but can be overridden by lever on bottom of steering wheel.

STEERING
Worm and nut (1939, Marles steering—B2MR).

JACKING SYSTEM
External jack carried in toolkit.

WHEEL
18 in. detachable wire wheels. Right- and left-hand threaded hub caps.

CHASSIS DETAILS
Overall length 154 in.
Overall width 69 in.
Wheelbase 126 in.
Track 56 in.
Ground clearance 6 in.
Turning circle R.H. 42 ft., L.H. 40 ft. 8 in.
Tyres 5.50 × 18 (1939, 6.50 × 17—B2MR) recommended pressures 30 lb./in.^{2}.
Weight: chassis (with tyres, battery, fuel, oil and water but excluding spare wheel, lamps and
    other accessories) 2,558 lb. approx.

CHASSIS NUMBERS
B2GA–B260GA; B1GP–B203GP; B2HK–B200HK; B1HM–B203HM;
    B2JD–B200JD   1936
B1JY–B203JY; B2KT–B200KT; B1KU–B203KU; B2LS–B204LS   1937
B1LE–B203LE   1938
B2MR–B200MR; B1MX–B205MX   1939

Note – GP, HM, JY, KU, LE and MX use odd numbers only and GA, HK, JD, KT, LS and
    MR even numbers: B2GA–B6GA are consecutive numbers, and then
    B8GA–B206GA are even numbers only. Number 13 was not used.

NUMBER PRODUCED
1,241

WRAITH
1938–1939

1939 Rolls-Royce Wraith saloon by James Young.

ENGINE

GENERAL Six cylinders, monobloc with detachable head, $3^{1}/_{2} \times 4^{1}/_{2}$, 4,257 c.c. (29.4 h.p. R.A.C. rating). Unit construction with gearbox in one unit, suspended at front by raised arch, with rubber mounting at rear. Compression ratio 6:1. Firing order 142635.

VALVES Overhead, operated by pushrods. Tappet clearance cold 0.008 in., inlet and exhaust.

CRANKCASE In two parts, the upper half carrying the crankshaft.

CRANKSHAFT Carried in seven bearings, with vibration damper at front end.

CAMSHAFT Carried in seven bearings.

LUBRICATION Gear type pump delivers oil at full pressure to crankshaft bearings, big ends and gudgeon pins. Relief valve lowers pressure for timing wheel case and overhead valve gear. Oil capacity 14 pints.

IGNITION Battery and coil with automatic control system. 12 V. 60 A.hr. battery. Six sparking plugs, stand-by coil fitted. Distributor gap 0.017–0.021 in., plug gap 0.025 in.

COOLING SYSTEM By centrifugal water pump and belt-driven fan. Thermostatically operated radiator shutters. Water capacity $2^3/_4$ gal.

CARBURETTOR Down-draught, with fixed jet. Idler system has adjustable needle, and accelerator pump is fitted. Air intake and silencer of R-R. design.

ENGINE CONTROL Hand throttle on steering wheel.

STARTER Of R-R. manufacture.

PETROL SYSTEM 18 gal. Tank at rear of chassis. Electrically operated duplex fuel pumps placed inside chassis frame. No reserve, but warning light on dash-board to indicate when fuel is low.

TRANSMISSION
GEARBOX Four forward gears and reverse. Synchromesh on all but first and reverse. Short right-hand gear lever isolated from engine. Oil capacity 5 pints. Gear ratios 3:1, 2.01:1, 1.35:1, 1:1.

CLUTCH Single dry-plate type.

PROPELLER SHAFT Totally enclosed all-metal universal joints, trunnions fitted with needle-type roller bearings.

FINAL DRIVE Hypoid gears, full floating, with road wheels mounted on extension of axle tubes. Ratio 4.25:1. Oil capacity 2 pints.

BRAKES
Internal expanding operated by mechanical servo in form of friction disc clutch rotated by transmission and mounted on side of gearbox. Handbrake operates on rear wheels (only model where same shoes are used for hand and foot operation).

CHASSIS LUBRICATION
Complete centralised system operated by pedal.

SUSPENSION
Rear semi-elliptic springs, front independent, with helical springs enclosed in casing which forms spring housing and hydraulic shock damper body. Hydraulic shock dampers have degree of damping automatically controlled by governor in accordance with speed of car

but can be manually overrridden by lever on top of steering wheel. Stabilising torsion rod coupled to shock damper arms.

STEERING
Marles cam and roller.

JACKING SYSTEM
Built-in hydraulic jacks fitted to front suspension and rear axle operated independently or together by hand pump under front passenger's seat. Hydraulic fluid reservoir on bulkhead.

WHEELS
Wire type with 17 in. well-base rims. Self-locking knock-off type hub caps.

1939 Rolls-Royce Wraith saloon by H.J. Mulliner.

CHASSIS DETAILS

Overall length 203 in.

Overall width 74 in.

Wheelbase 136 in.

Track $58^1/_2$ in. front, $59^1/_2$ in. rear.

Tyres 6.50×17, recommended pressures 30 lb./in^2

Turning circle $46^1/_2$ ft.

Ground clerance 7 in.

Weight: chassis (with tyres, battery, fuel, oil and water but excluding spare wheel, lamps and other accessories) 3,038 lb. (approx.).

CHASSIS NUMBERS AND SERIES

Series A: WXA1–109	1938
Series B: WRB1–81; WMB1–81; WLB1–41	1938–39
Series C: WHC1–81; WEC1–81; W25	1939

NUMBER PRODUCED

492

ROAD TEST

The Motor, 4 October 1938

    10–30 m.p.h. 4th gear, 9 sec.

                    3rd gear, 7 sec.

    10–50 m.p.h. 4th gear, 20 sec.

                    3rd gear, 15.7 sec.

  0–30 through gears 8 sec.

  0–50 through gears 16.4 sec.

  Standing $^1/_4$ mile 25 sec.

BENTLEY MK V

1939–1941

1940 Mk. V Bentley saloon by Park Ward in wartime use by a company official.

ENGINE

GENERAL Six cylinders cast in one block. $3\frac{1}{2} \times 4\frac{1}{2}$, 4,257 c.c. (29.4 h.p. R.A.C). Aluminium alloy pistons. Detachable cylinder head. Engine and gearbox in one unit. Compression ratio 6.4:1, firing order 142635.

VALVES Overhead valves, operated by pushrods. Valve rocker clearance cold 0.006 in., inlet and exhaust.

LUBRICATION Gear type pump delivers oil under pressure to all crankshaft and connecting rod bearings. Dual relief valve provides positive low-pressure supply to valve rocker shaft and to rockers, pushrods and tappets. Oil capacity 14 pints.

IGNITION Battery with automatic timing control (some chassis have hand control also). 12 V. system. Automatic regulation of dynamo output by vibrator control. 55 A.hr. battery. Plug gap 0.025 in.

302

Mk. V: saloon by Park Ward on chassis No. B16AW, 1940.

COOLING SYSTEM By pump and belt-driven fan, with thermostatic control. Water capacity 3 gal.

CARBURETTOR Two S.U. carburettors, with automatic closing of starting carburettor as engine becomes warm.

STARTER Pinion provides gentle engagement.

PETROL SYSTEM Dual electric pump mounted in offside of frame. 16 gal. Capacity (Corniche, 19 gal.). Warning light on dash indicates last 2 gal. of supply.

TRANSMISSION

GEARBOX In one unit with engine. Four forward speeds and reverse, with synchromesh on second, third (direct) and top (overdrive). Right-hand gear lever. Gear ratios 2.44:1, 1.43:1, 1:1, 0.836:1. Oil capacity 5 pints.

CLUTCH Single dry-plate type.

PROPELLER SHAFT Open, divided, with needle type universal joints and sealed intermediate bearing.

FINAL DRIVE Hypoid gears with bevel differential, fully floating rear axle (Corniche, semi-floating). Rear axle ratio 4.30:1 (Corniche 3.73:1). Oil capacity $1^{1}/_{3}$ pints.

BRAKES
Internal expanding type, assisted by mechanical servo.

CHASSIS LUBRICATION
Centralised lubrication system. Oil capacity of reservoir 2 pints.

SUSPENSION
Semi-elliptic rear, independent front with open helical springs and hydraulic dampers. Degree of damping of rear dampers adjustable by hand control above steering wheel.

STEERING
Cam and roller.

WHEELS
16 in. detachable wire wheels (Corniche, steel disc wheels with 5-bolt attachment). Right- and left-hand threaded hub caps (Corniche, right- and left-hand threads with snap-on hub discs).

CHASSIS DETAILS
Overall length 191 in.
Overall width 69 in.

Mk. V saloon by H.J. Mulliner.

Wheelbase 124 in.

Track, front 56¼ in., *rear* 58 in.

Ground clearance 6½ in. (unladen).

Turning circle, R.H. 43 ft., L.H. 44⅓ ft.

Tyres 6.50 × 16, recommended pressures 25 lb./in.^{2} front, 28 lb./in.^{2} rear (Corniche, for high-speed work in summer 30 lb./in.^{2} front, 35 lb lb./in.^{2} rear).

Weight: chassis (with tyres, battery, fuel, oil and water but excluding spare wheel lamps and other accessories) 2,719 lb. approx.

CHASSIS NUMBERS

B2AW–B38AW (even)   1939–41

NUMBER PRODUCED

19 (15 Standard, 4 Corniche).

BENTLEY MK VI

1946–1952

Mk. VI saloon coming off the production line.

ENGINE

GENERAL Six cylinders, $3^{1}/_{2} \times 4^{1}/_{2}$, 4,257 c.c. (1951, $3^{5}/_{8} \times 4^{1}/_{2}$, 4,566 c.c.—B2MD. R.A.C. rating 29.4 h.p. (1951, 31.5 h.p.—B2MD; 1954, 33.7 h.p.—BC1D). Aluminium alloy pistons. Firing order 142635. Compression ratio 6.4:1.

VALVES Overhead inlet valves, pushrod operated; side exhaust valves, operated from camshaft. Inlet valve rocker clearance 0.006 in., exhaust tappet clearance 0.012 in.

CAMSHAFT Driven by single helical fabric gears (1950, aluminium gears—B2HR) and carried in four plain bearings.

CRANKSHAFT Seven bearings, copper-lead-indium lined steel shells.

306

LUBRICATION Pressure feed to all crankshaft and connecting rod bearings at 25 lb./in.^{2}. Relief valve providing positive low-pressure supply to valve rocker shaft, from which inlet valves, pushrods and tappets are lubricated. By-pass filter (1951, full-flow filter—B2MD). Oil capacity 16 pints.

IGNITION Automatic regulation of dynamo output by vibrator control. 12 V. system with 55 A.hr. battery. Plug gap 0.025 in.

COOLING SYSTEM Centrifugal pump circulation and fan, thermostatically controlled. Water capacity 3¼ gal.

CARBURETTOR Right-hand-drive models, twin S.U.s 1½ in. bore (1950, 1¾ in.—B83HP); left-hand-drive models, Stromberg downdraught.

STARTER Reduction gear and pinion providing gentle engagement.

PETROL SYSTEM Twin electrical pumps. Petrol capacity 18 gal.

TRANSMISSION

GEARBOX Four forward speeds and reverse. Synchromesh on second, third and top, right-hand control lever for right-hand-drive cars, steering column mounted lever for left-hand drive cars. Ratios 2.99:1, 2.05:1, 1.33:1, 1:1 (1952, 3.80:1, 2.34:1, 1.28:1, 1:1).

CLUTCH Single-dry plate, 10 in. long type (1950, 11 in. light type—B2HR; 1951, 11 in. heavy type—B300LJ).

PROPELLER SHAFT Open type, fitted with needle-bearing universal joints.

FINAL DRIVE Semi-floating. Hypoid gears with differential. Oil capacity 1¾ pints. Rear axle ratio 3.73:1.

BRAKES

Internal expanding, hydraulic front, mechanical rear, servo assisted. Handbrake operates on rear wheels.

CHASSIS LUBRICATION

Centralised system supplied by foot-operated pump and reservoir on dash-board.

SUSPENSION

Independent front by open helical springs in combination with hydraulic shock dampers, semi-elliptic rear with controllable hydraulic shock dampers.

Fixed head coupé by Freestone and Webb, 1947.

STEERING
Cam and roller (1950, modified geometry—B1GT).

JACKING SYSTEM
Portable mechanical jack.

WHEELS
Steel, 16×5 well-base rims secured with five nuts.

CHASSIS DETAILS

*Overall length**	192 in., $196^{1}/_{2}$ in.
width	71 in.
height	$64^{1}/_{2}$ in.
Wheelbase	120 in.
Track, front	$56^{1}/_{2}$ in.
rear	$58^{1}/_{2}$ in.
Turning circle	$42^{1}/_{2}$ ft.
Weight, kerbside	4,088 lb.
Tyres	6.50×16
Recommended pressures,	
front	25 lb./in.^{2}
rear	30 lb./in.^{2}

*Depending on type of bumper.

1946 Mk. VI saloon, pressed steel body.

SERIES AND CHASSIS NUMBERS
MK. VI

A	Series:	B2AK–B254AK; B1AJ–B247AJ	1946–47
B	Series:	B2BH–B400BH; B1BG–B401BG	1947
C	Series:	B2CF–B500CF; B1CD–B501CD	1947–48
D	Series:	B2DA–B500DA; B1DZ–B501DZ	1948–49
E	Series:	B2EY–B500EY; B1EW–B501EQ	1949
F	Series:	B2FV–B500FV; B1FU–B601FU	1949–50
G	Series:	B1GT–B401GT	1950
H	Series:	B2HR–B250HR; B1HP–B251HP	1950
J	Series:	B2JO–B250JO; B1JN–B251JN	1950–51
K	Series:	B2KM–B200KM; B1KL–B201KL	1951
L	Series:	B2LJ–B499LJ; B1LH–B401LH	1951

M Series: B2MD–B400MD; B1MB–B403MB   1951
N Series: B2NZ–B500NZ; B1NY–B501NY   1951–52
P Series: B2PV–B300PV; B1PU–B302PU   1952

Notes – Chassis series starting with the number 1 use odd numbers only and those starting with the number 2 use even numbers only but continental models use all numbers. Left-hand-drive cars have L before chassis letters (B46LEY, BC8LH, for example). The number 13 was not used in any series. 1951, twin exhaust system on right-hand drive models—B2MD. Rear wing valances optional on all Mk VIs. 1951, side scuttle ventilators—B29MD.

NUMBER PRODUCED
5,201

SILVER WRAITH

1947–1959

Rolls-Royce Silver Wraith Limousine by H. J. Mulliner.

ENGINE

GENERAL Six cylinders, $3^1/_2 \times 4^1/_2$, 4,257 c.c. (1951, $3^5/_8 \times 4^1/_2$, 4,566 c.c.—WOF1; 1955, $3^3/_4 \times 4^1/_2$, 4,887 c.c.—DLW163). R.A.C. rating 29.4 h.p. (1951, 31.5 h.p.—WOF1; 1955 33.7 h.p.—DLW163). Compression ratio 6.4:1 (1952, 6.4:1 or 6.75:1 according to cylinder head—WVH1 (short wheelbase), BLW1 (long wheelbase); 1953, 6.75:1—CLW1; 1957, 8:1—FLW60). Firing order, 142635.

VALVES Overhead inlet valves, pushrod operated; side exhaust valves, operated from camshaft. Tappet clearances cold, inlet 0.006 in., exhaust 0.012 in.

CYLINDER HEAD Aluminium alloy.

1949 Rolls-Royce Silver Wraith Cabriolet by James Young.

CRANKSHAFT Seven bearings with spring-centre flywheel and torsional vibration damper.

CAMSHAFT Driven by single helical fabric gears (1950, aluminium gears—WHD87) and carried in four plain bearings.

LUBRICATION Submerged pump sends oil to two-stage relief valve, the first stage of which controls supply to crankshaft and other main bearings at full pressure and the second stage of which controls supply at reduced pressure to valve rockers, pushrods and tappets. Oil level recorded on dash-board, with dipstick also provided. By-pass oil filter (1951, full-flow filter—WOF1). Oil capacity, 2 gal.

IGNITION Automatic regulation of dynamo output by vibrator control. 12 V. system with 55 A.hr. battery. Distributor gap 0.020 in., plug gap 0.025 in.

COOLING SYSTEM Centrifugal pump, with thermostatically controlled radiator shutters. Water capacity, 4 gal.

CARBURETTOR Short-wheelbase model, dual choke downdraught Stromberg (1952, s.d. Zenith—WSG7). Long-wheelbase model, single downdraugth Zenith (1956, twin S.U.s with $1^3/_4$ in. bore—FLW1; 2 in. bore—GLW60).

Silver Wraith: sports saloon by Freestone and Webb on chassis No. WVA19, 1947.

STARTER Geared pinion for silent engagement.

PETROL SYSTEM Twin electric pumps, tank at rear. Petrol capacity, 18 gal.

TRANSMISSION

GEARBOX Four speeds (1952, automatic gearbox optional—H series (short wheelbase); standard—late D series (long wheelbase). Ratios 2.98:1, 2.02:1, 1.34:1, 1:1 (1952, 3.82:1, 2.63:1, 1.45:1, 1:1 with automatic gearbox). Oil capacity 6 pints (fluid capacity 20 pints with automatic gearbox).

CLUTCH Single dry-plate 10 in. long type (1947, 11 in. heavy type—WTA56), centrifugally assisted.

PROPELLER SHAFT Divided type.

FINAL DRIVE Hypoid rear axle, with semi-floating shafts. Oil capacity, $1^{3}/_{4}$ pints. Ratio SWB 11:41 (1951, 12:41 optional on some export cars—F series), LWB 11:41 and 12:41 optional (1955, 8:34—E series; 1956, 9:35—F series).

Rolls-Royce Silver Wraith Cabriolet by Park Ward.

BRAKES
Mechanical servo controlled from gearbox. Hydraulic front and mechanical rear operation.

CHASSIS LUBRICATION
Centralised system, operated by lever mounted on dash.

SUSPENSION
Independent front, with cross-coupled hydraulic dampers. Rear, half-elliptic, with hydraulic dampers controlled from steering wheel.

STEERING
Cam and roller (1950, modified geometry—WME1). 1956, power steering optional—FLW1.

JACKING SYSTEM
Portable mechanical jack.

WHEELS
Steel, 17 × 5 or 16 × 6.5 well-base rims.

CHASSIS DETAILS

	Short	Long
Overall length	200 in.	206 in.

Rolls-Royce Silver Wraith saloon by Hooper.

Overall width	75 in.	77 in.
Wheelbase	127 in.	133 in.
Track, front	58 in.	58 in.
rear	60 in.	64 in.
Tyres	6.50×17	7.50×16
	Recommended	Recommended
	pressures,	pressures,
	24 lb/in.² front,	24 lb/in.² front,
	33 lb./in.² rear	33 lb./in.² rear
	(1951, 7.50×16 on certain	
	export cars—WOF37)	
Turning circle	43 ft. 5 in.	45 ft. 5 in.
Ground clearance	8¼ in.	8¼ in.

SERIES AND CHASSIS NUMBERS

SHORT WHEELBASE

Series A	WTAI–85; WVA1–81; WYA1–87	1946–47
Series B	WZB1–65; WAB1–65; WCB1–73	1947–48
Series C	WDC1–101; WFC1–101; WGC1–101	1948–50
Series D	WHD1–101	1950
Series E	WLE1–35; WME1–96	1950–51
Series F	WOF1–76	1951
Series G	WSG1–76	1951–52
Series H	WVH1–116	1952

LONG WHEELBASE

Series A	ALW1–51	1951
Series B	BLW21–101	1952–53
Series C	CLW1–43	1953–54
Series D	DLW1–166	1954–55
Series E	ELW1–101	1955–56
Series F	FLW1–101	1956–57
Series G	GLW1–26	1957
Series H	HLW1–52	1958

Note – Left-hand drive cars have L before chassis letters (LWFC65, LFLW96, for example). The number 13 was not used in any series.

NUMBER PRODUCED
Short wheelbase, 1,144; long wheelbase, 639.

ROAD TEST
The Autocar 9 December 1949
Maximum speeds
Top (not given)
3rd 68 m.p.h.
2nd 44 m.p.h.
1st 24 m.p.h.

SILVER DAWN

1949–1955

Silver Dawn Special Saloon by Pininfarina, 1951.

ENGINE

GENERAL Six cylinders, $3^{1}/_{2} \times 4^{1}/_{2}$ (1951, $3^{5}/_{8} \times 4^{1}/_{2}$—SFC2). 4,257 c.c. (1951, 4,566 c.c.—SFC2). R.A.C. rating 29.4 h.p. (1951, 31.5 h.p.). Compression ratio 6.4:1 (1953, 6.75:1—SMF62). Firing order 142635.

VALVES Overhead inlet, side exhaust. Inlet rocker clearance 0.006 in., exhaust tappet clearance 0.012 in.

CRANKSHAFT Shaft main bearings, copper-lead-indium lined steel shells.

CAMSHAFT Driven by single helical fabric gears (1951, aluminium gears—LSCA23) and carried in four plain bearings.

Silver Dawn drophead coupé by Park Ward.

LUBRICATION Pressure feed to all crankshaft and connecting rod bearings by gear type pump with relief valve providing positive low-pressure supply to valve rocker shaft, from which inlet valves, pushrods and tappets are lubricated. Oil capacity 16 pints. By-pass filter (1951, full-flow filter—SFC2).

IGNITION Automatic regulation of dynamo output. 12 V. system. 55 A.hr. battery. Non-detachable plugs, gap 0.025 in.

COOLING SYSTEM Centrifugal pump circulation and fan. Thermostatically controlled. Water capacity 4 gal.

CARBURETTOR Stromberg downdraught (1952, Zenith—LSFC102).

STARTER Reduction gear and pinion providing gentle engagement.

PETROL SYSTEM Dual electric pump mounted in frame. Petrol capacity 18 gal.

TRANSMISSION

GEARBOX Four speeds (1952, automatic box optional—E series; 1953, standard—F series). Ratios 2.98:1, 2.1:1, 1.34:1, 1:1 (1952, 3.82:1, 2.63:1, 1.45:1, 1:1 with automatic gearbox). Oil capacity 6 pints (1952, fluid capacity 20 pints with automatic gearbox).

Silver Dawn standard saloon.

CLUTCH Single dry-plate 10 in. long type (1950, 11 in. light type—SCA27; 1951, 11 in. heavy type—SDB76).

PROPELLER SHAFT Universal joints fitted with needle roller bearings.

FINAL DRIVE Semi-floating type. Hypoid gears. Ratio 11:41 (1954, 12:41—SRH2). Oil capacity $1\frac{3}{4}$ pints.

BRAKES
Hydraulic operation on front wheels, mechanical on rear, servo assisted. Handbrake operates on rear wheels.

CHASSIS LUBRICATION
Centralised system supplied by foot-operated pump and reservoir on dash-board.

SUSPENSION
Independent front by open helical springs, assisted and controlled by hydraulic dampers. Rear, semi-elliptic with controllable hydraulic dampers.

STEERING
Cam and roller (1950, modified geometry—SCA1).

JACKING SYSTEM
Portable mechanical jack.

WHEELS
Steel 16 × 5 well-base rims secured by five nuts.

CHASSIS DETAILS
Overall length 192 in. or 196$^{1}/_{2}$ in., according to style of bumper fitted. (1952, 199$^{1}/_{2}$ in., 203$^{1}/_{2}$ in. or 210 in.—SKE2).
Wheelbase 120 in.
Track, front 56$^{1}/_{2}$ in., *rear* 58$^{5}/_{8}$ in.
Overall width 71 in., *height* 65 in.
Tyres 6.50 × 16. Recommended pressures 25 lb./in.^{2} front, 33 lb./in.^{2} rear.
Turning circle 41$^{1}/_{4}$ ft.
Ground clearance 7$^{1}/_{2}$ in.
Chassis weight 3,575 lb.
Riveted frame (1953, welded—SNF1).

SERIES AND CHASSIS NUMBERS
A series	SBA2–SBA138; SCA1–SCA63	1949–51
B Series	SDB2–SDB140	1951
C Series	SFC1–SFC160	1951–52
D Series	SHD1–SHD60	1952
E Series	SKE2–SKE50; SLE1–SLE51	1952–53
F Series	SMF2–SMF76; SNF1–SNF125	1953–54
G Series	SOG2–SOG100; SPG1–SPG101	1954
H Series	SRH2–SRH100; STH1–STH101	1954
J Series	SUJ2–SUJ130; SVJ1–SVJ133	1954–55

Note – Chassis series starting with the number 1 use odd numbers only, and those starting with the number 2 use even numbers only. Left-hand-drive cars have L before chassis letters (LSCA23, for example). Number 13 was not used in any series.

NUMBER PRODUCED
785

PHANTOM IV

1950–1956

Phantom IV Limousine owned by H.M. Queen Elizabeth II.

ENGINE

GENERAL Eight cylinders in line, $3^1/_2 \times 4^1/_2$, 5,676 c.c. (39.2 h.p. R.A.C.). Compression ratio 6.41:1. Firing order 16258374. Aluminium alloy pistons of split-skirt type.

VALVES Overhead inlet valves, pushrod operated; side exhaust valves, operated from camshaft. Inlet valve rocker clearance cold 0.006 in., exhaust tappet clearance 0.012 in.

CAMSHAFT Driven by single helical aluminium gears and carried in six plain bearings. Rubber tuned harmomic balancer to eliminate crankshaft vibration.

CRANKSHAFT Nine main bearings, copper-lead-indium lined steel shells.

LUBRICATION Pressure feed by gear type pump to all crankshaft and connecting rod bearings at 25 lb./in/^{2}. Relief valve provides positive low-pressure supply to valve rocker shaft, from which inlet valves, pushrods and tappets are lubricated. Oil capacity 18 pints. By-pass filter (1953, full-flow filter—4BP1).

IGNITION Automatic regulation of dynamo output. 12 V. system, with 78 A.hr. battery. Plug gap 0.025 in.

COOLING SYSTEM Centrifugal pump and fan. Radiator shutters thermostatically controlled. Water capacity $5\frac{1}{2}$ gal.

CARBURETTOR Stromberg dual downdraught.

STARTER Reduction gear and pinion providing gentle engagement.

PETROL SYSTEM Two sets of dual electric pumps mounted in frame: forward set is for main supply, and rear set is for 4 gal. reserve. Main petrol capacity 23 gal.

TRANSMISSION

GEARBOX Four forward speeds and reverse, with right-hand control lever. Synchromesh on second, third and top. Ratios 2.98:1, 2.02:1, 1.34:1, 1:1. Oil capacity 6 pints.

CLUTCH Single dry-plate 11 in. 'heavy' type.

PROPELLER SHAFT Universal joints fitted with needle roller bearings.

FINAL DRIVE Semi-floating type. Hypoid gears. Rear axle ratio 4.25:1. Oil capacity 3 pints.

BRAKES
Hydraulic front, mechanical rear assisted by servo. Handbrake operates on rear wheels.

CHASSIS LUBRICATION
Centralised system supplied by foot-operated pump and reservoir on dash-board.

SUSPENSION
Independent front suspension by open helical springs in combination with hydraulic shock dampers. Rear semi-elliptic in combination with controllable shock dampers.

STEERING
Cam and roller (Marles type).

JACKING SYSTEM
Portable mechanical jack.

WHEELS
Steel, with 17×5 semi-drop centre rims. Secured with ten nuts.

CHASSIS DETAILS
Overall length $229^{1}/_2$ in.
Overall width $75^{1}/_2$ in.
Wheelbase 145 in.
Track, front $58^{1}/_2$ in., *rear* 63 in.
Tyres 8.00×17. Recommended pressures 28 lb./in.^{2} front, 39 lb./in^2 rear.
Turning circle 49 ft. 1 in.

CHASSIS NUMBERS
4AF2–4AF22 (even); 4BP1–4BP7 (odd); 4CS2–4CS6 (even).

NUMBER PRODUCED
Made for Royalty and Heads of State only. 18 made.

BENTLEY R-TYPE AND BENTLEY R-TYPE CONTINENTAL

1952–55

R Type Continental (prototype): body by H.J. Mulliner, 1951.

ENGINE

GENERAL Six cylinders, $3^{1}/_{2}$ x $4^{1}/_{2}$, 4,257 c.c. (1951, $3^{5}/_{8}$ x $4^{1}/_{2}$, 4,566 c.c. – B2MD; (1954 Continental, $3^{3}/_{4}$ x $4^{1}/_{2}$, 4,887 .c.c—BC1D). R.A.C. rating 29.4 h.p. (1954, 33.7 h.p. – BC1D). Aluminium alloy pistons. Firing order 142635. Compression ratio 6.4:1 (1953, 6.75:1—B93TO; 1952 Continental, 7.27:1—BC1A; 1953 Continental, 7.1:1—BC19A; 1954 Continental, 7.2:1—BC4C).

VALVES Overhead inlet valves, pushrod operated; side exhaust valves, operated from camshaft. Inlet valve rocker clearance 0.006 in., exhaust tappet clearance 0.012 in.

CAMSHAFT Driven by single helical fabric gears and carried in four plain bearings.

CRANKSHAFT Seven bearings, copper-lead-indium lined steel shells.

LUBRICATION Pressure feed to all crankshaft and connecting rod bearings at 25 lb./in.^{2}. Relief valve providing positive low-pressure supply to valve rocker shaft, from which inlet valves, pushrods and tappets are lubricated. By-pass filter, oil capacity 16 pints.

IGNITION Automatic regulation of dynamo output by vibrator control. 12 V. system with 55 A.hr. battery. Plug gap 0.025 in.

COOLING SYSTEM Centrifugal pump circulation and fan, thermostatically controlled. Water capacity 3$^1/_4$ gal. (Continental 4 gal.). 1953, centre bar to radiator grill – B210TN.

CARBURETTOR Right-hand-drive models, twin S.U.s 1$^1/_2$ in. bore (Continental 2 in.); left-hand-drive models, Stromberg downdraught (1952, twin S.U.s – B2RT).

STARTER Reduction gear and pinion providing gentle engagement.

PETROL SYSTEM Twin electrical pumps. Petrol capacity 18 gal.

TRANSMISSION

GEARBOX Four forward speeds and reverse. Synchromesh on second, third and top, right-hand control lever for right-hand-drive cars, steering column mounted lever for left-hand drive cars (1952, automatic gearbox optional on left-hand-drive models – B2RT; 1952, optional on right-hand-drive models. 9B2SR; 1953, standard on left-hand-drive models, B1TO; 1954, standard on right-hand-drive models. B2WH; 1954–55, optional on Continental – BC1D). Ratios 2.99:1, 2.05:1, 1.33:1, 1:1 (1952, 3.80:1, 2.34:1, 1.28:1, 1:1. B2RT. Continentals, 2.64:1, 1.55:1, 1.22:1, 1:1).

CLUTCH Single-dry plate, 10 in. long type.

PROPELLOR SHAFT Open type, fitted with needle-bearing universal joints.

FINAL DRIVE Semi-floating. Hypoid gears with differential. Oil capacity 1$^3/_4$ pints. Rear axle ratio 3.73:1 (1952, 3.42:1 optional – B445SP; 1954, 3.42:1 standard – B1YA; Continentals, 3.07:1 standard).

BRAKES
Internal expanding, hydraulic front, mechanical rear, servo assisted. Handbrake operates on rear wheels.

CHASSIS LUBRICATION
Centralised system supplied by foot-operated pump and reservoir on dash-board.

SUSPENSION
Independent front by open helical springs in combination with hydraulic shock dampers, semi-elliptic rear with controllable hydraulic shock dampers.

STEERING
Cam and roller.

JACKING SYSTEM
Portable mechanical jack.

WHEELS
Steel, 16 x 5 well-base rims secured with five nuts.

CHASSIS DETAILS

	R type	Continental
*Overall length**	$199^{1}/_{2}$ in. $203^{1}/_{2}$ in., 210 in.	$206^{1}/_{2}$ in., $211^{1}/_{2}$ in.
Width	$71^{1}/_{2}$ in.	$71^{1}/_{2}$ in.
Height	$64^{1}/_{2}$ in.	63 in.
Wheelbase	120 in.	120 in.
Track, front	$56^{1}/_{2}$ in.	56 in.
rear	$58^{1}/_{2}$ in.	58 in.
Turning circle	$42^{1}/_{2}$ ft.	43 ft.
Weight, kerbside	4,212 lb.	3,696 lb.
Tyres	6.50 x 16	6.50 x 16
Recommended pressures,		
front 24 lb./in.2		
rear 33 lb./in.2		

SERIES AND CHASSIS NUMBERS
R-TYPE

R series	B2RT–B120RT: B1RS–B121RS	1952
S series	B2SR–B500SR; B1SP–B502SP	1952–53
T series	B1TO–B401TO; B2TN–B600TN	1953
U series	B1UL–B251UL; B2UM–B250UM	1953–54
W series	B2WH–B300WH; B1WG–B301WG	1954
X series	B2XF–B140XF	1954
Y series	B1YA–B331YA; B2YD–B330YD	1954
Z series	B1ZX–B251ZX; B2ZY6–B250ZY	1954–55

CONTINENTAL R-TYPE

A series	BC1A–BC26A	1952–53

* Depending on type of bumper.

Bentley Standard Saloon on Bentley R-Type chassis.

B series	BC1B–BC25B	1953–54
C series	BC1C–BC78C	1953–55
D series	BC1D–BC74D	1954–55
E series	BC1E–BC9E	1955

Notes –R type chassis series starting with the number 1 use odd numbers only and those starting with the number 2 use even numbers only but continental models use all numbers. Left-hand-drive cars have L before chassis letters (B46LEY, BC8LA, for example). The number 13 was not used. All but 16 Continentals had H. J. Mulliner coachwork.

NUMBER PRODUCED
R-type, 2,320; Continental R-type, 208.

SILVER CLOUD I AND BENTLEY S1

1955–1959

Rolls-Royce Silver Cloud I saloon.

ENGINE

GENERAL Six cylinders $3^{3}/_{4} \times 4^{1}/_{2}$, 4,887 c.c. (33.7 h.p. R.A.C.). compression ratio, 6.6:1; 7.25:1 on Continental S Type (1956, 8:1 on Continental S Type—BC21BG; 1957, 8:1 on models exported to United States and Canada—SDD136, B120EG; 1958, 8:1 standard—SFE23, B257EK). Automatic transmission in unit with engine. Aluminium pistons. Firing order 142635.

VALVES Overhead inlet valves, pushrod operated; side exhaust valves, operated from camshaft. Inlet rocker clearance cold 0.06 in., exhaust tappet clearance 0.012 in.

CRANKSHAFT Seven bearings.

328

Bentley S1 4-door saloon.

LUBRICATION Oil pump with helical displacement gears and integral relief valve. High-pressure feed to camshaft, connecting rods and crankshaft bearings; reduced feed to engine gears. Full-flow filtration. Oil capacity, 16 pints.

IGNITION Automatic regulation of output, 12 V. system with 55 A.hr. battery. Contact breaker gap 0.019–0.021 in. Sparking plug gap 0.025 in.

COOLING SYSTEM Centrifugal pump and fan, thermostatically controlled. Water capacity, $3\frac{1}{4}$ gal.

CARBURETTOR Twin S.U.s; $1\frac{3}{4}$ in. bore (2in. bore—8:1 compression engines). Automatic control for starting.

STARTER Fitted with planetary reduction gear.

PETROL SYSTEM Twin electric pumps at rear of chassis. Petrol capacity, 18 gal.

TRANSMISSION

GEARBOX Fluid coupling and four-speed automatic transmission in unit with engine: ratios 3.82:1, 2.63:1, 1.45:1, 1:1 (manual type available on Continental S type at customer's request but very few built).

PROPELLER SHAFT Two-piece divided type, with flexibly mounted centre bearing.

FINAL DRIVE Hypoid bevel with four-staff differential and semi-floating half shafts. Ratio 3.42:1 (Continental S Type, 2.92:1). Oil capacity $1^{1}/_{2}$ pints.

BRAKES

Mechanical servo assistance. Hydraulic (self-adjusting) front and combined hydraulic and mechanical at rear. Handbrake operates on rear wheels. Brake drums are cast iron.

SUSPENSION

Independent front by unequal-length wishbones and coil springs, with opposed piston hydraulic dampers and torsional anti-roll bar. Semi-elliptic rear with electrically controlled piston-type dampers and Z-type anti-roll bar.

STEERING

Cam and roller connected by transverse link to a three-piece track linkage (1956, power steering optional—middle of C series, SCI; end of C series, S1; all models, long wheelbase; early B series, Continental S Type).

WHEELS

15 in. steel disc wheels on five studs.

CHASSIS DETAILS

	Short	*Long*
Overall length	$211^{3}/_{4}$ in.	$215^{3}/_{4}$ in.
Overall width	$74^{1}/_{2}$ in.	$74^{3}/_{4}$ in.
Wheelbase	123 in.	127 in.
Track, front	58 in.	58 in.
rear	60 in.	60 in.
Width	$74^{3}/_{4}$ in.	$74^{3}/_{4}$ in.
Height, unladen	64 in.	64 in.

Tyres 8.20 × 15.00. Recommended pressure, 19 lb./in.^{2} front, 26 lb./in.^{2} rear.

Turning circle	41 ft. 8 in.
Ground clearance	7 in.

Weight, without passengers 4,368 lb.

SERIES AND CHASSIS NUMBERS

SCI

Series A	SWA2–250; SXA1–251	1955–56
Series B	SYB2–250; SXB1–251	1956
Series C	SBC2–150; SCC1–151	1956–57
Series D	SDD2–450; SED1–451	1957–58
Series E	SGE2–500; SFE1–501	1957–58
Series F	SHF1–249; SJF2–250	1958–59

Series G	SKG1–125; SLG2–126	1959
Series H	SMH1–265; SNH2–262	1959

S1

Series A	B2AN–B500AN; B1AP–B501AP	1955–56
Series B	B2BA–B250BA; B1BC–B251BC	1956
Series C	B2CK–B500CK; B1CM–B501CM	1956
Series D	B2DB–B350DB; B1DK–B351DK	1956–57
Series E	B2EG–B650EG; B1EK–B651EK	1957–58
Series F	B2FA–B650FA; B1FD–B651FD	1957–59
Series G	B1GD–B125GD; B2GC–B126GC	1959
Series H	B1HB–B45HB; B2HA–B50HA	1959

LONG WHEELBASE SC1

Series A	ALC1–26	1957–58
Series B	BLC1–51	1958–59
Series C	CLC1–47	1959

LONG WHEELBASE S1

Series A	ALB1–36	1958–59

CONTINENTAL S1

Series A	BC1AF–BC102AF	1955–56
Series B	BC1BG–BC101BG	1956–57
Series C	BC1CH–BC51CH	1957–58
Series D	BC1DJ–BC51DJ	1957–58
Series E	BC1EL–BC51EL	1958–59
Series F	BC1FM–BC51FM	1958–59
Series G	BC1GN–BC31GN	1959

Note – Chassis series starting with the number 1 use odd numbers only and those starting with the number 2 use even numbers only, but long wheelbase models use all numbers. Left-hand-drive cars have L before chassis letters (LSWA30, B202LAN, LALC15, LALB1, BC47LAF, for example). The number 13 was not used.

NUMBER PRODUCED
SC1, 2,238; S1, 3,072; LWB SC1, 121; LWB S1, 35; Continental S1, 431.

ROAD TEST

The Autocar 16 May 1958

Acceleration from constant speed, min.:

m.p.h.	Top	3rd	2nd
10–30	—	—	3.6
20–40	—	5.9	—
30–50	8.9	6.0	—
40–60	9.4	6.7	—
50–70	11.1	—	—
60–80	13.0	—	—

From rest through gears to:

m.p.h.	sec.
30	4.1
50	9.4
60	13.0
70	18.4
80	25.0
90	34.1
100	50.6

Time for standing $\frac{1}{4}$ mile, 18.8 sec.

Maximum speeds on gears m.p.h.

Top	106
3rd	63
2nd	34
1st	24

Fuel consumption, 12 m.p.g.

SILVER CLOUD II AND BENTLEY S2

1959–1962

Silver Cloud II: standard steel saloon, 1959.

ENGINE

GENERAL Eight cylinders, forming 90° V, 4.1 × 3.6, 6,230 c.c. Compression ratio 8:1. Firing order A1, B1, A4, B4, B2, A3, B3, A2 (A is offside bank).

VALVES Overhead pushrods and rockers, self-adjusting hydraulic tappets.

CYLINDER HEAD Aluminium alloy with austenitic steel valve seats.

CYLINDER BLOCK Cast aluminium, with wet cylinder liners of cast iron.

CRANKSHAFT Five main bearings. Nitrided chromium-molybdenum steel with integral balance weights.

CAMSHAFT *Monikrom* cast iron, driven by helical gears.

333

S2 drophead coupé by Park Ward, 1961.

LUBRICATION Oil pump with helical displacement gears and integral relief valve. High-pressure feed to camshaft, connecting rods, crankshaft bearings and hydraulic tappets: reduced feed to engine gears and hollow valve rocker shafts. Full-flow filtration. Oil capacity 12 pints.

IGNITION 12 V, system, 67 A.hr. battery, negative earth. Vacuum advance and retard mechanism. Sparking plug gap 0.025 in. Contact breaker gap 0.020 in.

COOLING SYSTEM Centrifugal pump mounted in tandem with fan and driven by V-belt. System pressurised at 7 lb./in.^{2}.

CARBURETTOR Twin s.d. S.U.HD6s $1^3/_4$ in. bore, with automatic choke.

STARTER Pre-engagement solenoid fitted.

PETROL SYSTEM Twin independent electric pumps. Petrol capacity 18 gal.

TRANSMISSION
GEARBOX Four speeds and reverse, automatic transmission through epicyclic gears; ratios 3.82:1, 2.63:1, 1.45:1, 1:1 (reverse 4.3:1). Fluid capacity 20 pints.

Bentley S2 drophead coupé with bodywork by Bentley Motors Ltd. in conjunction with H.J. Mulliner. Power operation of the hood and door windows is an optional extra.

PROPELLER SHAFT Divided type supported at centre by flexibly mounted ball race. Three universal joints fitted.

FINAL DRIVE Hypoid bevel with four-star differential and semi-floating half shafts. Ratio 3.08:1 (Continental S2, 2.92:1).

BRAKES
Mechanical servo assistance. Hydraulic front and combined hydraulic and mechanical at rear. Handbrake operating on rear wheels. Cast iron brake drums, with peripheral cooling fins.

CHASSIS LUBRICATION
21 points to be greased every 12,000 miles.

SUSPENSION
Independent front by unequal length wishbones and coil springs, with opposed piston hydraulic dampers and torsional anti-roll bar. Semi-elliptic rear with electrically controlled piston-type dampers and single radius rod.

Rolls-Royce Silver Cloud II long wheelbase saloon with division. A dual-purpose car designed to be either chauffeur- or owner-driven. The standard Silver Cloud chassis is lengthened by four inches aft of the centre column and converted to limousine form with an electrically operated central division. Electrically operated door windows are an optional extra.

STEERING
Cam and roller, with hydraulic power assistance.

WHEELS
15 in. steel disc wheels on five studs.

CHASSIS DETAILS

	Short	Long
Overall length	212 in.	216 in.
Overall width	74³/₄ in.	74³/₄ in.
Wheelbase	123 in.	127 in.
Track, front	58¹/₂ in.	58¹/₂ in.
rear	60 in.	60 in.
Height	64 in.	64 in.
Tyres	8.20 × 15	8.20 × 15
	(Continental S2 8.00 × 15)	
	Recommended pressures, front 22 lb./in.², rear 27 lb./in.².	
Turning circle	41 ft. 8 in.	
Ground clearance	7 in.	7 in.
Weight without passengers	4,558 lb.	

Rolls-Royce Silver Cloud II convertible by H.J. Mulliner.

SERIES AND CHASSIS NUMBERS

SCII

Series A	SPA2–326; SRA1–325	1959–60
Series B	STB2–500; SBV1–501	1960
Series C	SWC1–730; SXC1–671	1960–61
Series D	SYD2–550; SZD1–551	1961
Series E	SAE1–685	1961–62

LONG WHEELBASE SCII

Series A	LCA1–76	1959–60
Series B	LCB1–101	1960–61
Series C	LCC1–101	1961–62
Series D	LCD1–25	1962

S2

Series A	B1AA–325AA	1959
	B2AM–326AM	1959–60
Series B	B1BR–501BR; B2BS–500BS	1960
Series C	B1CT–445CT	1960
	B2CU–765CU	1960–61
Series D	B1DV–501DV	1961
	B2DW–376DW	1961–62

LONG WHEELBASE S2
| Series A | LBA1–26 | 1960 |
| Series B | LBB1–33 | 1961–62 |

CONTINENTAL S2
Series A	BC1AR–151AR	1959–60
Series B	BC1BY–101BY	1960–61
Series C	BC1CZ–139CZ	1961–62

NOTE – Chassis series starting with the number 1 use odd numbers only and those starting with the number 2 use even numbers only, but long wheelbase and continental models use all numbers. The number 13 was not used in any series.

NUMBER PRODUCED
SCII, 2417; LWB SCII, 299; S2, 1865; LWB S2, 57; Continental S2, 388

Rolls-Royce Silver Cloud II Saloon.

PHANTOM V

1959–1968

Phantom V: Sedanca de Ville by James Young, 1961.

ENGINE

GENERAL Eight cylinders, forming 90° V, 4.1 × 3.6, 6,230 c.c. Compression ratio 9:1 (8:1 also available). Firing order A1, B1, A4, B4, B2, A3, B3, A2, (A is offside bank).

VALVES Overhead pushrods and rockers, self-adjusting hydraulic tappets.

CYLINDER HEAD Aluminium alloy with austenitic steel valve seats.

CYLINDER BLOCK Cast aluminium, with wet cylinder liners of cast iron.

CRANKSHAFT Five main bearings. Nitrided chromium-molybdenum steel with integral balance weights.

CAMSHAFT *MONIKROM* cast iron, driven by helical gears.

LUBRICATION Oil pump with helical displacement gears and integral relief valve. High-pressure feed to camshaft, connecting rods, crankshaft bearings and hydraulic tappets:

339

Phantom V: touring limousine by James Young, 1962.

reduced feed to engine gears and hollow valve rocker shafts. Full-flow filtration. Oil capacity 12 pints.

IGNITION 12 V. system, 67 A.hr. battery. Negative earth. Vacuum advance and retard mechanism. Sparking plug gap 0.025 in. Contact breaker gap 0.020 in.

COOLING SYSTEM Centrifugal pump mounted in tandem with fan and driven by V-belt. System pressurised at 7 lb./in.^{2}. Water capacity, 21 pints.

CARBURETTOR Twin s.d. S.U. HD6s, with automatic choke (1964, S.U. HD8s).

STARTER Pre-engagement solenoid fitted.

PETROL SYSTEM Twin independent electric pumps on right-hand side of chassis frame. Petrol capacity, 23 gal.

TRANSMISSION
GEARBOX Four speeds and reverse, automatic transmission through epicyclic gears; ratios, 3.82:1, 2.63:1, 1.45:1, 1:1 (reverse 4.30:1). Fluid capacity, 20 pints.

PROPELLER SHAFT Divided type supported at centre by flexibly mounted ball race. Three universal joints fitted.

FINAL DRIVE Hypoid bevel with four-star differential and semi-floating half shafts.

Phantom V: state landaulette by Mulliner Park Ward, 1965.

Ratio 3.89:1. Oil capacity, $1^{3}/_{4}$ pints.

BRAKES
Mechanical servo assistance. Hydraulic front and combined hydraulic and mechanical at rear. Handbrake operating on rear wheels. Cast iron brake drums, with peripheral cooling fins. Two separate hydraulic systems and two master cylinders.

CHASSIS LUBRICATION
21 points to be greased every 12,000 miles.

SUSPENSION
Independent front by unequal length wishbones and coil springs, with opposed piston hydraulic dampers and torsional anti-roll bar. Asymmetric semi-elliptic rear with electrically controlled piston-type dampers and single radius rod.

STEERING
Cam and roller, with hydraulic power assistance.

WHEELS
15 in. steel disc wheels on five studs.

CHASSIS DETAILS
Overall length 238 in.
Overall width 79 in.

Wheelbase 144 in.
Track, front 60⅞ in., *rear* 64 in.
Tyres 8.90 × 15. Recommended pressures front 22 lb./in.^{2}, rear 30 lb./in.^{2}.
Turning circle 48 ft. 9 in.

SERIES AND CHASSIS NUMBERS

Series A 5AS1–101; 5AT2–100		1959–61
Series B 5BV1–101; 5BX2–100		1961–62
Series C 5CG1–79		1961–62

NEW SERIES

Series A 5VA1–123		1962–64
Series B 5VB1–51		1963–64
Series C 5VC1–51		1964
Series D 5VD1–101		1964–65
Series E 5VE1–51		1965–66
Series F 5VF1–183		1966–68

NOTE – Chassis series A and B use odd numbers only for those starting with the number 1 and even numbers only for those starting with the number 2. Number 13 was not used in any series.

NUMBER PRODUCED
832

Rolls-Royce Phantom V Limousine by Mulliner Park Ward.

SILVER CLOUD III AND BENTLEY S3

1962–1966

Silver Cloud III: standard steel saloon, 1962.

ENGINE

GENERAL Eight cylinders, forming 90° V, 4.1 × 3.6, 6,230 c.c. Compression ratio, 9:1 (8:1 for countries where 100 octane fuel not available). Firing order A1, B1, A4, B4, B2, A3, B3, A2 (A is offside bank).

VALVES Overhead pushrods and rockers, self-adjusting hydraulic tappets.

CYLINDER HEAD Aluminium-silicon alloy with austenitic steel valve seats.

CYLINDER BLOCK Cast aluminium, with wet cylinder liner of cast iron.

CRANKSHAFT Five main bearings. Nitrided chromium-molybdenum steel with integral balance weights.

S3 drophead coupé: by Mulliner Park Ward, 1963.

CAMSHAFT *Monikrom* cast iron, driven by helical gears.

LUBRICATION Oil pump with helical displacement gears and integral relief valve. High-pressure feed to camshaft, connecting rods, crankshaft bearings and hydraulic tappets: reduced feed to engine gears and hollow valve rocker shafts. Full-flow filtration. Oil capacity $12\frac{1}{2}$ pints.

IGNITION 12 V. system, 67 A.hr. battery. Negative earth. Vacuum advancer and retard mechanism. Sparking plug gap 0.025 in. Contact breaker gap 0.015 in.

COOLING SYSTEM Centrifugal pump mounted in tandem with fan and driven by V-belt. System pressurised at 7 lb./in.^{2}. Water capacity, 21 pints.

CARBURETTOR Twin s.d. S.U. HD8s 2 in. bore, with automatic choke.

STARTER Pre-engagement solenoid fitted.

PETROL SYSTEM Twin independent electric pumps on right-hand side of chassis frame. Petrol capacity, 18 gal. (auxiliary $3\frac{1}{2}$ gal. Tank available if required).

TRANSMISSION

GEARBOX Four speeds and reverse, automatic transmission through epicyclic gears: ratios, 3.82:1, 2.63:1, 1.45:1, 1:1 (reverse 4.3:1). Fluid capacity, 20 pints.

344

Silver Cloud III: two-door saloon by Mulliner Park Ward, 1964.

PROPELLER SHAFT Divided type supported at centre of flexibly mounted ball race. Three universal joints fitted.

FINAL DRIVE Hypoid bevel with four-star differential and semi-floating half shafts. Ratio 3.08:1. Oil capacity $1^5/_8$ pints.

BRAKES
Mechanical servo assistance. Hydraulic front and combined hydraulic and mechanical at rear. Handbrake operating on rear wheels. Cast iron brake drums, with peripheral cooling fins. Two separate hydraulic systems and two master cylinders.

CHASSIS LUBRICATION
21 points to be greased every 12,000 miles.

SUSPENSION
Independent front by unequal length wishbones and coil springs, with opposed piston hydraulic dampers and torsional anti-roll bar. Semi-elliptic rear with electrically controlled piston type dampers and single radius rod.

STEERING
Cam and roller, with hydraulic power assistance.

Rolls-Royce Silver Cloud III drophead coupé by Mulliner Park Ward (hood up). Fitted with automatic transmission, this car is powered by an eight-cylinder aluminium engine of 6,230c.c. The hood on this model is electrically operated.

WHEELS
15 in. steel disc wheels on five studs.

CHASSIS DETAILS

	Short	Long
Overall length	211 in.	216 in.
Overall width	$74^3/_4$ in.	$74^3/_4$ in.
Wheelbase	123 in.	127 in.
Track, front	$58^1/_2$ in.	$58^1/_2$ in.
* rear*	60 in	60 in.
Height	64 in.	64 in.
Tyres	8.20×15	8.20×15

(Continental S3 8.00×15)
Recommended pressures: front 22 lb./in.^{2}, rear 27 lb./in.^{2}.

Turning circle	40 ft. 8 in.
Ground clearance	7 in.
Weight, without passengers	4,558 lb.

SERIES AND CHASSIS NUMBERS
SCIII
Series A   SAZ1–61   1962
Series B   Not issued

Rolls-Royce Silver Cloud III drophead coupé by Mulliner Park Ward (hood down). Fitted with automatic transmission, this car is powered by an eight-cylinder aluminium engine of 6,230c.c. The hood on this model is electrically operated.

Series C	SCX1–877	1962–63
Series D	SDW1–601	1963
Series E	SEV1–495	1963–64
Series G	SGT1–659	1964
Series H	SHS1–357	1964–65
Series J	SJR1–623	1965
Series K	SKP1–423	1965

From G series onwards, coachbuilt cars are indicated by the letter C following the chassis number.

LONG WHEELBASE SCIII

Series A	CAL1–83	1962–63
Series B	CBL1–61	1963
Series C	CCL1–101	1963–64
Series D	DCL1–95	1964
Series E	CEL1–105	1964–65
Series F	CFL–41	1965
Series G	CGLI–29	1965

COACHBUILT SCIII
| Series B | CSC1B–141B | 1965 |
| Series C | CSC1C–83C | 1965–66 |

The first series of these cars was included with the standard saloons (*see above*).

S3
Series A	B2AV–26AV	1962
Series B	Not issued	
Series C	B2CN–828CN	1962–63
Series D	B2DF–198F	1963
Series E	B2EC–530EC	1963–64
Series F	B2FG–350FG	1964
Series G	B2GJ–200GJ	1964–65
Series H	B2HN–400HN	1965
Series J	B2JP–40JP	1965

LONG WHEELBASE S3
Series A	BAL2–30	1962–63
Series B	BBL2–12	1964–65
Series C	BCL2–22	1965

CONTINENTAL S3
Series A	BC2XA–174XA	1962–63
Series B	BC2XB–100XB	1963
Series C	BC2XC–202XC	1963–65
Series D	BC2XD–28XD	1965
Series E	BC2XE–120XE	1965–66

NOTE – Chassis series starting with the number 1 use odd numbers only (SCIII) and those starting with the number 2 (S3) use even numbers only. The number 13 was not used in any series.

NUMBER PRODUCED
SCIII, 2,044; LWB SCIII, 254; Coachbuilt SCIII, 113; S3, 1,286; LWB S3, 32; Continental S3, 312.

ROAD TEST
SCIII
The Autocar 9 August 1963

Maximum speeds		*Hill climbing at steady speeds*	
Top	117 m.p.h.	2nd	1 in 3
3rd	72 m.p.h.	3rd	1 in 5.3
2nd	40 m.p.h.	Top	1 in 7.9
1st	25 m.p.h.		

Top gear m.p.h. per 1,000 r.p.m., 27.8.
0–100 m.p.h. in 34.2 sec.

Note – The coachbuilt version of the SCIII and S3 remained in production after the introduction of the Silver Shadow and Bentley T in 1965, but was discontinued in March 1966.

SILVER SHADOW I AND BENTLEY T1

1965–1976

Silver Shadow drophead coupé by Mulliner Park Ward, 1969.

ENGINE

GENERAL Eight cylinders forming 90° V, 4.1 × 3.6, 6,230 c.c. (1970, 4.1 × 3.9, 6,750 c.c.—SRH 8742). Compression ratio 9:1 (1975, 8:1—SRD 22118, LRD 22073). Firing order A1, B1, A4, B4, B2, A3, B3, A2 (A is offside bank).

VALVES Overhead pushrods and rockers, self-adjusting hydraulic tappets.

CYLINDER HEAD Aluminium alloy with austenitic steel valve seats.

CYLINDER BLOCK Cast aluminium-silicon alloy, with wet cylinder liners of cast iron.

CRANKSHAFT Five main bearings. Nitrided chromium-molybdenum steel with integral balance weights (1969, bolted on balance weights—SRH 8742).

CAMSHAFT *Monikrom* cast iron, driven by helical gears.

350

T1 saloon, 1969.

LUBRICATION Oil pump with helical displacement gears and integral relief valve. High-pressure feed to camshaft, connecting rods, crankshaft bearings and hydraulic tappets: reduced feed to engine gears and hollow valve rocker shafts. Full-flow filtration. Oil capacity $14^{1}/_{2}$ pints.

IGNITION 12V system, 64 A.hr. battery. Negative earth. Generator with current/voltage compensated control (1969, alternator—SRH 7699). Vacuum and centrifugal advance and retard mechanism. Sparking plug gap 0.023 in.–0.028 in. Contact breaker gap 0.014 in.–0.016 in.

COOLING SYSTEM Centrifugal pump mounted in tandem with fan and driven by V-belt. System pressurised at 7 lb./in.^{2}. Water capacity 28 pints.

CARBURETTOR Twin s.d. S.U. HD8s with automatic choke.

STARTER Pre-engagement solenoid fitted.

PETROL SYSTEM Twin independent electric pumps. Petrol capacity 24 gal.

TRANSMISSION
GEARBOX Four speeds and reverse, automatic transmission: ratios 3.82:1, 2.63:1, 1.45:1, 1:1 (reverse 4.3:1). (1968, 3-speed gearbox and torque-converter transmission—SRH 4033, SBH 4478, SRH 4483 [except SRH 4487]). Fluid capacity, 24 pints.

1966 Rolls-Royce Silver Shadow 4-door saloon.

PROPELLER SHAFT Single piece, with ball and trunnion constant velocity universal joint and needle roller universal joint.

FINAL DRIVE Hypoid bevel. Ratio 3.08:1. Oil capacity 4 pints.

BRAKES
Hydraulically operated disc brakes at front and rear with power assistance. Handbrake operating on rear wheels.

CHASSIS LUBRICATION
Steering and height control ball joints to be greased every 12,000 miles.

SUSPENSION
Independent front, double triangle lever coil spring with hydraulic dampers and automatic height control (1969, deleted—SRX 7404 and LRX 7378), located by Panhard rod (1972, lower wishbone, complaint controlled upper levers, coil springs, telescopic dampers, anti-roll bar and anti-dive characteristics—LRX 13201 [and LRH 13084], SRH 13485 [and SRH 12586], SRX 12687, SRH 12583 and SRH 13066). Independent rear, coil spring and single trailing arm with hydraulic dampers and automatic height control, located by torque arm link.

STEERING
Recirculating ball, with power assistance (1969, higher geared steering 19.3:1—SRX 6429;

Bentley T1 4-door saloon.

1971, lower geared steering 17.5:1—SRX 11215, LRX 11290, SRH 11501, LRH 11551 [and LRH 11535, 11548 and 11549]).

WHEELS
Steel disc wheels on five studs.

CHASSIS DETAILS

	Standard	Long
Overall length	203^1/$_2$ in.	207^1/$_2$ in.
Overall width	71 in.	71 in.
Wheelbase	119^1/$_2$ in. (1974, 120 in.)	123^1/$_2$ in.
Track	57^1/$_2$ in. (1974, front 60 in., rear 59^5/$_8$ in.)	57^1/$_2$ in.
Height	59^3/$_4$ in.	59^3/$_4$ in.
Tyres	205 × 15 (1974, HR. 70, HR. 15)	205 × 15

Ground clearance 6^1/$_2$ in.
Weight, without passengers 4,558 lb.

CHASSIS NUMBERS
Chassis numbers started at SBH 1001 and ended at SRH 26700. Numbers run in

Rolls-Royce Silver Shadow 4-door saloon.

sequence, while letter prefixes were as follows: SRH, home Shadow: SRX, export Shadow; SBH, home T; SBX, export T; CRH (CBH), 2-door Shadow (T); DRH (DBH), drophead Shadow (T) (after 1971, a letter indicating the year of export was used instead of X: A, 1972; B, 1973, etc.). From January 1968, export models complied with U.S. Federal safety standards, and from May 1969 all models so complied. The long wheelbase model with division (which had a dual air-conditioning system) was one of the first production cars with division that complied with U.S. Federal safety regulations.

354

NUMBER PRODUCED
Shadow I, LWB Shadow I, 2,776; two-door Shadow I, 606; drophead Shadow I, 505; TI, 1,712; two-door TI, 99; drophead TI, 41.

ROAD TEST
The Autocar, 30 March 1967
Maximum speeds
Top 118 m.p.h.
3rd 72 m.p.h.
2nd 43 m.p.h.
1st 24 m.p.h.
0–100 m.p.h. in 37.8 sec.

The Autocar 1 May 1976
Maximum speeds
Top 120 m.p.h.
2nd 95 m.p.h.
1st 56 m.p.h.

NOTE
From 1971 onwards, two-door and drophead models were named Corniche (see pp. 359–62).

PHANTOM VI
1968–90

Rolls-Royce Phantom VI with coachwork by Mulliner Park Ward.

ENGINE

GENERAL Eight cylinders, forming 90° V, 4.1 × 3.6, 6,230 c.c. (1978, 4.1 × 3.9, 6,750 c.c.—PGH 101) Compression ratio 9:1 (8:1 also available). Firing order A1, B1, A4, B4, B2, A3, B3, A2 (A is offside bank).

VALVES Overhead pushrods and rockers, self-adjusting hydraulic tappets.

CYLINDER HEAD Aluminium alloy with austenitic steel valve seats.

CYLINDER BLOCK Cast aluminium, with wet cylinder liners of cast iron.

CRANKSHAFT Five main bearings. Nitrided chromium-molybdenum steel with integral balance weights.

CAMSHAFT *Monikrom* cast iron, driven by helical gears.

LUBRICATION Oil pump with helical displacement gears and integral relief valve. High-pressure feed to camshaft, connecting rods, crankshaft bearings and hydraulic tappets: reduced feed to engine gears and hollow valve rocker shafts. Full-flow filtration. Oil capacity 14 pints.

IGNITION 12 V. system, 68 A.hr. battery. Negative earth. Alternator with current/voltage compensated control. Vacuum and centrifugal advance and retard mechanism. Sparking plug gap 0.025 in. Contact breaker gap 0.015 in.

COOLING SYSTEM Centrifugal pump mounted in tandem with fan and driven by V-belt. System pressurised at 15 lb./in.^{2}. Water capacity, $28^3/_4$ pints.

CARBURETTOR Twin s.d. S.U. HD8s, with automatic choke (1978, twin s.d. S.U. HIF7s—PGH101).

STARTER Pre-engagement solenoid fitted.

PETROL SYSTEM Twin independent electric pumps on right-hand side of chassis frame. Petrol capacity, 23 gal.

TRANSMISSION
GEARBOX Four speeds and reverse, automatic transmission through epicyclic gears; ratios, 3.82:1, 2.63:1, 1.45:1, 1:1 (reverse 4.30:1) (1978, 3-speed gearbox and torque-converter transmission—PGH 101). Fluid capacity, 20 pints.

PROPELLER SHAFT Divided type supported at centre by flexibly mounted ball race. Three universal joints fitted.

FINAL DRIVE Hypoid bevel with four-star differential and semi-floating half shafts. Ratio 3.89:1. Oil capacity, $1^3/_4$ pints.

BRAKES
Mechanical servo assistance. Hydraulic front and combined hydraulic and mechanical at rear. Handbrake operating on rear wheels. Cast iron brake drums, with peripheral cooling fins. Two separate hydraulic systems and two master cylinders (1978, hydraulically operated at front and rear with power assistance).

CHASSIS LUBRICATION
21 points to be greased every 12,000 miles.

SUSPENSION
Independent front by coil springs, double wishbone hydraulic dampers and anti-roll stabiliser. Asymmetric semi-elliptic rear with electrically controlled piston-type dampers.

STEERING
Cam and roller, with hydraulic power assistance.

WHEELS
15 in. steel disc wheels on five studs.

CHASSIS DETAILS
Overall length 238 in.
Overall width 79 in.
Wheelbase 145 in.
Track, front $60^{7}/_{8}$ in., *rear* 64 in.
Tyres 8.90×15 cross-ply. Recommended pressures are decided upon for each car.
Turning circle 52 ft.

CHASSIS NUMBERS
First letter P, second letter R (4-speed gearbox) or G (3-speed gearbox), third letter H (right-hand drive) or X (left-hand drive).

CORNICHE
1971–1987

Pre-1977 Rolls-Royce Corniche saloon with chrome bumpers.

ENGINE

GENERAL Eight cylinders forming 90° V, 4.1 × 3.9, 6,750 c.c. Compression ratio 9:1. Firing order 1978: A1, B1, A4, B4, B2, A3, B3, A2. 1986: A1, A3, B3, A2, B2, B1, A4, B4 (A is offside bank).

VALVES Overhead pushrods and rockers, self-adjusting hydraulic tappets.

CYLINDER HEAD Aluminium alloy with austenitic steel valve seats.

CYLINDER BLOCK Cast aluminium, with wet cylinder liners of cast iron.

CRANKSHAFT Five main bearings. Nitrided chromium-molybdenum steel with bolted-on balance weights.

Bentley Corniche convertible, 1974. (Name changed to Continental in 1984.)

Pre-1977 Rolls-Royce Corniche convertible with chrome bumpers.

CRANKSHAFT *Monikrom* cast iron, driven by helical gears.

LUBRICATION Oil pump with helical displacement gears and integral relief valve. High-pressure feed to camshaft, connecting rods, crankshaft bearings and hydraulic tappets: reduced feed to engine gears and hollow valve rocker shafts. Full-flow filtration. Oil capacity $14^1/_2$ pints.

IGNITION 12V system, 68 A.hr. battery. Negative earth. Generator with current/voltage compensated control. Vacuum and centrifugal advance and retard mechanism. Sparking plug gap 0.023 in.–0.028 in. Contact breaker gap 0.014 in.–0.016 in.

COOLING SYSTEM Centrifugal pump mounted in tandem with fan and driven by V-belt. System pressurised at 15 lb./in.^{2}. Water capacity 28 pints, 50:50 water and anti-freeze.

CARBURETTOR Twin s.d. S.U. HD8s with automatic choke (1977, Solex 4A1 compound 4 choke—DRH 30003)

STARTER Pre-engagement solenoid fitted.

PETROL SYSTEM Twin independent electric pumps (1986, Bosch fuel injection system with one pump under floor and one in tank). Petrol capacity $23^1/_2$ gal.

TRANSMISSION

GEARBOX Three speeds and reverse, automatic with torque converter transmission. Fluid capacity, $19^1/_2$ pints.

PROPELLER SHAFT Single piece, with ball and trunnion constant velocity universal joint and needle roller universal joint.

FINAL DRIVE Hypoid bevel. Ratio 3.08:1 (1986, 2.69:1). Oil capacity $4^1/_2$ pints.

BRAKES

Hydraulically operated disc brakes at front and rear with power assistance. Parking brake operating on rear wheels.

CHASSIS LUBRICATION

Steering and height control ball joints to be greased every 12,000 miles.

SUSPENSION

Independent front, compliance rods, coil spring, anti-roll bar and hydraulic shock dampers together with brake dive compensation. Independent rear, coil spring, anti-roll bar and single trailing arm with hydraulic dampers; brake light compensation and automatic height

361

control, located by torque arm link (1979, smaller coil springs, auxiliary gas springs added—DRH 5003).

STEERING
Recirculating ball, with power assistance through rotary valve, torsion bar operated valve with collapsible steering column (1977 rack and pinnion, power assisted).

WHEELS
Steel disc wheels on five studs (1987, aluminium alloy).

CHASSIS DETAILS

	Two-door saloon	*Convertible*
Overall length	$203^1/_2$ in.	$203^1/_2$ in.
Overalll width	72 in.	$72^1/_3$ in.
Wheelbase	119 in.	$120^1/_2$ in.
Track	$57^1/_2$ in.	$57^1/_2$ in.
Height	$58^3/_4$ in.	$59^3/_4$ in.
Tyres	205×15	205×15

(1986, 235/70 **HR**15 radial ply)

Recommended pressure: 28 lb./in.^{2} front and rear (rear increased to 32 lb/in.^{2} with 4 occupants and luggage) (1986, 24lb/in.^{2} front, 28lb/in.^{2} rear)

Turning circle	$38^1/_2$ ft.	$38^1/_2$ ft.
(1984,	39ft.	1986, 39.8ft)

Ground clearance 6in.
Weight without passengers 5,200lb.

SERIES AND CHASSIS NUMBERS
Chassis numbers started at DRH 9770. The first letter of the chassis number indicates the body styling (C, two door saloon; D, convertible), the second letter indicates Rolls-Royce (R) or Bentley (B) and the third letter indicates left-hand (X) or right-hand drive (H). The prefix C was used to indicate coachbuilt cars up to CRX 6646.

ROAD TEST
The Autocar 6 April 1974
Maximum speeds
Top 122 m.p.h.
2nd 83 m.p.h.
1st 50 m.p.h.
0–100 m.p.h. in 30 sec.

SILVER SHADOW II, SILVER WRAITH II AND BENTLEY T2

1977–1981

Bentley T2.

ENGINE

GENERAL Eight cylinders forming 90° V, 4.1 × 3.9, 6,750 c.c. Compression ratio 8:1 (1980, 9:1—SRH 39628). Firing order A1, B1, A4, B4, B2, A3, B3, A2 (A is offside bank).

VALVES Overhead pushrods and rockers, self-adjusting hydraulic tappets.

CYLINDER HEAD Aluminium alloy with austenitic steel valve seats.

CYLINDER BLOCK Cast aluminium-silicon alloy, with wet cylinder liners of cast iron.

363

Silver Shadow II.

Silver Wraith II.

CRANKSHAFT Five main bearings. Nitrided chromium-molybdenum steel with bolted-on balance weights.

LUBRICATION Oil pump with helical displacement gears and integral relief valve. High-pressure feed to camshaft, connecting rods, crankshaft bearings and hydraulic tappets: reduced feed to engine gears and hollow valve rocker shafts. Full-flow filtration. Oil capacity $16\frac{1}{2}$ pints.

IGNITION 12V system, 69 A.hr. battery. Negative earth. Generator with current/voltage compensated control. Vacuum and centrifugal advance and retard mechanism. Sparking plug gap 0.023 in.—0.028 in. Contact break gap 0.014 in.–0.016 in.

COOLING SYSTEM Centrifugal pump mounted in tandem with fan and driven by V-belt. System pressurised at $7 lb/in.^2$ Water capacity $28\frac{1}{2}$ pints.

CARBURETTOR Twin s.d. S.U. H1F7s with automatic choke.

STARTER Pre-engagement solenoid fitted.

PETROL SYSTEM Twin independent electric pumps. Petrol capacity $23\frac{1}{2}$ gal.

TRANSMISSION
GEARBOX Three speeds and reverse, automatic with torque-converter transmission. Fluid capacity $18\frac{1}{2}$ pints.

PROPELLER SHAFT Single piece, with ball and trunnion constant velocity universal joint and needle roller universal joint.

FINAL DRIVE Hypoid bevel. Ratio 3.08:1. Oil capacity $4\frac{1}{2}$ pints.

BRAKES
Hydraulically operated disc brakes at front and rear with power assistance. Handbrake operating on rear wheels.

CHASSIS LUBRICATION
Steering and height control ball joints to be greased every 12,000 miles.

SUSPENSION
Independent front, lower wishbone, complaint controlled upper levers, coil springs, telescopic dampers, anti-roll bar and anti-dive characteristics. Independent rear, coil spring and semi-trailing arm, anti-roll bar and automatic ride height control.

STEERING
Rack and pinion, power assisted.

WHEELS
Steel disc on five studs.

CHASSIS DETAILS

	Shadow II and Bentley T2	Wraith II
Overall length	204$^1/_2$ in.	208$^1/_2$ in.
Overall width	72 in.	72 in.
Wheelbase	102$^1/_2$ in.	124$^1/_2$ in.
Track, front	60 in.	60 in.
rear	59$^1/_2$ in.	59$^1/_2$ in.
Tyres	HR70, HR15 or 235/70HR15 radial ply	
Ground clearance	61$^1/_2$ in.	61$^1/_2$ in.
Weight, without passengers	4,930 lb.	5,020 lb. (with division, 5,260 lb.)

CHASSIS NUMBERS
Chassis numbers started at SRF 30001 (Shadow II) and ended at SRL 41601; started at SBX 30046 (T2) and ended at SBH 41573; and started at LRX 30083 (Wraith II) and ended at LRL 41648.

NUMBER PRODUCED
Shadow II, 8,425; Bentley T2, 558; LWB T2, 10, Wraith II, 2,135.

ROAD TEST (WRAITH II)
The Autocar 21 October 1978
Maximum speeds
Top 120 m.p.h.
2nd 94 m.p.h.
1st 56 m.p.h.
0–100 m.p.h. in 32.4 sec.

VEHICLE NUMBERING SYSTEM FROM MODEL YEAR 1980

VEHICLE IDENTIFICATION NUMBER (VIN)

In October 1980 the USA 17-digit Vehicle Identification Number (VIN) was adopted by the International Standards Organisation for world-wide use. Consequently, instead of a chassis number, all Rolls-Royce and Bentley cars from the Silver Spirit on carry a unique VIN plate, usually on the inside of the A-pillar to which the front doors are hinged. The first twelve digits have specific meanings as detailed below, and the remaining five digits represent the car's sequential number. Reading and understanding VIN numbers provides important construction and equipment details about a particular car; they also reveal where, and for what model year the car was built.

In this and subsequent chapters the year indicates the model year (m.y.) for which a car was built: this is not necessarily the same as the calendar year in which it was actually built.

SAMPLE VIN OF THE FIRST PRODUCTION SILVER SPIRIT

S	C	A	Z	S	0	0	0	A	C	H	0	1	0	0	1

numbered 1 to 17 to give an explanation of the meaning of each of the above digits

1	2	3	4	5	6	7	8	9	10	11	12	13	14	15	16	17

1 – 3   Location & Manufacturer Identifier
1. S = Europe   2. C = UK   3. A = Rolls-Royce or B = Bentley

4   Chassis or Underframe Type
P = Phantom VI   Y = Camargue (and Corniche up to early in 1982)
Z = All other models except Rolls-Royce Silver Seraph, Park Ward, Bentley Arnage/RL/GL/BL/Le Mans/Birkin and lwb from 1998.

5   Model/Body Type
S = Saloon   N = Long wheelbase, no division
L = Long wheelbase with division D = Convertible
J = Camargue (until 1986)   T = Phantom VI Landaulette
M = Phantom VI Limousine   A = Phantom VI Protected Limousine
C = Corniche

367

NB. From 1987 L and T were dropped and the following digits indicating body types were added:

E = Bentley Eight (not USA)
N = Long wheelbase with or without division
R = Bentley Turbo R (from 1989)
X = Silver Spur and Mulsanne L Limousine
B = Bentley Continental R (1992 on) S (1994–95)
G = Flying Spur
K = Bentley Azure (from 1995)
Y = Extended wheelbase: Silver Spur Division
A = Silver Dawn (1994 USA. 1996 all markets)

M = Phantom VI (all coachwork types)
F = Bentley Eight lwb (1988, not USA)
P = Bentley Turbo RL lwb (from 1989)
W = Silver Spur II Touring Limousine
E = Bentley Brooklands (from 1993)

P = Bentley Turbo S (1994–95)
V = Silver Spur Park Ward Limousine
U = Bentley Continental T (from 1996)

4 and 5   Two-Digit Code Denoting Body Style and Model
From 1998 the 4th and 5th letters designate body style and model for the following models:
LA = Rolls-Royce Silver Seraph
LB = Bentley Arnage: Arnage Green Label: Arnage 4.4L Birkin
LC = Bentley Arnage Red Label: Arnage Le Mans
LD = Rolls Royce Park Ward
LE = Bentley Arnage lwb
LF = Arnage Black Label

6 and 7   Two-Digit Code Denoting Engine Type
NB. Cars for markets outside the USA, had 00 for unused digits 6 and 7 until they came into use for all markets.

Pre 1996 Model Year
00 – L410I naturally aspirated, non-catalyst equipped fuel injection
01 – Phantom VI Limousine 6.75 litre V-8
02 – L410I naturally aspirated, catalyst equipped fuel injection
03 – L410MTKR turbocharged, catalyst equipped
04 – L410MTER turbocharged
05 – L410MTKS turbocharged, catalyst equipped, power option
06 – L410MTKS turbocharged, non-catalyst equipped, power option
42 – All non-turbocharged catalyst equipped cars up to VIN 20000
80 – All non-catalyst equipped Bentley Eight cars up to 1987 model year
0T – All turbocharged non-catalyst equipped cars up to 1998 model year

From 1996 Model Year
11 – L410 naturally aspirated, catalyst equipped, Zytek control with OBD II
12 – L410 naturally aspirated, catalyst equipped, Bosch control with OBD I
13 – L410MNLT naturally aspirated, non-catalyst equipped, Zytek control (lead tolerant)

14 – L410MT2T turbocharged, catalyst equipped, Zytek control with OBD II

15 – L410MT1T turbocharged, catalyst equipped, Zytek control with OBD I

16 – L410MTLT non-catalyst equipped, Zytek control (lead tolerant)

17 – L410MN1T/Z naturally aspirated, catalyst equipped, Zytek control, traction assistance

18 – L410MNLT/Z naturally aspirated, non-catalyst equipped, Zytek control, traction assistance

From 1997 Model Year

19 – L410MT2V turbocharged, catalyst equipped, non-intercooled, Zytek control with OBD II

20 – L410MT1T turbocharged, catalyst equipped, non-intercooled, Zytek control with OBD I

21 – L410MTLV turbocharged, non-catalyst equipped, non-intercooled, Zytek control (lead tolerant)

22 – L410MT2T/S turbocharged, catalyst equipped, intercooled, Zytek control with OBD II

23 – L410MT1T/S turbocharged, catalyst equipped, intercooled, Zytek control with OBD I

24 – L410MTLT/S turbocharged, non-catalyst equipped, intercooled, Zytek control (lead tolerant)

From 1998 Model Year

25 – L410MT2W turbocharged, catalyst equipped, intercooled, Zytek control with OBD II

26 – L410MT1W turbocharged, catalyst equipped, intercooled, Zytek control with OBD I

27 – L410MTLW turbocharged, non-catalyst equipped, intercooled, Zytek control (lead tolerant)

28 – L410MT1T/R turbocharged, catalyst equipped, intercooled, Zytek control with OBD I

29 – L420MT2T/R turbocharged, catalyst equipped, intercooled, Zytek control with OBD II

30 – L410MTLT/R turbocharged, non-catalyst equipped, intercooled, Zytek control (lead tolerant) I

31 – L410MT2Y turbocharged, catalyst equipped, intercooled, Zytek control with OBD II

32 – L410MT1Y turbocharged, catalyst equipped, intercooled, Zytek control with OBD I

33 – L410MTLY turbocharged, catalyst equipped, intercooled, Zytek control (lead tolerant)

50 – Turbocharged, intercooled, non-catalyst, 4.4 litre V-8

51 – Turbocharged, intercooled, catalyst, 4.4 litre V-8

60 – Naturally aspirated, non-catalyst, 5.4 litre V-12

61 – Naturally aspirated, catalyst, 5.4 litre V-12, OBD II

62 – Naturally aspirated, catalyst, 5.4 litre V-12, EOBD

8   Occupant Restraint Systems

NB. Cars for markets outside the USA had 0 for the unused digit 8 until it came into use for all markets.

A = Active belts   B = Passive belts – front (USA only)
C = Twin air bags   D = Driver only airbag, passenger active belts
E = Twin air bags, seat belt pretensioners   0 = Other than USA prior to 1987

9   Check Digit

NB. Cars for markets outside the USA, had 0 for the unused digit 9 until it came into use for all markets.

0 to 9 or X = Check digit which is used in conjunction with a secret formulae to maintain security and preserve the integrity of the VIN as related to a specific car.

10   Year

NB. The year letter indicates the model year for which a car was built; this is not necessarily the same as the calendar year in which it was actually built. The Phantom VI is an exception in which the year letter indicates the year in which the chassis was laid down.

A = 1980	B = 1981	C = 1982	D = 1983	E = 1984	F = 1985
G = 1986	H = 1987	J = 1988	K = 1989	L = 1990	M = 1991
N = 1992	P = 1993	R = 1994	S = 1995	T = 1996	V = 1997
W = 1998	X = 1999	Y = 2000	1 = 2001	2 = 2002	3 = 2003

11   Factory

C = Crewe   W = Willesden

NB. This refers to the chassis, not the coachwork.

12   Steering Position

H = Right-hand drive   X = Left-hand drive

13 – 17   Five-Digit Sequential Identification Numbers

M.Y	No's.	M.Y.	No's.
1980	From 01001 on for all cars	1997	From 59001 on for 4-door cars
1985	From 12001 on for all cars	1997	From 61001 on (+53772) for Azure cars
1987	From 20001 on for all cars	1998	From 61501 on for Azure cars
1990	From 30001 on for convertible cars	1998	From 63001 on for Continental R cars
1990	From 31001 on for 4-door cars	1998	From 65001 on for Continental SC cars
1992	From 40001 on for convertible cars	1998	From 66001 on for 4-door cars
1992	From 42001 on for Continental R cars	1998	From 67001 on for Continental T cars
1992	From 44001 on for 4-door cars	1998	From 01001 on for Seraph/Arnage cars
1992	From 80001 on for Touring Limousine		

1993 From 46001 on for 4-door cars
1994 From 50001 on for convertible cars
1994 From 52001 on for Continental R cars
1994 From 54001 on for 4-door cars
1995 From 50801 on for Azure cars
1996 From 50401 on for convertible cars
1996 From 53001 on for Continental R cars
1996 From 53601 on for Azure cars
1996 From 57001 on for 4-door cars
1997 From 53301 on for Continental R cars
1997 From 53305 on for Continental T cars

2000 From 63301 on for Continental R/Mulliner
2000 From 65101 on for Continental SC/Mulliner
2000 From 67201 on for Continental T/Mulliner
2000 From 68002 on for Corniche cars
2000 From 04001 on for Seraph/Arnage cars
2000 From 07501 on for Park Ward cars
2000 From 62001 on for Azure/Mulliner cars
2001 From 05551 on for Seraph/Arnage cars
2001 From 07550 on for Park Ward cars

ROLLS-ROYCE

Silver Spirit 1980–89, Silver Spirit II 1990–93, Silver Spirit III 1994–95, Silver Spirit (96) 1996–97, Silver Dawn 1995–98, Silver Spur 1980–89, Silver Spur II 1990–93, Mulliner Spur 1990–91, Silver Spur III 1994–95, Silver Spur (96) 1996–97

BENTLEY

Mulsanne 1980–87, Mulsanne L 1981–87, Mulsanne S 1988–92, Mulsanne S L.W.B. 1988–92, Eight 1984–92, Brooklands 1993–97, Brooklands L.W.B. 1993–97, Brooklands R S.W.B. 1998, Brooklands R L.W.B. 1998–99, Brooklands R Mulliner 1998

Silver Spirit.

ENGINE

GENERAL L410 Eight cylinders in 90° V configuration, bore 4.1 in. (104.1 mm), stroke 3.9 in. (99.1 mm), cubic capacity 412 cu. in. (6,750 cc). Compression ratio 9:1 (8:1 on all cars for North America, Australia, Japan, the UK, and the rest of the world from 1986).

VALVES Overhead valves operated by helical gear-driven cast iron camshaft in V of engine. Hydraulic tappets.

CYLINDER HEAD AND CYLINDER BLOCK Aluminium cylinder head with austenitic steel valve seat inserts. Aluminium alloy monobloc casting with cast iron wet cylinder liners. From 1989 cross-bolted crankcase.

Silver Spur.

Bentley Brooklands, 1994.

Silver Dawn, 1997. Now the only non-turbocharged Rolls-Royce.

CRANKSHAFT Forged steel, counterweighted, statically and dynamically balanced five bearing crankshaft.

INDUCTION SYSTEMS Bosch K-Jetronic continuous fuel injection with 'closed loop' mixture control on cars for North America, Australia, and Japan, plus UK and other markets from 1986. Twin horizontal constant-vacuum HIF.7 $1^7/8$in. SU carburettors on other markets up to 1986. Bosch K-Motronic fuel injection and engine management system from 1989. Bosch M-3.3 fuel injection and engine management system from 1992. Low-pressure turbocharged engine with estimated 20 per cent more power (excluding Silver Dawn) from 1996. Zytek EMS3 engine management system from 1996.

EXHAUST SYSTEM North American and Japanese cars fitted with catalytic converters, from 1987–88 model year onward on all cars except those sold in the Middle East.
Cars not fitted with catalytic converters – twin pipe system with six silencer boxes.
Cars with catalytic converters: twin downtake pipes from engine merge into a single pipe prior to the catalytic converters, then revert to twin pipes with twin intermediate and rear silencer boxes.

POWER Unofficially, 200 b.h.p. plus using twin SU carburettors, 240 b.h.p. using Bosch K-Jetronic fuel injection on non-turbocharged engines from 1986, and 290/300 b.h.p. plus using low-pressure turbocharged engines from 1996.
Torque Not known.

TRANSMISSION
GEARS Until 1992, GM400 3-speed automatic transmission with torque converter. From 1992, GM4L80E 4-speed torque converter automatic transmission with overdrive top gear electronically linked to engine management system.

Electrically operated gear selection. Excluding the Bentley Brooklands, cars covered in this chapter have the gear selector mounted on the right side of the steering column. The Bentley Brooklands has a centre console-mounted gear selector.

RATIOS Up to 1987: 3.08:1, 4.56:1, 7.64:1. Final drive 3.08:1.
From 1987: 2.69:1, 3.98:1, 6.67:1. Final drive 2.69:1
From 1992: 2.31:1, 3.08:1, 4.56:1, 7.64:1. Final drive 3.08:1.

BRAKES
All four wheels fitted with 11-in (279-mm) disc brakes ventilated at the front. Each rear wheel fitted with one four-cylinder calliper and each front wheel with two twin-cylinder callipers. Two independent hydraulic circuits from separate high-pressure hydraulic systems operated via distribution valves operated by the brake pedal. Separate brake pads for foot-operated, hand-released parking brake. Anti-lock brakes (ABS) from 1986.

Bentley Brooklands, 1997. Twenty per cent more power from low-pressure turbocharged engine.

SUSPENSION

Front: independent by coil springs and telescopic dampers, with lower wishbones, upper compliant levers and anti-roll bar mounted on the front sub-frame. Rear: independent coil springs with semi-trailing arms and anti-roll bar. Telescopic hydraulic suspension struts and pressurised gas springs act in conjunction with the coil springs and incorporate both damping and self-levelling height control. The height of the car is maintained under all normal load conditions by the gas springs and suspension struts plus an automatic self-levelling system with restrictors in the pressure lines which ensure that the levelling responds slowly to suspension movements. Braking and self-levelling systems take Hydraulic System Mineral Oil pressurised up to 2,500 p.s.i. from two hydraulic accumulators mounted on the crankcase and fed by twin camshaft-driven hydraulic pumps. A safety valve ensures priority pressure to the braking system when pressure in the accumulators is low.

Automatic ride control capable of adapting to changing road conditions in a fraction of a second was introduced in 1992.

STEERING

Power-assisted rack and pinion with centre take-off. Power assistance by hydraulic pressure from engine-driven pump. Collapsible energy-absorbing steering column. 3.25 turns lock to lock. From 1996 electrically tilting steering wheel.

WHEELS AND TYRES

15-in. pressed steel wheels fitted with 235/70 HR15 steel-braced radial ply tyres were standard until 1986 when 15-in. aluminium alloy wheels became optional on the Bentley Eight and standard on other models. From 1996 16-in. aluminium alloy wheels fitted with 235/65 VR16 tyres were standard on the Bentley Brooklands, the Silver Spirit (1996) and the Silver Spur (1996).

375

Interior Bentley Brooklands.

UNDERFRAME

Separate front and rear sub-frames. Front: steel box section mounted to underframe with rubber mounts. Rear: suspension and final drive cross-members connected by bracing tubes to form rigid structure attached to underframe by rubber mounts with short horizontal telescopic dampers on front mounts.

COACHWORK

Pressed steel four-door monocoque construction with aluminium doors, bonnet (hood) and boot (trunk) lid. Electric lift windows, electric front seat adjustments, and fully automatic air conditioning. Electrically adjustable rear seats on some later long wheelbase cars.

DIMENSIONS

Standard wheelbase	10 ft. 0.5 in. (3,061 mm)
Long wheelbase	10 ft. 4.5 in. (3,162 mm)
Front track	5 ft. 0.5 in. (1,537 mm)
Rear track	5 ft. 0.5 in. (1,537 mm)
Overall length s.w.b.	17 ft. 3.4 in. (5,268 mm)

Silver Spur II, 1993.

Silver Spur (96), 1997. Twenty per cent more power from low-pressure turbocharged engine.

The Bentley Mulsanne.

Overall length l.w.b.:	17 ft. 7.4 in. (5,370 mm)
Overall width:	6 ft. 2.3 in. (1,887 mm)
Overall height:	4 ft. 10.5 in. (1,485 mm)

PERFORMANCE

1980–85 Models: Silver Spirit, Silver Spur, Mulsanne & Eight

Maximum speed:	119 m.p.h. (192 k.p.h.)	
Acceleration:	0–60 m.p.h.	10.0 sec.
Acceleration:	0–100 m.p.h.	30.8 sec.

1986–93 Models: Silver Spirit, Silver Spur, Mulsanne, Eight, Silver Spirit II, Silver Spur II, Mulliner Spur, & Mulsanne S

Maximum speed:	126 m.p.h. (202 k.p.h.)	
Acceleration:	0–60 m.p.h.	10.4 sec.
Acceleration:	0–100 m.p.h.	32.9 sec.

1993–95 Models: Silver Spirit III, Silver Spur III, Brooklands, & Silver Dawn

Maximum speed:	133 m.p.h. (214 k.p.h.)	
Acceleration:	0–60 m.p.h.	9.5 sec.
Acceleration:	0–100 m.p.h.	Not known

1996–99 Models: Silver Spirit (96), Silver Spur (96), Silver Dawn, Brooklands, Brooklands R & R Mulliner

Maximum speed:	140 m.p.h. (225 k.p.h.)	
Acceleration:	0–60 m.p.h.	7.9 sec.
Acceleration:	0–100 m.p.h.	Not known

VIN NUMBERS, FIRST AND LAST

Rolls-Royce Silver Spirit:	1980 First–SCAZS0000ACH01001:	1989 Last–SCAZS00A3KCH27798
Silver Spirit II:	1990 First–SCAZS00A7LCH31001:	1993 Last–SCAZS00A6PCX46740
Silver Spirit III:	1994 First–SCAZS02D5RCH54003:	1995 Last–SCAZS02CXSCH55760
Silver Spirit (96):	1996 First–SCAZS02C0TCH57003:	1997 Last–SCAZS12C5VCH59368
Silver Dawn:	1995 First–SCAZA02C4SCX54846:	1998 Last–SCAZA17C9WCH66305
Silver Spur:	1980 First–SCAZN0000ACH01006:	1989 Last–SCAZN02A4KCX27780
Silver Spur Centenary:	1985 First–SCAZN0004FCH14000.	
25 Replicas of above:	1985 First–SCAZN0004FCH14001:	1985 Last–SCAZN0004FCH14025
Silver Spur II:	1990 First–SCAZN02A7LCX31002:	1993 Last–SCAZN00AXPCX46781
Mulliner Spur:	1990 First–SCAZN02D5LCX33347:	1991 Last–SCAZN02A6MCH36065
Silver Spur III:	1994 First–SCAZN02D6RCX54001:	1995 Last–SCAZN02C5SCX55749
Silver Spur (96):	1996 First–SCAZNO2C1TCX57001:	1999 Last–SCAZN20E9XCH66585
Bentley Mulsanne:	1980 First–SCBZS0000ACHO1009:	1987 Last–SCBZS0004HCX21999
Mulsanne L:	1981 First–SCBZN0002CCH04010:	1987 Last–SCBZN0003HCH21373
Mulsanne S:	1988 First–SCBZS02B3JCK21058:	1992 Last–SCBZS02D5NCX44588
Mulsanne S l.w.b.:	1988 First–SCBZN00A6JCH22239:	1992 Last–SCBZN02A4NCH44582
Bentley Eight:	1984 First–SCBZS8004ECH08862:	1992 Last–SCBZE02A9NCH44552

The Silver Spirit II.

Bentley Brooklands:	1993 First–SCBZEO2D4PCX46004:	1997 Last–SCBZE20E5VCH60307
Brooklands l.w.b.:	1993 First–SCBZF02D4PCX46260:	1997 Last–SCBZY21C8VCX80505
Brooklands R s.w.b.:	1998 First–SCBZE20C4WCH66003:	1998 Last–SCBZE21C9WCX66400
Brooklands R l.w.b.:	1998 First–SCBZF20C9WCH66284:	1998 Last–SCBZF20C2WCH66420
Brooklands R Mulliner:	1998 First–SCBZF23E8WCH66802:	1999 Last–SCBZF19E7XCX66586

NUMBERS PRODUCED

Rolls-Royce: Silver Spirit, 8,125; Silver Spirit II, 1,152; Silver Spirit III, 234; Silver Spirit (96), 145; Silver Spur, 6,224; Silver Spur Centenary, 1; Silver Spur Centenary replica, 25; Silver Spur II, 1,658; Mulliner Spur, 71; Silver Spur III, 465; Silver Spur (96), 802; Silver Dawn, 237; Bentley: Mulsanne, 482; Mulsanne L, 47; Mulsanne S, 909; Mulsanne S l.w.b., 61; Eight, 1,734; Brooklands, 1,343; Brooklands l.w.b., 188; Brooklands R s.w.b., 79; Brooklands R l.w.b., 12; Brooklands R Mulliner, 100.

ROLLS-ROYCE
*Camargue 1981–87, *Corniche 1981–87, Corniche II 1986–89, Corniche III 1990–91, Corniche IV 1992–95, Corniche S 1995

BENTLEY
*Corniche 1981–85, Continental 1986–95, Continental Turbo 1992–95, Continental S 1995

NB. Although updated to the Silver Spirit technical specification from 1979 the *Rolls Royce Corniche and *Camargue models included in this chapter were actually in production from 1971 and 1975 respectively (see earlier specifications of Rolls-Royce Corniche).

Rolls-Royce Camargue, Mulliner Park Ward coachwork styled by Pininfarina.

ENGINE

GENERAL L410 Eight cylinders in 90° V configuration, bore 4.1 in. (104.1 mm), stroke 3.9 in. (99.1 mm), cubic capacity 412 cu. in. (6,750 cc). Compression ratio 9:1 (8:1 on all cars for North America, Australia, Japan, the UK and the rest of the world from 1986).

VALVES Overhead valves operated by helical gear-driven cast iron camshaft in V of engine. Hydraulic tappets.

CYLINDER HEAD AND CYLINDER BLOCK Aluminium cylinder head with austenitic steel valve seat inserts. Aluminium alloy monobloc casting with cast iron wet cylinder liners. From 1989 cross-bolted crankcase.

Rolls-Royce Camargue, 1980.

CRANKSHAFT Forged steel, counterweighted, statically and dynamically balanced five bearing crankshaft.

INDUCTION SYSTEMS Bosch K-Jetronic continuous fuel injection with 'closed loop' mixture control on cars for North America, Australia and Japan; also the UK and other markets from 1986. Four-barrel Solex downdraught carburettor for the UK and other markets until 1986. From 1980 Bentley Continental Turbo Garrett turbocharger from 1992. Bosch K-Motronic fuel injection and engine management system from 1989. Bosch M-3.3 fuel injection and engine management system from 1992.

EXHAUST SYSTEM North American and Japanese cars fitted with catalytic converters, then on all cars except those sold in the Middle East from the 1987/8 model year onward. Cars not fitted with catalytic converters: twin pipe system with six silencer boxes.
Cars with catalytic converters: twin downtake pipes from engine merge into a single pipe prior to the catalytic converters, then revert to twin pipes with twin intermediate and rear silencer boxes.

POWER Not available, except, unofficially, 240 b.h.p. using Bosch K-Jetronic fuel injection on non-turbocharged engines from 1986.

TORQUE Not available.

TRANSMISSION
GEARS: Until 1992, GM400 3-speed automatic transmission with torque converter. From 1992, GM4L80E 4-speed torque converter automatic transmission with overdrive top gear electronically linked to engine management system.
Electrically operated gear selection with the selector mounted on right side of the steering column.

RATIOS Up to 1987: 3.08:1, 4.56:1, 7.64:1. Final drive 3.08:1.
From 1987: 2.69:1, 3.98:1, 6.67:1. Final drive 2.69:1
From 1992: 2.31:1, 3.08:1, 4.56:1, 7.64:1. Final drive 3.08:1.

BRAKES
All four wheels fitted with 11-in. (279-mm) disc brakes ventilated at the front. Each rear wheel fitted with one four-cylinder calliper and each front wheel with two twin-cylinder callipers. Two independent hydraulic circuits from separate high-pressure hydraulic systems operated via distribution valves operated by the brake pedal. Separate brake pads for foot-operated, hand-released parking brake. Anti-lock brakes (ABS) from late 1986.

SUSPENSION
Front: independent by coil springs and telescopic dampers, with lower wishbones, upper compliant levers and anti-roll bar mounted on the front sub-frame.
Rear: independent coil springs with semi-trailing arms and anti-roll bar. Telescopic hydraulic suspension struts and pressurised gas springs act in conjunction with the coil springs and incorporate both damping and self-levelling height control.
The height of the car is maintained under all normal load conditions by the gas springs and suspension struts plus an automatic self-levelling system with restrictors in the pressure lines which ensure that the levelling responds slowly to suspension movements.
Braking and self-levelling systems take Hydraulic System Mineral Oil pressurised up to 2,500 p.s.i. from two hydraulic accumulators mounted on the crankcase and fed by twin camshaft-driven hydraulic pumps. A safety valve ensures priority pressure to the braking system when pressure in the accumulators is low.
From 1992 the Corniche IV has an electronic three-position ride control system capable of adapting to changing road conditions in milliseconds.

STEERING
Power-assisted rack and pinion with centre take-off. Power assistance by hydraulic pressure from engine-driven pump. Collapsible energy absorbing steering column. 3.25 turns lock to lock.

WHEELS AND TYRES
15-in. pressed steel wheels fitted with 235/70 HR15 steel braced radial ply tyres. From

1986 15-in. aluminium alloy wheels with stainless steel covers were fitted to Corniche models.

UNDERFRAME
Separate front and rear sub-frames. Front: steel box section mounted to underframe with rubber mounts. Rear: suspension and final drive cross-members connected by bracing tubes to form rigid structure attached to underframe by rubber mounts with short horizontal telescopic dampers at front mounts.

COACHWORK
Welded steel construction by Mulliner Park Ward on reinforced base unit with aluminium doors, bonnet (hood) and boot (trunk) lid. Electrically operated roof. Body stiffened by underfloor cruciform. Electric lift windows, electric front seat adjustments and fully automatic air conditioning.

DIMENSIONS
Wheelbase:	10 ft. 0.5 in.	(3,061 mm)
Front track:	5 ft. 0.5 in.	(1,537 mm)
Rear track:	5 ft. 0.5 in.	(1,537 mm)
Overall length:	17 ft. 0.5 in.	(5,194 mm)
Overall width:	5 ft. 11.7 in.	(1,821 mm)
Overall height:	4 ft. 11.75 in.	(1,518mm)

PERFORMANCE
1980–85 Models: Corniche, & Camargue from 1981
Maximum speed:	126 m.p.h. (202 k.p.h.)	
Acceleration:	0–60 m.p.h.	12.8 sec.
Acceleration:	0–100 m.p.h.	29.9 sec.

1986–93 Models: Corniche, Camargue, Corniche II, Corniche III, Corniche IV, Continental
Maximum speed:	126 m.p.h. (202 k.p.h.)	
Acceleration:	0–60 m.p.h.	10.4 sec.
Acceleration:	0–100 m.p.h.	32.9 sec.

1993–95 Models: Corniche IV, Corniche S & Continental
Maximum speed:	133 m.p.h. (214 k.p.h.)	
Acceleration:	0–60 m.p.h.	9.5 sec.
Acceleration:	0–100 m.p.h.	Not known

1992–95: Bentley Continental Turbo
Maximum speed:	140 m.p.h. (225 k.p.h.)	
Acceleration:	0–60 m.p.h.	7.9 sec.
Acceleration:	0–100 m.p.h.	Not known

VIN NUMBERS, FIRST AND LAST

*Rolls-Royce Corniche:	1981 First–SCAYD0009BCH01557:	1987 Last–SCAZD0001HCH21668
Corniche II:	1986 First–SCAZD42A5GCX13162:	1989 Last–SCAZD02A8KCX29289
Corniche III:	1990 First–SCAZD00AXLCH30001:	1991 Last–SCAZD02A4MCX30636
Corniche IV:	1992 First–SCAZD02A9NCX40001:	1995 Last–SCAZD02C5SCH50170
Corniche S:	1995 First–SCAZC03C7SCX50086:	1995 Last–SCAZC03C2SCX50156
*Camargue:	1981 First–SCAYJ42A8BCX01570:	1987 Last–SCAYJ42A1HCX10412
*Bentley Corniche:	1981 First–SCBYD42A7BCX02499:	1985 Last–SCBZD0004FCH10382
Continental:	1986 First–SCBZD42A8GCX13412:	1995 Last–SCBZD02C4SCX50167
Continental S:	1995 First–SCBZB05C1SCX52332:	1995 Last–SCBZB05C9SCX52451
Continental Turbo	1992 First–SCBZD04D6NCH40091:	1995 Last–SCBZCO3C2SCX50163

NB. *Prior to 1981 the Corniche and the Camargue were numbered on the old pre-VIN system.

NUMBERS PRODUCED
*Rolls-Royce: Corniche, 1,306; Corniche II, 1,226; Corniche III, 451; Corniche IV, 219; Corniche S, 25; *Camargue, 190. *Bentley: Corniche, 30; Continental, 430; Continental Turbo, 8: Continental S, 39.

NB. *Post-1980 numbers only

ROLLS-ROYCE

Silver Spur Limousine 1982-88, Silver Spur Division 1997–99, Silver Spur Non
Division 1998, Touring Limousine 1992–97, Park Ward Limousine 1996–99

Rear compartment of Silver Spur with division.

ENGINE

GENERAL L410 Eight cylinders in 90° V configuration, bore 4.1 in. (104.1 mm), stroke 3.9
in. (99.1 mm), cubic capacity 412 cu. in. (6,750 cc). Compression ratio 9:1 (8:1 on all cars
for North America, Australia, Japan, the UK and the rest of the world from 1986).

VALVES Overhead valves operated by helical gear driven cast iron camshaft in V of engine.
Hydraulic tappets.

CYLINDER HEAD AND CYLINDER BLOCK Aluminium cylinder head with austenitic steel
valve seat inserts. Aluminium alloy monobloc casting with cast iron wet cylinder liners.
From 1989 cross-bolted crankcase.

CRANKSHAFT Forged steel, counterweighted, statically and dynamically balanced five
bearing crankshaft.

Park Ward, 1997. Note the centre panel between front and rear doors.

Interior rear compartment of Park Ward, 1997.

Rolls-Royce Touring Limousine.

INDUCTION SYSTEMS Bosch K-Jetronic continuous fuel injection with 'closed loop' mixture control on cars for North America, Australia and Japan; also UK and other markets from 1986. Twin horizontal constant-vacuum HIF.7 $1^{7}/_{8}$in. SU carburettors for UK and other markets up to 1986. Bosch K-Motronic fuel injection and engine management system from 1989. Bosch M-3.3 fuel injection and engine management system from 1992. Low-pressure turbocharged engine with estimated 20 per cent more power from 1996. Zytek EMS3 engine management system from 1996.

EXHAUST SYSTEM North American and Japanese cars fitted with catalytic converters, from 1987–88 model year onward on all cars except those sold in the Middle East.

Cars not fitted with catalytic converters: twin pipe system with six silencer boxes.

Cars with catalytic converters: twin downtake pipes from engine merge into a single pipe prior to the catalytic converters, then revert to twin pipes with twin intermediate and rear silencer boxes.

POWER Unofficially, 200 b.h.p. plus using twin SU carburettors, 240 b.h.p. using Bosch K-Jetronic fuel injection on non-turbocharged engines from 1986, and 290/300 b.h.p. plus using low-pressure turbocharged engines from 1996.

TORQUE Not known.

TRANSMISSION

GEARS Until 1992, GM400 3-speed automatic transmission with torque converter. From 1992, GM4L80E 4-speed torque converter automatic transmission with overdrive top gear electronically linked to engine management system. Electrically operated gear selector mounted on the right side of the steering column.

RATIOS   Up to 1987: 3.08:1, 4.56:1, 7.64:1. Final drive 3.08:1.
            From 1987: 2.69:1, 3.98:1, 6.67:1. Final drive 2.69:1
            From 1992: 2.31:1, 3.08:1, 4.56:1, 7.64:1. Final drive 3.08:1.

BRAKES

All four wheels fitted with 11-in. (279-mm) disc brakes ventilated at the front. Each rear wheel fitted with one four-cylinder calliper and each front wheel with two twin-cylinder callipers. Two independent hydraulic circuits from separate high-pressure hydraulic systems operated via distribution valves operated by the brake pedal. Separate brake pads for foot-operated, hand-released parking brake. Anti-lock brakes (ABS) from 1986.

SUSPENSION

Front: independent by coil springs and telescopic dampers, with lower wishbones, upper compliant levers and anti-roll bar mounted on the front sub-frame.
Rear: independent coil springs with semi-trailing arms and anti-roll bar. Telescopic

hydraulic suspension struts and pressurised gas springs act in conjunction with the coil springs and incorporate both damping and self-levelling height control.

The height of the car is maintained under all normal load conditions by the gas springs and suspension struts plus an automatic self-levelling system with restrictors in the pressure lines which ensure that the levelling responds slowly to suspension movements.

Braking and self-levelling systems take Hydraulic System Mineral Oil pressurised up to 2,500 p.s.i. from two hydraulic accumulators mounted on the crankcase and fed by twin camshaft-driven hydraulic pumps. A safety valve ensures priority pressure to the braking system when pressure in the accumulators is low.

Automatic ride control capable of adapting to changing road conditions in a fraction of a second.

STEERING
Power-assisted rack and pinion with centre take-off. Power assistance by hydraulic pressure from engine-driven pump. Collapsible energy-absorbing steering column. 3.25 turns lock to lock. From 1996 electrically tilting steering wheel.

WHEELS AND TYRES
15-in. pressed steel wheels fitted with 235/70 HR15 steel-braced radial ply tyres were standard until 1986 when 15-in. aluminium alloy wheels were introduced. From 1996 16-in. aluminium alloy wheels fitted with 235/65 VR16 tyres.

UNDERFRAME
Separate front and rear sub-frames. Front: steel box section mounted to underframe with rubber mounts. Rear: suspension and final drive cross-members connected by bracing tubes to form rigid structure attached to underframe by rubber mounts with short horizontal telescopic dampers at front mounts.

COACHWORK
Pressed steel four-door monocoque construction with aluminium doors, bonnet (hood) and boot (trunk) lid. Electric lift windows, electric front seat adjustments and fully automatic air conditioning. Electrically adjustable rear seats.

DIMENSIONS
Wheelbase Silver Spur Limousine with 42 in. (1,067 mm) stretch: 13 ft. 6.5 in. (4,128 mm)
Overall length Silver Spur Limousine with 42 in. (1067 mm)
Stretch   20 ft. 9.5 in. (6,338 mm)
Wheelbase Silver Spur Limousine with 36 in. (914 mm) stretch: 13 ft. 0.5 in. (3,975 mm)
Overall length Silver Spur Limousine with 36 in. (914 mm)
stretch: 20 ft. 3.5 in. (6,185 mm)
Wheelbase Touring & Park Ward Limousines with 24 in.
(610 mm) stretch: 12 ft. 8.5 in. (3,770 mm)

Overall length Touring & Park Ward Limousines with 24 in. (610 mm) stretch:	19 ft. 7.4 in. (5,980 mm)
Wheelbase Silver Spur Division with 14 in. (356 mm) stretch:	11 ft. 6.6 in. (3,520 mm)
Overall length Silver Spur Non Division with 14 in. (356 mm) stretch:	18 ft. 11.2 in. (5,770 mm)
Front track all lengths:	5 ft. 0.5 in. (1,537 mm)
Rear track all lengths:	5 ft. 0.5 in. (1,537 mm)
Overall width all lengths:	6 ft. 2.3 in. (1,887 mm)
Overall height all lengths:	4 ft. 10.5 in. (1,485 mm)

PERFORMANCE

1980–85
Maximum speed: 119 m.p.h. (192 k.p.h.)
Acceleration: 0–60 m.p.h. 10.0 sec.
Acceleration: 0–100 m.p.h. 30.8 sec.

1986–93
Maximum speed: 126 m.p.h. (202 k.p.h.)
Acceleration: 0–60 m.p.h. 10.4 sec.
Acceleration: 0–100 m.p.h. 32.9 sec.

1993–95
Maximum speed: 133 m.p.h. (214 k.p.h.)
Acceleration: 0–60 mph 9.5 sec.
Acceleration: 0–100 m.p.h. Not known

1996–99
Maximum speed: 140 m.p.h. (225 k.p.h.)
Acceleration: 0–60 m.p.h. 7.9 sec.
Acceleration: 0–100 m.p.h. Not known

VIN NUMBERS, FIRST AND LAST

Silver Spur Limousine:	1982 First–SCAZN000600X06019:	1988 Last–SCAZX00A8JCH23441
Silver Spur Division:	1997 First–SCAZY20CXVCH80501:	1999 Last–SCAZY19E2XCX80541
Silver Spur Non Division:	1998 First–SCAZY21C7WCH80701:	1998 Last–SCAZY20C9WCH80720
Touring Limousine:	1992 First–SCAZW02D5NCX80001:	1997 Last–SCAZH20C8VCH80402
Park Ward Limousine:	1996 First–SCAZV12CXTCH80205:	1999 Last–SCAZV15E9XCX80258

NUMBERS PRODUCED

Rolls-Royce: Silver Spur Limousine, 101; Silver Spur Division, 39; Silver Spur Non Division, 20; Touring Limousine, 103; Park Ward Limousine, 52.
Also Armoured Silver Spur, 1 only (1999 SCAZY16E7XCX80801).
Bentley R Brooklands Division, 1 only (1998 SCBZY21C6WCX80536); Mulsanne L Limousine, 2 only (1986 SCBZN0006GCX14767 and 1987 SCBZN0000HCX20470).

BENTLEY

Mulsanne Turbo 1982–86, L.W.B. 1983–86, Turbo R & Turbo RL 1985–96,
Turbo R S.W.B. & Turbo R L.W.B. 1997, Turbo RT S.W.B. 1998, Turbo RT
L.W.B. & Turbo RT Mulliner 1998–99, Turbo S 1995

ROLLS-ROYCE

Flying Spur 1995

1996 Bentley Turbo R.

ENGINE

GENERAL L410 Eight cylinders in 90° V configuration, bore 4.1 in. (104.1 mm), stroke 3.9 in. (99.1 mm), cubic capacity 412 cu. in. (6,750 cc). Compression ratio 8:1 (9 :1 on Mulsanne Turbo, Turbo R and Turbo RL up to 1986.)

VALVES Overhead valves operated by helical gear-driven cast iron camshaft in V of engine. Hydraulic tappets.

CYLINDER HEAD AND CYLINDER BLOCK Aluminium cylinder head with austenitic steel valve seat inserts. Aluminium alloy monobloc casting with cast iron wet cylinder liners. From 1989 cross-bolted crankcase.

CRANKSHAFT Forged steel, counterweighted, statically and dynamically balanced five bearing crankshaft.

390

INDUCTION SYSTEMS Garrett turbocharger or Garrett turbochargers with intercooler and single Solex 4A1 four-barrel downdraught carburettor with fuel economy device operating during partial throttle openings. Carburettor was replaced in 1986 by Bosch K-Jetronic continuous fuel injection with 'closed loop' mixture control. From 1989, all cars MK Motronic fuel injection and engine management system. From 1996 Bentley turbocharged models, Zytek EMS3 engine management system.

EXHAUST SYSTEM North American and Japanese cars fitted with catalytic converters, then on all cars except those sold in the Middle East from the 1987/8 model year onward.
Cars not fitted with catalytic converters: twin pipe system with six silencer boxes.
Cars with catalytic converters: twin downtake pipes from engine merge into a single pipe prior to the catalytic converters, then revert to twin pipes with twin intermediate and rear silencer boxes.

POWER Unofficially, 298 b.h.p. using single Solex 4A1 carburettor, 330 b.h.p. from 1986 using Bosch K-Jetronic fuel injection. In 1994 an *Autocar* road test estimated 360 b.h.p. at 4,200 r.p.m. for the Rolls-Royce Flying Spur. Turbocharged engines officially quoted as 385 b.h.p. from 1995 but the 1998 Turbo RT was boosted to 400 b.h.p.

TORQUE From 1986 440 lb./ ft. From 1992 553 lb./ ft. on some models 590 lb./ ft. on others. From 1998 Turbo RT 590 lb./ ft.

TRANSMISSION
GEARS Until 1992, GM400 3-speed automatic transmission with torque converter.

From 1992, GM4L80E 4-speed torque converter automatic transmission with over-drive top gear electronically linked to engine management system. Viscous differential with traction control introduced on the 1995 Turbo S.

Electrically operated gear selection with the selector mounted on right side of the steering column on the Flying Spur which was only built for the 1995 model year. The Bentley Mulsanne Turbo also has the selector mounted on right side of the steering column, as do Bentley Turbo R models prior to the introduction of 4-speed automatic transmission in 1992. After 1992 all Bentley Turbo's have a centre-mounted console offering either standard or sports mode selection.

RATIOS Up to 1987:   3.08:1, 4.56:1, 7.64:1. Final drive 3.08:1.
   Bentley from 1987:   2.69:1, 3.98:1, 6.68:1. Final drive 2.69:1.
   From 1992:   2.31:1, 3.08:1, 4.56:1, 7.64:1. Final drive 3.08:1.
   From 1995:   2.02:1, 2.69:1, 3.98:1, 6.67:1. Final drive 2.69:1
   Rolls-Royce Flying Spur: 1.71:1, 2.28:1, 3.37:1, 5.65:1. Final drive 2.28:1.

BRAKES
340-mm front and 277-mm rear disc brakes ventilated at the front (Flying Spur and earlier

1994 Bentley Turbo R L.W.B.

The Bentley Mulsanne Turbo.

models 279-mm front and rear.) Each rear wheel fitted with one four-cylinder calliper and each front wheel with two twin-cylinder callipers. Two independent hydraulic circuits from separate high-pressure hydraulic systems operated via distribution valves operated by the brake pedal. Separate brake pads for foot-operated, hand-released parking brake. Anti-lock brakes (ABS) from 1986.

SUSPENSION

Front: independent by coil springs and telescopic dampers, with lower wishbones, upper compliant levers and anti-roll bar mounted on the front sub-frame.

Rear: independent coil springs with semi-trailing arms and anti-roll bar. Telescopic hydraulic suspension struts and pressurised gas springs act in conjunction with the coil springs and incorporate both damping and self-levelling height control.

The height of the car is maintained under all normal load conditions by the gas springs and suspension struts plus an automatic self-levelling system with restrictors in the pressure lines which ensure that the levelling responds slowly to suspension movements.

Braking and self-levelling systems take Hydraulic System Mineral Oil pressurised up to 2,500 p.s.i. from two hydraulic accumulators mounted on the crankcase and fed by twin camshaft-driven hydraulic pumps. A safety valve ensures priority pressure to the braking system when pressure in the accumulators is low.

STEERING

Power-assisted rack and pinion with centre take-off. Power assistance by hydraulic pressure from engine-driven pump. Collapsible energy-absorbing steering column. 3.25 turns lock to lock. From 1996 electrically tilting steering wheel.

WHEELS AND TYRES

15-in. pressed steel wheels fitted with 235/70 VR15 steel-braced radial ply tyres. 1984: Bentley Turbo R 15-in. aluminium alloy wheels with 275/55 VR15 low profile radial ply tyres – from 1986 255/55 VR15 option. Other Bentley models from 1986 15-in. aluminium alloy wheels. 1993: Bentley Turbo R 16-in. aluminium alloy wheels with 255/65 ZR16 low-profile radial ply tyres. 1994: 17-in. aluminium alloy wheels with 255/55 WR17 directional tyres introduced on the Bentley Turbo R and Turbo S – 225/65 VR15 on the Rolls-Royce Flying Spur.

UNDERFRAME

Separate front and rear sub-frames. Front: steel box section mounted to underframe with rubber mounts. Rear: suspension and final drive cross-members connected by bracing tubes to form rigid structure attached to underframe by rubber mounts with short horizontal telescopic dampers at front mounts.

COACHWORK

Pressed steel four-door monocoque construction with aluminium doors, bonnet (hood) and boot (trunk) lid. Electric lift windows, electric front seat adjustments, and fully automatic air conditioning.

DIMENSIONS

Standard wheelbase:	10 ft. 0.5 in.	(3,061 mm)
Long wheelbase:	10 ft. 4.5 in.	(3,162 mm)
Front track:	5 ft. 0.5 in.	(1,537 mm)
Rear track:	5 ft. 0.5 in.	(1,537 mm)
Overall length s.w.b.:	17 ft. 3.4 in.	(5,268 mm)
Overall length l.w.b.:	17 ft. 7.4 in.	(5,370 mm)
Overall width:	6 ft. 2.3 in.	(1,887 mm)
Overall height:	4 ft. 10.5 in.	(1,485 mm)

PERFORMANCE

1980–85 Models: Mulsanne Turbo & Turbo R
Maximum speed: 135 m.p.h. (217 k.p.h.)
Acceleration: 0–60 m.p.h. 7.0 sec.
Acceleration: 0–100 m.p.h. 17.9 sec.

1986–94 Models: Turbo R
Maximum speed: 143 m.p.h. (230 k.p.h.)
Acceleration: 0–60 m.p.h. 7.0 sec.
Acceleration: 0–100 m.p.h. 19.5 sec.

1995–99 Models: Turbo R, Turbo RT, Turbo RT Mulliner, Turbo S
Maximum speed: 151 m.p.h. (243 k.p.h.)
Acceleration: 0–60 m.p.h. 6.1 sec.
Acceleration: 0–100 m.p.h. 16.9 sec.

1995: Rolls-Royce Flying Spur
Maximum speed: 130 m.p.h. (209 k.p.h.)
Acceleration: 0–60 m.p.h. 6.9 sec.
Acceleration: 0–100 m.p.h. 21.0 sec.

VIN NUMBERS, FIRST AND LAST

Bentley Mulsanne Turbo:	1982 First–SCBZS0T05CCH04233:	1985 Last–SCBZS0T08FCH14162-
Mulsanne Turbo L:	1983 First–SCBZN0T04DCH06872:	1986 Last–SCBZN0TO1GCX15787
Turbo R:	1985 First–SCBZS0T04FCX12695:	1996 Last–SCBZR15C2TCX58286
Turbo RL:	1985 First–SCBZN0T04FCH12433:	1996 Last–SCBZP1SC9TCX58291-
Turbo R SWB:	1997 First–SCBZR15C6VCX59153:	1997 Last–SCBZR15E3VCH60314
Turbo R LWB:	1997 First–SCBZP15CXVCX59002:	1997 Last–SCBZP15C5VCH60321-
Turbo RT SWB:	1998 First–SCBZR23C6WCH66293:	1998 Last–SCBZR23C1WCX66392-
Turbo RT LWB:	1998 First–SCBZP23E4WCX66006:	1999 Last–SCBZP24E9XCX66583-
Turbo RT Mulliner:	1998 First–SCBZP27C9WCX66432	1999 Last–SCBZP25EXXCX66543

| Turbo S: | 1995 First–SCBZT05C8SCH56801: | 1995 Last–SCBZT05C2SCH56860 |
| Rolls-Royce Flying Spur: | 1995 First–SCAZG03C6SCX54974: | 1995 Last–SCAZG03C5SCX55761 |

NUMBERS PRODUCED

Bentley: Mulsanne Turbo, 496; Mulsanne Turbo l.w.b., 24; Turbo R, 4,450; Turbo RL, 1,044; Turbo R s.w.b., 8; Turbo R l.w.b., 480; Turbo RT s.w.b., 2; Turbo RT l.w.b., 250; Turbo RT Mulliner, 56; Turbo S, 60; Rolls-Royce: Flying Spur, 133.

BENTLEY

Continental R from 1992, Continental R Mulliner from 1999, Continental R Millenium 2000, Continental R Le Mans from 2001, Continental T from 1996, Continental T Mulliner from 1999, Continental T Le Mans from 2001, Continental SC 1998-2000, Continental SC Mulliner 1999-2000, Azure from 1995, Azure Mulliner from 1999, Azure Le Mans from 2001

ROLLS-ROYCE
Corniche from 1999

1993 Bentley Continental R.

ENGINE

GENERAL L410 Eight cylinders in 90° V configuration, bore 4.1 in. (104.1 mm), stroke 3.9 in. (99.1 mm), cubic capacity 412 cu. in. (6,750 cc). Compression ratio 8:1.

VALVES Two overhead valves per cylinder operated by helical gear-driven cast iron camshaft in V of engine. Hydraulic tappets.

CYLINDER HEAD AND CYLINDER BLOCK Aluminium cylinder head with austenitic steel valve seat inserts. Aluminium alloy monobloc casting with cast iron wet cylinder liners. From 1989 cross-bolted crankcase.

CRANKSHAFT Forged steel, counterweighted, statically and dynamically balanced five bearing crankshaft.

1999 Bentley Continental T, personal commission.

INDUCTION SYSTEMS Garrett turbocharger with Electronic Transient Boost Control and MK Motronic fuel injection and engine management system until 1995. From 1995, Zytek EMS3 engine management system. From 1997–9, intercooled Zytek EMS3 engine management system.

EXHAUST SYSTEM North American and Japanese cars fitted with catalytic converters, then on all cars except those sold in the Middle East from the 1987/8 model year onward.
Cars not fitted with catalytic converters: twin pipe system with six silencer boxes.
Cars with catalytic converters: twin downtake pipes from engine merge into a single pipe prior to the catalytic converters, then revert to twin pipes with twin intermediate and rear silencer boxes.

POWER 385 b.h.p. at 4,000 r.p.m. on some models 360 b.h.p. at 4,200 r.p.m. on others. From 1995, 400 b.h.p. at 4,000 r.p.m. From 1998, Continental SC and SC Mulliner 406 b.h.p. From 1999, Continental R Mulliner and Azure Mulliner 420 b.h.p. at 4,000 r.p.m. From 1999, Continental T and T Mulliner 426 b.h.p. Corniche 325 b.h.p.

TORQUE Estimated 440 lb./ft., later 553 lb./ft. on some models and 590 lb./ft. on others. From 1999, Continental T 650 lb./ ft. Corniche 544 lb./ ft.

TRANSMISSION
GEARS GM4L80E 4-speed torque converter automatic transmission with overdrive top

1997 Bentley Continental T, personal commission.

gear electronically linked to engine management system. The Corniche has an electrically operated gear selector mounted on the right side of the steering column, the others have electrically operated centre console-mounted selectors with sport and normal settings.

RATIOS   From 1992:   2.31:1, 3.08:1, 4.56:1, 7.64:1. Final drive 3.08:1.
          From 1995: 2.02:1, 2.69:1, 3.98:1, 6.67:1. Final drive 2.69:1

BRAKES AND TRACTION ASSISTANCE

279-mm front and 277-mm rear disc brakes (ventilated at the front). Each rear wheel fitted with one four-cylinder calliper and each front wheel with two twin-cylinder callipers. Two independent hydraulic circuits from separate high-pressure hydraulic systems operated via distribution valves operated by the brake pedal. Separate brake pads for foot-operated, hand-released parking brake. Anti-lock brakes (ABS).

Electronic Traction Assistance System (ETAS): EMS microprocessor monitors traction with wheel speed data and reacts via fuel metering to individual cylinders, significantly faster and more precisely than conventional throttle or brake intervention systems. Viscous limited slip differential eliminates need for individual wheel control. Adaptive Shift Control modifies the gear change points in 'normal' mode according to driving style.

SUSPENSION

Front: independent by coil springs and telescopic dampers, with lower wishbones, upper compliant levers and anti-roll bar mounted on the front sub-frame. Rear: independent coil

1998 Bentley Continental SC.

1998 Bentley Continental SC.

1997 Bentley Azure.

springs with semi-trailing arms and anti-roll bar. Telescopic hydraulic suspension struts and pressurised gas springs act in conjunction with the coil springs and incorporate both damping and self-levelling height control.

The height of the car is maintained under all normal load conditions by the gas springs and suspension struts plus an automatic self-levelling system with restrictors in the pressure lines which ensure that the levelling responds slowly to suspension movements.
Braking and self-levelling systems take Hydraulic System Mineral Oil pressurised up to 2,500 p.s.i. from two hydraulic accumulators mounted on the crankcase and fed by twin camshaft-driven hydraulic pumps. A safety valve ensures priority pressure to the braking system when pressure in the accumulators is low.

Automatic ride control capable of adapting to changing road conditions in a fraction of a second.

STEERING
Power-assisted rack and pinion with centre take-off. Power assistance by hydraulic pressure from engine-driven pump. Collapsible energy-absorbing steering column. Initial 3.25 turns lock to lock reduced to 3.1 turns, then 2.7 turns, at various dates on various models. From 1996, electrically tilting steering wheel.

WHEELS AND TYRES
16-in. aluminium alloy wheels with 255/60 ZR16 low-profile radial ply tyres from 1992

1998 Bentley Azure.

until fitted with 17-in. aluminium alloy wheels with 255/55 WR17 low-profile radial ply tyres in 1994. From 1996 18-in. aluminium alloy wheels with 285/45 WR18 low-profile radial ply tyres-on. Corniche 255/65 ZR17.

UNDERFRAME
Separate front and rear sub-frames. Front: steel box section mounted to underframe with rubber mounts. Rear: suspension and final drive cross-members connected by bracing tubes to form rigid structure, attached to underframe by rubber mounts with short horizontal telescopic dampers at front mounts.

COACHWORK
COUPÉ Pressed steel two-door monocoque construction with aluminium doors, bonnet (hood) and boot (trunk) lid. Electric lift windows, electric front seat adjustments and fully automatic air conditioning.

Later models also have anti-intrusion beams to all doors. Impact-absorbing body sections to front, rear and sides. Anti-trap windows. Anti-trap sunroof if fitted. High mounted rear stop lamp. Energy absorbing bumpers. Ten-stage anti-corrosion pre-treatment, including electro-coated galvanising. Lift-assisted luggage compartment lid with touch release and powered closing mechanism. Lift-assisted rear hinged bonnet. Elastomeric stone-chip protection to under body surfaces. From 2000, power folding door mirrors with electrochromic glass.

1999 Rolls-Royce Corniche.

CONVERTIBLE Welded steel construction by Mulliner Park Ward on reinforced base unit with aluminium doors, bonnet (hood) and boot (trunk) lid. Electrically operated roof. Body stiffened by underfloor cruciform. Electric lift windows, electric front seat adjustments and fully automatic air conditioning.

DIMENSIONS

Wheelbase except Cont. T & SC:	10 ft. 0.5 in.	(3,061 mm)
Wheelbase Cont. T & SC:	9 ft. 8.6 in.	(2,961 mm)
Front track:	5 ft. 0.9 in	(1,549 mm)
Rear track:	5 ft. 0.9 in.	(1,549 mm)
Overall length Cont. T & SC:	17 ft. 1.6 in.	(5,222 mm)
Overall length Corniche:	17 ft. 8.8 in.	(5,405 mm)
Overall length Azure & Cont. R & S:	17 ft. 6.6 in.	(5,350 mm)
Overall width:	6 ft. 9.0 in.	(2,058 mm)
Overall height Azure & Corniche:	4 ft. 10.1 in.	(1,475 mm)
Overall height Cont. R, T, & SC:	4 ft. 9.6 in.	(1,462 mm)

PERFORMANCE

1992–94

Maximum speed:	143 m.p.h. (230 k.p.h.)	
Acceleration:	0–60 m.p.h.	7.0 sec.
Acceleration:	0–100 m.p.h.	19.5 sec.

1995

(Azure about 5 m.p.h. slower)

Maximum speed:	155 m.p.h. (245 k.p.h.)	
Acceleration:	0–60 m.p.h.	6.1 sec.
Acceleration:	0–100 m.p.h.	16.9 sec.

Corniche

Maximum speed:	136 m.p.h. (220 k.p.h.)	
Acceleration:	0–60 m.p.h.	8.0 sec.
Acceleration:	0–100 m.p.h.	Not known

Continental T from 1996 & Mulliner models from 1999

Maximum speed:	170 m.p.h. (270 k.p.h.)	
Acceleration:	0–60 m.p.h.	5.7 sec.
Acceleration:	0–100 m.p.h.	Not known

VIN NUMBERS, FIRST AND LAST UP TO MODEL YEAR 2001

Bentley Continental R:	1992 First–SCBZB03D5NCX42001:	2001 Last–SCBZB22E01CX63564
Continental R Mulliner:	1999 First–SCBZB26E1XCX63141:	2002
Continental R Millenium:	2000 First–SCBZB22E3YCX63309:	2000-Last–SCBZB22E2YCX63320
Continental R Le Mans:	2001 First–SCBZB25E01CH63546:	2002
Continental T:	1996 First–SCBZU15C1TCH53159:	2002
Continental T Mulliner:	1998 First–SCBZU27E9XCX67107:	2001 Last–SCBZU25E51CX67535
Continental T Le Mans:	2001 First–SCBZU25E71CH67538:	2001 Last–SCBZU25E71CH67538
Continental SC:	1998 First–SCBZZ23E8WCX65001:	2000 Last–SCBZZ22E1YCX65104
Continental SC Mulliner:	1999 First–SCBZZ26EXXCX65000:	2000 Last–SCBZZ26E3YCX65101
Azure:	1995 First–SCBZK03C3SCH50801:	2002
Azure Mulliner:	1999 First–SCBZK25E2XCX61724	2002
Azure Le Mans:	2001 First–SCBZK25E11CX62659	2001 Last–SCBZK25E91CX62666
Rolls-Royce Corniche:	1999 First–SCAZK20EXXCH68001	2002

NUMBERS PRODUCED TO DATE (UP TO 2001 MODEL YEAR)

Bentley: Continental R, 1,299; Continental R Mulliner, 113; Continental R Millenium, 10; Continental R Le Mans, 25; Continental T, 2,292; Continental T Mulliner, 20; Continental T Le Mans, 1; Continental SC, 73; Continental SC Mulliner, 6; Azure, 1,015; Azure Mulliner, 86; Azure Le Mans, 3. Rolls-Royce: Corniche, 294.

ROLLS-ROYCE
Silver Seraph from 1998, Silver Seraph Last of Line 2001, Park Ward from 1999

Park Ward.

ENGINE

GENERAL Twelve cylinders in 60° V configuration. 5379cc, bore 85.0mm. stroke 79.0mm. compression ratio 10:1.

VALVES 24 valves (2 per cylinder) single overhead cam per bank.

CYLINDER HEAD AND CYLINDER BLOCK Both aluminium alloy.

CRANKSHAFT Forged steel, statically and dynamically balanced.

INDUCTION SYSTEMS Bosch Motronic 5.2.1 engine management system. Electronic throttle control.

EXHAUST SYSTEM North American and Japanese cars fitted with catalytic converters, then on all cars except those sold in the Middle East from the 1987/8 model year onward.
Cars not fitted with catalytic converters: twin pipe system with six silencer boxes.
Cars with catalytic converters: twin downtake pipes from engine merge into a single pipe prior to the catalytic converters then revert to twin pipes with twin intermediate and rear silencer boxes.
POWER 322 b.h.p. at 5,000 r.p.m.

TORQUE 361lb./ ft. at 3,900 r.p.m.

Park Ward.

TRANSMISSION

GEARS Five-speed automatic gearbox with electric gear actuation from steering column mounted selector. Adaptive shift management. Transmission torque reduction control. Brake pedal inhibit into reverse and drive.

Ratios/m.p.h. per 1,000 r.p.m: 1st 3.55/8, 2nd 2.24/12.7, 3rd 1.54/18.5, 4th 1.00/28.4, 5th 0.79/36.0. Final drive 2.93

BRAKES AND TRACTION ASSISTANCE

Power boost control system with 4-channel anti-lock braking. Fist brake calliper design. Hydraulic brake servo. Micro-alloy ventilated discs – 314-mm front, 305-mm rear. Foot-operated parking brake. Pad wear indicator system.

Automatic Stability Control (ASC). Engine torque reduction control. Speed sensors to all four wheels. Aquaplaning detection. Rear wheel stability braking. Driver-operated system on/off switch.

SUSPENSION

Double wishbone independent front and rear suspension. Computer-controlled adaptive hydraulic damping system – response time 1/100th second. Automatic ride height control with compensatory auto load and headlamp levelling. Weight distribution front:rear – 50:50.

Silver Seraph.

STEERING
Power-assisted rack and pinion steering with rotary open centre hydraulic control valve. Three-section steering column electrically adjustable for rake (memory-linked). Automatic position adjustment to facilitate easy entry/exit. 3.55 turns lock-to-lock.

WHEELS AND TYRES
7J by 16-in. wheels with cast aluminium spokes, locking polished stainless steel centre and painted feature ring fitted with 235/65 R16 tyres.

BODYSHELL
All steel four-door monocoque construction with high torsional rigidity. High strength door construction and single pressing body apertures. Anti-intrusion beams to all doors. Impact-absorbing body sections to front, rear and sides. Anti-trap windows. Anti-trap sunroof if fitted. High mounted rear stop lamp. Energy-absorbing bumpers. Ten stage anti-corrosion pre-treatment, including electro-coated galvanising. Lift-assisted luggage compartment lid with touch release and powered closing mechanism. Lift-assisted rear hinged bonnet. Elastomeric stone-chip protection to under body surfaces. From 2000, power-folding door mirrors with electrochromic glass.

INTERIOR AND EXTERIOR FEATURES DEPENDING ON MODEL AND YEAR

GENERAL Analogue instruments, driver information panel, trip computer. Steering wheel mounted cruise control. Electrochromic self-dimming rear view mirror. Exterior mirrors dip on selection of reverse gear. Four-way electrically adjustable front seats with four memory positions. Twin electric, independently adjustable rear seats. Two-stage seat heating and bi-level lumbar support to four main seats. Electric rake adjustable steering wheel with automatic easy entry/exit feature – memory linked to driver's seat and exterior mirrors. Self-adjusting front seat belts. Driver and front passenger airbags. Anti-submarine seats. Fuel shut-off, door auto-unlock and collapsible steering column safety systems triggered by impact. Picnic tables and magazine stowage to front seat backs. Heating, ventilation and air conditioning system with side-to-side, split level (face/feet), front/rear temperature regulation, pollen and dust micro-filters, dehumidifier and residual heating. Twin drink holders to front centre console and rear console. Dual mechanism electric window lift – one-touch open/close and linear. 4x35 Watt radio/cassette/6 CD autochanger audio system with remote control for rear passenger operation. Driver's door only unlock function. Walk-up/away courtesy headlamps. Auto door lock on selection of forward gear when engine running. Auto headlamps on fast wipe speed.

MULTI-FUNCTION PROGRAMMABLE ALARM SYSTEM Rolling code transponder immobilisation of both engine management and starter systems. Perimetric sensors to doors, bonnet, luggage compartment, glove box and Spirit of Ecstasy mascot. Microwave interior volume sensing. Glass break sensor. Central locking and deadlock system. Master and limited access valet parking keys. Air conditioning system and interior lights activate on disarming.

NB. For these models, the sub-headings 'Bodyshell' and 'Interior and exterior features depending on model and year' as used above are considered by the author (Brendan James) to be more appropriate than the two sub-headings 'Underframe' and 'Coachwork' as used in previous chapters for other models.

DIMENSIONS

Silver Seraph Wheelbase:	10 ft. 2.76 in.	(3,116 mm)
Park Ward Wheelbase:	11 ft. 0.62 in.	(3,366 mm)
Front track all models:	5 ft. 3.24 in.	(1,608 mm)
Rear track all models:	5 ft. 3.24 in.	(1,608 mm)
Silver Seraph overall length:	17 ft. 8.28 in.	(5,390 mm)
Park Ward overall length:	18 ft. 6.21 in.	(5,640 mm)
Overall width all models:	7 ft. 0.70 in.	(2,150 mm)
Overall height all models:	4 ft. 11.64 in.	(1,515 mm)

PERFORMANCE

Maximum speed:	140 m.p.h.	225 k.p.h.
Acceleration:	0–60 m.p.h.	6.9 sec.
Acceleration:	0–100 m.p.h.	17.2 sec.
Acceleration:	0–100 k.p.h.	7.0 sec.
Acceleration:	0–160 k.p.h.	17.1 sec.

VIN NUMBERS, FIRST AND LAST UP TO MODEL YEAR 2001

Silver Seraph:	1998 First–SCALA61E4WCX01002:	2001 Last–SCALA62E21CX99115
Silver Seraph last of line:	2001 First–SCALA61E91CX06558:	2002
Park Ward:	2000 First–SCALD61E1YCH07501:	2002

NUMBERS PRODUCED TO DATE (UP TO 2001 MODEL YEAR)

Rolls-Royce: Silver Seraph, 1,398; Silver Seraph last of line, 19; Park Ward, 72.

BENTLEY
Arnage 1998-99, Arnage Green Label 2000, Arnage 4.4 L Birkin 2000

1998 Bentley Arnage.

ENGINE

GENERAL Eight cylinders in 90° V configuration. 4398 cc, bore 92.0 mm. stroke 79.0 mm, compression ratio 8.5:1.

VALVES 32 valves (4 per cylinder) double overhead cam per bank.

CYLINDER HEAD AND CYLINDER BLOCK Both aluminium alloy.

CRANKSHAFT Forged steel, statically and dynamically balanced.

INDUCTION SYSTEM Digital pulsed sequential fuel injection system into each cylinder. Bosch Motronic 5.2.1 engine management system. Twin water-cooled, close-coupled Garrett turbochargers and engine mounted intercooler.

EXHAUST SYSTEM North American and Japanese cars fitted with catalytic converters, then on all cars except those sold in the Middle East from the 1987/8 model year onward.
Cars not fitted with catalytic converters: twin pipe system with six silencer boxes.
Cars with catalytic converters: twin downtake pipes from engine merge into a single pipe prior to the catalytic converters, then revert to twin pipes with twin intermediate and rear silencer boxes.

1998 Bentley Arnage.

POWER 350 b.h.p. at 5,500 r.p.m.

TORQUE 413 lb./ft. from 2500–4200 r.p.m.

TRANSMISSION

GEARS Four-speed automatic gearbox with electric gear actuation from selector located on centre console offers normal plus three sports modes. A winter programme is automatically selected when rear wheel slip is detected. Adaptive shift management. Transmission torque reduction control.

Ratios/m.p.h. per 1,000 r.p.m.: 1st 3.55/8, 2nd 2.24/12.7, 3rd 1.54/18.5, 4th 1.00/28.4, 5th 0.79/36.0. Final drive 2.93:1

BRAKES AND TRACTION ASSISTANCE

Power-assisted boost and four-channel electronic anti-lock braking system with single fist brake callipers and hydraulic brake servo. Micro-alloy ventilated discs – 334-mm front, 328-mm rear. Upgraded to 348-mm front, 345-mm rear in 2000. Electronic traction assistance and engine-braking system with engine torque control to counteract driven wheel spin.

SUSPENSION

Front and rear: double wishbone independent suspension system. Front upper wishbones in forged aluminium – high mounted to body. Automatic ride height control with auto load compensation. Computer-controlled electro-hydraulic suspension dampers with a response time of 1/100th second linked to transmission and steering input.

STEERING
Power assisted rack and pinion steering 3.3 turns lock-to-lock.

WHEELS AND TYRES
From 1998, 17-in. aluminium alloy wheels with low profile 255/55 R17 tyres. From 2000, six-spoke 18-in. aluminium alloy wheels with low profile 255/50 R18 tyres (optional five-spoke sports and chrome wheel).

BODYSHELL
Rigid all-steel monocoque with impact-absorbing body sections to front, rear and sides. Double-sided zinc-coated skin panels. High-strength door construction and single-pressing body apertures. Anti-intrusion beams to all doors. Impact-absorbing body sections to front, rear and sides. Anti-trap windows. Anti-trap sunroof if fitted. High mounted rear stop lamp. Energy-absorbing bumpers. Ten stage anti-corrosion pre-treatment, including electro-coated galvanising. Lift-assisted luggage compartment lid with touch release and powered closing mechanism. Lift-assisted rear-hinged bonnet.

INTERIOR AND EXTERIOR FEATURES DEPENDING ON MODEL AND YEAR
GENERAL Analogue instruments, driver information panel, trip computer. Steering wheel mounted cruise control. Electrochromic self-dimming rear view mirror. One-touch, power folding, electrochromic glass door mirrors which dip on selection of reverse gear. Four-way electrically adjustable front seats with four memory positions linking driver's seat to exterior mirrors, steering wheel, and self-dimming interior rear view mirror. Twin electric, independently adjustable rear seats. Two-stage seat heating and bi-level lumbar support to four main seats. Electric rake adjustable steering wheel with automatic easy entry/exit feature – memory linked to driver's seat and exterior mirrors. Self-adjusting front seat belts. Driver and front passenger airbags. Anti-submarine seats. Fuel shut-off, door auto-unlock and collapsible steering column safety systems triggered by impact. Picnic tables and magazine stowage to front seat backs. Heating, ventilation, and air conditioning system with side-to-side, split level (face/feet), front/rear temperature regulation, pollen and dust micro-filters, dehumidifier and residual heating. Twin drink holders to front centre console and rear console. Dual mechanism electric window lift – one-touch open/close and linear. 4x35 Watt radio/cassette/6 CD autochanger audio system with remote control for rear passenger operation. Driver's door only unlock function. Walk-up/away courtesy headlamps. Auto door lock on selection of forward gear when engine running. Auto headlamps on fast wipe speed. Park distance control.

MULTI-FUNCTION PROGRAMMABLE ALARM SYSTEM Rolling code transponder immobilisation of both engine management and starter systems. Perimetric sensors to doors, bonnet, luggage compartment, glove box and Spirit of Ecstasy mascot. Microwave interior volume sensing. Glass break sensor.

Central locking and deadlock system. Master and limited access valet parking keys. Air conditioning system and interior lights activate on disarming.

NB. For these models, the sub-headings 'Bodyshell' and 'Interior and exterior features depending on model and year' as used above are considered by the author to be more appropriate than the two sub-headings 'Underframe' and 'Coachwork' as used in previous chapters for other models.

DIMENSIONS

Wheelbase:	10 ft. 2.76 in.	(3,116 mm)
Front track:	5 ft. 3.24 in.	(1,608 mm)
Rear track:	5 ft. 3.24 in.	(1,608 mm)
Overall length:	17 ft. 8.28 in.	(5,390 mm)
Overall width:	7 ft. 0.70 in.	(2,150 mm)
Overall height:	4 ft. 11.64 in.	(1,515 mm)

PERFORMANCE

Maximum speed:	150 m.p.h.	240 k.p.h.
Acceleration:	0–60 m.p.h.	6.2 sec.
Acceleration:	0–100 m.p.h.	15.9 sec.

VIN NUMBERS, FIRST AND LAST UP TO 2001 MODEL YEAR

Bentley Arnage:	1998 First–SCBLB51E9WCX01001:	1999 Last–SCBLB51E1XCH99008
Arnage 4.4L Birkin:	2000 First–SCBLB51E4YCH05236:	2000 Last–SCBLB51E1YCH05498
Arnage Green Label:	2000 First–SCBLB51E2YCX04003:	2000 Last–SCBLB51F6YCX99044

NUMBERS PRODUCED TO DATE (UP TO 2001 MODEL YEAR)

Bentley: Arnage, 1,123; Arnage 4.4L Birkin, 50; Arnage Green Label, 9.

BENTLEY
Arnage Red Label from 2000, Arnage l.w.b 2001, Arnage Le Mans 2001,
Arnage Limousine 2000

2001 Bentley Arnage Red Label L.W.B.

ENGINE

GENERAL Eight cylinders in 90° V configuration, bore 4.1 in. (104.1 mm), stroke 3.9 in. (99.1 mm), cubic capacity 412 cu. in. (6,750 cc). Compression ratio 8:1.

VALVES Two overhead valves per cylinder operated by helical gear-driven cast iron camshaft in vee of engine.

CYLINDER HEAD AND CYLINDER BLOCK Aluminium alloy cylinder heads and aluminium-silicon alloy cylinder block with cast iron wet cylinder liners.

CRANKSHAFT Forged steel, counterweighted, statically and dynamically balanced five bearing crankshaft.

INDUCTION SYSTEMS Fuel injection, Garrett turbocharger with electronic transient boost control, intercooler and Zytek EMS3 engine management system.

EXHAUST SYSTEM North American and Japanese cars fitted with catalytic converters, then on all cars except those sold in the Middle East from the 1987/8 model year onward. Cars not fitted with catalytic converters: twin pipe system with six silencer boxes.

Arnage Le Mans.

Cars with catalytic converters: twin downtake pipes from engine merge into a single pipe prior to the catalytic converters, then revert to twin pipes with twin intermediate and rear silencer boxes.

POWER 400 b.h.p. at 4,000 r.p.m.

TORQUE 619 lb./ ft.

TRANSMISSION

GEARS Four-speed automatic gearbox with electric gear actuation from selector located on centre console offers normal plus three sports modes. A winter programme is automatically selected when rear wheel slip is detected. Adaptive shift management. Transmission torque reduction control.

Ratios/m.p.h per 1,000 r.p.m: 1st 3.55/8; 2nd 2.24/12.7; 3rd 1.54/18.5; 4th 1.00/28.4; 5th 0.79/36.0. Final drive 2.93:1

BRAKES AND TRACTION ASSISTANCE

Power-boost control system with 4-channel anti-lock braking. Fist brake calliper design. Hydraulic brake servo. Micro-alloy ventilated discs – 348-mm front, 345-mm rear. Pad wear indicator system.

Automatic Stability Control (ASC). Engine torque reduction control counteracts driven wheel spin. Speed sensors to all four wheels. Aquaplaning detection. Rear wheel stability braking. Driver-operated system on/off switch.

SUSPENSION

Front and rear: double wishbone independent suspension system. Front upper wishbones in forged aluminium – high mounted to body. Automatic ride height control with auto load compensation. Computer-controlled electro-hydraulic suspension dampers with a response time of 1/100th second linked to transmission and steering input.

STEERING

Power-assisted rack and pinion speed sensitive steering. Three-section steering column electrically adjustable for rake (memory linked). Automatic position adjustment to facilitate easy entry/exit. 3.2 turns lock-to-lock.

WHEELS AND TYRES

Six-spoke 18-in. aluminium alloy wheels with low profile 255/50 R18 tyres (optional five-spoke sports and chrome wheel).

BODYSHELL

Rigid all-steel monocoque with impact-absorbing body sections to front, rear and sides. Double-sided zinc-coated skin panels. High strength door construction and single-pressing body apertures. Anti-intrusion beams to all doors. Impact-absorbing body sections to front, rear and sides. Anti-trap windows. Anti-trap sunroof if fitted. High-mounted rear stop lamp. Energy-absorbing bumpers. Ten stage anti-corrosion pre-treatment, including electro-coated galvanising. Lift-assisted luggage compartment lid with touch release and powered closing mechanism. Lift-assisted rear-hinged bonnet.

INTERIOR AND EXTERIOR FEATURES DEPENDING ON MODEL AND YEAR

GENERAL Analogue instruments, driver information panel, trip computer. Steering wheel mounted cruise control. Electrochromic self-dimming rear view mirror. One-touch, power folding, electrochromic glass door mirrors which dip on selection of reverse gear. Four-way electrically adjustable front seats with four memory positions linking driver's seat to exterior mirrors, steering wheel, and self-dimming interior rear view mirror. Twin electric, independently adjustable rear seats. Two-stage seat heating and bi-level lumbar support to four main seats. Electric rake adjustable steering wheel with automatic easy entry/exit feature – memory linked to driver's seat and exterior mirrors. Self-adjusting front seat belts. Driver and front passenger airbags. Anti-submarine seats. Fuel shut-off, door auto-unlock and collapsible steering column safety systems triggered by impact. Picnic tables and magazine stowage to front seat backs. Heating, ventilation and air conditioning system with side-to-side, split level (face/feet), front/rear temperature regulation, pollen and dust micro-filters, dehumidifier and residual heating. Twin drink holders to front centre console

415

and rear console. Dual mechanism electric window lift – one-touch open/close and linear. 4x35 Watt radio/cassette/6 CD autochanger audio system with remote control for rear passenger operation. Driver's door only unlock function. Walk-up/away courtesy headlamps. Auto door lock on selection of forward gear when engine running. Auto headlamps on fast wipe speed. Park distance control.

MULTI-FUNCTION PROGRAMMABLE ALARM SYSTEM Rolling code transponder immobilisation of both engine management and starter systems. Perimetric sensors to doors, bonnet, luggage compartment, glove box and Spirit of Ecstasy mascot. Microwave interior volume sensing. Glass break sensor. Central locking and deadlock system. Master and limited access valet parking keys. Air conditioning system and interior lights activate on disarming.

NB. For these models, the sub-headings 'Bodyshell' and 'Interior and exterior features depending on model and year' as used above are considered by the author to be more appropriate than the two sub-headings 'Underframe' and 'Coachwork' as used in previous chapters for other models.

DIMENSIONS

Wheelbase:	10 ft. 2.76 in.	(3,116 mm)
Front track:	5 ft. 3.24 in.	(1,608 mm)
Rear track:	5 ft. 3.24 in.	(1,608 mm)
Overall length:	17 ft. 8.28 in.	(5,390 mm)
Overall width:	7 ft. 0.70 in.	(2,150 mm)
Overall height:	4 ft. 11.64 in.	(1,515 mm)

PERFORMANCE

Maximum speed:	155 m.p.h.	249 k.p.h.
Acceleration:	0–60 m.p.h.	5.9 sec.
Acceleration:	0–100 m.p.h.	15.4 sec.
Acceleration:	0–100 k.p.h.	6.3 sec.
Acceleration:	0–160 k.p.h.	15.3 sec.

VIN NUMBERS, FIRST AND LAST UP TO 2001 MODEL YEAR

Arnage Red Label:	2000 First–SCBLC32E9YCX04001:	2002
Arnage LWB:	2001 First–SCBLE31EX1CH07591:	2002
Arnage Le Mans:	2001 First–SCBLC31E01CX06341:	2002
Arnage Limousine:	2000 First–SCBLE32E0YCX07511:	2001 Last SCBLC31E81CH99113

NUMBERS PRODUCED TO DATE (UP TO 2001 MODEL YEAR)

Arnage Red Label, 2,114; Arnage L.W.B., 29; Arnage Le Mans, 139; Arnage Limousine, 2.

BENTLEY
Arnage T 2002

2002 Bentley Arnage T (front).

ENGINE

GENERAL Eight cylinders in 90° V configuration, bore 4.1 in. (104.16 mm), stroke 3.9 in. (99.06 mm), cubic capacity 412 cu. in. (6,750 cc). Compression ratio 7.8:1.

VALVES Overhead push rod operated through self-adjusting hydraulic tappets. The valve-gear has been totally renewed with a new camshaft featuring revised lift and duration. It operates on substantially strengthened push rods with a revised rocker ratio and new rocker pedestal fixings to cope with the higher engine speeds. Valve lift is increased and new Nimonic exhaust valves fitted; these are the same size as before but are much lighter and have reduced stem diameters to cope better with the higher potential engine speeds. The maximum permissible engine speed has been raised from 4,500 r.p.m. to 5,000 r.p.m. to suit new gearing but the power peak is at 4,100 r.p.m.

CYLINDER HEAD AND CYLINDER BLOCK Cast aluminium alloy engine block and cylinder head.

CRANKSHAFT Forged steel, counterweighted, statically and dynamically balanced five-bearing crankshaft.

2002 Bentley Arnage T (rear).

INDUCTION SYSTEMS Fuel injection, two Garrett T3 turbochargers and Bosch Mototronic ME 7 engine management system.

EXHAUST SYSTEM Three-way, catalytic air-fuel ratio control, converter, feedback. One 3-way catalytic converter per bank.

POWER 450 b.h.p. (336 Kw.) at 4,100 r.p.m.

TORQUE 645 lb. ft. (875 Nm.) at 3,250 r.p.m..

TRANSMISSION
GEARS Four-speed GM 4L80-E automatic gearbox with electric gear actuation from selector located on centre console. Ratios: 1st 2.48, 2nd 1.48, 3rd 1.00, 4th 0.75. Final drive 2.92:1

BRAKES AND TRACTION ASSISTANCE
Power boost control system with 4-channel anti-lock braking. Fist brake calliper design. Hydraulic brake servo. Micro-alloy ventilated discs – 348mm front, 345mm rear. Pad wear indicator system.
Bosch Electronic Stability Programme enabled by electronic 'fly by wire' throttle.

SUSPENSION

Front: quadrangle pressed steel sub-frame supporting the steering rack, with rubber-isolated lower wishbones. Independent front and rear suspension. Rear: a pressed steel sub-frame supporting rubber isolated upper and lower wishbones.

Plus: computer controlled 3-stage adaptive electro-hydraulic dampers and automatic ride height control with automatic load compensation.

STEERING

Power-assisted rack and pinion speed sensitive steering with compliant outer track rods. Ratio: 17.5:1. Turns lock to lock 3.11.

WHEELS AND TYRES

Wheels: 8J x 18 or optional 8J x 19 aluminium alloy. Tyres 255/50 R18 102Y or optional 255/45 R19 104Y. Inflation pressures: 18in. tyre or optional 19 in. tyre. Front 33 psi. Rear 36 psi.

BODYSHELL

Front-engine, rear wheel drive, 5-seat, 4-door saloon. Rigid all-steel monocoque with impact absorbing body sections to front, rear and sides. Double-sided zinc coated skin panels. High strength door construction and single pressing body apertures. Anti-intrusion beams to all doors. Impact absorbing body sections to front, rear and sides. Anti-trap windows. Anti-trap sunroof if fitted. High mounted rear stop lamp. Energy absorbing bumpers. Ten stage anti-corrosion pre-treatment, including electro-coated galvanising. Lift-assisted luggage compartment lid with touch release and powered closing mechanism. Lift-assisted rear hinged bonnet.

EQUIPMENT

STANDARD Standard equipment includes: Connolly leather; Wilton carpets; automatic climate control; driver, passenger and four side airbags, full length side air curtains; four channel anti-lock brakes; Bosch ESP stability control; flip up central navigation display with DVD satellite navigation; cruise control; electrically adjustable front seats with four memory settings, electrically adjustable rear seats; seat heaters in all four seats; audio system with six-CD stacker; front and rear parking distance control sensors; volumetric and perimetric alarm with rolling code transponder immobilisation and tow away protection.

PERSONAL COMMISSIONING Through its Personal Commissioning department, Bentley can tailor an Arnage to the precise specification of the customer. Customers can choose from an effectively unlimited resource of trim and specification possibilities that can turn a car into a mobile office or, by using a vast choice of hides, wood and upholstery possibilities, make a genuinely unique and luxurious travelling environment.

DIMENSIONS AND CAPACITIES

Wheelbase:	10 ft. 2.76 in. (3,116 mm.)
Front track:	5 ft. 3.12 in. (1,602 mm.)
Rear track:	5 ft. 3.12 in. (1,602 mm.)
Overall length:	17 ft. 8.76 in. (5,400 mm.)
Overall width across mirrors:	6 ft. 11.73 in. (2,125 mm.)
Overall width across body:	6 ft. 4.12 in. (1,932 mm.)
Overall height:	4 ft. 11.69 in. (1,515 mm.)
Kerb weight:	5,700 lb. (2,585 kg.)
Fuel tank capacity:	26.4 US galls. (100 litres)
Oil capacity:	22.2 US pints (10.5 litres)
Coolant capacity:	42.2 US pints (20 litres)

PERFORMANCE

Maximum speed:	168 m.p.h.	270 kph.
Acceleration:	0–60 m.p.h.	5.5 secs
Acceleration:	0–100 m.p.h.	13.5 secs
Acceleration:	0–100 k.p.h.	5.8 secs
Acceleration:	0–160 k.p.h.	13.4 secs

FUEL CONSUMPTION

	EU Cycle	
Urban:	9.2 m.p.g.	30.7 litres/100 km.
Extra urban:	19.1 m.p.g.	14.8 litres/100 km.
Combined:	13.7 m.p.g.	20.6 litres/100 km.
	EPA Cycle	
City driving:	11 miles per US gallon	
Highway driving:	16 miles per US gallon	
Combined:	13 miles per US gallon	

FIRST VIN NUMBER

Arnage T:	2002 First-SCBLF34F72CX08200

Index

Entries for ROLLS-ROYCE models and for BENTLEY models since 1931 will be found alphabetically under Rolls-Royce and Bentley specifications (figure-names are indexed as if the name were spelt out). Illustrations are indicated by page numbers in bold type. The letter 'n' after a page number means that the information will be found in a footnote on that page.

Oil level in early cars 55
Olds Motor Vehicle Company 14
Oldsmobile cars 14, 16, 24, 48,
  173
Oliver, George 117
Olympia Motor Show 37
'One-model' policy 50, 68–9, 105
One-shot chassis lubrication 156,
  157
Ormond Beach Races, 1907 67
Otto and Langen atmospheric gas
  engine 89
Overdrive 73

Packard cars 14, 15, 128
Panhard et Levassor cars 12–13,
  29, 30, 32, **32**, 35, 38, 39, 40,
  46, 49, 54, 56, 109, 148
  4 h.p. model bought by Ellis 30
  four-wheel brakes 93
  gear-change 25
  Panoramique 128
  6-cylinder engines 16
Paris-Bordeaux-Paris race (1895)
  38–9
Paris-Boulogne Race (1898) **36**
Paris-Vienna race, 1902 40
Park Ward, coachbuilders 119,
  143, 197, **267**, **281**, **283**, **288**,
  290, **302**, **303**, **314**, **334**
Parking Distance Control (PDC)
  208
Paulin (Bentley body designer)
  118
Peerless lorries 86
Pemberton, Sir Max, *The Life of
  Sir Henry Royce* 6, 79
Petrol rationing 135–6
Peugeot cars 12, 13, 29, 30, **30**,
  39, 49, 171
Phantom III Technical Society of
  America 122
Philip, HRH The Duke of
  Edinburgh 210, 211
Phoenix cars 74

Pierce cars 15, 171
Pininfarina, coachbuilders 190,
  317, **318**, **380**
Pistons, aluminium alloy, first
  used 91–2
Plastow, Sir David 185
Platford, Eric 23, 27, 57, 64, 83,
  84
Platform suspension 42, 54
Pomeroy, L.H. 153
Pomeroy, L.H. (senior) 54
Pressed Steel Co. 143
Prices of cars
  1900–1904 15–16
  1905 37–8
Prince Henry Tour, 1911 77
Princess R 170–71
Production experimental depart-
  ment 133, 134
Project Rolls-Royce 212–13
Prudential Assurance Company
  182
Punt, Alfred 19
Purchase Tax 137
Putch, Lem 143

Quadricycles 13, 85

Radiators
  Bentley **205**
  'Grecian shell' 34, 35, 106, 177,
    202
Radley, James 83, 84, 106
R.B. Two-Eleven engine 159
Rear-springs, *see* suspension
Red flag walking attendant 13, 30
Renault, Louis 14
Renault cars 14, 15, 42, 77, 95,
  100, 173
  10 h.p. 2-cylinder, price of 38
Ricardo, Harry 122
Richard, Georges 69
'Ride control' 128, 156
Riley cars 118, 170
Rippon Bros. **230**, **231**

Road & Truck report on Silver
  Shadow 167–8, 178
Robotham, W.A. 117
  Silver Ghosts and Silver Dawn 161
Roger, Emile 12
Roi-des-Belges body **230**
Roller dynamometer 91
Rolls, Hon. Charles Stewart **33**,
  36, 38, **78**
  early interest in motoring 29,
    30, 31
  engineering expertise 29, 31
  flying, interest in 69; fatal crash
    77
  40/50 R-R **70**
    gear-change, rough handling
    of 74
  Gordon Bennett Trophy 40
  meets Henry Royce 34
  sculpture of **155**
  sets up as dealer 32
  Silver Ghost trial run 64
  speech at opening of Derby fac-
    tory 68
  Technical Managing Director,
    1906–57; relinquished 77
  T.T. races 40–41, 42, 44–5, 59,
    60, 61, **62**
Rolls, C.S. and Co., agreement to
  sell Royce cars 34
Rolls-Royce aero engines *see*
  aero engines
Rolls-Royce of America Inc.
  annual output of cars 104
  coachbuilders bought up 103–4
  decline and failure 101, 104
  formation 101
  share capital 101
'Rolls-Royce Bible' 91–2
Rolls-Royce cars
  air-conditioning 181–2
  boot, smallness of 146
  brakes criticised 93–4, 153, 167
  dash-board criticised 146
  designwork by team 120